THE FRANCHISE AND POLITICS IN
BRITISH NORTH AMERICA

CANADIAN STUDIES IN HISTORY AND GOVERNMENT

A series of studies edited by Goldwin French, sponsored by the Social Science Research Council of Canada, and published with financial assistance from the Canada Council.

The Franchise
and Politics in
British North America
1755–1867

BY

John Garner

UNIVERSITY OF TORONTO PRESS

© University of Toronto Press 1969
Printed in Great Britain
Reprinted in paperback 2017
ISBN 978-0-8020-3219-5 (cloth)
ISBN 978-1-4875-9889-1 (paper)

To the Memory of

My Mother and Father

Pioneers in the Prairie West

PREFACE

THIS MONOGRAPH owes its existence to a casual remark made by Professor Frank Underhill that the Canadian franchise was a neglected field. Interested by the remark, I looked into the Canadian franchise and soon discovered that Confederation did not mark the beginnings of a new franchise; until 1885 the federal government chose to employ the provincial franchises at each federal election, and the provinces in turn continued for some years the franchises that had served their colonial predecessors. As it would have been impossible to tell the story of the development of the Canadian franchise and ignore the colonial era in which it had its origins, I have confined myself to the story of the development of the franchise in each of those British colonies which came to form the nucleus of the Dominion of Canada, from the establishment of their representative assemblies until they joined Confederation.

I wish to express thanks to those archives, libraries, and their staffs who were unstinting in their co-operation and hospitality over many months and years. Without wishing to depreciate in any way the assistance given by other institutions, I am particularly indebted to the Dominion Archivist, Dr. W. Kaye Lamb, and staff of the Public Archives of Canada; Dr. C. B. Fergusson and staff of the Public Archives of Nova Scotia; and Dr. F. A. Hardy and his former staff of the Library of Parliament. I would be remiss if I did not mention the help extended over a long period of time by Miss Norah Story, sometime head of the Manuscript Division, and Mlle Juliette Bourque, head of the Library Division, of the Public Archives of Canada. The debt Canadian historiography owes these public servants is immense.

I acknowledge with thanks the financial assistance given by the University of Toronto and the Social Science Research Council of Canada. The award of the Maurice Cody Research Fellowship from the University of Toronto allowed me to spend two years on uninterrupted research. The Social Science Research Council provided a grant that allowed material to be consulted in libraries and archives in various parts of the country, and as well sponsored the publication of the completed study.

Ottawa
July 1968

J. G.

CONTENTS

THE FRANCHISE AND POLITICS IN
BRITISH NORTH AMERICA

CHAPTER ONE

THE FRANCHISE

FROM THE INCEPTION of representative government in Nova Scotia in 1758 until the entrance of Prince Edward Island into Confederation in 1873, the franchise and its extension did not become a political issue of any magnitude in the British North American colonies. The quiet was not symptomatic of general political lethargy. The controversy over the alien question in Upper Canada with its ramifications for the exercise of the franchise must dispel any doubts about the vigour and persistence with which the colonists were prepared to challenge any tampering with the vote. If the franchise did not become, as in England, the centre of disputation it was because no numerous and important segment of the population was excluded from its exercise. The general populace had it within their power to choose general assemblies to their liking, friction arose because the general assemblies did not have the power to secure executives to their liking. The agitation in the British North American colonies was, in consequence, not a movement to secure control of the assemblies by an extension of the franchise but a movement of the majorities in the assemblies to secure control of their executives by an extension of the principle of responsibility. The political controversies in these colonies concerned the achievement of responsible government, not the achievement of representative government.

The radicals in these colonies never put franchise reform in the forefront of their programmes. Papineau, in his days of greatest power prior to 1837, never advocated an extension of the franchise, although he did advocate the extension of the elective principle to the Executive and Legislative councils. William Lyon Mackenzie, and no one cast his net of grievances wider, had no complaint against the franchise. It did not even claim his attention when he drafted a provisional constitution for Upper Canada in 1837. Mackenzie could scarcely have criticized a franchise which allowed the freeholders of the county of York to return him some seven times within a short space of years and which, following his exile, allowed him to be returned by the freeholders of Haldimand.

The absence of the franchise from controversy was due to its eminent suitability to the circumstances of life and the dominant interest in each colony. In Nova Scotia and New Brunswick the franchise was based on ownership of a freehold, but until the Crown was able to distribute land, the franchise in the first election was manhood suffrage in New Brunswick and a freehold of unspecified value and extent in Nova Scotia. In Prince Edward Island, where the inhabitants were tenants on the lands of absentee proprietors, the franchise was possessed by all resident freeholders, leaseholders, and householders. In the Canadas Whig criticism of the draft Constitutional Bill in the Imperial Parliament had resulted in a franchise so universal that the city of Montreal, in a petition of grievances tabled in the Assembly of 1832, signified its sincere attachment "To that part of the Constitution which, being wisely adapted to the state of society in this country where almost every father of a family is a freeholder, has rendered the right of voting at the election of members of the Assembly nearly universal."[1] In British Columbia the transient mining population had the Colonial Office bestow a franchise upon it unencumbered by any restraints.

The near universality of the colonial franchises might make it appear that the British Government, which favoured an antiquated and restrictive franchise at home, was in favour of manhood suffrage in the colonies. Such an appearance would be misleading; for the British Parliament and the Colonial Office were interested, not in giving the Canadian colonies manhood suffrage, but in establishing in the colonies as close a copy of the British constitution as the continuance of Imperial suzerainty would admit. The freehold franchise of rural England conferred on the colonies of Nova Scotia, New Brunswick, and the Canadas was transformed into virtual manhood suffrage by the abundance of land and the generosity of the Crown in its disposal.[2] The franchise possessed by Irish peasants who held leases for lives was transferred to the colony of Prince Edward Island where the freeholders, leaseholders, and householders were allowed to vote.[3] The British Columbia franchise had no English counterpart and was a concession to necessity and the fear of American expansion under the doctrine of manifest destiny. Franchises which had been restrictive at home became, when transplanted to the British North American colonies, tantamount to manhood suffrage in the circumstances of their new environment.

A franchise which achieved near universality in an era of free land might be expected to become more restrictive following the period when free land ceased to be available. This transition began to take place in the early 1830's when the Crown ceased its practice of free grants and substituted a policy of sale, and was reflected in the emergence of demands for a leasehold franchise in the Canadas and New Brunswick in the 1830's and the 1840's, for ratepayers' franchise in Nova Scotia in the 1840's, and for an assessment franchise in New Brunswick in the 1850's.[4] In every case the franchise was ultimately extended. In 1851 Nova Scotia gave the vote to all adult males who were assessed for and had paid the poor and county rates; in 1853 Canada extended the vote to all owners, occupants, and tenants of real property assessed for a specific actual or yearly value; in 1853 Prince Edward Island extended its already broad franchise to include all male citizens who were liable, but for a legal exemption, for statute labour on the roads; and in 1855 New Brunswick followed the trend and gave the vote to all male citizens who were assessed for a specific amount of real or personal property or for a specified annual income.

From the prompt accommodation of the demands for an expanded franchise, it might be supposed that the colonists were strongly inclined towards democracy, that the ideas of the French revolutionaries, of Thomas Paine, and of Jacksonian democracy about the rights, equality, and innate worth of the common man were firmly held. But in fact the ideas of these political movements were in advance of the political beliefs of the bulk of the colonists. No political party save the Parti Rouge espoused manhood suffrage—universal suffrage as it was then called—and its inclusion was more a gesture of piety to their French revolutionary gods than an entrenched belief; Antoine Dorion, the leader of the Parti Rouge, gave manhood suffrage little but lip service and spent his energies in the Assembly sponsoring improvements to the assessment franchise.[5] The political party most influenced by Jacksonian democracy, the Clear Grits, refused to endorse manhood suffrage although it was urged upon them by one of their ablest leaders, Peter Perry. Even he was forced to admit that the public mind was not prepared for so radical a departure.[6]

It is, moreover, possible to muster a roster of declamations against manhood suffrage by the leading public men and journals of the day. John A. Macdonald while Attorney General in 1858 is stated to have declared that "he was not in favour of universal suffrage but completely opposed to it."[7] The Attorney General of New Brunswick, Charles Fisher, in 1855 quoted with approval the opinion of Lord John Russell that "universal suffrage, in pretending to avoid it, gives the whole power to the highest and the lowest, to money and multitude, and thus disfranchises the middle class, the most disinterested, the most independent and the most unprejudiced of all," that "universal suffrage is calculated to produce and nourish violent opinions and servile dependence; to give in times of quiet a great preponderance to wealth, and in times of disturbance, additional power to ambitious demagogues. It is the grave of all temperate liberty and the parent of tyranny and license."[8] Alexander T. Galt thought the franchise should be based on a *bona fide* interest in the soil.[9] George Brown was unsympathetic to manhood suffrage.[10] Joseph Howe rejoiced that his Government had abandoned manhood suffrage although the immediate effect of the change had been disastrous to his administration, and the *Novascotian* agreed with him "that the change in the franchise from universal suffrage . . . was cheaply purchased by the downfall of the best Administration that ever existed in this Province."[11] The citizens of New Westminster repudiated the universality of the franchise given them by the Colonial Office and on their own volition established a propertied franchise.[12] *Haszard's Gazette* of Charlottetown could not "agree with those who base their argument upon abstract right and naked arithmetic, to whom the will of the majority is sacred; and in whose estimation one man is as good and as competent as another; and who hold that every man's claim to an equal share in the government is inherent and indefeasible" (February 26, 1853). And the St. Catharines *Evening Journal* of February 22, 1865, self-righteously pointed to the great corruption in American public life as evidence of the consequence of allowing the senseless and levelling rabble to vote.[13]

Despite the chorus of hostility, manhood suffrage was not without its proponents. The Upper Canada Central Political Union, as reported in the *Colonial Advocate* of December 13, 1832, was not alone in professing the just rights of man which included the right of every adult member of the community to an equal and in fact "a natural right to elect those who are to legislate for him." But the voices raised were not those of the leading and respected public men or the leading public journals. Yet bearing in mind the ease with which Nova Scotia slipped into manhood suffrage when her political leaders felt it to be politically beneficial, and the thin veneer of qualifications which separated Vancouver Island and Prince Edward Island from manhood suffrage, one is left to wonder if the abundance of abuse and paucity of praise were not due to its lack of respectability rather than to any rational opposition to the principles underlying manhood suffrage.

In consequence the British North American colonists could be charged with having no firm convictions about the nature of the franchise, with holding unreflectingly opinions which were the products in the main of English and American thought. There is much justification for such a charge. The colonists' opinions were the opinions current in England and America; and as these opinions were held with varying conviction and by varying numbers of people at any one time, the same individual was often found espousing different views about the proper franchise at various times.

There may, however, be detected three main views of the franchise current among the colonists during the century under consideration. The older and more traditional view looked upon the franchise as a privilege bestowed on the citizen by the state in its wisdom and magnanimity; the newer and democratic view looked upon the franchise as a right inherent in each man from his very nature; the third and more widely held view was somewhat of an amalgam of elements of the previous views and is probably most clearly stated in the following words of Montesquieu: "All the inhabitants . . . ought to have a right of voting at the election of a representative, except such as are in so mean a situation as to be deemed to have no will of their own."[14] While the mark of independence might be ownership of land, leasehold of land, or assessment for or the payment of taxes, the emphasis on these qualifications was merely as visual indications of the self-reliance of their possessors. The Attorney General of New Brunswick gave expression to this viewpoint when in a debate on an election bill in 1855 he stated that while "it was true that neither money nor the possession of property was conclusive evidence of a person possessing much brains . . . it was the best security that they could get that a person having gathered round him some property would not be likely to wish to see the laws and the institutions of the country disregarded."[15] It was to this school of thought that the advocates of what was often referred to as a stake-in-the-country franchise belonged.

The traditional view that the franchise was a privilege is probably best exemplified in a petition from the electors of Quebec Upper Town following the general election of August, 1827, wherein they complained of the returning officers' refusal to accept the votes of widows, for "neither in men nor women can the right to vote be a natural right; it is given by enactment. The only questions are whether women could exercise that right well and advantageously for the state and whether they are entitled to it."[16] Over the centuries of English constitutional development this privilege of voting had been bestowed on persons possessed of a specified property, status, or office so that the vote had become attached to or synonymous with the possession of land or the status of a knight or burgher and had become independent of the individual. If the property or status was lost the vote was lost, if property or status was gained the vote was won. By the nineteenth century, this view in its most absolute form had become the object of much ridicule and devastating attack from the supporters of the equality of all men, whether in Locke's state of naure and social contract, or in the puritan's equality of all men before God.[17] The ridicule generally took the form expressed in the *British Colonist* of June 8, 1859, where the editor argued that, if twenty acres of land constituted a vote, then he who had a thousand acres would be entitled to fifty votes; or in the mockery attributed to Benjamin Franklin and quoted in the *Colonial Advocate* of December 27, 1827: "Today a man owns a jackass worth fifty dollars, and he is entitled to vote, but before the next election the jackass dies . . . and the man cannot vote. Now gentlemen pray inform me in whom is the right of suffrage in the man or in the jackass?" The weight of rational argument and ridicule made it unlikely that many colonists would make overt attempts to promote the privilege theory of the franchise. Yet there were many British North Americans whose attachment to the British constitution led them to silently support this view by quietly following Burke's admonition to understand it according to their measure and to venerate where they were not able presently to comprehend.[18]

The democratic view that each man possessed an inherent right to the franchise had ranged on its side a formidable array of religious and philosophical argument. The puritan emphasis on the equality of man whether lay or clerical before God gave to this theory the sympathetic attention if not the active support of that large body of colonists who belonged to the non-conformist religions, although there were ranged against it those colonists who adhered to the teachings of the episcopal churches. The St. Catharines *Evening Journal* of February 22, 1865, exemplifies this contradiction: "the Constitution which makes the vox populi the 'all in all' political or governmental power has an inherent weakness which must result in its own death" for if "God has recognized distinctions in the government of His Church where there are some greater than others, surely it cannot be expected that poor finite humanity could improve on the Divine Model."

If the dissenting churches gave a religious sanction to this theory of the franchise, the philosophical postulates of the schools of Locke and Rousseau about the state of nature and social contract had given a rational justification which Thomas Paine popularized on the American continent in his "Rights of Man." As "men are born, and always continue, free and equal" and as "the end of all political associations is the preservation of the nature and imprescriptible rights of man," Paine deduced that "the right of voting for representatives is the primary right by which other rights are protected. To take away this right is to reduce man to slavery, for slavery consists in being subject to the will of another, and he that has not a vote in the election of representatives is in this case. The proposal therefore to disfranchise any class of men is as criminal as the proposal to take away property."[19] The arguments for this theory of the franchise were persuasive, and the *British Colonist* of November 19, 1870, had to admit that "the theory of universal suffrage is one which is most naturally and almost universally embraced by nearly all classes and ranks of men and it is a theory which cannot be successfully opposed by legitimate ethical logic." At an earlier day no less a personage than John Adams, second President of the United States, had perceived the same difficulty and the likely consequences. "It is hard to say that every man has not an equal right, but admit this equal right and equal power and an immediate revolution would ensue."[20]

Although manhood suffrage was difficult to oppose logically, the majority of British North Americans found it easy to oppose in practice. In their minds its logical appeal had been sullied and nullified by the American and French revolutions, and by the excesses of Jacksonian democracy as evidenced in the American cities and the frontier of the Middle West. William Lyon Mackenzie testified in the *Montreal Gazette* of December 16, 1854, that "he had seen how the franchise was exercised by drunkards and the refuse of society in the cities of New York, Albany, Rochester and elsewhere, where universal suffrage prevailed"; and the St. Catharines *Evening Journal* of February 22, 1865, stated: "Our Yankee neighbours have given evidence of the greatest corruption in the government of their country, a corruption unparalleled in the annals of nations, and the direct effect of universal suffrage and dollar worship." To the conservative agrarians of British North America manhood suffrage was condemned not by logic but by the excesses attributable to it. While manhood suffrage in consequence made no irresistible appeal, yet when the economy was depressed, and when creditors pressed hard, the country folk frequently shed their native conservatism and espoused manhood suffrage. Needless to say these conditions were not always wanting in British North America. Let one example suffice. The member for the rural New Brunswick riding of Kent during the agricultural depression of the mid 1850's was led to declare "that the right to vote was an inherent right of every freeborn man. The right itself existed from the creation of the world, and its exercise only was made the subject of legislative restriction. The right to vote was as much an inherent right appertaining to freemen as any other natural right that a free born man enjoyed."[21]

The independence or stake-in-the-country theory of the franchise had the virtue of accommodating characteristics of both the privilege and the natural right theories of the franchise. For while it rejected the dogma that the franchise was a privilege and admitted that the franchise was the right of every man, its insistence on a property, assessment, or tax-paying qualification was an insistence on the very qualifications through which the privilege franchise had been traditionally bestowed. The proponents of the stake-in-the-country franchise were thus able to have a foot in each camp and the colonial politicians found such a theory made it easy for them to slip in and out of freehold, assessment, tax-paying, and manhood franchises as political advantage warranted.

The supporters of this school of thought encompassed a wide range of interests. The pseudo-traditionalist and the pseudo-radical could each find a haven there. The thinking, the unthinking, the politicians suffering from a claustrophobia of principles, and those yearning after respectability could all be accommodated. For had not that idol of colonial lawyers, William Blackstone, supported this theory of the franchise? In his *Commentaries on the Laws of England*, "as to the qualifications of electors," he had stated:

the true reason of requiring any qualification with regard to property in voters, is to exclude such persons as are in so mean a situation that they are esteemed to have no will of their own. If these persons had votes, they would be tempted to dispose of them under some undue influence or other. ... If it were probable that every man would give his vote freely and without influence of any kind, then, upon the true theory and general principles of liberty, every member of the community, however poor, should have a vote in electing those delegates to whose charge is committed the disposal of his property, his liberty and his life. But since that can hardly be expected in persons of indigent fortunes, or such as are under the immediate dominion of others, all popular states have been obliged to establish certain qualifications; whereby some, who are suspected to have no will of their own, are excluded from voting. ... [22]

What a solace to a colonist's vanity to know that he as a voter would by implication be a stalwart and upright citizen and not a will-o'-the-wisp like his unfranchised neighbour. To advocate this franchise was to be respectable, to be an independent pillar in the community. It allowed colonial editors to point out self-righteously the moral excesses of Brother Jonathan and to draw repeated homilies from the fearful struggle going on in the United States. There, in the words of the *Courier* of July 18, 1863, "the admission of men of every class and degree, literate and illiterate, civilized and brutish, to the exercise of the elective franchise has produced, as it inevitably must always produce, its natural effects, the degradation of the electoral privilege itself, the demoralization of the electors, the lowering of the status of the elected, the consequent commitment of the reins of power to unqualified, incompetent and unprincipled hands and heads, and general corruption, malversation and mismanagement in all the departments of government and state affairs."

While the Blackstone cult in the legal world widened the support for the stake-in-the-country theory of the franchise, the religious climate of Calvinism inclined a wider segment of the community to the theory. Calvinism, which had dignified ordinary economic activity by the name of callings—tasks assigned to men directly by God—gave to those who pursued honesty, thrift, and industry the satisfaction of serving God and revealing to other men their state of grace. It raised the honest and industrious farmer, merchant, and artisan to a new social status, drove them to value and acquire property and to scorn the shiftless labourers of the cities. This point of view was reflected in the thinking of the Reformers of Upper Canada who never tired of eulogizing the sturdy yeomanry and industrious tradesmen on whose shoulders they professed the government of Upper Canada should rightfully rest. In a letter addressed on September 24, 1834, "To the Reformers of Upper Canada" William Lyon Mackenzie reveals the sobering effect of his Presbyterian background on his excitable personality: "Unless a legislature elected by the freeholders have the control of the public lands and the whole revenue raised from the people with the power to enact laws of general utility and to repeal statutes found inconvenient, this fine country cannot flourish as it otherwise would."[23] The same viewpoint was held by those colonists who coming from America had imbibed Jeffersonianism. In his *Notes on Virginia* Thomas Jefferson proclaimed his conviction that

those who labour in the earth are the chosen people of God, if ever he had a chosen people, whose breasts he has made his peculiar deposit for substantial and genuine virtue . . . Corruption of morals in the mass of cultivators is a phenomenon of which no age nor nation has furnished an example. It is the mark set on those, who not looking up to heaven, to their own soil, and industry, as does the husbandman, for their subsistence, depend for it on casualties and caprice of customers. Dependance begets subservience and venality, suffocates the germ of virtue and prepares fit tools for the designs of ambition . . . generally speaking the proportion which the aggregate of the other classes of citizens bears in any state to that of its husbandmen, is the proportion of its unsound to its healthy parts, and is a good enough barometer whereby to measure its degree of corruption.[24]

In agricultural communities where the self-interest of the agriculturists would alone dictate a propertied franchise, such sentiments confirmed the most independent-minded farmer to the support of a franchise which demanded a stake in the country. Extracts taken from two Nova Scotian newspapers of 1865 serve to confirm the widespread presence of this sentiment. The *Novascotian* of May 29 was of the opinion that "The amended franchise act is a truly conservative measure, an assertion of the rights of property, a vindication of the policy that the franchise should not be indiscriminately exercised by men who have no stake in the country, or by those who are mere birds of passage, here today and away tomorrow."[25] The *Acadian Recorder* of March 24 editoralized in a somewhat similar vein: "a property qualification will at once cut off large numbers, a great majority of whom have very little right and very little desire to exercise the privilege of the voters. They have little right because it will be found that nearly all the legislation of the country has reference to property. When we say they have little desire, we mean little desire, save the desire they have to secure a substantial quid pro quo for their votes, in the way of an order on the grocer, or absolute current coin of the realm."

Because of its breadth, the supporters of the stake-in-the-country theory of the franchise were to find it exceedingly difficult to oppose demands for changes in suffrage qualifications. Theoretical foundations which would accommodate change with relative ease gave an inherent instability to the franchise which would, had conflicting pressures existed, have allowed the suffrage qualifications to change with all the rapidity of a weather cock. But in fact the conflicting pressures did not always occur.

In Lower Canada the patriarchal and rural society found the freehold suffrage which disfranchised few heads of rural families so eminently suited to their condition of life that they never agitated change. In the other colonies the hostility between the old settlers and the new immigrants inclined many colonists to support an exclusive freehold suffrage and to oppose any departure from it, while the "Canada Firsters," the speculators, and those envious of America's rapid development were inclined to urge extensions to the franchise as one of the several devices that were to check the departure of new immigrants to the United States. The result was numerous technical but few fundamental changes in the franchise.

The re-emigration may in part account for the absence of any large number of fundamental changes. This migration had a profound effect on colonial politics and consequently on colonial political thought. It was the radical emigrants who, dissatisfied with Canada, passed on to the United States. The less venturesome and more conservative immigrants tended to stay and they were not of the inflammable material that was producing Jacksonianism in the immigrant-crowded cities of the eastern United States and in the waking Middle West. The British North American colonies exported their radicals and retained their conservatives at home. Nevertheless, while the colonists might profess disdain for Jacksonian democracy, it was a virulent and persuasive infection against which abhorrence was inadequate protection. This was especially true after England with the first Reform Bill had laid hands on its ancient constitution and had thereby unsettled the philosophical foundations of all those colonists whose politics were a reflection of their veneration for British laws and British traditions. In consequence, the colonists and the politicians of British North America, caught between English liberalism and American democracy and between divergent colonial pressure groups, and possessed of a pliable theory of the franchise, were prone to drift from one franchise to another with little forethought but with sharp sensitivity to shifting pressures and to political advantages.

CHAPTER TWO

NOVA SCOTIA, 1755–1830: THE ESTABLISHMENT AND CONSOLIDATION OF REPRESENTATIVE INSTITUTIONS

NOVA SCOTIA was the oldest of the British possessions which were to form the nucleus of the Dominion of Canada, having come into the final possession of the British Crown in 1713 on the conclusion of the Treaty of Utrecht. Nova Scotia acquired a legislative assembly in 1758. This Assembly, elected on a freehold franchise of such liberality as to ensure virtual manhood suffrage, was the consequence of a well-intentioned but premature decision taken by the British Government at the time of Cornwallis' appointment as Governor of Nova Scotia in 1749. In the Commission of Appointment, the Board of Trade had formally instructed Cornwallis to be guided by:

> such reasonable laws and statutes as hereafter shall be made or agreed upon by you with the advice and consent of our Council and the Assembly of our said Province under your government hereafter to be appointed. . . . And we do hereby give and grant unto you full power and authority with the advice and consent of our said Council from time to time as need shall require to summon and call General Assemblys of the said freeholders and planters within your government according to the usage of the rest of our Colonies and Plantations in America.[1]

To the dispute surrounding the implementation of this proviso of the Governor's Commission and to the subsequent strivings of the Governor and Council to ensure a politically compatible assembly it is necessary to turn in order to understand the nature of the initial franchise and its immediate development.

Cornwallis and his successors, Hopson and Lawrence, were not inclined, either by their military background or by the circumstances in which they found Nova Scotia, to establish an elective legislature. The restoration of Louisbourg to the French by the Treaty of Aix-la-Chapelle in 1748, the renewed restiveness of the Acadians and Indians, and the preliminary skirmishes preceding the Seven Years' War were not propitious for the establishment of elective institutions in Nova Scotia. It was not until the arrival in 1754 of Jonathan Belcher, as first Chief Justice of Nova Scotia, that a jurist's concern for legality disinterred the Commission to the Governor.

The Chief Justice, having been reared in the democratic atmosphere of New England where his father had served as Governor both of Massachusetts and of New Jersey, had been nurtured by birth and by professional training in the principles of parliamentary government. This background led him quickly to strike at the very basis of the existent government by questioning the legality of the ordinances passed by the Governor and Council. He based his opinion on the ground that the enactment of laws without the concurrence of an assembly was contrary to the Governor's Commission. The Chief Justice, while expressing such a legal opinion, was not, however, in favour of the creation of an assembly at that time. His New England background notwithstanding, Belcher, in the letter covering his observation on the power of the Governor and Council to make laws, stated that to convene "an Assembly would at present be not only impolitick but almost impracticable, and tho' Halifax should be divided into districts, it would be difficult to find persons qualified for representatives either as freeholders or otherwise."[2]

While the Chief Justice seems to have desired the Board of Trade to reconsider the wisdom of its Commission to the Governor, the Board instead took a legalistic approach. It referred Belcher's observation to the Law Officers of the Crown, and when, on April 29, 1755, the Law Officers handed down their opinion "that the Governor and Council alone are not authorized by His Majesty to make laws,"[3] the Board ordered Governor Lawrence to make preparations to call an assembly. For in the words of the Board:

tho' the calling of an Assembly may in the present circumstances of the colony be difficult, and attended with some inconveniences, yet as the Attorney and Solicitor General are of opinion that the Governor and Council have no power to enact laws, we cannot see how the Government can be properly carried on without such an Assembly. We desire, therefore, you will immediately consult with His Majesty's Chief Justice, in what manner an Assembly can be most properly convened, of what number of members it shall consist, how these members shall be elected and what rules and method of proceedings it may be necessary to prescribe for them; transmitting to us as soon as possible your opinion and report thereupon in as full and explicit a manner as possible, to the end we may lay this matter before His Majesty for His Majesty's further directions therein.[4]

The authorization of an assembly by the Board of Trade received a mixed reception in Halifax. Chief Justice Belcher, fortified by the opinion of the Imperial Law Officers, set about resolutely to consider the constitution of the new legislative body. Governor Lawrence, more conscious of the practical and military difficulties facing the colony, turned rather to engage in a protracted correspondence to dissuade the Board of Trade.[5] He considered the necessity of convening an assembly in order to validate the ordinances of Governor and Council to be merely "a point of law"; the ordinances were "chiefly such as appeared indispensably necessary to make for the good regulation of the town of Halifax and the encouragement of its commerce"; "the people whom they concerned . . . have never made the least question of their validity."[6] The Board of Trade was totally unimpressed by Governor Lawrence's objections and in 1756 firmly, almost brusquely, ordered the establishment of an assembly.[7]

Chief Justice Belcher, in his effort to devise the manner and means of convening a representative assembly, found little official guidance in the Instructions issued to Governor Lawrence. The Instructions simply stated that in case the Governor should "find it necessary for our service to call an Assembly within our said Province, you shall take care that the members thereof be elected only by the freeholders as being more agreeable to the custom of this Kingdom."[8] The extent of the freehold franchise, the manner of representation, and the number of representatives were left to the discretion of the Governor. Earlier instructions issued to Cornwallis and Hopson had been more explicit. Governors Cornwallis and Hopson had been directed "to issue writs in His Majesty's name" to return two representatives from each township in the General Asembly "as soon as any of the said townships have fifty or more families settled therein. . . ."[9] The Chief Justice did not, however, feel that the conditions of settlement in Nova Scotia warranted representation by township: "Under the present circumstances of the Province of Nova Scotia, it would be impracticable to constitute an Assembly by members from the respective towns as is customary in all other colonys, the people, compared with them being very inconsiderable in number, and the inhabitants, except in Halifax, being chiefly either foreigners or soldiers, who ought not to be qualified to be electors."[10] Rather, he proposed that the first Assembly should consist of twelve members elected by the province at large, and that qualifications for voting should be either a personal estate of £30 or a freehold of 40s. a year. He felt that this franchise should only be temporary, and that when population warranted the colony should be divided into counties with both the county and the county town returning representatives.

The Chief Justice's proposals were not brought before the local Executive Council for consideration until some fourteen months later.[11] The delay was occasioned by Governor Lawrence forwarding them to the Board of Trade accompanied by a critical dispatch.[12] The Board was not to be dissuaded nor was it to be drawn into an expression of opinion on the proposed franchise. It replied that the decision as to the membership and the qualifications of electors and elected had to be made by those with a first-hand knowledge and experience of the conditions, but it did imply that within specified limits it was prepared to allow considerable latitude to the Governor and Council. For the Board conceded that "the first Assembly . . . be it in what form it will, must necessarily consist of persons or property in trade, because there is no person who can be truly said to have any considerable landed interest until the country is cleared and the lands laid out; yet it may be proper, and it will be necessary to take care, that a certain landed property, be it ever so small, be the qualification as well of the electors as the elected, because the Commission directs, that the Assembly shall be chosen by the majority of the freeholders."[13]

When the Chief Justice's proposals were placed before it the Council spent an entire month in discussion; and it was not until January 3, 1757, that it set forth its decisions in a series of resolutions.[14] The membership of the Assembly was to be twenty-two; twelve members to be elected for the province at large, and the remainder for the townships as follows: Halifax, four; Lunenburg, two; Dartmouth, Lawrencetown, Annapolis Royal, and Cumberland, one each. Representation would be subsequently extended to other townships when they possessed twenty-five qualified electors. All Protestants of twenty-one years of age who possessed a freehold, unspecified as to value or extent, should be electors. Each elector was to be entitled to as many votes as there were members to be returned from his place of residence. The Council, in view of the large military establishment at Halifax and the outlying garrisons, felt obliged to disfranchise all private soldiers and non-commissioned officers unless they possessed a registered freehold. The civilian settlers were required to possess a freehold but it did not have to be registered. This additional requirement for the lower ranks of the military seems to have been motivated by the fear that the merchants or citizens of Halifax might sway the elections through granting unregistered freeholds to any number of soldiers, for in 1757 Halifax was the operational base of Lord Loudoun, Commander in Chief of the British Colonies in America, from which base he was preparing the attack to reduce Louisbourg.

In a general way the Council determined the manner of the conduct of elections. For each election the Governor was required to issue a writ to the Provost Marshal ordering him or his deputies to summon the freeholders to meet within their respective districts at a convenient place and time to be determined by the Provost Marshal. It was specified that he was to give twenty days' notice of the election and that the writ was to be returnable within sixty days, thus leaving forty days in which the vote might be taken. Within this interval each township poll was to remain open two days, and the polls for the province at large, four days. At these polls, before the assembled multitude, each elector was to declare publicly his name and the persons for whom he voted. From these votes recorded in the poll book by the returning officer and his assistants, the candidates with the largest votes were to be ascertained and declared elected.

Lawrence did not put the resolutions of his Executive Council into immediate operation. To their exasperation, he dispatched the resolutions to the Board of Trade for review.[15] The Halifax civilians utilized this delay to approach the Board of Trade and in the name of "the wisdom of the British nation" demand the immediate calling of an assembly. They took marked exception to the proposed plan of representation and especially to that part which granted representation to the outlying townships. The population of Cumberland Township consisted, they said, of "five old sergeants and soldiers, all settlers to the garrison and subject to military law, for none else was ever heard of in that Fort"; they were equally contemptuous of the population of Annapolis; that of Lawrencetown was "composed of three settlers (subject to the Proprietors who are all Placemen or expecting Places)."[16] The petitioners had objected to the granting of such unequal representation, not merely on the grounds that these townships lacked a settled civilian population, but on the further basis that their population was not free from the official control of the Governor.

The main concern of the petitioners, however, was not the townships of Lawrencetown or Cumberland, but rather the more populous township of Lunenburg. They claimed Lunenburg, on account of its greater freehold population, would determine the twelve seats allotted to the province at large, and with its two township members would control fourteen of the twenty-two seats in the Assembly.[17] The petitioners feared that the citizens of Lunenburg would be submissive to the desires of the Governor, who had provided and was still providing these settlers with the necessities of life. The Halifax petitioners were looking ahead, for the settlers at Lunenburg, while not yet eligible for the franchise, would on their completion of seven years' residence acquire British citizenship and the vote. The agent of the Halifax merchants before the Board of Trade estimated the Governor would be able to nominate two-thirds of the members of the projected Assembly. The estimate may be extreme, but undoubtedly the Governor, as captain general of all the military establishments in Nova Scotia and as dispenser of Crown lands and relief supplies to the settlers at Lunenburg, should have been able to exercise a marked, if not determinate, influence on the electorate. On a plea of democratic justice and as loyal Englishmen in danger of being swamped in their own Assembly by a foreign vote, the Halifax merchants pressed their own plans for control of the Assembly.

The petitioners were concerned not merely with the mutilation of the franchise through over-representation of the outlying townships and the vote of foreigners and placemen, but also with the lack of a fixed freehold valuation as a qualification for the franchise. They complained to the Board of Trade that "the value of such freehold . . . is not at all limited, so that persons of the very lowest condition, if they have but any such freehold of ever so mean a value, may elect, or be elected, which is conceived not to be agreeable to the British constitution, nor to the practice in other Colonies and whereby the members may possibly consist of the lowest and the most unfit persons to the exclusion of those of the best property and substance."[18] The petitioners were also exercised over the possibility of the soldiers' vote swamping the civil population, for they put no faith in the requirement that soldiers' freeholds must be registered before they could vote. The fears of the merchants were in some measure real and for this reason the Board of Trade stated "that the freeholders [might] rest assured that His Most Sacred Majesty and the Lords of Trade intended they should have an Assembly not in name only but in reality, to be freely elected by the persons of property settled there, and not to be either directly or consequentially nominated by the Governor or elected by the Troops, and are perfectly satisfied that their Lord-ships know what is best and most fit for the service of the Province and will advise the Assembly to be constituted under such regulations as to answer His Majesty's most gracious intentions."[19]

In spite of such assurance to the merchants, the Board of Trade in its new directions to Governor Lawrence took no steps to insist on a freehold franchise of a stated and appreciable value. The Board instead simply reiterated the part of its Instructions to Governor Hopson which had required each township to have fifty settled families before it should be granted two representatives in the Assembly.[20]

The Executive Council of Nova Scotia, in the light of the directive of the Board of Trade, struck the townships of Dartmouth, Lawrencetown, Annapolis Royal, and Cumberland from the privilege of representation, thereby augmenting the representa-tion of the province at large to sixteen instead of twelve and leaving Halifax and Lunenburg as the only represented townships.[21] While Governor Lawrence by this action had removed one of the grievances of the merchants of Halifax, he took steps to make certain that they would not achieve their second objective, the disfranchise-ment of Lunenburg. Although the writs for elections as determined by the Executive Council in their resolutions of January 3, 1757, were to be returnable sixty days from the date of issue, Lawrence made them returnable October 2, 1758, over four months from date of issue. By this action he enabled some of the Lunenburg settlers to com-plete their seven years' residence and thereby obtain their citizenship and the fran-chise.[22] The franchise was left at an unspecified amount of freehold property which save in the case of soldiers, need not even be registered. By this broad provision in a land-poor colony the worst fears of the Halifax merchants were confirmed for every man who owned "but the hundredth part of an acre" had a vote.

The first Assembly of Nova Scotia was, as previously mentioned, elected in October, 1758, on a freehold franchise of such liberality as to ensure virtual manhood suffrage. The representatives were apportioned sixteen to the province at large, with four to the township of Halifax and two to the township of Lunenburg. In actual practice the "sixteen for the Province at large were returned by the freeholders of Halifax and Lunenburg jointly"; for the sparsity of population and poor communications, as well as the besieging of Louisbourg, physically prevented the extension of the franchise to all those citizens who possessed the qualifications.[23]

The first Assembly of Nova Scotia was of short duration. It was dissolved in 1759 after its second session. The collapse of French resistance first at Louisbourg and then at Quebec was expected to lead to an influx of New England settlers into the vacant farmsteads of the Acadians and Lawrence and his Council feared that they would swing the pendulum of political power to the discomfiture of the Executive. To fore-stall this danger, the prerogative power of the Governor was called into play, to create counties and townships, and to adjust the representation and the franchise. The dissolution of the Assembly was accordingly followed by the immediate creation of five counties and two townships, the lands of which the Governor proceeded to grant to seven members of the Executive Council and nineteen lesser officials. This action was accompanied by the abolition of representation for the province at large and the substitution of representation based on county and township. In order not to reduce the effect of the change, the new freeholders of Kings County were granted permission to cast their votes for the county members for Kings at Halifax. The result of this move was that nineteen of the twenty members returned to the second Assembly had been recipients of land grants from the Governor.[24]

With regard to the franchise the Governor and Council modified the qualification that had granted the vote to all owners of freeholds, regardless of value or extent. The new requirement allowed the vote only to those freeholders whose holdings provided a clear yearly return of 40s. In other respects the franchise remained as before with all "Popish recusants" and all under twenty-one years barred.[25] As there was no machinery with which to determine the yearly value of freehold property, the qualification was to place no new limit on the franchise. Each freeholder could be expected to declare a yearly revenue of 40s. The franchise was in fact limited only by the ability of the settlers to acquire grants of land from the Crown. In adopting the 40s. franchise, Governor Lawrence and Council brought the Nova Scotia franchise into harmony with that of the English counties; and as this centuries-old franchise had been copied in many American colonies, its adoption by Nova Scotia was not novel.

While Lawrence had brought the franchise into harmony with the English county franchise largely on his own and his Council's initiative, in the matter of the change in representation he had had the suggestion of the Board of Trade to guide his hand. Lawrence had adopted the procedure which the Board of Trade had suggested when commenting on the proposals of Chief Justice Belcher in 1756. At that time the Board had stated: ". . . although Halifax is at present the only town, in which there are any inhabitants qualified to be electors or elected, yet, as it is not proposed that actual residence should be required, in order to qualify a person to act in either one or other of those capacities, the making of a few grants of land in any of the districts, as Minas, Chignecto, Piziquid, Cobequid, etc., will remove this difficulty; and if this can be done, the first Assembly will bear the nearer resemblance to the form in which it must be convened when the Province becomes better peopled and settled."[26]

The adjustment of the franchise and representation by the Governor and Council indicated that they did not consider that the establishment of an Assembly limited in any way the Governor's prerogative respecting either the franchise or representation. The Council, sitting in its legislative capacity as the Legislative Council, had already rejected a bill to regulate elections passed by the first Assembly on the grounds that it was "contrary to His Majesty's Instructions and the resolution of the Governor and Council settled and confirmed by His Majesty."[27] The legislative councillors undoubtedly believed that they were acting in harmony with the intent of the Imperial authorities, although the Instructions had not specifically forbidden the Assembly to legislate on such matters nor had the Board of Trade officially confirmed the franchise as established by Minute of Council in 1757.

It is necessary to consider the struggle to establish legislative control over representation in the Assembly because the resolution of this dispute also determined who should define the franchise. The relative authority of the Board of Trade, the colonial Executive, and the colonial Assembly over the determination of the legislative representation and the franchise had to be resolved and defined. The problem was merely compounded by the fact that in Great Britain itself both the Crown and Parliament had each on past occasions independently granted representation in the Commons and that, at each colony's commencement, necessity had placed the right of granting representation in the hands of Governor and Council.

In Nova Scotia as long as the official Halifax circle and its friends dominated the Executive and the Assembly no complaints were to be expected. There were no complaints when, on the dissolution of the second Assembly in 1761, Lieutenant Governor Belcher arbitrarily dropped the county and township of Cumberland from representation and added two members for each of the townships of Falmouth, Cornwallis, and Liverpool; nor in 1765 when the new Governor, Montagu Wilmot, after dissolving the third Assembly modified the representation. As the families settled in the townships of Falmouth, Cornwallis, and Liverpool were mainly tenants on the lands granted by Lawrence to the Halifax official circle in 1759, the representatives granted these townships by Belcher merely enhanced the control the Halifax circle exercised over the Assembly. Governor Wilmot's adjustment of the basis of representation was also designed to ensure the continuance of their control.

During the life of the third Assembly considerable immigration occurred and a number of new townships were settled. If the Minute of Council of August 22, 1759, had continued to govern representation these new townships would have been entitled to two members and Halifax's control of the Assembly imperilled. It was this danger Montagu and his Council sought to forestall when they changed the basis of representation in the Assembly. The county representation was allowed to remain at two members each save for the county of Halifax whose representation was raised to four; but the representation of all townships was reduced by one-half, that is, the representation of Halifax Township was reduced from four to two, and the representation of all the other townships was reduced from two to one.[28]

Complaints did arise in the fourth Assembly when the animosity between Belcher and certain Halifax merchants engendered by a controversy over a debt moratorium shattered the unity of the Halifax interests.[29] The representatives of the outsettlements, as a consequence, found themselves possessed of a new influence in the Assembly and they set about to challenge the prerogative right of the Governor to adjust the representation. They demanded "that the Assembly be put on the footing it ever has been since the convention of a General Assembly in this province, that is to say, that each township should have the privilege of sending two members."[30] They asserted that Governor Lawrence's proclamation of 1758 and subsequent practice was "the foundation of their constitution or plan of government which they humbly are of opinion cannot be altered without their own consent."[31] The Governor refused to accede to the full demands of the Assembly that the representation be based on statute and on Lawrence's plan of two representatives to each township. He informed the Assembly he would only go so far as to "confirm by law the present representation in General Assembly."[32] The Assembly accepted the compromise. The spring season was threatening to draw the members from the outsettlements back to their farms, and the Assembly believed it had established the principle that all subsequent changes in representation would have to be sanctioned by the Assembly.

In this belief the Assembly was doomed to disappointment; for the Board of Trade had just been induced to take the first step to regularize the procedure governing the granting of representation in colonial assemblies. In the face of the deluge of colonial representation acts following the peace of 1763, the Board in September 11, 1767, issued a circular instruction to all colonial governors which forbade the governors giving assent to any bill originating in a colonial legislature altering the representation or franchise.[33] The Board had taken the view that colonial assemblies were inferior legislative bodies, constituted by royal grace and favour, limited in powers, and their membership a fit subject for the exercise of the royal prerogative. In anticipation of the Instruction, the Nova Scotia statute was disallowed by Order in Council on June 26, 1767.[34]

It was not until some years later that the hopes of the Assembly to control electoral matters were revived following the departure of Hillsborough and the arrival of Dartmouth at the Board of Trade. Under Dartmouth's presidency the policy of the Board underwent a change, and the change was reflected in the Instructions issued in 1773 to the next Governor of Nova Scotia, Francis Legge. Legge was instructed to allow the Assembly to legislate on representation and the franchise if the legislation had received prior approval from the Board of Trade, or if the legislation contained a suspending clause.[35] Dartmouth intended the change to be a real grant of power to the Assembly and in the following year, when the Governor and Council requested the exercise of the royal prerogative to modify the representation and the size of the Assembly's quorum, Dartmouth refused and advised Legge to secure the change by statute.[36] Legge and his Council had desired to reduce the Assembly's quorum from twelve to nine, and to give to Halifax Township and County two additional members each, thereby assuring ten members to Halifax in an Assembly whose quorum was to be nine.

On learning of the request the Assembly rose in righteous indignation. In the shadow of Concord and Lexington, it complained to the Governor that:

the method proposed . . . is replete with mischief, subversive of real representation and in its consequences must render a Governor of this Province absolute . . . and when we consider that four additional members are proposed for the town and County of Halifax, in order to command a quorum at all times on the spot, we own we are alarmed at seeing a plan proposed so subversive of our freedom. With a dependent Council and a majority of such a quorum of Assembly, what might not an ambitious Governor affect.[37]

The Assembly then proceeded to send a secret address to the King and Parliament which, after a compilation of grievances, requested protection from the arbitrary discretion of the Governor and Council, the prohibition of Crown employees from serving as representatives in the Assembly, the establishment of triennial assemblies, and the statutory fixation of elections.[38]

While in this frame of mind the Assembly passed a bill to regulate elections. The bill sought to establish a property qualification for members, fix the life of parliament at three years, introduce the ballot, fix the hours of polling and the period of notification of elections, fix the quorum at sixteen, and make the Assembly and not the Governor the sole judge of elections and qualifications of members.[39] The Legislative Council handled the bill harshly, striking out the ballot, triennial parliaments, the fixation of the Assembly quorum, and the clause establishing a poll in each township. The Assembly refused to accept the amendments and the bill died. The third attempt of the Assembly to limit the Governor's discretionary power over electoral matters had failed.

A fourth attempt was made by the same Assembly some years later. It was a modest attempt occasioned by the undue length of the fifth General Assembly and the irregularity of the sessions. The Assembly sought the minimum of yearly meeting and a maximum life of seven years.[40] The bill would have ensured that a governor could not govern without an assembly and that the personnel of the Assembly would be renewable at periodic general elections. No more was asked than that the laws and customs which regulated the life of the Imperial Parliament should be extended to the Assembly of Nova Scotia. Despite the fact that the bill contained a suspending clause the Board of Trade refused to confirm the measure, insisting that it should also have been submitted in draft form for the prior approval of the Crown.[41] With Dartmouth gone from its presidency, the Board of Trade was again determined to maintain the prerogative powers of the Governor. The Assembly was not to be allowed to regulate the representation, elections, or the franchise.

While the pre-loyalist Assembly never secured a law to regulate the elections, it did, in an indirect and limited way, reduce executive control over them. This gain was occasioned by the Assembly's securing the abolition of the office of Provost Marshal and the creation of the office of county sheriff.[42] The Provost Marshal, being an appointee of the Governor and Council, was suspected of being partial in elections to the Halifax interests. The Assembly, in its secret address to the King and Parliament in 1775, had begged to be delivered "from a Provost Marshal presiding over this whole province, whose influence, owing to the nature of his office and the number of his deputies, must be excessive, and whose power is absolute"; otherwise they could "have no pretensions even to the name of freemen."[43] The Assembly hoped the abolition of the office would reduce centralized control of the elections. While the Governor and Council were to appoint the sheriffs, their choice was limited to a list of three names provided for each county by a judge of the Supreme Court. The sheriffs, residing in their county town, were more independent of the official circle at Halifax and in any election where a conflict arose between local and Halifax interests, Halifax direction tended to be less influential.

The conclusion of the American Revolutionary War produced the conditions that led to the achieving of the Assembly's ambition, the statutory control of representation and the franchise. The advent of the loyalists had not merely the effect of separating the St. John valley and Cape Breton from Nova Scotia,[44] but it created a political cleavage within Nova Scotia between the old settlers of pre-revolutionary origin and the new loyalists. This cleavage was clearly evidenced in 1784 when Governor Parr dissolved the fifth General Assembly. Despite its fourteen-year life, the loyalists were "confident that the Governor had been advised to dissolve the present House and have a new one elected, before the Loyalists should be in a condition to become electors within the sense of the provincial law."[45] The suspicion was not justified, for the dissolution of the Assembly had been ordered by the Secretary of State as early as 1781, but on account of the failure of the despatch to reach Halifax it had been necessary in 1783 for the order for dissolution to be reissued.[46]

Prior to the dissolution and in order to placate the loyalists, Parr had requested the Secretary of State to increase the membership of the Assembly by Royal Instruction. Parr had felt that "nothing [would] contribute more to quiet the minds of the Loyalists in this Province than being represented in the House of Assembly."[47] In reply Parr was instructed to increase the representation by assenting to any bill found necessary for increasing the number of counties or townships and their representation.[48] In consequence, a joint committee of the Legislative Council and the Assembly, in the dying hours of the fifth General Assembly, drafted and passed a representation act which created two new counties, Shelburne and Sydney, and two new townships, Shelburne and Digby, and assigned them representation.[49] The act was not a consolidation of the existing representation, it simply granted representation to the new settlements. It did not confirm the existing representation which continued to rest on minutes of the Executive Council; but it established a precedent which enabled the Assembly, in the years immediately following, to extend its control over the franchise.

It should be said that in the pre-loyalist period, while the franchise and representation remained under the absolute discretion of the Governor and Council, it was fashioned on British precedents. The ancient English principle of representation, two knights from each shire, was applied from the second General Assembly to each county, as was the English county franchise. As mentioned, the change in the franchise between the first and second assemblies was of no practical effect. No election was ever set aside throughout this period because a freehold was less value than 40s. per annum. If an elector possessed a freehold of any size and in some state of productivity, it appears to have been universally accepted that it was of the requisite value. There was, however, as evidenced in the Cape Breton election of 1766, an insistence that each elector possess a freehold.

Cape Breton had been annexed to Nova Scotia in 1763, but the Board of Trade had ruled, in order to reserve the coal and fisheries to the Crown, that no freehold grants should be given to settlers. In consequence the settlers in Cape Breton possessed their holdings on certificates of occupation. When on December 16, 1766, the Governor of Nova Scotia issued a writ for the election of two county members from Cape Breton, the Assembly voided the return on the grounds that the members were not returned by freeholders.[50] Cape Breton was left without representation until the dissolution of the Assembly in 1770 when the Executive Council refused to issue a writ for the Island "because of the want of freeholders to make an election" and decreed instead "that the said Isle be deemed to be represented by the members for the County of Halifax unto which it has been resolved and become a part thereof as heretofore."[51]

The first loyalist Assembly promptly set out to secure statutory control of the franchise. A select committee under the chairmanship of the Solicitor General, R. J. Uniacke, was immediately set up to consider the status of the Assembly in relation to the passage of legislation to regulate elections.[52] At this point the attention of the House was diverted for two sessions by a struggle between the loyalist and pre-loyalist factions to secure a contested seat for Annapolis County; and it was not until the Assembly was jolted by a fracas at a Halifax by-election that it returned to consider legislation to regulate elections. The Assembly then endorsed a resolution "that the House has the sole and exclusive power of examining and determining the rights and qualifications of electors and elected, together with return of writs, and all matters incidental to elections,"[53] and followed their resolution by passage of "an Act for the better regulation of Elections."[54] When the act was approved by the Board of Trade, the Assembly had achieved control of the franchise and ended the days when the whim of the Governor could enfranchise and disfranchise Nova Scotian citizens.

The Election Act retained the 40s. freehold franchise but extended the suffrage to include all men who possessed a dwelling house of any value and the ground on which it stood, or one hundred acres of cultivated or uncultivated land. The extension was of especial benefit to urban residents, to those engaged in the fishing industry, and to the new settlers. The latter further benefited by a relaxation in the requirements as to tenure. In addition to freehold tenure, a licence of occupation from the Crown was to entitle occupants of the requisite property to be electors or candidates. Many licences of occupation had been issued to the loyalists on unsurveyed land or on land which the Crown had already alienated but on which the grants were to be revoked. These licences of occupation were to be replaced by freehold grants once the lands were surveyed or the process of escheat had been completed. Besides easing the economic barriers to the franchise, the act also removed the religious barriers. All religious tests were abolished and henceforth Roman Catholics and Jews were not to be denied the vote on account of their religious beliefs.

The Election Act also dealt with the conduct of elections. Little change was introduced, the act being in the main a statutory confirmation of the practices established by minute of Executive Council in 1757. The returning officer was still to appoint electors to assist him to record the votes, and the candidates were to nominate inspectors. The electoral assistants were reduced from three to two and each candidate was to be privileged to appoint not merely an inspector but also a clerk. This innovation meant each candidate would be able to take down a record of the votes cast which would serve as a check on the official record taken by the returning officer's assistants. The period of public notification of elections was set at twenty days,[55] a reversion to the practice of the first general election. The condition of communications made this a welcome extension over the five days' notice which had been required since the second general election.

The period of polling was set at six days unless sooner concluded with the consent of all the candidates or by the failure of any elector to come forward during a one-hour period, and the poll was not to move about the county unless all candidates agreed. The single-day poll which had been the prevailing practice until the 1785 election had confined the franchise to the county town and had led to a minority of the freeholders returning the elected member. When a candidate was returned on the vote of five electors in a 1783 by-election for Sunbury,[56] the Executive Council decided a single-day poll was inadequate; and at the next general election the Council ordered the polls to be kept open from day to day until all electors were polled or until no electors presented themselves within the space of one hour.[57] In face of the increasing dispersion of settlement and poor communications, the Assembly had to decide whether to revert to the single-day poll and establish a multitude of polls or to continue the single poll and maintain a lengthy period of polling. They chose the latter.

This issue had almost destroyed the act in the Assembly, and was the reason why the bill narrowly passed third reading on a vote of 16 to 15.[58] The loyalists and members from the outsettlements voted against the bill because they wanted the poll adjourned around the county in order that the privilege of voting might be placed within the reach of each elector. Halifax influence prevailed and the bill was carried, the only concession being the provision to allow the pool to adjourn around the county on the unanimous consent of the candidates, a condition unlikely to be fulfilled. The failure of the Assembly to require either a multitude of polls or the compulsory adjournment of the single poll resulted in the disfranchisement of those electors located some distance from the single stationary poll for each riding. What may be described as territorial disfranchisement was a recurrent problem in Nova Scotia and in all the British North American colonies. The degree of disfranchisement occasioned becomes evident when the returns for an election in which the poll did adjourn around the county are observed. By the time of the Halifax County election (1799) whose returns are shown below, the single poll was required to adjourn to two places outside the county town. The returns, which show each candidates' total

vote at the completion of the poll in each place, indicate the degree of disfranchisement that would have occurred had the poll been held only at the county town, as
well as the different four members that would have represented Halifax County.[59]

	Halifax	Onslow	Walmsley
Morris	756	782	1000
Stewart	621	626	627
Wallace	596	636	888
Hartshorne	578	597	605
Tonge	392	889	1257
Mortimer	109	621	1077
Fulton	86	603	1001

In the next forty years four problems concerning the effectiveness of the franchise
drew the attention of the Assembly. These involved a renewal of executive discretion
as respects the franchise, the lack of any limit on the life of the Assembly, the need to
curb the increase in electoral corruption, and, most important of all, renewed attempts
to overcome territorial disfranchisement.

While the first Assembly that had been under the influence of the loyalists has been
credited with asserting legislative control of the franchise, the reannexation of Cape
Breton to Nova Scotia in 1820 brought a re-emergence of executive control. The
Royal Instructions ordering the reannexation reached Nova Scotia after the Assembly
had been dissolved. As the laws of Nova Scotia did not extend to Cape Breton, the
Governor and Council, anxious to give Cape Breton representation in the new Assembly, determined the franchise and the conduct of the election. The election was required to conform to the procedure established by the Executive Council in 1759
rather than that established by the statute of 1789, and the franchise was to be open
to leaseholders on Crown lands.[60] The Executive Council harboured no sinister design
on the powers of the Assembly. They were merely anxious to have Cape Breton represented in the new Assembly and were conscious of the fact that Cape Breton possessed few freeholders; from 1763 to 1784 land had been held only by Crown lease or
licence of occupation, and freehold grants issued after 1784 had generally been given
in large blocks to speculators, as for instance the Mire grant of 100,000 acres given in
1787 by Governor DesBarres to one hundred associates. It was estimated in 1821
that of the 685,640 acres taken up, 229,220 acres were held in fee simple, 98,600 acres
by Crown leases, 15,000 acres by licences of occupation, and 342,820 acres by warrants of survey.[61] The majority of the residents of Cape Breton were either tenants
or occupants on lands of the Crown or of private speculators.

Before the next general election the Assembly extended the laws of Nova Scotia to
Cape Breton.[62] While the 40s. freehold franchise was to be the governing qualification,
the Assembly did not restrict the franchise from that decreed by the Executive Council, for the legislation equated leases and licences of occupation on Crown lands in
Cape Breton with freehold tenure.[63] As the franchise was not extended to tenants on
the lands of private citizens and as the leases and licences on Crown lands were to be
replaced with grants in fee simple, the Assembly was not seriously departing from the
freehold franchise. Nevertheless this leasehold franchise did not go unnoticed at the
Colonial Office and the Governor was required to give an explanation.[64] As he had
already made considerable progress in turning the Crown leases into grants in fee
simple and had given land to the squatters under ticket of location with the prospect
of a grant when the conditions of settlement had been completed, Kempt confiden-

tially replied that there was no real need to extend the franchise to leaseholders and that he was "now disposed to think that it [would] be better in all respects to place the whole Province on the same footing and confine the right of voting in Cape Breton to freeholders as in Nova Scotia proper."[65] Kempt's recommendation arrived too late for the bill to be disallowed and a leasehold franchise, although applicable only to Cape Breton, became incorporated in Nova Scotia law and was to serve as a precedent on a future occasion.

For a short period the franchise was jeopardized by the lack of any limit to the duration of the Assembly. Attempts had been made in 1775 to limit the life of an future Assembly to three years, and in 1780 and again 1790 to seven years. But in the first instance the Legislative Council objected, in the second the Board of Trade disallowed the act, and in the third Lieutenant Governor Parr, guided by the Board of Trade precedent, refused his assent. The Assembly took advantage of Parr's death and passed a second septennial bill in 1792. This bill, after being endorsed by Lieutenant Governor Wentworth, received the approval of the Secretary of State.[66] For the future there could be no repetition of the virtual disfranchisement occasioned by the fourteen-year life of the fifth General Assembly.

The strong factional spirit coupled with the multiple days of polling led in Nova Scotia to a growth in electoral corruption. There was, in fact, less need to liberalize the franchise in the decades following the American Revolutionary War than to purify its exercise. The act of 1789 had made fraudulent conveyances to multiply votes a crime, but as the act had not required that the freeholds be registered, it was impossible to prevent such a multiplication of votes. The Assembly found that in two controverted elections, Kings and Hants, brought before the House following the general election of 1793, the sitting members had achieved their majorities by the transfer of property.[67] In the investigation of the Kings County election, the sitting member was proved to have granted away one hundred acres to each of twenty-nine persons for a payment of £5 and his vote, all transfers having taken place within the ten days previous to the opening of the adjourned poll at Parrsborough. The Assembly ruled "that deeds executed subsequent to the teste of the writ for electing members to serve in General Assembly are illegal and insufficient, to entitle a person to vote under such deeds" and voided the election.[68] As a result of this experience the Assembly set up a select committee to prepare a remedy.[69] The end result was the passage of an act, some four years later, which, while confirming the essentials of the 1789 franchise, ended the right to vote on licences of occupation, required those possessed of one hundred acres of land to have at least five acres under cultivation, and required all freeholds to be registered at least six months before the issuance of the writs of election.[70] The changes reflected the transition of the loyalist settlements from raw to mature communities and the attempt of the Assembly to end voting on fraudulent conveyances. The latter provision would have been of more value if the registration of property could have been effectively carried out, but the state of communications in Nova Scotia and the state of its local government were grave handicaps. Two complaints from the county of Annapolis illustrate this fact. In 1800 the freeholders petitioned that their votes had been refused on the grounds their property was not registered although their deeds had been deposited in the sheriff's office many months before the teste of the writ; in the following general election a freeholder from the same county complained that the sheriff had refused the petitioner a vote although his deed had been in the sheriff's office for over two years.[71]

B

Similarly, the failure to define the hours of polling by statute allowed sharp practices. While the act of 1789 had stated that the sheriff should commence the election on its first day between 10 A.M. and 12 noon, there was no further provision as to the times of opening and closing the polls, save that the sheriff was to proceed from day to day until all the electors were polled or until no elector appeared for one hour after the sheriff had made a public proclamation summoning lethargic freeholders to vote. The custom developed that the candidates would agree on the hours of opening and closing the poll but the custom was often honoured in the breach. On one occasion at Halifax, the sheriff insisted on closing the poll at the firing of the garrison's gun at sunset, although the candidates were tied and the poll thronged with voters; on another occasion in Digby, the sheriff would not close the poll until midnight, and at Newport a sheriff took the opportunity to close the poll in the middle of a wind- and rainstorm.[72] In 1824, to regularize the polling and prevent citizens being disfranchised by the eccentricities of the returning officers, the hours of closing the polls were fixed at 4 P.M. between September 22 and March 22 and at 6 P.M. during the rest of the year.[73]

As mentioned, the act of 1789 had not accommodated the outsettlements by the establishments of peripatetic polls, to take the election from settlement to settlement in each county and township. In the following year, the Assembly returned to a consideration of territorial disfranchisement when two remedies for the evil were presented to it. One proposed remedy came in the petitions from Pictou and Merigomish in Halifax County advocating the subdivision of the larger counties into new counties and townships, thereby multiplying the polling facilities; the other remedy took the shape of a bill sponsored by Major Milledge, loyalist member for Digby Township, to adjourn the poll to specific places beyond the county towns in Halifax, Annapolis, and three other counties.[74]

The Assembly was to try both remedies. A bill to create peripatetic polls passed the Assembly but perished in the Legislative Council, which was filled with Haligonians who had no desire to see their influence weakened by the admission of Colchester and Pictou settlers to the Halifax County franchise. Foiled, the Assembly appointed a committee to prepare an Address to the King that the Assembly be allowed to create new counties. The petition declared that "the principal settlements now forming in the remote parts of the county of Halifax are Pictou and Merigomish Harbour, in which are now settled upwards of twelve hundred inhabitants who, from want of roads, find their communications with Halifax at all times difficult; they being nearly ninety miles distant from it, and in consequence thereof are deprived of the inestimable privilege of British subjects, the giving of their suffrage to elect a person to represent them in General Assembly."[75] The Assembly confirmed the Address and requested the King to allow them to divide the counties of Halifax and Annapolis. Lieutenant Governor Parr forwarded it with a covering dispatch advising its rejection. The request was contrary to the personal inclination of the Governor and his Council, who felt the augmentation of the county representation would only add to the factious group of loyalists and others who were demanding the impeachment of the judiciary.[76]

No further action was taken until 1792, after Parr's death, when Sir John Wentworth, a loyalist, succeeded to the office of Lieutenant Governor. The bill of 1790 was revived, and the sheriffs in five counties, Halifax, Annapolis, Shelburne, Sydney, and Kings, were to be required to adjourn the election to specified polls in each county on the request of any candidate.[77] The bill was accepted by the Legislative Council and received the express approval of the Lieutenant Governor on the grounds that it gave accommodation "to the voters in elections, by saving expensive and difficult travelling, and may tend to moderate the warmth and indiscretion which often results from more numerous meetings."[78]

In the following years the Assembly continued intermittently to reduce the territorial disfranchisement by extending the device of the peripatetic poll to other counties. Queens and Cumberland counties were given a perambulating poll in 1817, Hants in 1824, and Lunenburg in 1835, and Cape Breton was given the same facilities in 1820 and 1826 by minutes of the Executive Council when legislative oversight failed to provide them by law.[79] While the peripatetic poll was a help, it did not eliminate territorial disfranchisement, as in Halifax County for example, where the poll reached only the three towns of Halifax, Truro, and Pictou.

Unless elections were to be unduly prolonged there was a limit to the extension of polling circuits. In 1811 and 1814, it had been impossible to complete the polling for Sydney County within the time allowed by the writ of election.[80] In consequence, the request to the Colonial Secretary to allow the subdivision of counties, which the Assembly had tried to secure in 1792 and which had occasioned a second address from the Assembly in 1801, was effectively renewed by Dalhousie.[81] The Colonial Office, convinced of the inconvenience and injustice imposed on the electors of Halifax and Annapolis counties, granted the Assembly the right to erect new counties.[82]

Freed by the Colonial Office, the Assembly found that localism made it difficult to apply the new remedy. The Assembly was prepared to subdivide Annapolis County into Digby and Annapolis, and to subdivide Halifax County into Colchester, Pictou, and Halifax, but the Legislative Council had other designs.[83] It was not prepared to subdivide Annapolis, and while determined to subdivide Halifax County, wanted to retain the larger representation customarily accorded that county.[84] The Halifax-dominated Legislative Council schemed to get its way by offering to divide the extensive but numerically smaller county of Shelburne and thus throwing the Assembly into jealous local factions. The result was such bitter rivalry between Halifax and Annapolis that all adjustments in county structure were delayed for over a decade.[85]

In retrospect the half century following the American Revolutionary War was a period of quiet growth. The loyalists brought to Nova Scotia an energetic and conservative people who were not lacking in self-reliance. Their independence led them to assert legislative control over the franchise, representation, and the mode of election. They maintained the traditional foundation of landed property for the franchise, but they were not averse to modifying the 40s. freehold franchise when they perceived it was not entirely suitable to a colony possessing its wealth in large virgin tracts of land or in the teeming offshore fisheries. For these reasons they extended the franchise to include all owners of one hundred acres of land and all home owners. These changes served to enfranchise most rural settlers, merchants, town dwellers, and fishermen. As the years advanced and virgin tracts were cleared, they required each owner of one hundred acres to possess at least five acres cleared, a requirement justly discriminating against the speculators to the advantage of those worthy settlers who worked to clear a home in Nova Scotia's valleys and uplands.

CHAPTER THREE

NOVA SCOTIA, 1830–67: THE FRANCHISE AND POLITICS

THIS PERIOD opens with a quickening of the political tempo in Nova Scotia. The brandy dispute of the early 1830's which involved a contest between the Assembly and the Council over control of custom revenue, the libel suit brought by the magistrates of Halifax against Joseph Howe, and the struggle to separate the personnel of the Executive and Legislative councils stirred political passions. The evangelical movement in the Protestant churches was equally important. It synchronized with and gave impetus to the rise of the temperance societies and both influences working together profoundly stirred the righteous souls of Nova Scotia.

Afire with moral fervour, the temperance movement set about to eliminate debauchery and corruption from elections. They sought to reduce the carousals occasioned by large numbers congregating at the two or three polls for each county by creating more polls, suppressing open houses, and adopting the voters' register. These reforms were instrumental in reducing territorial disfranchisement and in bringing the Assembly to contemplate the adoption of an assessment franchise.

The General Assembly elected in 1830 turned its immediate attention to the subdivision of counties and the provision of more polling facilities. While the temperance advocates supported the reform on moral grounds, the outsettlements supported it in order to overcome inequalities in a representation which had remained virtually unchanged since 1785.[1] The growth of settlement had seriously distorted representation. Cape Breton, for instance, returned two members, although it was geographically as large as Annapolis and Shelburne which returned ten members, and twice as populous as either Annapolis, Shelburne, or Pictou.[2] This distortion might have been overcome by the simple procedure of augmenting the representation but this solution would not have remedied territorial disfranchisement. An extension of the polling circuits in each county would have reduced territorial disfranchisement, but it would not have overcome the inequalities in representation and would have prolonged elections which were already unduly protracted. The 1832 by-election in Cape Breton, necessitated by the grant of an additional member, dispelled any doubts on this matter. The election lasted over a month, and the intense rivalry between the candidates, William Young, and Richard Smith of the General Mining Association, produced open and prolonged rioting.[3] Young, describing the riot at Sydney, had reported in the *Novascotian* of January 3, 1833, that:

The town was filled with vast bodies of men drawn from the mines, houses thrown open in every street, an expenditure of unexampled profusion and amount incurred, and a degree of excitement created and kept up which rendered it dangerous in the last degree for any man to espouse my interest. . . . The door of my apartment was broken in and forced and its privacy invaded the same evening by a lawless mob, my friends and myself obliged to abandon the house . . . and to fly under the shades of night for protection, two of my supporters subjected to personal outrage, and a universal terror diffused, which few indeed could be expected to withstand.

As territorial disfranchisement and inequalities in representation had to be solved by a subdivision of the larger counties, it might have been expected that the Assembly would have taken advantage of the census of 1827 and proceeded to a general redivision of the province. A select committee was established by J. B. Uniacke, member for Cape Breton, for this purpose, but a general revision had to be abandoned in favour of particular legislation when the secession movement in Cape Breton made delay dangerous.[4] Although the Solicitor General subsequently tried for three sessions to obtain a general revision, it was never possible to secure, as local jealousies and hostility led to a piecemeal settlement. In the years to 1837, the particular legislation was devised and secured. In spite of bitter rivalry between Halifax and Annapolis, the five larger counties were subdivided into a total of twelve counties, and except for the further division of Cape Breton County in 1851, the county structure was finalized.[5] The worst inequalities in representation were corrected and territorial disfranchisement was reduced but not eliminated when each new county was provided with its own polling circuit. Territorial disfranchisement was not finally eliminated until 1847, when political circumstances led Nova Scotia to adopt the practice of the English Reform Bill and divide each county into a number of polling subdivisions.

The temperance advocates were less successful in their attempts to abolish the practice of candidates maintaining open houses. They did not receive sympathetic support from the general public as they had done in their move to subdivide the counties. It had become an established custom that candidates should maintain open houses at each poll to provide free food and drink for their supporters. While the practice had been legally discouraged since the first election act, it had grown in popularity until the candidates had become victims of their own hospitality. A report in the *Acadian Reporter* of December 10, 1836, of a contest in Colchester County may serve as an illustration:

The polling commenced with much merit and before the hour of adjournment the Attorney General stood 404 and Mr. Logan 130. The adjournment was hailed by all present with uncommon pleasure, as a fear was abroad that Mr. Logan would resign the first day, and deprive them of the amusement they anticipated in the contest of another. The night was one of great excitement. Many of the Attorney General's warmest friends huzzaed for Logan to give confidence to his party. His commissariat, however, was very deficient, and many of his pretended friends quartered upon the enemy where they were well entertained.

Although the cost had begun to bear heavily on the candidates, the temperance advocates were unable to secure passage of a bill to deny a seat to any member who provided entertainment at his election.[6] They had to content themselves with forbidding candidates to distribute liquor on pain of a £100 fine at the hands of any common informer.[7] The practice was too firmly entrenched in popular expectations to be eradicated by such legislation.

The voters' register and the ballot, which had been espoused by the temperance advocates as part of their programme to end electoral corruption, appear to have been adopted primarily because these reforms had been in the forefront of the English electoral reform movement. When the ballot failed to be carried into the first Reform Bill, the temperance advocates ceased to press for its adoption in Nova Scotia and directed their efforts towards securing the voters' register. It was expected to curtail fraudulent voting, end the need for scrutinies, and by reducing the need to swear electors, facilitate polling and reduce the excitement of the crowds at the polls. The struggle to secure its adoption, however, revealed difficulties. Could it be established cheaply? Could it be established in the absence of an efficient system of municipal government and a province-wide assessment of propety? When the deliberations of four select committees were unable to devise satisfactory answers, interest in the voters' register flickered out.[8] It was to be revived in the partisan politics of the 1840's.

While the deliberations of the select committees did not lead to the adoption of the voters' register, they were not without effect on the franchise, as a by-product of the decision of the select committee established in 1837 to proceed to a consolidation of the laws governing elections and the franchise. The consolidating statute retained the 40s. freehold franchise but abolished the right to vote on possession of one hundred acres of land, or of a dwelling house and the land on which it stood.[9] At first sight this change might appear to have disfranchised the speculators who held tracts of uncultivated lands, the owners of urban property, and the fishermen who possessed homes and staging areas on Nova Scotia's rocky coast. But though the speculators were in fact disfranchised, urban property owners and fishermen were not, for the concept of a freehold was broadened to include real estate as well as land and the value of a fisherman's staging was to be determined by the annual harvest of his nets.[10] Crown leases and licences of occupation remained valid titles in Cape Breton, and to accommodate progress, mortgagors, co-partners, tenants in common, and joint tenants might vote if their individual interest in any property was equal to 40s. yearly value.

When in December, 1843, Howe withdrew from the Executive Council, Nova Scotia embarked on a new era. The disintegration of the coalition in mutual recrimination led to the formation of rival political parties, the struggle for responsible government and its establishment. The ensuing rivalry to secure and retain public office forced the parties to espouse in rapid succession simultaneous polling, a ratepayers' franchise, manhood suffrage, equalization of representation and finally the abolition of manhood suffrage in favour of an assessment franchise, and the voters' register. These progressive modifications of the franchise were not the products of an unfolding of the democratic ideal but rather the by-products of the search for public favour by political parties.

The franchise was thrown into the political arena by the excessive violence exhibited at Pictou in the general election of 1843. It was reported that:

the polling was held in the second storey of the Court House, which was reached by a broad staircase. One party hit upon the device of packing this stairway with its own men, who overflowed into the corridor above and the room in which the votes were given. The process of voting was made slow by protests and other means. This forced monopoly of space stirred resistance in the hearts of the other party. From a number of outlying sections the voters had not arrived. Messengers were, therefore, sent to let them know the state of things at the polling place. The result was that in a short time about one hundred men appeared, each having a dangerous looking stick in his hand. In an incredibly short time the stairway and upper space was cleared. . . . When the struggle was over, in one house, near the polling place, there were seventeen men in the hands of the doctors. To storm and take the stairway was not enough; it must be held day and night by all means. A man now living remembers that with other boys he walked upon the shoulders of the men holding the fort, carrying them food and pails of rum and water, to keep up their strength and spirits day and night in defending this vantage ground gained in a violent struggle.[11]

Because of this election the leader of the new government, Attorney General Johnston, abolished the polling circuits and the multiple polling days.

In the new Assembly, following the deliberations of a select committee, Johnston asked the House to consider the adoption of "registration and simultaneous polling unitedly, or if registration be impossible at present . . . simultaneous polling without registration, and also . . . the propriety of basing the election franchise on the payment of rates."[12] The controversial nature of these alternatives and the state of party feeling in the House were not conducive to a unified solution. In consequence when Johnston, in 1845, introduced a resolution to establish simultaneous polling, the Liberal party leaders, Uniacke and Howe, insisted that simultaneous polling must be accompanied by a registration of voters.[13] The Conservatives agreed that fraudulent voting would not be eliminated by simultaneous polling unaccompanied by the voters' register, but they rejected the Opposition's proposal, fortified in the knowledge Canada and New Brunswick had established simultaneous polling without a voters' register. The Conservatives, were undoubtedly influenced by the absence of effective local machinery to prepare and revise annually a voters' register, and by the failure of the registration of voters in England. There the neglect of the overseers of the poor law to prepare the lists and the pernicious activity of party agents had resulted in the wholesale perversion of the voters' register.[14]

The simultaneous polling established in Nova Scotia differed from that adopted in Canada and New Brunswick in that the entire colony had to be polled in one day whereas Canada and New Brunswick required only that each constituency be polled in one day. This reform radically modified election procedure. While the old county and township representation was retained, the division of each constituency into many polling subdivisions, to allow the completion of polling in one day, necessitated the separation of nominations from elections.[15] Election writs had to be issued simultaneously to all sheriffs setting forth the day of nomination, which was to be followed one week later by the day of polling. As the sheriff could no longer personally conduct each poll, he assumed the role of the modern returning officer. He gave ten days' notice of nomination day, presided over the sheriff's court to receive nominations, and selected a presiding officer and clerk for each poll. These officers, assisted by a clerk, an inspector, and an agent from each candidate, were to conduct the recording of the vocal votes of the electors between the hours of 8 A.M. and 5 P.M. on the day of election. On completion of the poll, the presiding officer was to seal the official poll books and return them to the sheriff. The sheriff was to retain the poll books until the reassembling of the sheriff's court five days after the election, when the seals would be broken, the vote officially tabulated, and the result of the polling declared.

While the changes wrought by simultaneous polling were procedural, they also affected the franchise. Simultaneous polling restricted the voting privileges of the extensive property owners. Although the right of property owners to vote in any township or county in which they held property remained, the time limit on voting could not but curtail the vote of non-resident property owners. The creation of polling subdivisions on the other hand extended the franchise. Polls were for the first time placed within convenient reach of all residents, and territorial disfranchisement was eliminated. The separation of nomination from polling day and the creation of polling subdivisions reduced the violence at elections and ended the disfranchisement of the faint-hearted.

When the bill to establish simultaneous polling had been before the Assembly, the Liberals had espoused a concept that was to constitute the next reform in the franchise. Their advocacy of a voters' register ceased, and was replaced by the demand that all taxpayers should be entitled to a vote. The ratepayers' franchise was in use in the English boroughs and had been in use in many American states following the Revolution, but its adoption at this time by the Liberals seems to have been motivated by its rhetorical value on the hustings and their belief that a ratepayers' franchise would provide a ready-made voters' register. In the following general election, the Liberals were returned on their promise to institute responsible government and a ratepayers' franchise and before the Assembly was again dissolved both promises had been implemented.

The act establishing the ratepayers' franchise was put on the statute books in 1851.[16] It enfranchised all males of twenty-one years who had been assessed for and had paid the poor and county rates in the year previous to any election. No limits were placed on the rates required to confer the franchise, the legislation merely stating that the rates must be levied and paid. The collector of the poor and county rates was annually to prepare the assessment roll and to indicate which ratepayers had paid their rates. This record of assessments and collections would serve as a voters' register.

The ratepayers' franchise should have meant a major extension in the electorate, as the poor and county rates were assessed on both real and personal property.[17] There must have been a need to extend the franchise. The Crown had ceased since 1832 to make free grants of land, and while Crown lands could be purchased at an upset price of 1s. 9d. the lands which were both accessible and arable must have been limited. In the decade and a half since the cessation of free land grants there must have grown up in town and country a class of men who did not possess a freehold. There was considerable uncertainty as to the size of this class. Howe, as late as 1847, had not considered it large, for "from the abundance and low price of land this qualification [40s. freehold] is easily acquired by an industrious person";[18] the *Acadian Recorder* of March 22, 1851, on the passage of the act stated: "It is supposed it will add one-fourth to the numerical increase of the franchise. This is high we think. In some localities it may add more, but generally less. We doubt if it will add over one-eighth in the whole Province." In the face of these estimates it was with some surprise that the public witnessed a 30 per cent increase in the vote cast in the general election of 1851 as compared with the previous election of 1847.[19]

The answer to the discrepancy between the estimates and the reality was to be found in the fifteen election petitions that reached the new Assembly. These petitions protested against the conduct of the election, against the tampering with the assessment rolls, and against the fraudulent creation of votes through the presentation of fake collectors' receipts. The latter abuse had arisen out of a safeguard inserted in the act to protect the legitimate taxpayers against any laxity on the part of the collectors. Since no elector could vote on the ratepayers' franchise unless he had been assessed and paid poor and county rates, the failure of the collector to record the payment of rates on the assessment roll meant disfranchisement. Consequently, an elector was allowed to vote on presentation to the returning officer of a collector's receipt for the tax even though his payment had not been recorded on the assessment roll. The election also revealed that the assessors possessed the power to contract or expand the size of the electorate at will. The law governing assessment procedure had left to the discretion of the assessors the amount of real or personal property that made a citizen eligible to pay county or poor rates.[20] The assessors were placed in a position of being able to equate the ratepayers' franchise with manhood suffrage or to make it somewhat less. Leaving aside all differences in assessment inspired by villainy or partisanship, the discretion of the assessors made it inevitable that the franchise was extended to dissimilar classes of citizens in adjoining counties and townships.

The ratepayers' franchise necessitated the presence of competent municipal personnel and the annual imposition and collection of poor and county rates. These ingredients were frequently lacking. In Victoria County, it was subsequently revealed that the two assessors were illiterate, and in Halifax County it was reported some years earlier that the collections had amounted only to £36 and that even this small sum had not been paid to the county treasurers or any other officer authorized to receive it.[21] The county and poor rates were neither imposed nor collected annually, but were sporadically imposed when necessity demanded. Even "in the county of Halifax, it was a fact that the people of St. Margaret's Bay, of Musquodoboit, and of other outlying parts of the county paid no taxes."[22] The Government had foreseen this possibility and for that reason the legislation establishing the ratepayers' franchise had not abolished the 40s. freehold franchise. Where the rates were not assessed or collected the continuance of the 40s. freehold franchise maintained the voting rights of the traditional electors.

When the ratepayers' franchise had been before the House, the Conservatives had resolutely opposed it. Their opposition had not been based on hostility to the principle of a vote to every taxpayer, but on the practical difficulties of implementing such a franchise. When it had become clear the Liberals were determined to carry the measure, the Conservatives had turned from mere denunciation to urge the substitution of manhood suffrage. As the ratepayers' franchise should have extended the franchise to all male members of the families of freeholders and tenants who possessed any real or personal property on which the smallest county or poor rate might be imposed, the Conservatives had had to adopt manhood suffrage in order to outbid the Liberals. The Conservative motion was defeated on a straight party vote as was their subsequent motion to grant the franchise to all males who had performed statute labour;[23] but the Conservatives were led to renew their advocacy of manhood suffrage following the fiasco of the ratepayers' franchise.

When the Liberal Government, preoccupied with Howe's railway projects and hampered by the failing health of the Government leader, J. B. Uniacke, took no steps to improve the ratepayers' franchise, the Conservatives began to act. Johnston secured the establishment of a select committee to review the operation of the franchise. In the words of its report the committee was "unable to frame any plan for reducing the ratepaying franchise into a simple uniform and practically working system, and they recommended . . . that the house should substitute a franchise based on universal suffrage qualified by residence."[24] On the basis of this report, Johnston, in the following session, introduced a bill to abolish the ratepayers' franchise and establish manhood suffrage. The bill passed the Assembly without division, and had the Legislative Council not added an amendment incorporating the ballot, the bill would have passed into law. While the lack of opposition in the Assembly was astonishing, the Government's action in allowing the Leader of the Opposition to introduce and pilot through so important a measure was astounding. The answer seems to lie in Howe's overwhelming concern to secure legislative approval of his plans for an interprovincial railway. His party was divided on aspects of his railway programme, and Howe appears to have been desirous of appeasing the Opposition. He judged in all probability that the political gain accruing to the Liberal Government from the railway programme would far outweigh any political capital the Conservatives might secure from manhood suffrage.

When Johnston reintroduced the manhood suffrage bill in the following session,

B*

Howe, no longer dependent on the Opposition to carry his railway programme, allowed the Liberals to oppose it. Their criticism raised sufficient misgivings in the minds of some Conservative members that one, Martin Wilkins, was led to refer the bill to a select committee from which his leader, the sponsor of the bill, was excluded.[25] The sixteen-member committee which included Howe and eight other Liberals reviewed the problem of the franchise. They felt it was impossible to retain the ratepayers' franchise, for as Howe stated, "if continued the assessment franchise would lead to universal corruption and rascality."[26] They did not wish to proceed to manhood suffrage for Howe insisted that manhood suffrage had to be preceded by the adoption of universal education. Howe regretted that the 40s. freehold franchise had been disturbed, but the committee did not feel it was politically wise to return to it. The committee finally decided to adopt the franchise of the English Reform Bill of 1832. When the committee returned the bill to the House, it had been amended to establish a freehold and tenant franchise.[27] The bill was to retain the 40s. freehold franchise and to extend the vote to all occupants of property valued at £5 per annum. Despite the backing of Howe and William Young, the Speaker, the amended bill received rough treatment in the House. Fortified by the experience of New England, Johnston fought tenaciously to restore manhood suffrage. He was successful. The Liberals split, the House rejected the amendments made by the select committee, and the bill passed in the form Johnston had introduced it.[28]

The new franchise gave the vote to all British male subjects who had resided five years in Nova Scotia and one year in the county and township in which they would vote. The residence clause had been opposed but it was ultimately retained because of the expected influx of Irish labourers with the commencement of railway construction. Being under no illusion as to the manner in which employees of the Crown voted, the legislation for similar reasons denied the franchise to Indians and all paupers in receipt of aid from the government or from the county poor rates.[29] The 40s. freehold franchise was retained and within the limitations of simultaneous polling property owners could still cast their votes in all counties and townships in which they held property. The retention of the traditional franchise maintained a bias in favour of property and allowed British emigrants of substance to become enfranchised prior to the completion of five years' residence in the colony. The acquisition of property would enable its owners to vote as soon as the property had been registered in their name for six months.

In the absence of a voters' register the precise degree to which the electorate was extended by the adoption of manhood suffrage is uncertain. From the returns available in the newspapers for eight counties and seven townships, the vote cast in the election of 1855 was 52 per cent greater than in the election of 1851. While the addition of one elector for the township of Halifax meant the addition of four votes, two for the county and two for the township, the increase of 44 per cent is still large when we avoid this duplication by confining the comparison to the counties. As might have been expected, the increase was most substantial in the urban townships. The vote increased by 117 per cent and 90 per cent for Halifax and Lunenburg townships respectively, and the increase in the electorate drops to 36 per cent if the counties with the larger urban centres are excluded from the calculations. It may, therefore, be said that manhood suffrage chiefly benefited the labouring and tenant class of the towns, the tenant farmers, farmers' sons and farm labourers of the counties, and the fishermen's sons and the crews of the fishing fleets in the outports.

The increase of 44 per cent in the electorate occasioned by manhood suffrage and the 30 per cent increase occasioned by the ratepayers' franchise meant that the voting population of Nova Scotia increased by approximately 87 per cent between the elections of 1847 and 1855. These figures would seem to indicate that the freehold franchise had become restrictive, but against these figures must be placed the wide prevalence of fraudulent voting which manhood suffrage without a voters' register encouraged and the natural increase in the population. The extent of the fraudulent voting is impossible to gauge but the population increased by 20 per cent during this period. If the effects of fraudulent voting are ignored but the increase due to population growth is deducted, the resultant 56 per cent increase in the electorate between the 40s. freehold electorate of 1847 and the manhood electorate of 1855 remains substantial.

Although Nova Scotia was the first British colony in North America to introduce manhood suffrage, or universal suffrage as it was then known, there was no deep affection for it. It had been adopted as partisan tactics to extricate the franchise from the intolerable conditions attendant on the adoption of the ratepayers' franchise. Few of its proponents seem to have sincerely believed in it. As most members had supported its adoption because they believed it politically unwise to return to a freehold franchise, it is not surprising that manhood suffrage was readily abandoned when its demise would benefit the party in office. The Liberals were returned to power in the first manhood suffrage election in 1855, but they were the party destined to abolish manhood suffrage.

Howe had been personally defeated by Charles Tupper in this election and, although he was the chief Liberal strategist, he had not sought a second seat but had remained in public life as chairman of the provincial railway board. While he was engaged in this work, the Lieutenant Governor was asked by the British Government to secure recruits for the British forces in the Crimea. The Nova Scotia Government agreed to help, and Howe was dispatched, ostensibly in search of labourers for railway construction, to secure recruits in the cities of New England and New York. While he was engaged in this dubious venture, the President of the Charitable Irish Society in Halifax, William Condon, wired an Irish newspaper in New York that Howe's labourers were being transported to Halifax and the British army. The effect was immediate. The Irish Americans created a major political storm, Howe was forced to flee New York and return to Halifax, and President Pierce dismissed Crampton, the British Ambassador.[30]

The incident strained Irish tempers in Nova Scotia. Riots occurred between Irish Catholics and Protestant labourers on railway line construction between Windsor and Truro. The riots, popularly known as the Gourlay Shanty riots, were suppressed by troops from the Halifax garrison, but the odium fell on Howe under whose jurisdiction the railways lay. The presentation of a public address to Crampton, who stopped at Halifax on his way back to England, was marred by heckling. This discourtesy so exasperated Howe that he publicly rose and denounced the Irish and Catholicism in unmistakable terms. When he followed up this denunciation with bitter attacks in the press and on the public platform, Nova Scotia was plunged into a politico-religious war.

Howe's recognized position as leader of the Liberal party turned the wrath of the Irish Catholics on the Government and despite Howe's subsequent return to the House in a by-election, he was unable to maintain party solidarity. On a motion of want of confidence the Catholics deserted the Liberals and the Government fell. The assumption of office by the Conservatives led to a further reduction in the political influence of the propertied class and prevented the immediate repeal of manhood suffrage.

The curtailment of the political influence of property owners was not unrelated to the religious controversy. The *Acadian Recorder* of April 17, 1858, intimated as much when it declared that "the bill, with all its gross injustice to freeholders in all parts of the province, must have been intended to meet some particular case. Somebody's seat must be endangered by the votes of freeholders from some other county, and this bill is forced through the House to ensure its safety." The member was Tupper and the seat was Cumberland. Tupper, seeking re-election following his appointment as Provincial Secretary, had nearly been defeated when residents of Westmorland County in New Brunswick had crossed over to vote on woodlots they owned in Cumberland.[31] These electors had been drawn to the polls by the money and horses of W. A. Black, a Legislative Councillor and prominent Methodist of Cumberland, to play their part in the politico-religious feud dividing Nova Scotia. As Howe had begun to recoup the strength of the Liberal party by organizing the "Protestant Alliance," the mantle of Protestantism was being gathered around the Liberal party and that of Catholicism cast around the Conservatives. The Conservatives had recognized the danger and took steps to offset it. Since the Irish Catholic population was mainly labourers and the Protestants, comprising 60 per cent of the population, owned the greater part of the provincial real estate, the Conservative Government had decided that any curtailment of the freehold vote would work to its advantage.

The act of 1854, while it had enabled all British males of full age to vote after a period of five years' residence to Nova Scotia and a year's residence in a constituency, had continued the 40s. freehold franchise and the political influence attached to extensive ownership of property. The Conservative Government now curbed the influence of property but did not abolish the 40s. freehold franchise. All owners of real estate were forbidden to vote on their property unless they had resided three months within the county in which their property lay.[32] The special voting power which had formerly accrued to property was ended. The only preference remaining was the ability of a property owner to become enfranchised following three months' residence in a constituency rather than after a year's residence as was required of non-propertied voters.

Despite this legislation and because of the covenanting zeal of the Protestant Alliance, the Conservatives were defeated in the bitter election campaign of 1859. The ensuing term of office was not a happy one for the Liberals. The American Civil War put an end to the provincial railway schemes, and for some years adversely affected the shipping trade and general prosperity of the province. The Protestant Alliance disintegrated and the Conservatives made capital out of the depression by demanding a major retrenchment in government expenditures. The change in public sentiment was brought home to the Government when two by-elections in Cumberland and Victoria went against them, and as a consequence Howe felt obliged to attempt to repair his breach with the Catholics. He dissociated himself from the Protestant Alliance and began to offer cabinet appointments to Roman Catholic members of the Assembly.[33] When his overtures failed, his two colleagues, Archibald and McCully, Attorney General and Solicitor General respectively, turned to contain the growing hostility to their Government by manipulating the franchise.

Their plan was to abolish manhood suffrage and revert to an assessment franchise.

The assessment franchise, as brought forward by Archibald, was to limit the vote to all British subjects of twenty-one years who had been assessed for real property to the amount of $150 or assessed for personal estate, or personal and real estate, to the value of $300.[34] Although it did not require the payment of rates, it was similar to the ratepayers' franchise of 1851 in that it presumed the existence of a comprehensive municipal assessment of the province. While the latest measure did establish a court of revision to be staffed by appointees of the General Session of the Peace, its successful operation was to be dependent, as was the success of its predecessor, on the county assessors and clerks of the Peace. The administration of the counties had not improved perceptibly since the fiasco of the ratepayers' franchise, and there was no reason to believe a similar failure would not follow the adoption of the new assessment franchise. The danger was greater because, where the former suffrage had been saved from total disaster by the retention of the 40s. freehold as a supplementary franchise, now the 40s. freehold franchise was abolished. The entire electorate was to be determined by the competence and industry of the county assessors.

The Conservatives naturally opposed the measure. If manhood suffrage had increased the electorate by 44 per cent, it might be assumed the reversion to an assessment franchise would reduce the electorate by a comparable amount. Evidence was produced to prove that in one electoral district in Richmond County where there had been 110 electors under manhood suffrage, there would be but 16 under the assessment franchise.[35] The dissatisfaction of New Brunswick with similar legislation was pointed out. It was charged that the assessors and clerks of Peace, on whose ability and impartiality the success of the franchise would depend, would be partisans of the Government as they were appointees of the magistrates in General Session. Solicitor General McCully had his condemnation of some three years previous against the old ratepayers' franchise quoted against the new franchise: "There never was . . . so much corruption at any election as that held under the ratepaying bill. . . . Under the taxation principle the dominant party can manufacture as many votes as they please; the assessors, in fact, become vote manufacturers. At a meeting of the General Sessions in one county the whole magistracy were fighting day after day for a week nearly, as to who were to be the assessors. The bystanders were perfectly amazed at this but it was soon found out that the real question was how the next election was to be decided and it was felt that the question depended upon who were to be the assessors."[36] Arguments were, however, of no avail. The Protestant Alliance was crumbling; the Catholic vote was adamant against the Government; and the political effect of this hostility had to be contained. Despite seven motions for deferment moved by the Conservatives and fifty petitions protesting the repeal of manhood suffrage, the Liberals carried the measure through the Assembly.

The legislative contest did not conclude with the passage of the bill by the Assembly. The Liberals possessed only a majority of one in the Legislative Council, and the Conservatives turned their attention to that body. Tupper was successful there; he persuaded H. G. Pineo, a Liberal Legislative Councillor from Cumberland, to vote not against the new franchise but for an amendment that would delay its coming into effect until June, 1864, when the life of the existing Assembly would have expired. Tupper had outmanoeuvred the Government. They capitulated and accepted without division the bill as amended in the Legislative Council.

The reason for the Liberals' acquiescence seems to lie in Howe's realization that the sponsorship of the bill by Archibald and McCully had already irretrievably damaged the popular prestige of the Liberal party.[37] The error had been committed when consequent upon his appointment as Imperial Fishery Commissioner and his decision to retire from public life, Howe had relaxed his direction of the Liberal party. The acquiescence did mean, however, that the Liberals had to go into the election bearing all the ignominy of having disfranchised the artisans and labourers of Nova Scotia and the sons of fishermen and farmers, while deprived of any immediate benefit accruing from that disfranchisement.

Tupper exploited his opportunities to the utmost. He formed early in 1863 a "Constitutional League" in Halifax which published an organ *Public Opinion* to denounce Howe's persecution of a religious minority, his extravagance in Government, his reactionary disfranchisement of the electorate, and his unconstitutional acceptance of an Imperial appointment while remaining leader of the Government. The Liberals suffered a rout in the ensuing election; nine Conservatives were elected by acclamation, and of the remaining forty-six seats, the Liberals carried fifteen. Howe, who had been reluctantly persuaded to run again, went down to defeat.

Tupper, securely returned to power, might have been expected to repeal the assessment franchise and restore manhood suffrage which the Conservatives had fathered in 1854 and which they had fought to retain in the late Assembly. It was therefore with some surprise that the Assembly heard Tupper refuse to repeal the assessment franchise because ". . . a very decided majority of that Branch [Legislative Council] gave their firm and unqualified adhesion to the law as it is now on the statute book. The Government cannot, if they would, shut out that fact from their consideration. It has occurred to the Government that it would be better to let the law go to the country as it is, and let the objections to it develop themselves. If the objections are such that the law should be repealed, the House will hear it, and hear it in no measured tones."[38] This excuse was mere camouflage. Tupper wished to retain the assessment franchise because he had determined to bring free compulsory education to Nova Scotia and he was under no illusion as to the hostility it might arouse.

The hostility came from two sources, popular opposition to direct taxation, and Roman Catholic opposition to public schools. The Roman Catholics had in existence a system of parochial schools which the Government wished to replace with a sysem of free non-sectarian schools, supported by public taxation, whose teachers, courses of study, and text books would be under the control of a Council of Public Instruction. Politically this measure meant the alienation of the Catholic vote which had stood by the Conservatives in the last two elections. Despite the resignation of the Financial Secretary, the Protestant representative of the Catholic county of Richmond, Tupper persisted and to sounds of noisy resentment in the country the educational measure came in effect in 1865.[39]

With Catholic support alienated by the education act, and Nova Scotian nationalism outraged by the Quebec Conference, Tupper did not risk the restoration of manhood suffrage. If, as his former Financial Secretary declared, the assessment franchise would reduce the number of enfranchised fishermen from 400 to 55 in one district in the county of Richmond,[40] he might have expected this franchise to check the voting power of his opponents. At the same time Tupper believed that the assessment franchise would work better than the ratepayers' franchise. The laws governing assessments had been overhauled and the nature of the real and personal property to be subjected to taxation had been clarified.[41] The assessors were to be appointed annually by the Grand Jury or in case of default by the magistrates. On completion of the assessment, the magistrates were to divide each county into revisal sections and were to appoint three revisors for each section from a list of six presented by the Grand Jury. The revisors were to prepare an alphabetical list of qualified electors from the assessment rolls, and these provisional lists, after public exhibition for one month, were to be revised publicly at the revisors' courts. The lists as finally revised were to serve as the voters' registers. It must, however, have been less the revision of the laws governing assessments that gave Tupper confidence in the working of the assessment franchise than the knowledge that free public education would annually necessitate a detailed and proper assessment of each county.

Nevertheless the hostility to the education act and the heavy financial and administrative burden placed on the elementary municipal machinery did create difficulties. The first difficulty was occasioned by the popular belief that the Conservatives would repeal the assessment franchise. When Tupper had dispelled this belief, there was still considerable reluctance to proceed to the revision of the assessment rolls and the preparation of the voters' list.[42] The reluctance was encouraged by the administrative burden involved and by the cost which was to be borne in its entirety by the counties. As late as 1865 members of the Assembly reported instances of such neglect; in Lunenburg and Victoria counties, the grand juries were reported to have ignored the requirement to appoint revisors, while in Guysborough, the Grand Jury was reported to have refused to act.[43] By the time of the next general election, however, the reluctance had departed before the anxiety of all Nova Scotians to express themselves on the issue of Confederation.

The abandonment of manhood suffrage encountered little lasting opposition in Nova Scotia. The 50 petitions hostile to repeal which reached the Assembly in 1863 appear to have been party generated, and not the reflection of any fixed attachment to manhood suffrage. Archibald, the leader of the Liberal Opposition, publicly informed Tupper in 1864 that "if the Government are desirous of still farther elevating the franchise they will find no difficulty on this side of the House";[44] and Howe in a letter to the Colonial Secretary rejoiced at the abolition of manhood suffrage. "Lord Mulgrave will have described our political 'bouleversement'. Many causes combined to produce the result but the chief one was the rather plucky effort to try back from universal suffrage. Though we got our bill through it did not apply to the first election, and of course all the disfranchised and a good many who were not but were made to believe they were, took sweet revenge for an Act which I rejoice is on the statute books, although the immediate effect upon the administration was disastrous."[45]

The distate for manhood suffrage was rooted in the society of small farmers, merchants, and owners of fishing smacks. These men took pride in their independent status and disapproved of political power being entrusted to men unable to be their own masters. The *Acadian Recorder* reflects this view in an editorial of March 24, 1856:

. . . any comparison between the character of Assemblies where a universal is put against a limited franchise, whether as regards the character of public men, insecurity of government or corruption and profligacy in the management of public affairs must tell strongly against universal suffrage. . . . However corrupt a man may be, if he is above the strong current of necessity, if he is tolerably well-to-do, he wishes to preserve a certain air of respectability, and he can have little temptations of another nature to lead him to decide at the polls against what he thinks will better subserve the common good. But if you bring into the decisions of the polls abandoned men, hardened by culpable poverty and impoverished by idleness and vice, there is no guarantee that they will not assist in destroying the best elements of the commonwealth. There is little danger of making the franchise too restricted.

The independence, bred of the frontier, had left its conservative imprint on Nova Scotia.

The Conservative ministry, which had assumed office following the defeat of the Liberals on a want of confidence motion in February, 1857, had secured two measures which had an important bearing on the franchise. The least important of these measures has already been mentioned, and involved the abolition of the multiple voting rights attached to ownership of property. The second and more important measure was the equalization of the franchise within each county through the abolition of township representation. It had long been a grievance that electors in the townships voted for both county and township members whereas electors outside the enfranchised townships found their vote confined to the county members. The grievance had not disappeared although the adjustment of representation in the 1830's had evolved the principle that each county, with the exception of Halifax, should have one member if it contained an enfranchised township, and two members if it did not. For instance, in Annapolis, the townships of Annapolis and Granville returned members but the township of Wilmot, equal in size, had to share the county member; in Colchester, the township of Onslow with one-thirtieth of the county's population returned a single member as did the county; in Cape Breton, the township of Sydney, dominated by the General Mining Association, selected its own representative and the representative for the fisherfolk and farmers of the county; and in Hants, three townships huddled in one corner of the county returned three members.[46] There were sporadic remedies proposed and applied, new townships were enfranchised, old townships were extended to encompass their county, and new counties erected and township representation abolished.[47] These remedies had been inadequate and the Conservatives desired to reorganize and equalize the representation of the whole colony.

Although Johnston first introduced the bill as a non-Government measure, the bill did not escape partisan politics. It was caught up in the unreasonable suspicions accompanying the politico-religious feud that was distressing Nova Scotia, and in the political suspicions that are attributed to all legislation as the life of an Assembly draws to a close. The measure sought to abolish township representation and allot representation on the basis of one member per 5,000 population. The large counties of Halifax and Pictou were to be divided into two ridings each, while members were to be transferred from the over-represented counties of Colchester, Hants, Kings, Shelburne, and Queens to the under-represented counties of Halifax, Pictou, Inverness, Sydney, and Cape Breton.[48] When the Liberals accused Johnston of adjusting the representation to favour the Roman Catholics and when many Conservatives proved hostile to the diminution of the representation of their counties, the bill was not pressed.

In the following session the bill, much amended, was reintroduced as a Government measure. The new bill did not remove the inequalities in representation both within counties and between counties as had its predecessor but mainly confined itself to adjusting the inequalities within counties. The representation of only one county, Hants, was reduced, and the total membership of the Assembly was increased to overcome the under-representation of Halifax, Pictou, and Inverness. The township representation was abolished in all counties but Yarmouth, Shelburne, and Queens where the townships already encompassed the county. The representation possessed by the abolished townships was transferred to the county at large in all cases except Halifax, Pictou, Colchester, Hants, and Kings where the counties were divided into two ridings.[49] The opposition to the new bill was no less intense that it had been to its predecessor. The Liberals claimed that the 1851 census on which the bill was based was antiquated in 1859, that the bill selected population as the sole basis of representation to the exclusion of property and industry, and that the bill was a new "Popish Plot" to "Romanize the Assembly." They complained that Protestant Hants was deprived of a member while Catholic Halifax and Inverness were augmented, that the Protestant township of Sydney was dissolved into the Catholic county of Cape Breton while the Catholic township of Argyle was not dissolved into Protestant Yarmouth. It was claimed by William Young, a leading Liberal, that the Government bill was to ensure the return of sixteen Catholic members.[50]

The absurdity of the charges was evidenced in the following general election when seven Catholic members were returned, two less than in the sitting Assembly. The Liberal charges were specious. While it was true Protestant Hants had lost a member, Pictou had gained one. Catholic Halifax had gained a member, but whereas the city formerly might return four members, its own and the two county members, the division of the county into two ridings ensured that the Protestant Eastern District might return two members and the city but three. While the Protestant township of Sydney had been abolished, the same fate had befallen the Catholic township of Clare. After careful consideration it may be said that the act could have increased the Catholic representation by one, whereas the bill of the previous year would have given the Catholic population a possible gain of six seats. In truth the representation act forced through the Assembly on strict party lines left a religious bias in the representation in favour of the smaller Protestant counties.

In the heat of the politico-religious quarrel, sound judgment had departed the electorate. They readily accepted the Liberal charges that the bill ending the voting rights attached to extensive property holdings and the bill to equalize representation were designed to strengthen the Catholic vote. The *Novascotian* of March 21, 1859, declared

that this bill is the result of a cool premeditated deliberate plot . . . and Mr. John Tobin, Rome's vice regent in the Assembly had the boldness, yes the effrontery, to cry out in this Protestant country "the bill, the whole bill and nothing but the bill." Protestants remember that ! . . . Make no terms with them [the Romanizing administration] under any circumstance whatever. Stand for the dear faith, now in jeopardy. Strike for the principle of the Reformation. Stay not to enquire whether the candidate is Conservative or Liberal, that is immaterial, sink all smaller distinctions and party now, and go in for a strictly Protestant Government.

In the face of the clamour of the Protestant Alliance, it is remarkable that the Conservative Government persisted with the reform. The Assembly had received ninety-eight petitions against the equalization bill and but two in its favour; and Stayley Brown, the Receiver General, could perceive "that the bill [would] have the reverse effect from what [was] supposed, that it [would] lessen the influence of the present Government instead of increasing it . . . that it [would] do more to damage and prejudice the Government than any measure that they have ever introduced."[51]

The answer to the Conservatives' persistence in pressing this reform would seem to lie in the strained personal relations within the party between Tupper and Johnston. Johnston, who was being gradually displaced from the party leadership, had come to resent his eclipse and had determined to reassert his authority. The bill to equalize the representation was the measure he adopted to show Tupper and the public that he remained master. Irrespective of motive, Nova Scotia sorely needed its representa-

tion rationalized and Johnston's measure was a step in this direction. It served fur-
thur to equate the political influence of each citizen, a process which the temporary
adoption of manhood suffrage had commenced. The further attempts to rationalize
the representation, and to adjust the assessment franchise belong to the post-Con-
federation era.

CHAPTER FOUR

PRINCE EDWARD ISLAND

PRINCE EDWARD ISLAND was detached from Nova Scotia to form a distinct colony by Imperial Order in Council in 1769. During the six years it was under the jurisdiction of Halifax, it did not participate in the political life of Nova Scotia, for neither membership in the Assembly nor the exercise of the franchise was extended to it. With the erection of the Island into a distinct colony, the Commission authorized its first Governor, Walter Patterson, "so soon as the situation and circumstances of our Island under your government will admit thereof . . . to summon and call General Assemblies of the freeholders and planters within the Island."[1] The lack of a sufficient population and the lack of funds to establish the most elementary administration prevented the immediate creation of an assembly. As in Nova Scotia, the want of validity of the ordinances of the Governor and Council and the need to raise revenue finally forced Patterson to lay the question of the establishment of an assembly before the Council.[2]

In February, 1773, the Governor and Council unanimously decided to call an assembly. The Commission and Instructions to Patterson required him to confine the the electorate to "freeholders and planters," to follow Holland's survey when creating the electoral divisions, and in all other details to follow the example of Nova Scotia and Georgia. Local circumstances made it impossible to carry out the instructions as regards confining the franchise to freeholders; the total population was estimated to be 1,215 and they were all tenants or squatters on the lands of the absentee proprietors.[3] Consequently the Council opened the franchise to all Protestant residents on the Island.[4] The Council did not specify any regulations as to age, nationality, or sex, but as the Provost Marshal was to conduct the elections in the manner made "use of upon elections for Knights of Shire to serve in the Parliament of England," it was apparent that the franchise was to conform to Imperial practice unless otherwise specified.

The liberality of the franchise was approved by the Secretary of State as was the device of electing the members of the Assembly for the province at large.[5] The latter device had been used in Nova Scotia at the first commencement of representation there, but Prince Edward Island hedged this practice with the requirement that each elector vote for eighteen members or have his vote rejected. This requirement prevented the practice of "plumping" and had the indirect effect of assisting in the creation of two political parties. Hindering the emergence of independent candidates, it prevented the representation of local interest and submerged local personalities and issues beneath the political aspirations of the capital. As long as Charlottetown was politically unified, the elections amounted to little more than the confirmation of a list of candidates drawn up by the official circle at Charlottetown.

For the first eleven years there were no political divisions within the Assembly or between the Assembly, the Governor, or Council. It was not until the Governor committed an indiscretion with the wife of the Chief Justice[6] that political divisions emerged. The electoral system thereupon transformed what was essentially a personal feud into a political feud and imposed this political division right across the Island. In the 1784 election the Island electors were consequently faced with the choice of two lists of candidates, the "Country" list, sponsored by John Stewart, son of the Chief Justice, and the Attorney General's list sponsored by Captain James Campbell and other friends of Governor Patterson.[7] The divisions established at this election were repeated at the two ensuing general elections and laid the basis for a party system in Prince Edward Island which never entirely disappeared.[8] The electoral system assisted in the establishment of the party lines but it must be said that, despite a favourable system and an inflammable issue, the two parties were never able to present two distinct slates of candidates. Each list contained a number of common candidates whose neutrality made them inoffensive to both parties or whose vote-gathering powers in outlying points made their presence on the party list essential.

As in Nova Scotia the first Island franchise had been determined by the Executive Council and it continued to rest at the discretion of the Executive until 1801. In Nova Scotia the first loyalist Assembly had ended executive control but its cessation was achieved more slowly in Prince Edward Island. While the loyalist migration to the Island and its corresponding impact on Island political life was negligible, the failure of the Assembly to assert itself lay in two other reasons. The Island Executive did not tamper with the representation as did the Nova Scotia Executive. The Assembly remained unchanged at eighteen members from 1773 to 1838. The change that did occur involved the abolition of representation at large and the substitution of representation based on town and county. This change was so generally approved that the Assembly returned after its introduction, although hostile to the Lieutenant Governor, did not chide him for an abuse of executive power.[9] Secondly, the Executive and the majority of the Assembly were generally in agreement. On those occasions when they were not, the Governor either dissolved the Assembly or governed with the aid of his Council alone. In 1784 Patterson, faced with a hostile Assembly, dissolved it before the first session had completed any legislation. In 1788 Fanning allowed a hostile Assembly to meet for one session and then had it rusticate for two years at which time with the Speaker ill and six members absent from the Island he took occasion to dissolve it. The dissolution resulted in the return of an Assembly so favourable to Fanning that he found no need to dissolve it for twelve years.

The first change in the franchise took place in 1787 on the election of the fifth General Assembly. The election writ not only abolished representation at large but modified the franchise. The writ continued the first franchise of "freeholders, leaseholders and resident housekeepers" but confined it to the county elections and instituted a new franchise for the royalties of Princetown, Georgetown, and Charlottetown.[10] In the latter cases the franchise was confined to the owners of lots of land. The division of the electoral franchise into two parts, virtual manhood suffrage in the counties and a freehold suffrage in the royalties, had political significance. Of all the lands in the Island only the three royalties had not been granted away to proprietors. These royalties contained the only lands which the Governor and Council had at their disposal. In the ensuing election it was no accident that the supporters of the Executive were elected by the royalties.

The fifth General Assembly, although hostile to the Executive, took no action to end this discretion. It was left to the sixth General Assembly to pass the first franchise act. This Assembly, which had been returned in 1790 with a majority favourable to the Executive, ultimately became hostile. Over the length of its twelve-year life the Stewart party lost by-election after by-election, as the electorate returned members of the old Patterson party. These members began to sponsor bills to regularize the franchise, and on their fourth attempt with John Stewart, the Speaker, absent in England, they secured the passage of the first franchise act.[11]

The act confirmed the franchise as set forth by Fanning in the election writ for the previous general election. The dual franchise was retained, the electors for the royalties were required to be freeholders of lots within those town sites, while the county electors were all freeholders, leaseholders, and resident housekeepers who were Protestant. The retention of the duality in the franchise cannot be explained by a desire to curb the political influence of transients for the three towns were not major ports of entry. It appears to have been retained because the Stewart party controlled the Legislative Council, and the Assembly faced the alternative of securing a statutory basis for the franchise by confirming the existent suffrage, or of having their legislation rejected and the franchise left to the continued discretion of the Executive. The Assembly would not have have achieved this much if Lieutenant-Governor Fanning had not been desirous of conciliating the Patterson faction.[12]

A too abrupt calling of the 1806 general election became the occasion for the next adjustment of the franchise. Opportunity was taken of the resultant outcry to amend both the law governing election procedure and the franchise. The changes made in the franchise were a reflection of the concern of the old inhabitants at the pauper immigration that was beginning to press into the Island from the Scottish Highlands. The act continued to allow Protestant freeholders, leaseholders, and resident housekeepers to vote for each county but hedged these qualifications with limitations. An elector was required to possess a freehold estate of the value of 20s. per annum or a leasehold estate of 40s. annual rent, or if a resident housekeeper, to occupy premises of a yearly rental of £3. These qualifications had to be held six months before the issuance of an election writ and the possession had to be registered at the Registry Office for three months.[13] While the act curbed the virtual manhood suffrage that had prevailed for the counties, it extended the franchise in the royalties. Whereas the suffrage in the royalties had been confined to the owners of freeholds, the electorate was now enlarged to include housekeepers of no fixed valuation who had been resident in the royalty for six months prior to the teste of the writ. The act did not extend the leasehold qualification to the royalties but enfranchisement of the resident housekeepers would of necessity enfranchise any resident leaseholders. The act further specified that a freeholder of a royalty was henceforth entitled to vote only for the royalty and not in the adjacent county. In this respect Prince Edward Island early ended a privilege that existed in Nova Scotia and Lower Canada, where freeholders of townships and parliamentary boroughs voted both for the township or town and for the county in which they were located.

This curtailment of the franchise was associated with the transition of the Stewart party from the ranks of the tenant class to the ranks of the propertied class. During the long regime of Lieutenant Governor Fanning these individuals had accumulated landholdings by devious means substantially aided by the fact that John Stewart was Receiver General of Quit Rents. Their desire to limit democratic influences had been sharpened by the emergence of an escheat party, the "Club of Loyal Electors," which was organized to urge the Crown to revoke the land grants made in 1767 to the absentee proprietors and to regrant the lands to the tenants who were resident on the lands and were responsible for bringing them into productivity. The growing support for the escheat party had led the Assembly dominated by landowners and the agents of landowners to restrict the franchise and to establish a qualification for members of the Assembly. Previously a candidate for membership had been required simply to be a Protestant resident of the Island;[14] henceforth the candidates were to be Island residents who had possessed, twelve months prior to the day of election, a freehold or personal estate of the value of £50. Politically motivated as this election act may have been, it was not without its virtues. Aside from regularizing the notice required for elections, it also placed a seven-year limit on the life of the Assembly to prevent a repetition of the "Long Parliament" of 1790 to 1802.

The following decades were filled with personal political warfare of a bitterness equalled only by the politics of Lower Canada. The Lieutenant Governor stood against the Chief Justice and the Attorney General while the Assembly supported the Attorney General but fought the Lieutenant Governor and Chief Justice. These quarrels diverted attention from the franchise and it was not until the third decade of the century that the Assembly became again concerned with the franchise.

The issue was brought to the fore by pressure from the growing numbers of Irish immigrants to secure the enfranchisement of Roman Catholics. While the opposition was sufficiently strong to contain the strivings for emancipation until the Colonial Office ordered the Assembly to hedge no longer, the debate brought the Assembly to the realization that the pauper immigrants were not all Roman Catholics, and that the existent franchise was an inadequate barrier. The Lieutenant Governor was of this opinion, for writing to Huskisson he stated, "as the law now stands every squatter has a vote (a description of persons far below the travelling tinker at home) and placed on the footing of one holding a freehold."[15] The Assembly made a determined effort to raise the franchise in 1828 and would have succeeded but for the Legislative Council. The Council rejected the bill, not because of any democratic bias on its part, but through pique. It had become involved in a dispute with the Assembly over appropriations, and had suspended all legislative activity.

The bill of 1828 had sought to increase the county franchise from a freehold of 20s. annual value to one of £5 annual value, from a leasehold of 40s. yearly rent to one of £7/10 and from a resident housekeeper occupying premises of £3 yearly rent to one of £10; the royalty franchise remained at ownership of a town or pasture lot with an increase in the qualifications for resident housekeepers from a rental of unspecified amount to a rental of £15. The restrictive intent of the bill was made more evident by the increased qualification required of candidates for the Assembly. In place of the £50 freehold or personal estate specified by the act of 1806, the qualification based on personal estate was to have been abolished and possession of a freehold of £100 value or a leasehold of £150 substituted.[16]

The move to restrict the franchise was renewed at the next session. But such is the influence that one or two men could wield in an assembly as small as that of Prince Edward Island that the death of the Attorney General, William Johnston, and the resignation of Dugald Stewart meant the bill was not again introduced in its full reactionary form. The act[17] as passed by the Island Legislature raised the county franchise for freeholders from property of a yearly value of 20s. to one of 40s.; for leaseholders, the qualification remained unchanged at a yearly rent of 40s.; resident householders were required to occupy premises whose yearly rent was £5 rather than £3. The royalty franchise remained unchanged for freeholders at ownership of a town or pasture lot but for housekeepers it was raised from occupancy of property of unspecified value to occupancy of property bearing a yearly rent of £10. A further innovation was introduced; whereas formerly any freeholder who owned less than a town or pasture lot could not vote save as a resident housekeeper, now any owner of real property could vote if the property had a yearly value of £10. The predilection towards a propertied franchise was accentuated by an increase in the county polls from two to three and a curtailment in the time required for freeholders and lease-holders to qualify. Formerly householders, leaseholders, and freeholders had to possess their qualification six months before the teste of the election writ; this act reduced the qualifying period to one month for all but householders. The qualification for candidates and the religious restraint on the franchise remained unaltered.

The retention of the religious restraint brought the measure to momentary grief. The Imperial Parliament had ended the disfranchisement of Roman Catholics by the time the Island franchise act reached the Colonial Office. In consequence the Colonial Secretary informed Lieutenant Governor Ready that the bill would not be sanctioned until the clauses confining the vote and membership in the Assembly to Protestants were repealed.[18] In the following session the Assembly re-enacted the 1829 bill verbatim with two exceptions. The franchise was opened to Roman Catholics, and the qualifying period was changed back to six months for freeholders and leaseholders, and raised to twelve months for resident housekeepers in the royalties.[19]

The act was designed to exclude squatters, labourers, and transients from the exercise of the franchise, for virtually any freehold could produce an annual revenue of 40s. and as the rents for leaseholds ran from 1s. to 5s. per acre, a small leasehold of forty acres would enfranchise a rural tenant.[20] However, the increase in the suffrage requirement for rural housekeepers was found on application to exclude some old and respected farmers. Through the years the sales by proprietors of their original grants or their deaths and lack of heirs had introduced an uncertainty as to the actual owner of large blocks of land. The resident farmers on these lands had been unable to secure title or lease to the property on which they lived and were legally in the category of mere squatters.[21] The plight of these individuals was brought to the attention of the Assembly by a petition from Kings County.[22] William Cooper, leader of the escheat party which possessed a narrow majority in the House undertook to sponsor the cause of this rural class. As a result a bill was passed by the Assembly to consolidate the election laws and to extend the elective franchise to these rural residents.[23] The bill, which had received a mixed reception in the House because this rural class had always shown itself quick to respond to radical panaceas such as escheat, was given the three months' hoist in the Legislative Council, a body particularly unsympathetic to the levelling tendencies of the escheat party.[24] There had been some urgency on the part of the escheat party to secure the passage of this franchise, for the 1830 act, which had raised the franchise, had received royal assent on February 6 1832, and was to come into effect with the next general election. Frustrated, the Assembly had to content itself with passing a series of resolutions denouncing the Council for denying the right of freemen to "a numerous and respectable class of His Majesty's loyal and deserving subjects" and to demand the removal of all executive officers from the Legislative Council.[25]

The anti-escheat or proprietors' party was returned to power in the next general election and its victory was followed by a confirmation of the restrictive franchise of 1830 in the election consolidation act of 1836.[26] The consolidation for the first time specifically limited the franchise to males, raised the qualifying period to twelve months for all electors, and further tightened the qualification for candidates to the Assembly by requiring them to possess £50 real property, freehold, or leasehold, rather than £50 real or personal property.

The proprietors' party's oppressive tactics against the leaders of the escheat party occasioned the next adjustment in matters pertaining to the franchise. Emboldened by the disallowance of the act to establish an escheat court, the main achievement of the escheat party in the previous Assembly, the proprietors' party took steps to repress the agitation for escheat. They commenced by ordering the leader of the escheat party, William Cooper, and two associates, John LeLacheur and John MacKintosh, to apologize to the Assembly for their conduct at public meetings on the land question. When they refused, the Assembly ordered their arrest and confinement in the custody of the Sergeant at Arms for the two remaining sessions of the Assembly.[27] During the last session LeLacheur escaped from custody, was hunted across the Island, captured, dragged back to Charlottetown, and tossed into jail.[28] These vindictive tactics re-established the popularity of the escheat party, and its opponents in the Assembly were obliged to resort to adjusting the representation to escape their folly.

There was a need to adjust the repesentation. It had been fixed at eighteen since 1773 and the last adjustment had been in 1788 when representation at large had been abolished in favour of representation by county and royalty. In the interval the population had increased many times and discrepancies were manifest. The proprietors' party decided to increase the membership of the House, adding two members to each county while leaving the representation of the royalties unchanged. The partisan aspect of the measure was not the increase in representation but the decision to abolish representation at large for each county and to divide each into three electoral districts, for these were designed to localize the influence of the escheat party by confining its voting strength. Cooper and his followers claimed that the bill would "disfranchise the people and deprive them of two-thirds of their former privileges by confining the elector to a small district and to two representatives"; they claimed the electoral districts had been drawn with an eye to party purposes and that the measure was an attempt to escape from the verdict of the people.[29] Its leaders being under arrest, the escheat party petitioned the Legislative Council and the Lieutenant Governor to stop the bill and, when those appeals failed, carried its protest to the Colonial Office. The Lieutenant Governor, however, had pressed upon Glenelg the urgency of approving the bill,[30] and when the Island delegation reached London with a petition demanding the withholding of royal assent, the bill had already been confirmed.[31] The change in the representation was of little avail, for the proprietors' party had so outraged the electorate's sense of decency that Cooper and his followers were returned at the ensuing election, taking seventeen of the twenty-four seats.

Returned to power, the escheat party might have been expected to repeal the franchise restrictions imposed in 1830 and re-enfranchise the rural squatters. This was not done. When the Imperial authorities absolutely refused to facilitate escheat, the death knell of the party was sounded; to have re-enfranchised the rural squatters would have brought them no political strength. The dispirited escheat party did no more than secure legislation to clarify some ambiguities in the existing law governing the franchise.[32]

In the interregnum between the defeat of the escheat party and the final struggle for responsible government, a bipartisan Executive Council abetted by the Lieutenant Governor and the Colonial Secretary secured the adoption of simultaneous polling, which had already been adopted in neighbouring New Brunswick and Nova Scotia as well as Canada and Great Britain. The immediate impetus in Prince Edward Island was a series of election riots at Belfast in the third district of Queens. These riots, between the older Scottish Presbyterian settlers and the newer Irish Catholic immigrants, had marred and voided the general election in that district in August, 1846, had frustrated the subsequent by-election in March, 1847, and had necessitated the presence of a detachment of troops at the next by-election.[33] The suggestion of the Colonial Secretary conveyed to the Assembly in the Speech from the Throne was readily agreed to, and simultaneous polling was incorporated into the 1848 legislation consolidating the franchise and electoral procedure.[34] As Nova Scotia had done the previous year, the Island divided each electoral district into as many polling subdivisions as were necessary to poll the entire colony on one and the same day. By increasing the number of polls and shortening the duration of the polling, the act had the effect of curtailing the intimidation of electors, reducing territorial disfranchisement, and thereby extending the effective franchise.

Following the concession of responsible government to Nova Scotia and the reorganization of the remnants of the escheat party into the Liberal party to seek responsible government for Prince Edward Island, interest in the franchise sharply revived. The official circle in Charlottetown, knowing the land question merely slumbered, feared the refurbished escheat party concealed sinister designs behind its advocacy of responsible government.[35] When the Liberal party captured control of the Assembly in the general election of 1850 and refused to pass supply bills until responsible government was granted, the Governor and Council were driven to find a specific that would make the concession politically safe. The safeguard devised was revealed in two lengthy dispatches from Lieutenant Governor Campbell to the Colonial Secretary.[36] In his public dispatch Campbell stated that "before the people of the Island can be safely entrusted to carry out the system of responsible or self-government, it will be necessary to place a greater restriction on the right of voting for members of the House of Assembly, to abolish the electoral districts and throw open the counties, to reduce the number of members and to increase the amount of their qualifications."[37] The proposed changes in the franchise were detailed in a bill appended to this public dispatch. The county franchise was to remain unchanged for freeholders, but the housekeeper franchise was to be abolished and the requirements for the leaseholders sharply increased. It was proposed that a leaseholder, instead of possessing for twelve months a lease valued at 40s. per annum, had to have possessed continuously for twenty years a lease on fifty acres at an annual rental of 50s. and to have made improvements valued at £200 on the leased property. Campbell anticipated that the leaseholders who constituted in his estimate four-fifths of the county electorate would have their voting strength so diminished as to permit a reversion to the election of members for the county at large. Further to ensure the control of the Assembly by the property owners, the qualification for membership in the Assembly was to be raised from possession of real property of £50 value to ownership of real property valued at £200. The plan was designed to destroy the political basis of the Liberal party by disfranchising the classes interested in escheat and to ensure that responsible government could be conceded with safety to the proprietors.

The plan involved the passage of the franchise bill through the Imperial Parliament, to be followed by the dissolution of the existent Assembly and the concession of responsible government to the party returned under the restricted franchise. This appeal for the legislative intervention of the Imperial Parliament was postulated on the precedent set by the Canadian Act of Union.[38] The climate at the Colonial Office, however, had changed and the Colonial Secretary refused to ask the Imperial Parliament to intervene.[39] When in October, 1850, Campbell died and Bannerman arrived authorized to grant responsible government, the total failure of the conspiracy to disfranchise the bulk of the Island electors was evident to Council.

After Bannerman called George Coles, leader of the Liberal party, to form an Executive Council responsible to the Assembly, the new Premier appointed a select committee to look into the election laws.[40] Composed of five Liberals, four of whom were executive councillors, the select committee was designed to ferret out the substance in the rumours of constitutional change that had circulated under the previous administration. When the revelations had produced the requisite public outrage, the Government moved to extend the franchise. A bill was introduced to unify the franchise in county and royalty and to grant the vote to any twelve-month occupant of premises valued at 40s. annually.[41] There was to be no legal requirement that the premises be held in freehold or leasehold tenure; mere occupancy was to be sufficient. In consequence, the franchise would have been extended to virtually all householders, if the bill had not run into difficulties in the Legislative Council. There the opposition concentrated its attack on a clause which sought to abolish all property qualifications for members of the Assembly. This clause had been introduced into the bill by the Premier late in the committee stage and after Palmer, the leader of the Opposition, had challenged the qualification of a member of the cabinet, Hon. Edward Whelan.[42] Although the Assembly, on a partisan vote, subsequently declared Whelan's qualification adequate both currently and at the time of his candidature, the Legislative Council interpreted the amendment as designed to succour Whelan should the Assembly have found his qualification inadequate. This interpretation led Rice, a colleague of Whelan, to cross the floor and vote against the franchise bill fathered by the Government of which he was a member.[43] His defection spelled the defeat of the measure.

The defeat made the Government more determined to extend the franchise. Its determination was undoubtedly enhanced by the unpopularity of the direct taxes which it had imposed on the property owners for the provision of free education.[44] As a consequence Coles introduced a bill, in the following session, which sought to extend the franchise beyond the occupancy franchise of the previous year and to proceed to virtual manhood suffrage. The bill, which was passed into law, granted the franchise to every British male of twenty-one years who had been resident in the Island for twelve months previous to the date of election, and who was liable to perform statute labour, or was liable to statute labour but for the exemption accorded his office or occupation, or was allowed by law to commute his statute labour by the payment of a sum of money.[45] As the Statute Labour Act[46] required all male inhabitants of the Island between the ages of sixteen and sixty years except school teachers to contribute yearly four days' labour or its monetary equivalent towards the construction of roads, this extension of the franchise to all who *were liable* to statute labour amounted to the enfranchisement of the entire male population from twenty-one to sixty years. The act also extended the vote to all British males of twenty-one years who "own or are entitled to a freehold estate or are in the actual possession or use and occupation however derived or acquired" of any town lot, or real property in town or county worth 40s. per annum for twelve months prior to the teste of the election writ. Any leaseholder who might still be excluded because his yearly rent was less than 40s. was to be allowed to vote if the fee simple value of the farm leased was £35 currency.

The act was essentially a combination of the occupancy franchise of the previous year and manhood suffrage. The statute labour clauses allowed all men to the age of sixty to vote, and the occupancy clauses allowed all men who owned, leased, or occupied property a second vote if the property lay in an electoral district other than the district in which they resided and in which they were liable to statute labour. These two franchises reflected a conservative predilection on the part of the Island politicians. The propertied franchise had not been abandoned, and the Island mind did not equate the statute labour franchise with manhood suffrage. They considered manhood suffrage to imply that all adult males were entitled to the franchise as an inherent attribute of citizenship, whereas the statute labour franchise gave the vote to all adult males because they had a duty to discharge towards the community. While the Island franchise was not in theory manhood suffrage, the Conservative Opposition was under no illusion as to its actual effect. They forecast that the new franchise would "effectually place the basement class of our social edifice in a position to over-rule all the others; it will give to those who toil the power to govern those who think; and impart to those who labour with the hands a supremacy over those who labour with the brain."[47]

The franchise, as was required by Royal Instruction, contained a suspending clause. Colonial Office approval had become a nominal requirement but on this occasion the bill was subjected to close scrutiny. The late effort to obtain security for the proprietary interests by manipulating the franchise had opened the eyes of the Colonial Office to the implication of changes in the Island suffrage. Its concern was not allayed by Bannerman's bland assurance that the extension was of little moment as the franchise was already so wide, especially when he had dissolved the Assembly before the new franchise might come into effect.[48] Its misgivings were heightened by the receipt through John MacGregor, Member of Parliament for Glasgow and late member for Georgetown in the Island Legislature, of a petition from Island landowners and merchants against the bill.[49] Bannerman had to make an additional report. When he replied that the increase in the electorate occasioned by the bill could not swamp the existing electorate which at the late election numbered 7,000 out of an adult male population of 10,000, Newcastle was satisfied and the act was approved.[50] There can be little doubt that the implications of the act were hostile to the propertied class. The Liberal party, as heir of the escheat party, had found its main support among the tenantry. Although it had now abandoned escheat in favour of the buying out of the proprietors by the colony, it still needed the support of the non-propertied. Its establishment of free education sustained by a tax on property had been proving more costly than originally estimated and to meet the hostility attendant on the increase in taxation, it had sought to broaden the electorate. The Conservatives, scions of the proprietors' party, might have been expected to repeal this franchise but by the time they were returned to office the concession of manhood suffrage had had too profound an effect on their platform. They had ceased to consider the statute labour franchise a political disability when some six years later on their return to office their platform endorsed escheat and temperance.

Accepted by both parties the franchise established in 1853 remained essentially un-changed for the remainder of the colonial period. The changes that were introduced were attempts to eradicate abuses that became evident on its use. These abuses con-cerned electors who voted in spite of their failure to perform or commute their statute labour, and electors who voted on lands they did not possess, lease, or occupy. Such defects had been encouraged by the law which allowed all men liable to statute labour to vote and which placed the onus to prove a vote was invalid on the objecting party. The remedy followed the bitter general elections of 1859, when the Conservatives were returned after the loss of two leading members through fraudulent voting. The resul-tant legislation required the electors to be both liable to statute labour and to have performed it or have paid the commutation money.[51] On the request of the returning officer the electors were to present a receipt for the same from the overseer of statute labour. The onus of proof as to the legality of a vote was placed on the recipient of the vote rather than on the objector.

There was no political storm of sufficient intensity to force a retreat from the statute labour franchise. Prince Edward Island did not experience a controversy such as forced Nova Scotia back from manhood suffrage. But there was an incident that gave the Government cause to consider such a possibility. A Tenants' League had been formed to urge tenants to cease to pay their rents in order to force the proprietors to sell their lands on terms agreeable to the League. In 1865 when a mob organized by the League prevented the deputy sheriff of Queens County seizing property in lieu of rent, the Government arrested the ringleaders of the League and maintained order with troops from the Halifax garrison. The resulting loss of popularity with the tenantry led the Conservative administration to toy with the prospect of restricting the franchise. But the Conservatives were unable to steel themselves to the ruthless curtailment of the franchise that would have been necessary to save them, and the end product of their vacillation was a feeble move to enhance the influence of the propertied class.

Whereas property owners had always been entitled to vote in as many electoral districts as they possessed property, the introduction of simultaneous polling in 1848 had reduced the value of this privilege. The simultaneous polling legislation had made provision for the poll personnel who were electors in several districts to vote by special return at the poll where they were officiating. The Government now resolved to extend this privilege to all property owners. Following 1866 owners of property were to cast all their votes at their nearest poll and the sheriff was made responsible for the distribution of the votes to their proper electoral division.[52] This meagre attempt to strengthen the political influence of property and the 1861 curtailment of the vote to those who had completed their statute labour were the only changes made before Confederation to the dual franchise established in 1853.

A second franchise was operative on the Island in the elections for the Legislative Council. The incidents leading to the institution of an elective Legislative Council need not detain us but suffice it to say that the reform was secured in 1862.[53] Follow-ing the precedent set by the Province of Canada in 1856, the Island Legislature had desired to retain the same franchise for both the Legislative Council and the Assembly but to increase the qualifications required of candidates for the Council.[54] To this end the Legislature passed a measure which set the qualifications of candidates for the Legislative Council at British citizenship, age of thirty years, five years' residence on the Island, and legal possession of a freehold or a leasehold estate to the value of

£600 above all encumbrances.[55] The measure did not receive the approval of the Colonial Office. Newcastle was of opinion that "a well chosen constituency will choose a good representative and any limitations imposed upon its choice can only operate by occasionally preventing them from choosing the best. An ill chosen constituency on the contrary will tend to choose an indifferent representative but this tendency will not be controlled by any property qualification which can never be so stringent as to prevent their finding within the prescribed limits some such men as they may desire."[56] Newcastle was of the opinion there should be "a tolerably high property qualification in the case of electors but of the candidate I would require that he should be a British subject resident in the colony and 30 years of age."[57] The Legislature carried out Newcastle's wishes. Councillors were required to be British subjects, thirty years of age, and five years resident on the Island, but they were not required to possess a property qualification, a privilege not possessed by the members of Assembly. They were to be elected from an electorate which had to possess all the qualifications of electors of the Assembly and to possess in addition a freehold or leasehold estate to the value of £100 currency above all encumbrances.[58] Newcastle's insistence on a restrictive franchise may not have been divorced from a consideration of the Island land question. In the same month that he rejected the Legislative Council bill he had rejected the recommendations of a royal commission designed to resolve the land quandary. His advice may have been prompted by fear of a revival of the latent radicalism of the tenantry.

Complementary to developments in the franchise were developments in the procedure governing elections. It may be recalled that the entire membership of the Assembly was initially elected at large and at one poll. The remotest resident on the Island had to travel to Charlottetown if he wised to exercise his suffrage. The first relief for this territorial disfranchisement had come on the accession of Lieutenant Governor Fanning in 1787. Under the influence of the Stewart faction, he had dissolved the Assembly, dominated by the Patterson faction, and ordered the sheriff to hold polls at Princetown, St. Peters, and Charlottetown for the election of the members at large.[59] Fanning might have deserved praise for this change if it had not been politically inspired, for the strength of his friends lay outside of Charlottetown and environs.[60] When the modification failed to secure the return of the Stewart faction, the sheriff, a partisan, refused to return the Patterson candidates on the pretext the election at Charlottetown had been marred by violence and military interference. Since all members were elected at large and on one writ, the sheriff's refusal was considered to have voided the election. The Executive Council, on ordering a new election, took the opportunity to modify a second time the procedure governing elections. They abolished representation at large and issued distinct writs to each county and town that they might separately return four and two members respectively.[61]

Many had been dissatisfied with the modification of the election procedure by executive decree prior to the above incident. In the writ directed to the Provost Marshall for the first two general elections, he had been instructed to give thirty days' notice of the election in all inhabited parts of the Island, but his task had been rendered difficult by the freedom with which the Executive changed the election date. For instance, in calling the second general election, the Executive Council on February 18, 1774, had set the date for June 28, on the day previous to the election they had postponed it to September 12, and on August 16 it had been again deferred to October 3, on which day it had been allowed to proceed.[62] In consequence the Assembly had passed its first election act, which required the Provost Marshal within fourteen days of the receipt of the election writ to give public notice of the place and date of each election.[63] The act was postulated on the assumption that the Executive would issue the writ sufficiently in advance of the election date to allow the Provost Marshal to give adequate notice, but when the Executive at the next general election had issued the writ the day previous to the day set for the election, the above requirement was of no avail.[64] When the Assembly was again dissolved the Executive Council took cognizance of the complaints and the writ ordered twenty days' notification. Indeed the Executive Council was so accommodating that when the condition of the roads made it impossible to give the specific notice to all settlements, it ordered the extension of the polling time by three days.[65]

It was not until 1801, however, that the opponents of the Executive Council secured control of the Assembly. They marked this achievement with the passage of a statute to formalize the franchise and election procedure. The procedure adopted was largely a composite of the Nova Scotia procedure as set forth in 1789 and 1792. The sheriff was required to post a notice of election in each inhabited place on the Island within fourteen days of the receipt of the writ. The polling was to commence on the same day in each county and royalty, proceed for a maximum of three days at the county court house, and then adjourn to a second place of polling in each county at which the poll could remain open two days.[66] The adoption of multi-day polling and the creation of additional polls must have materially overcome disfranchisement caused by distance and time.

In spite of previous experience, the legislation had not required that the writ be issued sufficiently in advance of election day to allow the sheriff to give the required notice. The neglect became apparent when Lieutenant Governor DesBarres issued the writ for the next general election. Issued on October 24, 1806, the writ specified the date of election for the counties and royalties as November 4 and November 7 which enabled the sheriff to give but five to ten days' notice.[67] Peter MacGowan, the Attorney General, urged the Lieutenant Governor to reconsider and delay the election as his action would "be productive of much murmuring and discontent amongst the inhabitants from the shortness of the notice.[68] He refused to reconsider on the grounds that in England elections had to be completed within ten to sixteen days of the issuance of the writ.[69] His analogy with Imperial practice was inappropriate for, as MacGowan pointed out, "in a county in England where they have the advantages of post offices, open roads and circulating prints, I should think nine days would afford a more general notice to the electors than thrice the time in either Kings county or Prince county . . . owing to the remoteness of the settlements and the difficulty of access to them by means of the unimproved state of the roads or paths through the woods."[70] Following the election the legislation was amended to require the issuance of the writs thirty and twenty days before the election for county and royalty respectively, and the sheriff was required to have the notices posted seven days after the receipt of the writ.[71]

Incidents similar to those at a by-election for Kings County in July, 1831, led to the next modification of the election procedure. The supporters of the trailing candidates at this by-election, anxious to have the election terminated without the sheriff making a return, had engaged in riotous conduct. They had demolished the hustings, forced the sheriff to retire to a barn to continue the polling and, availing themselves of the dark, thrown showers of stones at the lamps, repeatedly plunging the poll into darkness, until the sheriff closed the election at half-past nine without declaring any candidate elected.[72]

Such incidents led the Assembly to extend the polling circuit to three polls per county and to regularize the hours of polling.[73] The hour of commencement had been set between 10 A.M. and 12 A.M. by the act of 1806 but except for one occasion in 1787 the hours of polling had been left to agreement among the candidates or the failure of electors to appear. The Assembly now ruled that the polls were to close at 7 P.M. between April 1 and October 1 and at 5 P.M. during the rest of the year.[74]

Continuing violence at elections led the Island to adopt simultaneous polling. This device, made popular by the English Reform Bill, was adopted by Prince Edward Island in 1838 when the elections in each county were made simultaneous.[75] Each county was divided into three electoral districts with two polling places per district, and the duration of the election was reduced from fifteen to five days in all districts but one. The reform proved inadequate to curb violence; the duration of polling and the fact the elections were not simultaneous throughout the Island allowed crowds to gather and violence to occur. The previously mentioned Belfast riots, during which many were injured and three lives were lost, induced the Island Legislature in 1848 to take the final step and establish simultaneous one-day polling for the entire Island. Each electoral district was divided into sufficient polling subdivisions, complete with election staffs, to permit the polling of the entire Island on the same day.[76] The brevity of the polling, the dispersal of the crowds, and the separation by one week of the day of nomination and the day of polling reduced the electoral violence. While not eradicated, it did cease to be a feature event of every election.

There were to be no further procedural changes before Confederation. The colonial period was to come to an end with simultaneous single-day polling of an extensive electorate. The electorate, determined by the occupancy and statute labour franchise, embraced virtually the entire male population of Prince Edward Island. With the exception of British Columbia, no colony entered Confederation with a broader franchise. As in British Columbia the reason for the liberal franchise was to be found not in democratic sentiment but in local circumstances. The liberal character of the Island franchise was historically determined when the Board of Trade in 1767 granted the lands of the Island to claimants on the favour of the Crown. An exclusive freehold franchise was forever rendered inappropriate where men were tenants and squatters on the lands of absentee proprietors.

CHAPTER FIVE

NEW BRUNSWICK

In August, 1784, the colony of New Brunswick was created out of Nova Scotia, and Thomas Carleton became Governor. The separation of New Brunswick from Nova Scotia was made necessary by the influx of loyalists into the St. John Valley on the termination of the American Revolution. Carleton was given the usual intructions. He was to govern with the advice of an executive council until such times as the situation and circumstances of the colony would allow the calling of a general assembly. Sydney, the Secretary of State, made it clear that Whitehall believed there were already a sufficient number of settlers present to warrant an assembly.[1] Carleton, nevertheless, did not call an assembly on his arrival in November, 1784, since he was fully occupied with providing shelter for the refugees, and with surveying and allocating lands.

It was not until the following autumn that Carleton undertook to establish a representative government. In October, 1785, he and his Council, bearing in mind their Instructions to "summon and call a General Assembly of the freeholders . . . in such numbers and for such districts and parts thereof as shall appear to form an equal representation of the said freeholders," divided the colony into eight counties and ordered the sheriff for each county to return a specified number of representatives.[2] After representation had been assigned with some approximation to population, they proceeded to determine the franchise. For guidance they had the Instructions which confined the franchise to freeholders, Carleton's Commission which confined it to "freeholders and settlers," and the past practice in the St. John Valley which, as the county of Sunbury, had returned members to the Assembly of Nova Scotia on a 40s. freehold franchise. Having in mind the local circumstances the Governor and Council ignored the official emphasis on property and conferred the franchise on on all white males of twenty-one years who had resided in the colony three months and were willing to take the oath of allegiance. It was made quite clear that freeholders were not entitled to vote as such but as inhabitants only which confined the vote of each elector to the county in which he lived.[3]

As the writs of election were issued on October 15, 1785, all inhabitants of New Brunswick who had arrived in the colony as late as July 15, 1785, were legally entitled to vote. This liberality was necessitated by circumstances of which Carleton thought proper to remind Sydney.[4] The bulk of the settlers were settled on lands to which they did not possess titles in fee simple. The need to escheat previous grants and to conduct surveys had forced the Council to assign lots of land to loyalists on no more permanent authority than a Minute of Council. The Council hoped the completion of titles would not necessitate a repetition of this indiscriminate extension of the franchise.

In the first session of the General Assembly, the Legislature took up the question of formalizing the franchise. This action was taken on the advice of Governor Carleton who in the Speech from the Throne directed the Assembly to consider "a bill provid-ing for the election of members to serve in Assembly, and for regulating all such elec-tions, as well as determining the qualifications of electors."[5] This direction from the Governor was in sharp contrast with Nova Scotia's experience, where for thirty years the Assembly had fought unsuccessfully to remove the franchise from executive control. The changed attitude cannot be attributed to Carleton but rather to the Board of Trade who had instructed Carleton to secure an immediate statutory basis for the franchise and representation.[6] As directed, the franchise bill was drawn up by a select committee of the Assembly consisting among others of the Attorney and Solicitor General; the bill successfully passed both Houses and was sent to England for con-firmation.[7]

The bill confirmed in most respects the franchise decreed by the Minutes of Council of October 11 and 21, 1785. The electors were required to be twenty-one, resident in the county, and to have possessed for three months before the teste of writ a freehold of the clear value of £20 above all encumbrances. Why the Assembly selected a free-hold of £20 value as the criterion for enfranchisement is uncertain. It may have been a 10 per cent capitalization of the Imperial and Nova Scotian franchise which was a freehold yielding a yearly revenue of 40s.; or it may have been the value ascribed to the minimum grant of land given to loyalists and other settlers in the province; or a modi-fied version of the franchise of the "loyalist" colony of New York where ownership of real property to the value of £40 was required.[8] The franchise contained a requirement which had been omitted by the Executive Council in 1785; all residents to secure the franchise were to take the oaths to sustain the Protestant succession. This restriction was included to remedy an oversight in the Minute of Council which had allowed the Roman Catholic Acadians to vote in the first election. The bill detailed the same representation as prescribed by the Minute of Council on October 11, 1785, with the exception that, while the city and county of St. John were to continue to return six members, four were to be returned by the freeholders of the city and county, and two by the freemen of the city. The bill then concluded by outlining the regulations to govern future elections.

The election bill had been sent home for approval in June, 1786, but by March, 1790, the Secretary of State had still not informed Carleton of the fate of the bill, at which time Carleton, with four vacancies in the Assembly, was anxious to invoke the new act.[9] As a result of his prodding, the Privy Council came to a decision. The bill was not to be allowed because of a technical mistake in transcription. The body of the bill specified an elector's qualification as property of the value of £20, but a mar-ginal note set the qualification at ownership of property of £20 yearly value. While this was the reason for disallowance, Grenville made it clear the qualification itself was not entirely satisfactory.[10] Grenville judged the qualification to be too low, but inti-mated that the Colonial Office would accept the present franchise if the Assembly insisted and if the textual error was corrected. This information was conveyed by Carleton to the Assembly and in 1791 a second election bill was passed.[11]

In line with the suggestion of Grenville, the franchise qualification was raised. The county electors were divided into two classes, resident and non-resident; the former had to possess a freehold of £25 clear value in the county, the latter a freehold of £50 clear value. This requirement was subject to the proviso that any elector who remained in possession of his property and enjoyed its revenue would vote even if the property was mortgaged. The electors were required to be twenty-one years of age, and have

C

their titles registered six months before the teste of the writ; to exclude aliens and Roman Catholics, the electors, on request of a candidate, were obliged to take the state oaths. This bill established a higher qualification than the previous bill and was to establish in law the most restrictive franchise in the British North American colonies. Nova Scotia at this time gave the franchise to any citizen who possessed a dwelling house, or a hundred acres of cultivated or uncultivated land, or real estate which provided a revenue of 40s. per annum; Prince Edward Island enfranchised all freeholders, leaseholders, and housekeepers; and the Canadians by Imperial enactment allowed all 40s. freeholders to vote in county elections.

The conservative nature of the New Brunswick franchise act was not entirely owing to Grenville's suggestion, for it also reflected the political temperament of the leading public men in the colony. New Brunswick received a high percentage of loyalists who had possessed high public and military office, and who in New Brunswick through public appointments and substantial land grants had resumed their old ascendancy. The ideals of this class and the autocratic tendencies of Lieutenant Governor Carleton inclined them to confine the franchise to the larger property holders. Their conservative inclinations were strengthened by the smouldering democratic fervour which had produced the St. John riot in the first general election and had led to the election of Elias Hardy for Northumberland in 1785 and James Glenie for Sunbury in 1791 against official opposition. This conservative attitude was reflected in the special qualifications required of candidates for the Assembly. Where Nova Scotia required the same qualification from a candidate as an elector, New Brunswick required a candidate to possess £200 of real estate in the county he sought to represent, and while the candidate himself need not be a resident of the county, his property in that county must have been registered six months before the teste of writ. All were requirements which would limit the class from which candidates might come.

The second election act was dispatched to the Home Secretary for royal approval with the request that the act be confirmed at once, as the life of the Assembly was drawing to a close. The act became lost in the maze of Imperial red tape and, despite frequent reminders from Carleton, was not confirmed until June 3, 1795.[12] Meanwhile Carleton had been obliged to dissolve the first Assembly and elect a second House in 1793 on the franchise established by Minute of Council in October, 1785. On receipt of confirmation of the act, Carleton dissolved the Assembly a second time and called a general election, and on the basis of the new and restrictive franchise, members were returned for the third General Assembly.

The election act had carried to a logical conclusion the change in representation accorded the county and city of St. John intimated by the defunct bill of 1786. The county and city were accorded distinct representation, and the franchise applicable to the city was distinct from that applied to the county. The city of St. John was to return two members who, in the words of the act, were to be "chosen by the freemen being inhabitants and the freeholders thereof." The institution of freemen was an Old World practice that Carleton transferred to the New when he incorporated the city of St. John. The charter of incorporation authorized the mayor under the common seal to make any resident of the city who was a natural-born British subject, or a subject by naturalization or denization, a freeman on the payment of a fee not exceeding £5. The freemen were to enjoy the liberty to engage in any occupation or trade within the city but, as all the white residents of the city on the date of its incorporation were automatically to be made freemen on registering with the Common

Clerk, the privilege was not restrictive.[13] The freemen, to enjoy the franchise, were required to have been a freeman for six months, to have lived in the city for six months before the teste of the writ, and to possess personal property to the value of £25. In addition the franchise for the city was to include freeholders. The wording of the statute is uncertain as to the qualification of these freeholders, it did not specifically state that they were required to possess property to the same value as that required of county electors, and it would appear a freehold of any value was sufficient.[14]

The franchise requirements in New Brunswick, as mentined, were legally the highest in British North America. The £25 freehold qualification for residents and the £50 freehold qualification for non-residents would at the current valuation placed on New Brunswick lands have enfranchised freehold estates of two hundred and fifty and five hundred acres respectively.[15] As the minimum grant of land authorized by the Royal Instructions of July 28, 1784, was one hundred acres for each head of a family together with fifty acres for each additional member, the minimum grant would have enfranchised all married couples with two children (or servants).[16] Since the Instructions had allowed larger grants to all applicants capable of working the same, the Commissioner of Crown Lands had made it a practice to allow three hundred acres to every married man and two hundred acres to every single man.[17] As these grants were freely given, few were disfranchised and the highest franchise requirements did not in practice produce a restricted electorate.

While the franchise requirements were initially not restrictive, a change in Imperial policy made them so. On March 6, 1790, an additional Instruction was issued to Dorchester, as Governor of British North America, to the effect that all grants of land were to be suspended until further notice. An accompanying dispatch to Carleton alleviated the severity of the Instruction; the Lieutenant Governor was to continue to issue a grant of land in all cases where an "antecedent step" had been taken to secure a Crown grant.[18] The effect of this change in policy was not immediately apparent, as grants continued to be issued for some years. When the restraint on free land grants stretched into a decade the problem began to assume serious proportions. The young and the immigrants had to secure land by purchase or by mere occupation. The majority were forced to become squatters, and as such were legally excluded from the franchise.

The Executive Council in order to counteract the adverse effects on immigration and to prevent emigration continued to receive applications for Crown grants. The applicants were allowed to settle on the land applied for with the expectation that the lands would be granted on the cessation of the embargo.[19] The general expectation that grants would be renewed had an adverse effect on the franchise; it led to the subversion of the franchise as legally established. While the franchise continued to be confined to registered freeholds of £25 or £50 depending on residence or non-residence, in practice the franchise was extended to all occupants of land. When in 1802 the granting of land was resumed by Royal Instruction, the practice of ignoring the strict terms of the franchise was continued and all resident farmers were allowed to vote. This condition was clearly brought out in the election of 1828. This election was particularly bitter as it marked the overthrow of the political dominance of the first loyalist families. As a result of the strong feelings many elections were disputed and the investigations revealed that in the rural counties of Kings and Charlotte over 28 per cent of the votes cast were not legal. These controverted elections served to show that, while a quarter of the electorate might not be legally entitled to vote, the practice of allowing all occupants of land to vote had persisted.

The large percentage of unqualified voters was not due to any lack of land or curtailment in the issuance of grants, for as late as 1825 over fourteen million acres were still at the disposal of the Crown. The main reason lay in the inability of many settlers to acquire a grant because they were too poor to pay the fees and costs of survey, or because they had failed to satisfy the conditions of settlement which after 1802 were required to be completed before title deeds were issued.[20] Each grantee was required to clear three acres of land for every fifty acres received within a period of three years or the grant would be forfeited to the Crown. The grants were seldom forfeited except in cases of abandonment but by 1825 one-half of the grantees had failed to complete the conditions of settlement and were not in possession of their title deeds.[21] A secondary reason why there were a large number of disqualified voters in 1828 was the failure of grantees to register their title deeds at the county registry. The franchise act required each elector to have registered his deeds at least six months prior to the issuance of the election writ but this provision had been so repeatedly ignored that the select committee on the Kings County election had to inquire of the Assembly if the provision was still in effect.[22]

The Assembly took no notice of the public revelation that a large part of the populace was legally disfranchised. No steps were taken to bring the franchise requirements into harmony with prevailing conditions or to ensure that the franchise would be confined to those legally qualified. The Assembly decided to ignore the situation and in so doing gave tacit recognition to the extension of the franchise to occupants of Crown grants on a warrant of survey, or a licence of occupation as it was called in the Canadas. This class of *de facto* electors was long a feature of the New Brunswick franchise.

The step that the Assembly did take to modify the election law was in a small way a reflection of their recognition of these *de facto* electors. An election act was passed raising the qualification required of members of the Assembly and requiring the registration of the freemen of the city of St. John.[23] Candidates for the Assembly had been obliged to possess real estate in the county they sought to represent to the extent of £200 but the freehold could be mortgaged without invalidating the candidate's qualification. Candidates were now to be possessed of a freehold property to the value of £200 over and above all encumbrances. For the freemen of the city of St. John the electoral qualification had been personal property to the value of £25 and six months' residence in the city as a freeman before the teste of the election writ. The freemen were now to be denied the franchise unless they had taken the trouble to be duly registered in the table of freemen at least six months before the teste of the writ. This requirement prevented the enfranchisement of the wandering residents of this seaport town who had often been polled on the assumption they were freemen.[24] The Assembly had by the virtual establishment of a voters' register for freemen ensured that none but the qualified might vote, but for the counties they had taken no such step. The convention that all occupants of Crown lands were electors was allowed to remain and as a safeguard against democratic radicalism the qualification for members of the Assembly was raised. In allowing this convention to survive, the Assembly was aware that the policy of free land grants was coming to an end. The Colonial Office had intimated the previous year that Crown lands would in the future be sold to the highest bidder, and the Assembly must have foreseen that the poor immigrants would become either tenants or squatters on the public domain. The Assembly was thus prepared to give tacit but not legal recognition to manhood suffrage in the rural areas.

This laxity may have been due to the lack of strong party divisions in New Brunswick. What party divisions did exist were largely geographical; the Fundy counties were united to secure the transfer of the seat of government to St. John, and the lumbering counties of the North Shore were hostile to the settled agricultural counties of the St. John Valley. In this rivalry the franchise played little part although the adjustment of representation was of vital importance.

Efforts to purify the elections and to overcome territorial disfranchisement require consideration. The movement to purify elections was sparked in New Brunswick as in Nova Scotia by the rise of the temperance movement. In New Brunswick the temperance movement reached its greatest influence; beginning in 1830 it grew steadily until the passage of the prohibitory liquor act in 1855. The greater strength of the New Brunswick temperance movement was due to the active support of both the Protestant and Roman Catholic churches. Whereas in Nova Scotia temperance received strong support from the Methodist and Baptist churches, the Churches of England and Rome gave indifferent support and the Presbyterian Church was too distracted by internal feuding to be united on the issue of temperance.

Temperance began to be associated with a demand for electoral reform in the Assembly of 1831. Stephen Humbert, who had been returned for the county of St. John after having suffered defeat in his first attempt at election, attributed his defeat to the riot, confusion, and drunkenness accompanying elections. He desired to curtail the evils associated with elections by reducing the time allowed for polling and facilitate polling by limiting the number of oaths required of electors.[25] Humbert failed to carry his reform but support grew, aided by the British adoption of two-day polling in the Reform Act of 1832. In 1835 Lemuel Wilmot took up the issue and had a select committee established which recommended that the time of polling be reduced from a maximum of fifteen days as under the existing law to a maximum of eight days, and that it be made mandatory for the sheriff to move the poll about the county at the request of at least one-half the candidates.[26] This recommendation was prompted by incidents such as the by-election for York County in 1822 where four candidates offered for the vacant seat but after the poll had been kept open four days, three had withdrawn because the sheriff refused to hold the poll elsewhere than the town of Fredericton.[27] Fredericton on the eastern edge of the county was 150 miles from its northern extremity and 65 miles and 100 miles respectively from the settlements of Woodstock and Andover. The sheriff had by his refusal disfranchised all the inhabitants of the county of York except those in Fredericton and environs. The recommendations of Wilmot's select committee was referred the following session to a second select committee to embody into a bill.

The bill, as introduced into and passed by the Assembly in 1837, was somewhat in advance of the recommendations of the select committee of 1835.[28] The select committee had recommended the period of polling be reduced from fifteen to eight days but in the bill the period had been shortened to four. The poll was to commence at the county town and continue for four days but on the third day the polls at all the specified places in each county were to open and continue for two days. This approximation to simultaneous polling allowed the nominations to be made at the county town, and the official list of nominees circulated to the presiding officers of each county poll before those polls opened on the third day. If the Assembly had conceived of the idea of separating nominations from the days of polling, it would have been possible to have had simultaneous polling. The Assembly by this provision expected to extend the franchise and reduce the bribery, corruption, and treating by shortening the period of election and dispersing the election crowds among the several polls.

The bill also incorporated a recommendation of the 1835 select committee that any person who voted illegally at an election might be made liable to legal action at the suit of any candidate. The select committee had suggested this restraint on the exercise of the franchise by the non-qualified when the freeholders of the county of St. John petitioned the Assembly to confine voting to freeholders legally qualified.[29] This clause was the first sign that the Assembly might be aware of a need to confine the electorate to those enfranchised by law, and not merely by custom. While the efficacy of the clause may be questioned, yet it was the first time the Assembly had placed a penalty on persons who voted although not qualified by law. The Assembly accepted this restraint on illegal voting in place of a voters' register which they felt would be too difficult and expensive to establish although there existed in each county a registrar of titles who might have been required to provide a list of all registered freeholds. The exclusion of unqualified electors from the polls was to be left to the self-interest of the candidates.

Although there were many protests that the four-day period of election was too short, the bill passed the Assembly. In the Legislative Council it was completely re-written. The four-day elections and the approximation to simultaneous polling were replaced by the recommendations of the 1835 select committee. The period of election was fixed at eight days, a polling circuit was set up for each county, and to remove any discretion on the part of sheriff or candidates, the locations, duration, and order of each poll were specified in the act. The act as amended ended the sheriff's discretion, for he had to commence the county election circuit on the request of any candidate or of two electors. The Legislative Council removed the penalty against unqualified voters and allowed the exercise of the franchise by the unqualified to remain unpunishable in law. The majority of the Assembly, relieved at the extension of the time of polling from four to eight days, accepted the bill as amended by the Legislative Council and it became law.[30]

The attempt to purify the election and reduce drunkenness and corruption by confining the voting to eight days and establishing a specific polling circuit was not considered adequate by the advocates of temperance. Before the act had been tested at a general election, petitions were reaching the Assembly to reduce polling to one or two days.[31] Fisher, the Liberal member for York County, took up the cause and in 1842 introduced a bill into the Assembly to shorten the period of election and establish simultaneous polling in each county. While he was unable to secure a majority, the riots at Fredericton, St. John, and the county of Northumberland during the ensuing general election brought the issue to a head.

The violence of these riots may be judged from the Northumberland election. This county was divided in allegiance to two lumber firms, Gilmour, Rankin and Co., and J. Cunard and Co., rivals both in trade and politics. A participant describes the election:

The Rankin party were not only forewarned but forearmed, as they had piles of stones placed at convenient places, covered with sods or grass, so as not to attract attention, and a cable stretched on stakes, so as to divide the courthouse entrance door, with the intention to have the Rankin voters go in one side of this dividing rope and the Cunard voters on the other. The Chatham party were late in appearing, and did not arrive till 11 a.m. They took in part of the situation, and Hea gave the command in Irish, to clear away the cable, which was done instanter. They were about two hundred or three hundred strong. The Rankin-Street party, through Big Jim Bass, then got the order to charge, which they did, and the air was immediately full of stones, sticks, and other missiles, and a battle royal commenced, but the Chatham party were overpowered at last and fled in different bodies —one through the woods, coming out that night about Lamont's mill; another through the woods, but only came out next day at Mill Bank, and the third made directly back to their wharf, followed by the crowd of victorious Street men. They crowded on board the steamer St. George. . . . There was a heap of coals lying on the wharf, which the Street party used as missiles, and when she arrived at Chatham there was four inches of coals all over the decks, mute witnesses of the battle.

Some days later, when the poll had moved to the south bank of the Miramichi, the report continued,

The Chatham folks were not to be caught napping, so every one was astir bright and early and down on Peabody's wharf watching for developments, except those that were preparing the barricades. These consisted of two 14-inch squared timbers . . . three cannon were lashed to these and loaded with scrap iron and spikes and cart loads of stones were dumped down there to form an obstruction or defence wall and furnish ammunition for the unarmed. These two barricades commanded perfectly the egress from Peabody's wharf, the only point where the enemy could well land. . . . The woman and children were sent out of town for safety. The morning was beautifully bright and clear, and the red shirts could be seen quite distinctly at Douglastown, embarking in eight or nine vessels. But now, a thunderstorm, with lightning of unprecedented severity, set in with floods of rain and the wind veered to the east; but not a man left his post, and after the storm had partially passed, the vessels were seen heading down the river towards Chatham.[32]

As a result of these outrages, Lieutenant Governor Colebrooke intervened and called upon the Assembly to revise the election laws to secure public peace at elections and restore the privileges of the franchise to those constitutionally enfranchised. Fisher chaired the select committee and a bill was prepared and passed the Legislature to revise and consolidate the election laws.[33] This act adopted one-day polling and simultaneous elections within each county. The act separated the process of nomination from the day of polling. The day that the sheriff was to open his nomination court was set by the writ, and he was required to hold the election throughout the country not less than three nor more than six days after the day of nomination. The sheriff was to open polls at the several places specified by the act in his country, provide a polling booth, and appoint presiding officers and poll clerks who would between the hours of 8 A.M. and 4 P.M. record the votes, name, and residence of all electors. The poll books were then to be sealed and returned to the sheriff, who would at his declaration court within four days of the election open the poll books, tabulate the vote, and return the candidates possessing a majority. This procedure was in many respects a copy of the Imperial act of 1835 and the Canada act of 1842. The single-day polling was to be held simultaneously throughout each county but not simultaneously throughout the province. New Brunswick never followed Nova Scotia's example of 1847, when simultaneous voting was made province-wide. Nevertheless New Brunswick's separation of the exuberance of nomination day from the day of polling, and the division of the electorate into a series of simultaneous and distinct polls did help to reduce the chances of riot, intimidation, and excess that had characterized past elections.

This act and its predecessor of 1837 by establishing election circuits materially reduced the disfranchisement occasioned by distance and poor communications. The extension of the polling to six or eight places in each county was still not sufficient to end territorial disfranchisement where a county such as Northumberland was allowed to encompass one-third of the province. If territorial disfranchisement was to be overcome, the establishment of an election circuit had to be accompanied by the subdivision of electoral districts. Subdivision was made difficult by the association between representation and county. As long as an electoral district had to be synonymous with a county, no subdivision of electoral districts could occur without the subdivision of the county. This fact introduced a rigidity in the physical limits of electoral districts, for the creation of a new county was expensive because of the need to establish a new and complete local administration, together with registry and court buildings. Closely associated with the need to adjust the size of electoral districts was the need to maintain some relationship between representation and population. Although it was possible by addition and subtraction of members to overcome maladjustments in representation without overcoming territorial disfranchisement itself, it was customary to remedy both evils by the same means.

The Assembly had been early concerned with the adjustment of representation. As early as 1793 the first petition had reached the Assembly to increase the representation for Kings. This petition had been followed in succeeding years by the introduction of a variety of bills to equalize the representation of individual counties or of the province as a whole. All the bills had been defeated in the Assembly or the Legislative Council. It was more often the former, for the shifting combination of the St. John Valley counties against the North Shore, or the Fundy counties against the others proved fatal to each measure. The first attempt to readjust representation and also overcome territorial disfranchisement occurred in 1823 when the upper parishes of York County petitioned to be erected into a distinct county. This petition was occasioned by the refusal of the sheriff in the 1822 by-election to remove the poll from Fredericton on the extreme eastern edge of the county. The petitioning parishes lay 100 miles above Frederiction, and although they were unsuccessful in their immediate request, they had pointed out a remedy that was to be increasingly adopted.

In 1825 Lieutenant Governor Douglas toured the county of Northumberland and at its next session he recommended to the Assembly that it subdivide the county and increase its representation.[34] Douglas had found that Northumberland in area encompassed one-third of the province and contained a population larger than any other county and that its population per member was 7,914 in contrast to only 2,853 for the province as a whole.[35] Under official pressure the Assembly trisected Northumberland and created the new counties of Kent and Gloucester and assigned one representative to each.[36] The Assembly by this action created a third level in the representation accorded counties. As originally established by Minute of Council in 1785 and confirmed by statute in 1791 the counties had been divided into two classes; the "Fundy" counties of Charlotte, St. John, and Westmorland and the capital county of York had been granted four representatives each, and the remaining counties were granted two.

The way had now been opened and in 1831 the upper parishes of the county of York achieved their desire and were erected into a distinct county.[37] The county town for Carleton was placed at Woodstock and the territorial disfranchisement of the residents of the upper St. John was materially reduced. Carleton was accorded one representative but the new county was not satisfied with being ranked as a third-class county and as a result of their agitation the representation of the counties of Carleton, Kent, and Gloucester was raised to two members each in 1834.[38] In 1837 the county of Gloucester, which was geographically divided into two parts by the valleys of the Nipisiguit and Restigouche rivers and in whose valleys the lumber trade had built two distinct economic and political centres, was divided into two parts by the erection of Restigouche County. Local administration and the exercise of the franchise were both facilitated.

The following years witnessed repeated attempts by interested parties to secure division of Charlotte, Westmorland, and Carleton and to increase the representation accorded Kings and Restigouche. In 1844 and 1845 the final adjustments were made. In order to overcome the isolation of the settlers on the furthest reaches of the St. John above Grand Falls and to reach the Madawaska settlers, Victoria County was carved out of Carleton; to overcome the isolation of the western residents of Westmorland occasioned by the need to ford the Memramcook and Petitcodiac rivers to reach Dorchester, the county town, Albert County was created out of Westmorland.[39] To overcome the under-representation of Kings and Northumberland counties, their representation was augmented, and although their populations were nearly equal, the representation of Kings was raised to three, but that of Northumberland to four. The special concession to Northumberland was a political necessity. The sharp cleavage in politics and commercial interests between Rankin and Cunard interests on the north and south shores of the Miramichi meant equal representation had to be accorded each side of the river. The province was now divided into fourteen counties, aligned in conformity with geography and settlement. The creation of these new electoral districts, each with its electoral circuit, and the gradual building of roads reduced to a considerable degree the disfranchisement caused by distance and difficult communications.

The next change in the franchise makes it necessary to consider again the condition of settlement and disposal of Crown lands. As mentioned, Crown lands had been given gratuitously to each applicant until 1827, at which time Bathurst had ordered them to be disposed by public auction, or leased to those unable to purchase.[40] This change in land policy had created a large class of leaseholders, squatters, and occupants who, having purchased land at auction, had failed to pay the instalments and remained on the land as occupants without titles, and were by the franchise laws excluded from the vote.[41] These three classes were in a somewhat different category from those who in former times voted on warrants of survey; the former groups had no prospects of ever receiving title deeds to the property they occupied, while the latter group ultimately did. Yet the convention had become firmly established that occupants of the proper quantity of landed property were eligible to vote the law notwithstanding.

Periodic attempts were made by individual reformers in the Assembly to remedy the legal situation and to give to the unqualified the right to exercise the franchise legally and openly and not by stealth. The purification of the exercise of the franchise was approached from two different points of view depending on whether the reformer had liberal or conservative inclinations. Fisher, a future Liberal Premier, sponsored bills on two occasions to grant the franchise to leaseholders;[42] Street, Boyd, and Brown two Conservatives and an Independent, sponsored a bill on five occasions to enforce the current franchise by the establishment of a voters' registry.[43] The moves to establish the voters' registry fared no better than the move to extend the franchise. Despite the precedent set by the Imperial Reform Act of 1832 and the support of Lieutenant Governor Colebrooke, the amorphous political state of the Assembly was unable to bring either reform to fruition. Unable to resolve the problem in a forth-

c*

right manner, the Assembly took the hesitant step of further raising the qualifications required of candidates from £200 to £300 over and above all encumbrances.[44]

For the second time the Assembly had increased the qualifications of members of the Assembly. It was a precautionary measure against the radical ramifications they feared from a franchise which had been allowed to deteriorate into a chaotic condition. The Assembly through both fear and lassitude refused to enforce or expand the franchise. From 1791 to the 1850's there was no change in the franchise except the enfranchisement of the Roman Catholics in 1810; yet in that period New Brunswick had increased in population tenfold, the French Revolution had come and gone, the conservative reaction had ebbed before the democratic revival in Europe, and Jacksonianism flourished in America, but New Brunswick lay in the arms of the old tradition. In New Brunswick there was no consistent advocacy for reform; men of liberal ideas entered the Legislature and for a few sessions advocated change, received their reward in minor offices, and became staunch upholders of the *status quo*. G. E. Fenety, after a lifetime of political journalism, wrote in his introduction to *Political Notes and Observations* that:

there was not as a rule a concentration of talents, a steady perseverance, for the attainment of a particular object, the correction of great political abuses. . . . In the absence of a steady purpose, then, the country was in want of the needful materials at this early day, out of which to present or give embodiment to a grievance. There being no fixity of principles, no sufficient number of able, disinterested men, to take the lead, the practice for many years among our representatives was but a nibbling at constitutional questions. . . . Our House of Assembly was but a reflex of the old party, completely beneath its control in all matters affecting individual rather than public interests. It was nearly as impossible to gather roses from thorns, as to extract liberal ideas from those to whom the people had confided conservative trusts. There were but few men bold enough to don the reform armour, and whet their swords for an encounter with the foe; and what were these among a party so numerous and interested in maintaining the status quo. . . . The attempts at reform therefore were only spasmodic, and for a long time seldom resulted in anything but failures.[45]

While the Assembly lacked the political fortitude to remedy the current chaos in the franchise, the situation was becoming rapidly untenable. It was no longer uncommon for large numbers of unqualified persons to march to the polls and vote, the rush at times being too great and the political excitement too strong for the candidates or poll clerks to stop and challenge doubtful applicants. Boyd of Charlotte, who had endured a controverted election in 1847, was satisfied that "had there been a Registry Bill in operation during the last election, he would not have been put to the trouble which he had since experienced. The fact was, that the rabble would pour in from all quarters, who had no right whatever to vote, and yet they would and did vote during the last election."[46] Fenety, speaking of this condition, said:

The number of scrutinies that followed every general election was the result of this lax system. The time of the House, or rather that of Committees drawn from the House, was usually occupied, a large part of the session dissecting the electoral lists, separating the genuine from the spurious votes, and striking a balance between the member in possession and the member in expectancy. Day after day the floors of the House . . . were all but deserted, the real business of the House in the meantime being at a standstill. Thus was time frittered away; and no wonder that a Registration Act was called for as a remedy for the mischief. But what concerned the public interests in this respect, did not appear to suit the convenience of those honourable gentlemen whose private influence at the polls sometimes brought more votes for them than could be possibly commanded by the legitimate operations of their opponents. The principle with them appeared to be—it were better to stick to a bad cause, and be on the winning side, than honestly assist to do right in the House, and consequently risk defeat at the polls.[47]

While the Assembly was incapable of remedying the chaos into which the franchise had fallen, the Executive Council took a step in 1848 which was to enfranchise legally a large number of the electorate.[48] Since the institution of the disposal of Crown lands by sale in 1827, many freeholders had been disfranchised because they lacked title deeds, having failed to complete the purchase of their lands. The Executive Council determined that title deeds should be given to the property at the time of purchase, the terms for the sale of Crown land remaining otherwise unaltered: one-quarter downpayment and the remainder in yearly payments secured by the purchaser's bond. This change enfranchised all purchasers of Crown lands and was in harmony with the current franchise law which allowed mortgagors to vote as long as they were in possession of the property. While the action of the Executive brought a numerous class legally within the franchise, it did not affect leaseholders or squatters who were unable to make the downpayment on Crown lands. These two classes of subjects, together with the pauper Irish who had emigrated into the towns and lumber camps of New Brunswick in the 1840's, formed a substantial class who were legally disfranchised although most of them as occupants of land exercised the franchise on sufferance and by convention.

The condition of the franchise was not merely irksome to the members through the involved scrutinies it precipitated but it was becoming dangerous as a result of the radicalism abroad among the new emigrants. In 1850 the citizens of the city of St. John became sufficiently alarmed to petition the Assembly for the incorporation of a voters' register into the election law of the province. The object of the petition was to prevent "a vast amount of imposition which takes place at the polls by persons who exercise what they frequently do not possess—the elective franchise and . . . the prevention of perjury which is too frequently committed by unprincipled men, upon these exciting occasions."[49] Although on previous occasions bills had been introduced in the Legislature to establish a voters' register, this was the first occasion in which the public had expressed their support of the measure. The alarm that precipitated this expression of support was economic. The adoption of free trade by Great Britain in 1846 had brought economic depression to the timber trade, the merchants, and shipping interests of New Brunswick. This economic stress produced a political radicalism among the unemployed and created a political awakening among the propertied class. The result was the establishment of a Colonial Association in St. John to advocate reciprocity with America and to secure among other reforms a voters' register and vote by ballot.[50] The Colonial Association's political programme was endorsed in petitions from the counties of York and Carleton in the ensuing year.[51] This programme received support from an unexpected source; the moralists associated with the temperance movement, desiring to bring purity and sobriety to elections, sponsored prohibition, vote by ballot, and a voters' registration. These planks were always espoused by the temperance candidates at a time when it was not fashionable for candidates to commit themselves at elections.[52]

The immediate result of this agitation was the incorporation of the voters' register and vote by ballot in the municipal corporation act of 1851 and in the act amending the incorporation of Fredericton.[53] The adoption of the voters' register and the ballot remained confined to municipal elections; the Assembly was not sufficiently enthusiastic to extend them into the provincial field. The edge was taken off the reform movement by the deflection of Wilmot and Gray from the ranks of the Liberal Opposition to the Government benches and the subsequent resignation in disgust of three prominent Liberals, Tilley, Ritchie, and Simmonds, when the electors of St. John returned Gray and Wilmot in the ministerial by-elections.[54] A few individual members continued to introduce bills to establish these reforms. Gray, the renegade Liberal, even sponsored a bill to establish a voters' register, but the Government was hostile and the measures were sidetracked by railway legislation.

The Government was not adverse to sidetracking the reforms because of the implications of the voters' register. If a voters' register was conceded, something would have to be done about the franchise. The adoption of a voters' register and the enforcement of the present franchise would result in the disfranchisement of large numbers who had long been accustomed to vote. If the franchise was extended, where should it stop? Should it be extended to leaseholders and to ratepayers? The latter extension had just proved such a failure in Nova Scotia that the province had had to adopt manhood suffrage, a prospect that appalled many members of the Government. The issue, however, could not be long evaded. Controverted elections from Westmorland and Charlotte counties were before select committees. Both elections had ultimately to be set aside when scrutinies stretching over two and three sessions respectively proved three hundred of the voters had been unqualified.[55] The publicity accompanying these scrutinies and the proddings of the Lieutenant Governor, Sir Edmund Head, forced a reluctant and divided Government to introduce legislation in 1853 to amend the election act.

The debate on the Speech from the Throne revealed the divisions in the Government. The Provincial Secretary, J. R. Partelow, indicated he supported vote by ballot and the voters' register, while the Attorney General, J. A. Street, and the Surveyor General, R. D. Wilmot, were opposed to the ballot.[56] When the legislation was introduced into the Assembly by the Attorney General, it made no provision for vote by ballot or a voters' register. It merely extended the franchise to leaseholders and placed the determination of controverted elections in the hands of commissioners independent of the Assembly. In committee, several amendments were moved to the bill by the Liberal Opposition, and after several attempts an amendment was carried by a vote of 18 to 17 incorporating the vote by ballot. The amendment was carried on the vote of the Provincial Secretary who voted against the Attorney General and the Surveyor General. When Gray, another member of the Government, moved and the Assembly adopted an amendment to establish a voters' register, the Attorney General washed his hands of the measure and declared that those of his colleagues who supported the amendments could now conduct the bill to its conclusion.[57]

In the face of its splintered ranks, the Government allowed the bill to die. In the ensuing session the Liberal Opposition and the Liberal press continued the pressure on the Government to introduce the ballot and the voters' register and extend the franchise. From Carleton County alone came five petitions pressing for these reforms. But the Government would not be forced into a repetition of its unseemly conduct of the previous session. The Attorney General refused to bring forward an election bill on the grounds that a voters' registry must form an integral part of such a measure and that the Assembly was too close to a general election to allow its establishment.[58] Unable to secure leave to introduce embarrassing legislation in the Assembly, the Liberals were able to secure the introduction into the Legislative Council of a bill to establish vote by ballot and a voters' register without instituting a change in the franchise. This bill, after a stiff battle, was given the three months' hoist in the Legislative Council on the grounds it was an infringement on the privileges of the Assembly.

In each case a main argument against the adoption of the voters' register was the cost of its establishment. Gray in 1853 would have placed the preparation of the voters' register in the hands of the same commissioners that were to determine controverted elections. These commissioners, being barristers of several years' standing, were competent to undertake the task, but the cost of employing such professional skill was prohibitive. While the Legislative Council bill, by retaining the existent franchise, would have disfranchised many conventional voters, it would have simplified the task of establishing a voters' register. As freeholders whose titles were registered were alone entitled to vote, it should have been simple to establish a voters' register from the records in the land titles office in each county.

The defeat of the Legislative Council bill brought the four-year life of the fifteenth General Assembly to a close with only the most minor change in the franchise. Any person possessing a freehold interest in real estate held in trust for charitable, educational, burial, or ecclesiastical purposes was to be disqualified from voting.[59] This statute had a distinct Orange flavour and was a reprisal against the Roman Catholic clergy for their success in preventing the incorporation of the Orange Society in 1850.

The four-year contest in the Assembly, while it had borne no fruit, had committed the Liberal press and many Liberal politicians to a reform of the franchise. The ballot was universally accepted as a party measure; its successful application in the municipal elections for Fredericton and St. John had silenced the sceptics. The voters' register was accepted in principle although the cost factor raised strong practical doubts. Over the extension of the franchise itself, there was little agreement. Some advocated the extension of the vote to leaseholders, while others advocated its extension to ratepayers, or to owners of a specified quantity of personal property.[60] The complexity of assessing personal property, the lack of municipal organization in many counties, and their lack of ratepayers all posed the question whether there was any half-way house between a freehold franchise and manhood suffrage. The failure of Nova Scotia to find a suitable intermediate franchise filled New Brunswick reformers with misgivings. These misgivings led the Liberal press into contradictions. It found itself advocating the extension of the franchise to ratepayers and to the assessed owners of real and personal property, while declaring in the same editorial that "we do not regard an extension or diminution of the suffrage of much importance."[61]

The Liberals had little time left to determine their stand on the extension of the franchise. The forces of the Sons and Daughters of Temperance were gathering to destroy the Conservative administration. The Conservatives had toyed with the affections of the temperance societies by passing a bill to prohibit the manufacture of intoxicating liquors. Having watched the mass evasion of this law by a conniving Government and a populace reduced to a nation of importers, the temperance societies were prepared to seek revenge. The election came and despite the vigour of the Orange support the Conservatives were returned as a minority Government. After a motion of want of confidence was moved and carried, the Conservative administration, conceding the principle of responsible government, resigned and the Liberals took office.

During the election, the temperance societies had sought to commit candidates to an acceptance of their triple platform of prohibition, the ballot, and the voters' register. While individual temperance candidates were numerous, the temperance workers in most constituencies endorsed the Liberal candidates, and by this transmutation the Liberal party became heir to the temperance platform. The temperance societies were not disappointed in their expectations. Within a year all three reforms were on the statute books under the Liberal administration of S. L. Tilley, the Provincial Secretary and a Most Worthy Patriarch of the Sons of Temperance.

If individual Liberals had had misgivings as to the need for electoral reform, the general election dispelled them. There were sixteen elections scrutinized and seven later reached the Assembly for final adjudication.[62] In the bitter St. John County election, the Conservatives were found to have created 250 fraudulent freeholders on swampland to take advantage of a ruling of a former controverted election committee that they would not inquire into the value of a freehold. If an elector was proved to possess a freehold, it was to be considered of the requisite value.[63] While the ruling was essentially a violation of the law, the controverted election committees, bearing in mind the customary size of freeholds, had adopted this rule to facilitate the determination of disputed returns. In the same county four hundred votes were objected to because those who tendered them did not possess a freehold. These squatters, leaseholders, and occupants of Crown and private lands had voted out of custom long standing, but the increasing political controversy attendant on the rise of political parties led the Liberal press to expostulate: "Here are four hundred men claiming to be freeholders and exercising their rights as such, yet who are not known to their neighbours or to the assessors to be possessed of any property and who do not contribute a penny towards the ordinary expenses of the county when at least one thousand men who pay over £3 a year of assessed taxes are excluded from voting."[64]

In the session of 1855 the Liberal Government under the auspices of the Attorney General, Charles Fisher, introduced the bill to regulate elections. The bill established the ballot, the voters' register, and extended the franchise. The latter issue produced the most controversy in the Assembly. The House divided across party lines on the extension. A few urged manhood suffrage based on the natural right of all free-born men to exercise control over the civil power, but these democrats did not reflect the overwhelming opinion of the Assembly.[65] The vast majority were obsessed with finding an electoral qualification that would enlarge the legal franchise but not start a chain reaction that would ultimately lead to manhood suffrage. The experience of Nova Scotia still served as a stern object lesson. Many Liberals as well as Conservatives were so impressed by Nova Scotia's plight that they were determined not to abandon even the current unsatisfactory freehold franchise.[66] Others like Street, the Conservative leader, felt the franchise could with safety be extended to leaseholders. Fisher destroyed the case of those who urged the retention of the current freehold franchise when he reminded the Assembly that the select committees on controverted elections had for years considered as valid the vote of any freeholder regardless of the value of his freehold. Thus in the late controverted election for Charlotte County, the select committee had confirmed votes of freeholders who owned a cranberry bog and a few acres of rock. Fisher was less successful in repudiating the leasehold franchise of which he had himself been an advocate as early as 1840. He simply stated that a leasehold franchise and a cheap voters' register were incompatible. He did not explain how an assessment franchise would produce a less costly voters' register.

The Liberal Government had determined on an assessment franchise. The vote was to be exercised by all freeholders assessed for real estate to the amount of £25, all owners of personal property or personal and real property to the value of £100, and all persons assessed as recipients of an annual income of £100.[67] This franchise extended the right to vote to all property owners, to urban artisans and rural leaseholders, and even to rural squatters whose personal and real property was assessed for £100. In addition those tradesmen and professionals receiving an income of £100 a year were to be enfranchised. The intention of the Government was to avail itself of the assessments made by the overseers of the poor in each parish as the basis of the voters' register and of the franchise. The assessors under the poor law were required to assess all real and personal estates within each parish and the incomes of the inhabitants of the same.[68] The extent of the franchise would in these circumstances depend on the breadth and thoroughness of the poor law assessment.

The assessment list of the parish assessors was to be the basis of the voters' register subject to revision by three revisors. The three revisors were to be elected or appointed annually according to the customary method of selecting officers in each parish; in incorporated counties the two councillors representing each parish together with a third person to be appointed by the county council would act as revisors; in the cities of St. John and Fredericton the revision was to be made by three aldermen appointed by the council for such purposes. These revisors were to be furnished each year by August with an assessment list by the parish assessors. From these lists they were to select and publish an alphabetical list of all qualified electors by September 1, and by the end of that month all claims to have electors added or struck from the list were to be in their hands. By October 10 they were to post a list of all electors protested against or seeking to be added to the voters' register, and two weeks later, on October 25, they were to hold their revision court and adjudicate claims for addition or subtraction from the register. They were then to draw up the final and corrected voters' list for each polling district and transmit it to the clerk of the Peace for the county by November 10. This list of electors was to serve as the voters' register for the ensuing year.

Why Fisher expected this assessment franchise to succeed when the ratepayers' franchise had failed in Nova Scotia is puzzling. It is true the municipal machinery in New Brunswick was somewhat better than in Nova Scotia, for the establishment of a general system of education dependent on a degree of local financial support had helped to strengthen the municipal organization and improve the assessment rolls provided by the poor law assessors. But there was no uniformity in the manner of assessment, it was adjusted to local prejudice, and local prejudice could not be expected to produce an assessment which would enfranchise the same class of people in adjacent counties. There was the added danger that the assessors in the absence of set rules of assessment could easily become political agents by slight adjustments in the valuation of real and personal property. This danger was enhanced by the fact that there was no deterrent such as the requirement in the ratepayers' franchise that taxes must have been paid on the assessment before one exercised the franchise. The Government in fact was dissuaded from accepting a ratepayers' franchise by the experience of Fredericton where candidates had created municipal electors by paying up their taxes and by this form of bribery had placed them under obligation at the polls.[69] When the Legislative Council had come dangerously close to incorporating this requirement in the bill, the Government had taken steps to safeguard their assessment franchise by the addition of two new legislative councillors.[70] The bill extended the legal franchise beyond that on the statute books since 1791, but since the franchise law had seldom been enforced there was legitimate reason to believe that the new franchise enforced by a voters' register would actually curtail the franchise. The knowledge that the voters' register would reduce the electorate was probably the reason why the Government pressed for an assessment franchise although the municipal machinery on which it would depend for its successful operation was less than adequate. Destined to suffer from a lack of uniformity in assessment methods, and from assessments conducted only at irregular intervals, the voters' register was further endangered from the refusal of the Government to bear any part of the cost of the preparation and revision of the voters' lists. The financial burden was left to the county, a condition not likely to induce its co-operation.

The act continued to accord the vote to non-resident property owners and indeed reduced the qualification from £50 to £25 as well as extending the privilege to owners of personal property where applicable. The act abolished the right of freemen of the city of St. John to vote for representatives of the city; but these tradesmen and merchants were not disfranchised as they would qualify on the assessment of their real or personal property. The qualification of members remained unchanged at £300 freehold property over and above encumbrances. The routine of the election remained unaltered except that no person could vote unless on the voters' register, and the result of the elections would not now be known at the end of polling but only some three days later when the sheriff would open the ballot boxes at his declaration court.[71] The act was not to be effective until January 1, 1857, although the machinery was to become operative a year earlier to allow for the preparation of the voters' register. As a result the act was not in effect when the Liberal Government was forced to go to the country. The financial effect of the Prohibition Act of 1855 on the provincial revenue had so alarmed the Lieutenant Governor that he dissolved the Assembly against the wishes of his ministers. The Liberals were defeated and the Conservatives assumed the reins of office faced with the responsibility of implementing a voters' register which they had not favoured.

The new Government found that in only five counties, Carleton, Sunbury, Albert, Restigouche, and York, had the voters' register been satisfactorily prepared. The city of St. John and the remaining nine counties had failed to complete the process of assessment and revision required by the election act.[72] The parties levelled charges at each other, the Liberals blaming the Government for every error and neglect of the assessors and revisors, and the Government charging the Liberals with disfranchising near 16,000 electors by establishing a faulty voters' register. Both claims were unjust. The Government could not be charged with the neglect of local officers over whom they had no control. In fact, considering the novelty of a voters' register the local officials had proved surprisingly resourceful, for at the parish level the voters' lists had been completed in all but 21 of the 108 parishes into which the counties of New Brunswick were divided. The new franchise established by the act had also proved less restrictive than some had feared. In four out of five counties in which the registers had been completed, the number of eligible voters were larger, in some cases substantially larger, than the voters at the previous election in 1856. While it is unjust to compare the number who voted with the number of potential voters, nevertheless, the resultant increase in the electorate was unexpected.

The surprise was mainly attributable to the eccentricities of the assessment system. Where the assessment franchise act appeared to increase the electorate in the frontier counties of Gloucester and Restigouche anywhere from 50 per cent to 30 per cent, it appeared to reduce the electorate in Sunbury by 20 per cent and appeared likely to reduce the electorate of the city and county of St. John by 40 per cent. The decline in the St. John electorate under the new franchise was not attributable to the disfranchisement of freemen or the "swamp" voters first created by the Tories in the election of 1854. The reason was the manner of assessment. In St. John, a low assessment and a high mill rate had discouraged many former electors from adjusting their assessment to retain their vote under the new franchise law.

The Conservative government, never enthusiastic about the assessment franchise, contemplated the abolition of the measure. But they were divided over the form of franchise they would substitute. Some of the party wished to proceed to manhood suffrage, others favoured a return to a simple freehold franchise.[73] The balance appeared to be swinging in favour of the latter when the designs of the Government on the franchise were cut short by a vote of want of confidence introduced by the Liberal Opposition. The motion critical of the Government's administration of the electoral and railway acts was defeated but only on the casting vote of the Speaker.[74]

Humbled by the motion of want of confidence, the Government felt that it dare go no further than delay the operation of the assessment franchise for another year. Elated, the Opposition was determined to force the government to accept immediately the new franchise regardless of the defective voters' registers. The Government, foreseeing the Opposition's intentions, moved that Lewis, the Liberal member from Albert County, should chair the Committee of the Whole and thereby release the Speaker for party divisions in the committee. The tactic paid off and the Government was able on a vote of 21 to 19 to defeat an Opposition amendment decreeing the last assessment roll the voters' register in all parishes where the revisors had failed to prepare a proper voters' register.[75] The Government then thought it wise to accept an amendment to its measure. The assessment franchise was to be immediately operative in the five counties in which the voters' register had been satisfactorily completed and delayed for one year in all other counties. Although the Liberals made a further attempt in the Legislative Council to substitute the raw assessment rolls for defective or non-existent voters' registers, the bill finally passed as approved by the Assembly.[76]

The operation of the assessment franchise was by this act deferred in all but the counties of York, Carleton, Sunbury, Albert, and Restigouche until January 1, 1858. As the Government fell before the session was completed, the Assembly was dissolved and a general election was conducted on two distinct franchises. In five counties all subjects assessed for £25 freehold, £100 personal property, or £100 income voted by ballot if their names were entered in the voters' register; in the remaining nine counties residents of the county voted by open declaration if they possessed a £25 freehold, non-residents if they possessed a £50 freehold; and in the city of St. John, freemen of the city also voted if they possessed £25 personal property.

The Liberals were returned to office and the continuance of the assessment franchise, the ballot, and the voters' register was assured. The new administration made no attempt to standardize provincial assessments; but both parties, finally convinced that the assessment franchise was not likely to be repealed, worked with vigour to overcome the delinquencies of the assessors by appeals to the revisors. So vigorously did the parties work that the voters' list prepared for the county and city of St. John lists as potential voters 70 per cent and 17 per cent more persons respectively than had polled in the late election.[77] With active party participation the voters' registers were completed in all counties and the ballot, the voters' register, and the assessment franchise were applicable to the next general election in 1861.

The remaining years to Confederation were so filled with controversy over railways and union that New Brunswick politicians made few attempts to change the franchise. Attempts were made to increase the representation but these attempts were as unsuccessful as was the campaign conducted by W. J. Gilbert of Westmorland to establish simultaneous polling throughout the province. For three successive sessions Gilbert sponsored bills to secure "the expression of the people between the rising and setting of the sun, all over the Province, the country speaking with one voice, in one day, on any question coming before them."[78] New Brunswick had had simultaneous voting within each county since 1843 but the politicians had proved that by adjusting election dates this procedure could be used to party advantage. The 1861 general election is an example. Early in that year, it had been revealed before a committee of the Assembly that Fisher, the Attorney General and leader of the Liberal government, had used his office to engage in speculation in Crown lands. The charges had been so damaging that his entire Council, led by Tilley, resigned. Tilley was then asked to form a new government and Fisher was removed from office. This incident precipitated a general election. After a preliminary test in a Liberal county had defeated the sitting Liberal member, the Liberals decided to attack their opponents rather than defend their own record. The Government called the elections for the city and county of St. John, a Conservative stronghold; a Liberal cabinet minister was moved from Victoria to run with Tilley, and the whole Liberal organization went into action. The result was the rout of the Tories. Wilmot and Gray, their leaders, went down and their defeat so prejudiced the Tory chances that the Liberals were returned to office with their majority unimpaired despite the scandal and internal division. While this was not the usual pattern which the Government of the day followed in calling the county elections, it illustrates the influence political success in one county exercised on party fortunes in another.

Although Gilbert's simultaneous election bill was supported by Nova Scotian example and it was public knowledge that the present method of calling elections had partisan implications, the Assembly would not adopt the practice. It was argued that province-wide simultaneous elections would deprive the country of the services of able politicians if they were denied the privilege of going from county to county offering their services until such time as they were accepted by the electors. It was also argued that it would allow a government to call a province-wide snap election and disfranchise multitudes as had happened at a late election in Charlotte when the sheriff called the election while the men were back in the bush. There was further opposition from the pro- and anti-Confederation members, who were loathe to caste aside any political device that might be exploited to advantage.

In conclusion it may be said the New Brunswick franchise was until 1855 legally confined to freeholders but was in practice open to all occupants of land. While the assessment franchise of 1855 gave political voice to tradesmen, professionals, and the upper level of clerical workers, it did not enfranchise the labouring class who were in the census of 1861 calculated to comprise 21 per cent of all males over sixteen years.[79] There was no pressure to extend the franchise to this class, for public opinion was veering away from manhood suffrage, the American Civil War being considered an object lesson to proponents of manhood suffrage.[80] Nova Scotia was to abandon it in 1864 and the Australian state of Victoria was reported as looking for a road back. The colonial period closed in New Brunswick as in Nova Scotia with a franchise legally more liberal than at the colonies' origins but, because of changes in the economic life of the colonies, in practice less liberal.

CHAPTER SIX

THE CANADAS

I. Lower Canada

FOLLOWING THE CESSION of Quebec to the British Crown, the colony was governed for nearly thirty years without benefit of representative institutions. Although there had been intermittent agitation on the part of the British settlers for an assembly, the agitation did not receive attentive consideration until after the American Revolutionary War. On Dorchester's reappointment as Governor General, and because of the influx of loyalists and the continuing controversy over the retention of the French Civil Code, he was instructed to report on public sentiment.[1] When Dorchester, by nature hostile to democracy, had to report that the agitation for an assembly would annually increase and when the agitators were successful in presenting their case at the Bar of the House, the Home Government determined to revise the government of Quebec.[2]

The decision to concede an assembly to Quebec required Imperial legislation. The other British North American colonies had received an assembly through the exercise of the royal prerogative, but in Quebec it was necessary first to repeal the Quebec Act. Grenville, the Home Secretary, in whose department the administration of the colonies rested, was required to prepare the necessary legislation. He decided to create two distinct colonies, Lower and Upper Canada, and in order to end the racial and legal controversy, to allow Lower Canada and its French Canadian majority to retain the French Civil Code while Upper Canada was to follow the Common Law.

The draft bill,[3] submitted to Dorchester for comment, make it plain that no religious restraint was to be placed on the exercise of the suffrage, that the franchise was to be confined to persons of twenty-one years who were natural-born British subjects or were residents of the province and had been born within the province prior to the conquest. The decision to grant the French Canadians the right to vote and the right to membership in the Assembly was a continuation of a policy first evidenced by the Quebec Act when Roman Catholics were appointed to the Governor's Council. It was a concession to necessity and it was acquiesced in by the English population.[4]

Dorchester approved of this concession and recommended its extension to all inhabitants of Quebec who had resided in the province prior to the conquest although they might not be native born. Hopeful of augmenting the population by immigration, Dorchester also recommended the extension of the franchise to all foreigners who were naturalized under Imperial or provincial law.[5] While Grenville agreed to the enfranchisement of all residents of Quebec at the conquest whether native or foreign born, he at first demurred at extending the right to naturalized subjects,[6] but he ultimately relented sufficiently to allow foreigners naturalized by Imperial statute to vote and be members of the Assembly. In addition, Dorchester had recommended that all persons attainted for treason, felony, militia desertion, and bankruptcy should be disqualified from the franchise. Grenville accepted his recommendation as regards those convicted of treason or felony but felt that further disqualifications were a matter of local regulation and should not be incorporated in the constitution. The Constitutional Act,[7] thereupon, specified that all persons over twenty-one years who had not been convicted of treason or felony and were not disqualified by provincial law might vote, if they were natural-born British subjects or if they had become British subjects by cession of Canada to the Crown, or had been naturalized by an Imperial act and if they possessed the requisite property qualifications.

The property qualifications specified in the Constitutional Act were the result of political pressures in the British House of Commons. Grenville, in dispatching the first draft to Dorchester, had left the section dealing with the property qualifications blank so that Dorchester with his knowledge of local conditions might fill in the detail. Grenville, however, had taken the liberty to suggest in marginal notes what qualifications he considered proper. He suggested that electors in counties should be confined to owners of property of a yearly value of £5, and in urban centres to owners of a dwelling house or to residents possessed of £100 personal property. Dorchester had incorporated these suggestions without change in his revision of the draft and it was these property qualifications that had been presented to the House of Commons.

These qualifications were higher than any prevalent in the other British North American colonies. While a New Brunswick bill which would have confined the franchise to freeholders possessing an estate valued at £20 awaited approval at the Home Office, it was not as stiff a qualification as possession of an estate valued at £5 per annum. The conservative nature of the qualifications suggested by Grenville may have been inspired by the plan for an assembly drawn up by a citizens' committee in Quebec and Montreal in 1784 but not presented to Grenville until 1789. This plan had suggested the franchise should be confined to owners of urban property valued at £40, and to owners of a farm at least one and a half acres in front by twenty acres in depth.[8] It appears unlikely, however, that this petition did more than confirm a conclusion drawn from the American Revolution that a low franchise encouraged democratic and republican sentiments.[9]

When the bill came before the House of Commons, the franchise qualifications came under the attack of the Whigs. Fox was critical of the establishment of a restrictive franchise at a time when the principles of freedom were so much abroad in the world, and he felt it would undermine and contradict the professed purpose of the bill which was the introduction of popular government.[10] Its critics made the disturbing comparison "that the laws of this country, where money is more plentiful, considering a freehold of forty shillings per annum a sufficient qualification, do strongly decide against the clause of this Bill which requires a freehold of five pounds per annum as a qualification in a country where money is less plentiful, the price of labour much higher and the best directed industry less productive."[11] Pitt, who prided himself on bringing a government to Quebec as near as nature and the situation would admit to a copy of the British Constitution, was forced to agree to the enfranchisement in the counties of the owners of real property producing a yearly revenue of 40s. rather than £5. In towns the owners of a dwelling house and lot of ground worth £5 per annum were enfranchised, as were householders resident twelve months in the town who rented a dwelling house for £10 per annum. As a result of Whig intervention, the franchise given Lower and Upper Canada was as liberal as any in British North America. Few heads of rural families should have been disfranchised.

The Constitutional Act specified that the property conferring the franchise might be held *en fief, en roture*, in freehold, or by certificate issued under the authority of the Governor and Council of the Province of Quebec. The first two forms were tenures that had prevailed in Quebec during the French regime and were the basic tenures of the seigniorial system. Tenure *en fief* involved the possession of land by grant from the Crown on certain specific obligations, an obligation of fealty and homage, an obligation of military service, an obligation to pay the Crown a mutation fine or quint equivalent to one-fifth of the value of the seigniory on all cases of transfer except by direct descent, and from 1711 an obligation to subgrant the seigniory to habitants.[12] The conquest of Quebec by British arms involved a transfer of the seigniors' obligations from the French to the British Crown and in no way invalidated the tenure. The seignior in turn subgranted his lands to habitants who were under specific obligations to the seignior. Holding their lands *en roture*, they were obliged annually to pay *cens et rentes*, a nominal sum payable in money or kind which was a combination rent for the use of the land and a recognition of the seignior's authority. The habitants were obliged to provide a fixed number of days of labour, *corvée*, to their seignior and to conform to the seignior's banal rights such as having their grain ground at the seignior's mill. On transfer of their farm by sale or descent, the habitants were obliged to pay a mutation fine, *lods et ventes*, to the seignior equivalent to one-twelfth of the value of the farm, of which sum by custom the seignior remitted one-third. These were the main obligations the seignior owed his lord, and the habitant, his seignior. If the seignior and habitant met their obligations they could not be dispossessed, and were able to sell or convey by gift or demise as freely as if they held their property by freehold tenure.[13]

The two forms of tenure, freehold and seigniorial, were both prevalent in Quebec. Freehold tenure had been introduced into all new land grants for a brief period following the completion of the Treaty of Paris in 1763, but grants in this form had been suspended on the recommendations of Governor Carleton. In July, 1771, an additional Instruction to Carleton had authorized that lands for the future be granted in seigniorial tenure only, and this Instruction was continually renewed.[14] The advent of the loyalists introduced no change in this policy.[15] The loyalists disliked seigniorial tenure and Dorchester in 1787 had to advise the Home Secretary that there should be a return to freehold tenure.[16] The advice was taken and the Constitutional Act decreed that lands in Upper Canada were to be granted in freehold and those already granted on seigniorial tenure were to be regranted. In Lower Canada lands were to continue to be granted *en fief* unless the grantee specifically requested a freehold which request was to be accommodated.

Tenure under certificate of occupation had grown up because the authorities had not been able to handle the sudden influx of loyalists. The Royal Instructions having required grants *en fief* to be made only after a satisfactory survey would ensure a correct title, the Governor and Council had had to issue certificates of occupation or warrants of allotment and survey. These certificates were to have been temporary and were to have been replaced by titles *en fief* when the surveys were completed, but the hostility to tenure *en fief* had delayed their disappearance.

In the matter of representation the Constitutional Act left the creation of representative districts and the assignation of representatives to the governors of each province with the proviso that there should be a minimum of sixteen and fifty members for Upper and Lower Canada respectively. Grenville, having found the seven judicial and administrative districts into which Quebec had been divided[17] too massive for representative purposes, had suggested to Dorchester that the Governor General should be authorized to divide the province into counties and towns and to assign representation subject to the proviso that the bill would determine the number of counties and the number of representatives for each province. Dorchester redrafted the bill to remove any limit on the discretion of the Governor General as to the number of counties or members but specified that the representation in Lower Canada should not be less than thirty and in Upper Canada not less than sixteen.

In this form the bill had reached the House of Commons where the Whigs were very critical of the power vested in the Governor to create counties and allot representation.[18] They had, however, to acquiesce as the Imperial Parliament lacked the local knowledge necessary to specify these details in the Imperial act. They then concentrated their attack on the small size of the assemblies, Fox charging "that sixteen was a good number for an aristocracy but by no means for a democracy."[19] Pitt, under strong pressure for a people "fully and freely represented," refused to raise the minimum representation for Upper Canada above sixteen but agreed to raise the minimum representation of Lower Canada to fifty.[20] In consequence when the Constitutional Act came into effect in 1792 the lieutenant governors of Lower and Upper Canada by proclamation divided each province into counties and allotted fifty and sixteen members respectively.

The establishment of representative government by Imperial enactment posed a unique problem. The franchise, representation, appointment of returning officers, the duration, time, and place of elections were all regulated by an Imperial act. Was there any way in which the assemblies of Lower and Upper Canada could modify the franchise or representation? The Constitutional Act itself gave permissive authority to the provincial assemblies to modify the allocation of representation, the numbers of representatives, the appointment of returning officers, the duration, time, and place of elections; but the act did not permit them to modify the franchise. Aside from the power to disqualify specific professional or criminal classes from the franchise, the provincial assemblies were obliged to allow all possessors of land of 40s. yearly value to vote until such times as the Imperial Parliament should amend the Constitutional Act.

The inability to alter the franchise locally proved of little consequence. In the political turmoil incident to the workings of representative government in Lower Canada, when no institution or personality was above criticism or abuse, the franchise came in for no share of the denunciation. On March 1792, the *Quebec Gazette* commended the wisdom and justice of the British Parliament in "qualifying almost every inhabitant in the Province to vote"; and in 1832 a petition of grievances from the city of Montreal stated that the petitioners were sincerely attached "to that part of the Constitution which being wisely adapted to the state of society in this country where almost every father of a family is a freeholder, has rendered the right of voting at the election of members of the Assembly nearly universal."[21] These opinions from divergent sources and spanning forty years of political strife indicate that the franchise as set forth in the Constitutional Act was eminently satisfactory to the majority of Lower Canadians.

This satisfaction was due to the universality of the franchise. The suffrage, extending in the counties to all who possessed land in freehold, *en fief*, or *en roture* which yielded an annual revenue of 40s., was easily met. The minimum holding held *en roture* had been set by royal ordinance prior to the conquest at a farm with a frontage of one and a half lineal arpents and thirty to forty arpents in depth.[22] This edict issued in 1745 had been necessary to curb the effect of the laws of inheritance[23] which were leading to an uneconomic subdivision of the habitants' holdings. Placing a limit of from forty to fifty acres on the holding of each habitant, the edict had created a floor as to the size of rural holdings and as a result the franchise "scarcely excluded one farmer in a thousand."[24]

While there was no mention of the franchise in the 1834 compilation of grievances known as the ninety-two resolutions, it was nevertheless true that consideration had been given to changing the franchise during the life of the Lower Canada Assembly. When Craig's tactless administration had changed the temperate rivalry of two cultures into an implacable fight of two races, an adjustment of the franchise had been contemplated. The English controlled the governorship and the Executive and Legislative councils, while the French Canadians controlled the Assembly. The latter had only gradually come to recognize the importance of the Assembly and of using their franchise to make it subservient to their wishes.[25] As the number of English and pro-administration French noblesse in the Assembly declined before the expressed votes of the habitants, consideration had been given to adjust the franchise in order to curb the political power of the French Canadian party.

Sir James Craig initiated action in 1810 after he had had to prorogue the Assembly for a second dissolution within the year because of a deadlock between the two legislative chambers over a bill to disqualify judges from voting or sitting in the Assembly. Although Craig employed John Henry, a secret service agent, to devise a new franchise, the scheme had to be abandoned.[26] It was found impossible to fashion a franchise which would curb the habitant vote but not obliterate it. The difficulty was occasioned by the near uniformity of each habitant's holding. Craig was forced to conclude that nearly every farm exceeded the value required by the existing franchise but "the farms in general run so nearly of the same value, or vary only on account of being in a more or less favorable part of the Province, that any qualification under the general average would bear the right of suffrage very near where it now is, and if it were established at a higher rate, it might perhaps narrow the right below its fair limits."[27] Afraid to provoke the outrage of a mass disfranchisement, the Governor felt obliged to leave the franchise unchanged.

While the administration never again contemplated a revision of the franchise, changes were urged upon the Colonial Office on several subsequent occasions. Rev. John Strachan and Chief Justice Willian Campbell of Upper Canada urged the heightening of the franchise.[28] Campbell felt the unrest in Lower Canada originated in the premature conferment of virtual manhood suffrage which had "unfortunately placed it completely in the power of the most numerous tho' least useful and important part of the community, to exclude the other part from any effective share in the representation." This "great injustice," he felt, could "only be remedied by a change in the qualification of electors and elected both which should be very considerably raised in value." Strachan suggested that the franchise be confined to persons possessing a freehold of £5 per annum in the counties, £10 per annum in the town or a year's residence in a house whose rent was £20 per annum. Campbell suggested ownership of one hundred acres of land in the counties, ownership of a house or lot in the towns or tenancy of a house whose annual rent was £50. Their advice was never acted upon, for these eminent Upper Canadians in ignoring seigniorial tenure revealed their ignorance of the Lower Canada scene. The modification of the urban franchise as distinct from the rural was agitated by the Lower Canada commercial interests. Following the 1834 general election the adjustment of the urban franchise became an urgent rather than an academic issue to the commercial interests, for in that election "the whole of the population not of French origin in the cities and counties of Quebec and Montreal, although they nearly equal the French population in number, have not been able to return one member of their choice, out of twelve."[29] The agitation continued without success until the suspension of representative government.

The English commercial interests had not been alone in desiring changes in the urban franchise. The French and rural party had become concerned with this franchise when they had seen the seat of their chief, Louis Joseph Papineau, rendered insecure by the increasing English vote in the West ward of Montreal. They took positive steps to contain this danger prior to the 1834 general election. Taking advantage of the provision in the Constitutional Act which allowed the Assembly to prescribe who should be disqualified from voting, they disqualified all proprietors in common.[30] These citizens, known commonly as co-proprietors, were partners in commercial ventures and had been allowed to vote on their real property held in common. Racial discrimination was clearly evident in the nature of the disqualification and the manner in which it was secured. While commercial partners were common among the English the disqualification had specifically excepted co-heirs who were common among the French because of the manner of equal succession. The French party had taken advantage of the establishment of two select committees to revise the election law and the law relative to controverted elections to secure the disqualification.[31] When Neilson, chairman of the former committee, had opposed the disqualification[32] and internal bickering had rendered its deliberations abortive, the Papineau forces had attached the disqualification as a rider to the controverted election bill emanating from the second select committee. In the excitement attendant on the passage of the ninety-two resolutions this bill with its offending rider passed the Legislative Council unobserved.

The oversight was forcefully brought home to the Montreal and Quebec merchants in the ensuring general election. Enraged, they sought through the agency of the Constitutional Association to bring pressure to secure repeal of the disqualification.[33] They were fortunate in that the Colonial Secretary had disapproved of another clause in the act which would have sustained select committees beyond the prorogation of the Assembly and he had ordered the Governor General to secure repeal of this clause or the act would be disallowed.[34] When the Legislative Council made the repeal of the latter clause contingent on the Assembly re-enfranchising the co-proprietors, the amendment was not passed and the act was disallowed.[35] The disallowance terminated the disqualification of the co-proprietors.

On balance the English commercial interests were not treated as badly as they claimed. By convention urban property owners were allowed to vote in the urban elections and in the elections for the encircling county. The convention was doubtless fostered by the lack of distinct urban municipal governments, the urban centres remaining for administrative and judicial purposes part of their county. This convention accrued to the primary benefit of the English merchants of Montreal, Quebec, and Three Rivers. While the rural electors of these counties did petition the Assembly to secure the abolition of this privilege, Papineau with his control of the Assembly secure did not bother to act.[36]

There remain two problems to consider: the attempts to increase the qualifications of members of the Assembly and the attempts to adjust the representation. These issues were approached by the English party from the same point of view from which it had approached the franchise. Members' qualifications and representation were to be adjusted in such a manner as to increase disproportionately the English strength in the Assembly. Throughout the life of Lower Canada it was the constant object of the English party to change a racial minority in the country into a political majority in the Assembly. While its goal was never achieved during the life of Lower Canada, it was achieved on the passage of the Act of Union.

The Constitutional Act had specified that a member of the Assembly must be twenty-one years, a British subject, and not a member of the Legislative Council or of a religious order. The Act did not specify that a member should possess even the property qualification of an elector. The seigniors had taken up this lack of qualification in the first Assembly but the bill to establish qualifications was lost when the English members refused to give their support.[37] The English members came to regret this refusal, for the habitants soon replaced the seigniors in the Assembly, and by 1800 when the English members decided qualifications were advisable they were unable to carry the measure.[38] Recourse was then had to the Imperial Parliament. In 1810, among his suggestions for a reunion of the provinces, Craig urged the establishment of a stiff property qualification for members. He suggested members should be required to possess land producing a clear annual revenue of £100 or personal property to the value of £2000 above all encumbrances.[39] It was his belief that this qualification would exclude from the Assembly the excessively ignorant, a class that had been the subservient tools of men like Papineau, Bedard, and Bourdages.[40] When the reunion of the colonies was before the House of Commons in 1822–23, Dalhousie strongly endorsed the qualification that future members be required to own real property to the clear value of £500.[41] The union bill failed of passage but the Colonial Office was again urged in 1828 to amend the Constitutional Act to establish a stiff qualification of £500 clear annual income in the expectation that "it would be attended with the additional benefit of giving a fair chance to the British part of the community to obtain a share in the representation which they can never have as the law stands at present."[42] When the life of the Lower Canada Assembly was terminated, the Legislative Council had under consideration an address to the Crown with a similar object. The desire to disfranchise the French Canadians by limiting their choice of representatives had failed in Lower Canada but the agitation was not unfruitful; Poulett Thomson became enamoured of the idea and on his recommendation the Act of Union set the qualification for members of the Assembly of the Province of Canada at ownership of real property to the value of £500 above all encumbrances.[43]

The question of representation in Lower Canada was closely associated as elsewhere with the problem of territorial disfranchisement; but nowhere else was the association so bedevilled by race and creed. Territorial disfranchisement in Lower Canada had been initially accentuated by Lieutenant Governor Clarke's manner of dividing the colony. Clarke had divided the colony into twenty-one counties on the basis of their population with little regard to their territorial area or potentialities. He had made no attempt, as had been done in Upper Canada, to strike a balance between population and area. The county of Buckingham, for example, extended for more than sixty miles down river from the head of Lake St. Peter and reached inland to encompass all the land between the St. Lawrence and the American border. It exceeded in area the combined counties of Kent, Surrey, Montreal, Leinster, and Warwick.[44] Since the large as well as the small counties possessed a single poll, the lack of roads and the great distances meant proximity to a poll was of greater importance in enfranchisement than a liberal franchise.[45]

It must be said, however, that the situation was, at the commencement of representative government, rendered less acute by the manner of settlement. The main settlements, being on the seigniories, formed one continuous line along the banks of the St. Lawrence and the river served as an avenue of communication to the polls. But as time passed and settlement spread from frontage on the St. Lawrence to the tributary rivers and the back lots in the seigniories, the disfranchisement occasioned by isolation increased. The evil was made worse by the original location of the county boundaries. These had not been designed to follow the natural configuration of the land but had been delimited by lines running straight into the interior and perpendicular to the St. Lawrence. As a result the tributaries of the St. Lawrence could not serve their natural function as avenues of movement from the interior to the polls situated on the north and south shores of the St. Lawrence.

The initial sparsity of petitions confirms the view that the populace did not at first view territorial disfranchisement as a serious problem; but the spread of settlement soon led to complaints. The Assembly, taking cognizance of the changing conditions, in 1800 created a second poll in nine counties and in 1807 added a second poll in a further two counties.[46] The Assembly might have gradually continued to overcome the problem by the creation of additional polls had the racial issue not intruded. The growth of English settlement in the townships laid out on the waste lands of the Crown beyond the seigniories became appreciable after 1800, and the worst features of territorial disfranchisement came to coincide with an area settled by a racial minority.

The settlers in the Eastern Townships and at a later date the settlers in the townships on the Ottawa[47] became aroused at their inability to exercise their franchise and at finding themselves represented in the Assembly by French Canadians returned by the residents of the seigniories. They sought a remedy not alone in the provision of more numerous and convenient polls but in the erection of the townships into distinct counties.[48] Whereas the erection of counties had been originally accomplished by executive proclamation, it was impossible to repeat this procedure as the Constitutional Act had required all subsequent changes in county structure to be made by an act of the Assembly.[49] In a racially sensitive Assembly, the creation of new counties in the Eastern Townships with the ensuing increase in English representation could be accomplished only with the exercise of great tact. Craig's appointment as Governor General was therefore most unfortunate. He had no sympathy for or understanding of the French Canadians and envisaged his mission in Canada to be the seizing of control of the Assembly for the English race.[50] The French Canadians were quick to discern his intentions and were unprepared to assist in their own destruction. Craig converted the remedy for territorial disfranchisement into a bitter bone of contention between the two races. His conduct was to embroil the Imperial authorities in the racial struggle. For as he foresaw, the intransigency of the Assembly would inevitably lead to appeals from the English citizens for Imperial legislative intervention.[51]

The events transpired as foreseen. The French Canadians, who had come to regard the Legislative Assembly as a bulwark of their racial survival, refused to open its doors to increased English representation. The township petitions, which became an annual event from 1819, were disregarded. The estimates[52] of township population were considered fanciful, a suspicion which the annual refusal of the Legislative Council to authorize a provincial census did nothing to dispel. Imperial intervention, which the Colonial Secretary had refused to contemplate in 1810, was by 1822 sought from the Imperial Parliament by an Under-Secretary for the Colonies.[53] In the bill to reunite the Canadas (necessitated by a deadlock over the distribution of the Montreal customs revenue), the Colonial Office had included a provision to allow the Governor General to erect every six townships into a county and assign it a represesentative.

The bill failed to pass the House of Commons, but it generated, a sharp change in the attitude of the contending parties. The obduracy of the French Canadian majority in the Assembly was softened on the realization that their control of representation might be breached if they did not make concessions. The arrogance of the English Canadians was heightened by their confidence that the Imperial Parliament would not remain indifferent to their plight. The Assembly, commencing in 1823, now annually sponsored a bill to augment the representation and the Legislative Council annually rejected it.[54] The Legislative Council claimed the bills were racial gerrymanders, which was the object of its own connivings. For its assertion that the increase in representation should be confined to the townships and its denial of the assertion of the Assembly that the province-wide growth in population warranted a general increase in representation, stemmed from the attempt to augment the slender English bloc in the Assembly at the expense of the increasing population of the seigniories.[55]

The Legislative Council was confident that in time it would secure its object by Imperial intervention and each year saw the demand for township representation passed on to the Colonial Office. It was, therefore, with the utmost satisfaction that it saw a select committee of the House of Commons established in 1828 to investigate Lower Canada's affairs. The issue of representation was brought before the committee. Nielson and Cuvillier were sent over to present the French and Assembly point of view that the Assembly had been and was willing to adjust the representation of the townships and seigniories on the basis of population. Gale and Ellice appeared to present the English and Legislative Council point of view that representation in a new and rapidly developing country should not be based on population but rather should be based on territorial area.[56] After laudatory passing references to the Upper Canadian method where representation was based on a joint consideration of area and population,[57] Gale and Ellice struck out for the adoption of the system prevailing in the state of Vermont. That state had adopted area as the sole basis for representation. It has been divided into 246 townships, each six miles square, and if possessed of any settled inhabitants each township returned one representative regardless of any disparity in their populations.[58] When the report of the select committee was received it was a disappointment to the English interests for it did not recommend Imperial intervention. It left the remedy to the Legislative Assembly of Lower Canada with the recommendation that they might adopt the representative system operating in Upper Canada.[59]

After initial attempts of both chambers to get their principle of representation adopted, the Assembly and Legislative Council jarred to a compromise on the Upper Canada principle of balancing territory and population.[60] The legislation reorganized the county boundaries, created nineteen additional counties, and assigned one representative to each county with a population of 1,000 and a second to each county whose population was in excess of 4,000.[61] When eight representatives reached the Assembly from the Eastern Townships in 1830, the racial and territorial disfranchisement which they had suffered for a quarter of a century was ended.

The representation act of 1829 did not end English complaints that they were discriminated against.[62] Nor did the revelation of the census of 1831 that representation was heavily weighed in favour of the less populous counties still their clamour.[63] What the English wanted was not equality of treatment but preferential treatment. The Assembly was undoubtedly never motivated by a desire to enhance English influence, but the population figures could nevertheless justify its action. The English population was somewhat less than one-quarter of the total provincial population and was so scattered among the French Canadian population that except in the townships it could not legitimately expect independent representation. The Gosford Commission in 1836 rejected the charge that the redistribution of 1829 could be charged with unfairness, but to accommodate the English clamour it did suggest the adoption of a system of proportional representation.[64] The existing constituencies were to be abolished and replaced by large constituencies returning a number of representatives in proportion to their population. Each elector was to be allowed one vote and by the machinery of proportional representation it was believed the nationality of the elected members would bear a close approximation to the numbers of each race. This suggestion never gained the acceptance of the English population, who wanted not representation in proportion to their numbers but representation in proportion to their "commercial enterprize and active intelligence."[65] During the separate existence of Lower Canada, they never achieved their aim. They were to press their case on Lord Durham without success; but when the Imperial Parliament came to unite the Canadas on the basis of equal representation in a joint Assembly, the English were to achieve their goal and turn a racial minority into a political majority.

While the representation act of 1829 had reduced territorial disfranchisement, it was by no means eliminated. French outsettlements, which had long suffered in silence lest their complaints should bolster the English case, began to demand an improvement in polling facilities. In the five years following 1829 eight counties ranging from the Magdalen Islands to the Ottawa petitioned for additional polls;[66] and the creation of eleven new counties was sought as another means of securing improved facilities. Provisional steps to ease the situation were taken by the erection of additional polls in seven counties;[67] but the political turmoil during the final years of the life of Lower Canada prevented the preparation of a thorough-going remedy.

II. Upper Canada

THE FRANCHISE of Upper Canada was similar to that of Lower Canada, both being determined by the Constitutional Act. All residents of the province who were twenty-one years, natural-born British subjects, subjects naturalized by act of the Imperial Parliament, or subjects by the conquest and cession of Canada, and who had not been convicted of treason or felony nor disqualified by provincial statute, were eligible to enjoy the franchise. These residents could exercise the franchise if as residents in a rural riding they possessed for their own use property to the yearly value of 40s. sterling above all charges, or as residents in an urban riding they possessed for their own use a dwelling house and lot of ground of the yearly value of £5 sterling or having been residents within a town for twelve months had paid a year's rent for a dwelling house to the amount of £10 sterling.

The Constitutional Act had declared that the property the electors were required to possess was to be held in freehold, *en fief*, *en roture*, or by certificate issued by the Governor and Council of the Province of Quebec. In the first election for Upper Canada the large majority of the settlers appear to have voted on certificates of occupation issued by the Governor of the Province of Quebec as a preliminary stage to the establishment of seigniorial tenure, while a few electors voted on seigniorial tenure especially in the counties of Essex and Kent.[68] This election was the first and last occasion in which seigniorial tenure can be said to have formed the basis of the Upper Canada franchise. For the Constitutional Act had declared all future grants of land in Upper Canada were to be in freehold and the certificates of occupation issued by the Governor and Council of Quebec were to be replaced by grants in freehold.

While these certificates were recognized by the Constitutional Act as a title of sufficient validity to confer the franchise, the question arose whether such certificates issued by the authority of the Lieutenant Governor and Council of Upper Canada conferred the same privilege. It was not until 1821 that the question was brought before the Assembly by a controverted election in the county of Durham. In this election the returning officer had struck off votes tendered by holders of certificates of occupation, popularly called location tickets, and in so doing had reversed the standing of the candidates.[69] The Assembly, after two weeks' debate, ruled that location tickets granted under the authority of the Lieutenant Governor and Council of Upper Canada did not confer such a freehold qualification as to entitle the resident holder to vote.[70]

This decision, reached on a vote of 25 to 10, was surprising. The privilege of the franchise conferred by the Constitutional Act on holders of certificates of occupation issued by the Governor and Council of Quebec might by corollary have been expected to apply to their counterpart issued under the authority of the Lieutenant Governor and Council of Upper Canada. Until 1818, the certificates issued by the authorities in Upper Canada had been verbatim copies of the certificates issued by the Governor of Quebec; the holder was merely required "to occupy and improve" his property and the title deeds would be issued. In both cases only non-residence could prevent the ultimate issuance of the titles, and the law had always treated the holders as possessing an equitable freehold in their land.[71] After October, 1818, when the settlement duties were stiffened, the ultimate transition from location ticket holder to freeholder became less certain, and the Assembly could have used this fact as an argument to support their decision.[72] They did not. The reasons put forward in opposition to the enfranchisement of the holders of location tickets were the power it gave to the Executive to swamp the Assembly with subservient men by saturating counties with location tickets before each election; and the lack of wisdom in giving the immigrant settlers a voice in the government of the country before they had become "permanently established and possessed of such a stake as could be deemed a sufficient pledge for their future conduct and interestedness in the general prosperity of the colony."[73] The latter reason weighed most heavily with the Assembly and explains why members normally supporters of the administration joined with the opposition to deny the vote to holders of location tickets.

The fear that the old settlers might lose control of the Assembly was occasioned by the upsurge in immigration that had followed the end of the Napoleonic Wars, the disbandment of Wellington's armies, and the attendant depression in the manufacturing and agricultural industries in Great Britain. It was not that the Assembly as such was opposed to the principle of extending the franchise, rather they were afraid of the effect of such an extension on their hegemony. Gordon, member for Kent, gave voice to this fear. He approved the extension of the franchise, and had he the power would have extended the right "to all land occupants being natives of the country, or who by long residence or personal services in its defence had proved their fidelity and attachment to it; but he should doubt the wisdom of including in such extension the number of strangers who were daily flocking in upon them. . . . in many sections of the country they already outnumber the old inhabitants and might very soon do so in all."[74] The Durham County election itself had been an illustration of this danger. It was the Ulstermen from the newly settled township of Cavan who, denouncing the old settlers of Port Hope as Yankees, had given the majority to their candidate, George Boulton.

The Ulstermen of Cavan did not accept the ruling of the Assembly as final but dispatched to the Lieutenant Governor a petition for His Majesty. Maitland forwarded the petition under a covering letter which impartially explained the attitude of both parties, and while he expressed no preference, he did indicate that a large portion of the population of the province was in the same situation as the petitioners, being recent immigrants.[75] Maitland urged for a speedy and authoritative decision on the question whose agitation was maintaining feelings of jealousy and distrust between the old and new settlers.

While the Law Officers of the Crown laboured over a period of five years to deliver an opinion, the Province of Upper Canada was subjected to a general election. In this contest the holders of location tickets were disfranchised by the aforementioned resolution of the Assembly, and there seems reason to believe that this was the first occasion on which they were debarred from voting.[76] The sudden emergence in the records of a new electoral service on the part of the candidates, the securing of title deeds for constituents,[77] and the complete absence of complaints against the voting of holders of location tickets in all controverted elections previous to the Durham election leads one to believe that voting on location tickets had formerly been customary. On the other hand it must be borne in mind that the loyalists, their children, and the soldiery disbanded in Upper Canada received titles without payment of fees and after the completion of settlement duties which until 1818 was one of residence, title deeds should have been easy to secure for a large part of the populace.

In late 1827 the opinion of the Law Officers reached Upper Canada. They were of the opinion that the privilege of voting on certificates of occupation issued by the Governor and Council of Quebec did not extend to certificates of occupation issued by the Lieutenant Governor and Council of Upper Canada.[78] The Law Officers were further of the opinion that, since possession of equitable freeholds had by decisions of the British House of Commons been interpreted as conferring the right to vote, possession of a certificate of occupation on which the settlement duties had been performed ought to confer the vote. For once the conditions of settlement were met, the occupant was entitled to a patent, whereas prior to their fulfilment he was not so entitled and might never be. This decision of the Law Officers would have placed the franchise in an unhappy state, for while it was relatively easy to determine if a farmer possessed patent deeds or a location ticket, it was a matter of opinion if settlement duties had been satisfactorily performed. The Assembly did not rescind its resolution disfranchising holders of location tickets and these settlers continued to be without the vote. Some five years later, for instance, the Assembly unseated the sitting members for Lanark and Carleton counties on the grounds a ticket of location did not qualify the holder to vote or to be elected a member of the Assembly.[79]

Periodic attempts were made to enfranchise this class. In 1827 a select committee of the Assembly in response to a petition from the Bathurst District urged that those possessed of an equitable right to their property should be entitled to vote; and in 1836 Dunlop, M.P.P. for Huron, sponsored a bill to extend the franchise to holders of location tickets, letters of licence, and leaseholds.[80] These reforms all perished on the fear of the old settlers, that the new immigrants would make common cause with the Family Compact Tories and the Governor. The *Brockville Recorder*, commenting on Dunlop's bill, stated: "the effect of this would be to place an engine in the hands of the executive, calculated to control the elections. The issue of patent deeds was sufficiently iniquitous without this addition to the power of our irresponsible Governors."[81] The supporters of the administration were of the same opinion. One writing to the Secretary to Sir Francis Bond Head stated;

I feel . . . that if the election franchise can be made available to those who have not paid up the whole instalments on their lands it would be the means of returning to the House of Assembly a very different class of men to the present, the British feeling of loyalty to the King and respect to the Constitution will become pre-eminent in the House as it now is in the mass of the people, and instead of factious opposition to the measures of Government, the House would be composed of those who would actively coincide with the Governor in those measures which he wishes to effect for the sound prosperity of the Province.[82]

After 1827 the cessation of free Crown grants produced two new classes of settlers, leaseholders and purchasers of farms on time. The growth in their number is uncertain. Certainly their number did not rapidly exceed the number of location ticket holders. For the Crown continued to grant free lands to those who had prior claims on the Crown such as the sons and daughters of the United Empire Loyalists. In the years 1827–38 the Crown sold 100,317 acres but granted free about 2,000,000 acres.[83] The acreage sold by the Crown does not give an indication of their number, for the Crown sales were insufficient to accommodate the great number of new settlers who were becoming leaseholders or purchasers of farms from the old settlers, the speculators, and more particularly the Canada Company and the Talbot settlement.

Although leasing of lands had been going on for decades, (the Crown had issued leases on clergy reserves as early as 1799) the problem of the status of these settlers as regards the franchise did not engage the attention of the Assembly until 1831. In that year the election of John Brant for the county of Haldimand was disputed on the grounds that Brant had been returned by the votes of leaseholders on the lands of his father's tribe. The Indians of the Six Nations had for years been leasing lands on the Grand River reserve to white settlers for a term of 999 years. The Assembly refused to consider a leasehold a sufficient title to secure the franchise and Brant was unseated.[84] This ruling of the Assembly inspired many protests. Haldimand County petitioned for an extension of the franchise to leaseholders, and Prince Edward District petitioned on behalf of the leaseholders of clergy reserves.[85] Heartened by the first Reform Bill, which extended the vote to rural leaseholders in England, bills were sponsored in the Assembly to extend the franchise to the same class in Upper Canada.[86] The measures never passed into law. Doubts as to the constitutional power of the Assembly to extend the franchise, and doubts as to the political effect of such an extension, led to their defeat.

If the Reform party had been reluctant to extend the franchise to location ticket holders, to leaseholders, and to purchasers of lands on terms because these British immigrants had little sympathy with their radicalism, the administration forces had been as active in attempting to curb the voting power of the American element in the province from whom the Reform party received its strongest support. By 1800 many Tories had become alarmed at the number of immigrants into Upper Canada from the United States; and in the representation bill of that year, a rider was added to exclude from the franchise all persons who had sworn allegiance to or had lived in a foreign state, until such time as they had lived in a British dominion for seven years and had taken the oath of allegiance.[87] The rider was designed to disfranchise Americans or former residents of the United States, "many of whom," in the opinion of the Solicitor General, were "not altogether destitute of the democratical principles which prevail in that country nor is it always known whether their motives for coming into the Province are good or bad."[88] Members of the Assembly sympathetic to the American immigrants tried repeatedly but ineffectually to repeal the residentiary limit on the franchise. Until 1804 loyalist strength was too great in the Assembly, and after 1804 when hostility to Administrator Peter White's large land grants to favourites had given control of the Assembly to the Reform element the Legislative Council blocked repeal.[89] The outbreak of the War of 1812 and the defection of two members, Wilcocks and Markle, and of one former member, Mallory, merely ensured the permanency of the disqualification.

After the alien controversy[90] had clarified the national status of Americans resident in Canada, the residentiary qualification was rendered less necessary. It was clearly understood, following 1824, that immigrants from the United States, having taken an oath of allegiance to a foreign state, were not British subjects and were debarred from voting by the Constitutional Act. In consequence the qualification was redundant to the extent it declared voters who had taken an oath of allegiance to a foreign power were not eligible to vote until they had resided seven years in the province. The qualification had in practice become applicable only to British subjects who had entered Upper Canada after residence abroad. The Reformers, to whom the qualification had always been politically distasteful, renewed their agitation for repeal. Mackenzie, when in England as representative of the York Central Committee of the Friends of Civil and Religious Liberty in 1832, brought this disability to the attention of Goderich,[91] who ordered the residentiary qualification repealed, and the Assembly complied.[92] There was no subsequent change in the franchise during the life of the Assembly of Upper Canada; two attempts to disfranchise participants in the rebellion of 1837 were stillborn, the Constitutional Act's disqualification of subjects guilty of treason or a felony being considered adequate.[93]

The disqualifications based on tenure and residence were the main adjustments made to the franchise in Upper Canada. But as evidenced in Lower Canada, the franchise can be indirectly limited by the establishment of stiff qualifications for members of the Assembly. The residence requirement put on voters in 1800 had merely been the extension of a disqualification which had first been applied to members of the Assembly. In 1795 Simcoe, for similar reasons, had secured an act to disqualify from membership in the Assembly all former citizens of a foreign state until they had resided seven years in Upper Canada.[94] The defections occasioned by the War of 1812 led to an extension of this period from seven to fourteen years,[95] and where the restraint had formerly applied only to subjects who had sworn allegiance to a foreign power and resided in that foreign country, it now applied to all citizens who had merely resided for any length of time in a foreign state. The act remained unaltered until 1818 when a controverted election for Halton County revealed an incongruity. The act had stated that anyone who came into the province from a foreign country after its passage had to reside fourteen years in the province before he might be be eligible for a seat in the Assembly, but the act had not stopped there. It had gone on to state that those who were already in the province must have spent fourteen years in the province prior to the passage of the act in order to be eligible to be a candidate. Moses Gamble, the member-elect for Halton, was found to have come into Upper Canada from the United States prior to the passage of the act and to have resided within the province ever since. But he had not been resident in the province for fourteen years prior to the act's passage and by its terms he was permanently ineligible to be a member of the Assembly.[96] As a result in 1818 the act was repealed and replaced by a measure which declared an alien or a British subject who had been resident in a foreign country could not be a candidate for the Assembly until he had resided in Upper Canada seven years.[97] While Mackenzie's agitation secured the repeal of the residence qualification in respect of voters, the qualification was not repealed in respect of members of the Assembly.

The residentiary qualification had served as a safeguard against British subjects who might have imbibed republican sentiments on their passage through the United States, but it had not served to curb that small group of English radicals, such as Willcocks and Gourlay, who had come to Upper Canada directly from England. For this reason, the act of 1814 had introduced a property qualification for members of the Assembly. Upper Canada adopted what Craig had advocated for Lower Canada, a stiff property qualification to overcome the liberality of the franchise. The Upper Canada statute required each candidate to possess an unencumbered freehold in land to the assessed value of £40 currency and other ratable property to the assessed value of £160 currency.

This qualification was rendered workable by the mode of assessment practiced in Upper Canada. At the time of passage of the qualification, the assessments were governed by 51 Geo. III, c. 8 (1811) which determined what real property should be ratable and fixed an arbitrary valuation. Arable and pasture lands were to be assessed at 20s. per acre and uncultivated lands at 4s. per acre, and squared log houses, frame houses, brick houses, grist mills, saw mills, shops, warehouses, oxen, milch cows, and so on, were given a stated valuation. When in 1818 the Assembly found itself unable, in a disputed return for Wentworth County, to determine whether the member-elect owned sufficient livestock to fulfil the qualification in respect of non-landed property, the qualification in property other than land was abolished and the landed qualification was doubled to £80 currency.[98] This qualification was not difficult to achieve; eighty acres of cultivated land or four hundred acres of uncultivated land would be adequate; but it did ensure that the candidates had resided in the province and had wrested a farm out of the wilderness, or were immigrants of sufficient wealth to have purchased an improved farmstead, or of sufficient influence to have secured

D

a land grant in excess of the basic grant of two hundred acres. It was hoped that this qualification would prevent radicals becoming members of the Assembly and was in the same vein as the resolution of the House of October 20, 1818, which had denied a seat in the Assembly to any elected representative who had been a delegate to Gourlay's convention at York in July of that year.[99]

As in the other colonies, it is necessary to consider the distribution of representation and the mode of elections to determine if the franchise was in any way restricted by factors other than mere qualifications. In 1792 Simcoe, by proclamation, had divided the province into nineteen counties and had assigned to them a total of sixteen representatives, the minimum prescribed by the Constitutional Act. The representation assigned the counties was based on population as evidenced in the militia returns and bore no relationship to area.[100] For example, the county of Glengarry was divided into two ridings with one member each, but the combined counties of Durham, York, and Lincoln, first riding, that extended along Lake Ontario from Port Hope to Grimsby received one member. Since there was only one poll for each constituency, it is needless to say that distance proved a greater obstacle to the exercise of the franchise than did the franchise qualifications themselves.

The first change in representation was occasioned by a better reorganization of the province for administrative purposes. As it had been customary for a close relationship to exist between county and constituency, the members of the Assembly were not unmindful of the political consequence of the reorganization. For this reason there was a severe contest in the Assembly between the American and administration factions. Both factions agreed each settler should be placed within a day's journey of his county town but the American faction wanted the counties to be erected not on the basis of current settlement needs but on the expectation of future settlement needs. Such a division would mean a departure from the principle of representation based on population to representation based on area. A compromise was reached, the county reorganization was based on area but when the representation was assigned, it was allocated not on the basis of area alone but on the basis of area and population.[101] The more populous counties were assigned one or two members and of the less populous two or more were combined and assigned one representative. Unfortunately the representation act had not included an escalator clause which would have allowed representation to be adjusted to increases in population. In consequence as the pressure of a new immigrant population built up, the Assembly was flooded with petitions from the new settlements and with bills from interested members for adjustments in the representation.[102]

Piecemeal adjustments were inadequate to still the demands for increases in representation. Yet the Tories were reluctant to engage in a major revision because they feared the increased influence that might accrue to the American settlers. It was not until the cessation of hostilities in Europe had brought an influx of British immigrants that their fears were allayed and a general readjustment of the representation was made.[103] It was decided to end the rigidity which had characterized the adjustment of representation. To accommodate a population shifting rapidly before waves of immigration, a sliding scale of representation was introduced. All counties with a population of 1,000 were to return one member, and all counties with 4,000 population were to return two members.[104] The act placed in the hands of the Lieutenant Governor the responsibility for adjusting the representation prior to each general election in the light of the population returns each township clerk was required to

transmit annually. The act had the great virtue of restoring flexibility to the apportion-
ment of representation, and through its combination of area and population as the
criterion of representation, it increased the political influence of the new settlements
beyond their statistical due.

The principle of weighing the representation in favour of the less settled and frontier
counties, a principle the English party in Lower Canada never tired of eulogizing,
came under serious attack from the Upper Canadian Reformers and more particularly
William Lyon Mackenzie. Although Mackenzie was first elected to the Assembly
in 1828, he did not turn his attention to the representation until the rout of the Reform
party in the subsequent general election. Then casting about for an explanation, he
noticed that all the small single-member constituencies had returned members of the
administration party to the number of ten, while York and Leeds, their equal in
population, had gone Reform but contributed only four members to the House.
Mackenzie argued that a majority of the whole House represented less than a third
of the population and, based on assessment returns, property was even more mis-
represented than population. He was especially critical of the representation accorded
the towns where the Quarter Sessions met. He termed them rotted boroughs, whose
small population was influenced by officers of "the Bank," judicial and district officials,
always found in the ranks of the Government party.[105]

Many members of the administration party were equally critical of the system of
representation. Middlesex, the third largest county in the province, felt under-represented with two members; Lanark and Carleton resented the statute which denied
them representation in accordance with the act of 1820. As a result when Mackenzie
moved for the establishment of a select committee on representation, although it was,
composed entirely of Reformers he received support from both sides of the House.[106]
The select committee failed to report before the House prorogued, but the committee
was known to have decided to recommend a general equalization of the constituencies,
either on the basis of population or the combined principle of population and of
assessed property, and require that towns should not be represented until their
population reached 4,000.[107] While no adjustment in representation took place, the
House did show its agreement with the committee on town representation, for in
erecting Prince Edward County into a distinct judicial district, it refused to authorize
representation for the town of Hallowell. The House was not prepared to reproduce in
Prince Edward the conditions in Leeds where at the late election sixty electors had
returned a member for Brockville while 1,200 electors had returned but two members
for the county.[108]

Mackenzie kept the issue of representation before the House and brought it to the
attention of the Colonial Office. In his memorial to the Crown for a redress of grievances, the state of the representation appears as one of the main planks. His complaints were those found by the select committee of which he had been chairman. The
Colonial Secretary refused to interfere in the adjustment of representation. He merely
recalled the principle on which the act of 1820 had been founded and left it to the
Assembly to decide if this principle should be abandoned in favour of representation
proportional to population or to population and property.[109] The issue was kept before the House during Mackenzie's absence in England by a legacy of seventy-eight
petitions he left the Assembly. These petitions, all virtual copies of the parent petition
that had been prepared by Mackenzie and friends in Vaughan Township, demanded
among other things an equalization of the representation.[110] The Assembly, on the

recommendation of a select committee to which the petitions were referred, refused to abandon the compound principle of population and territory on which the 1820 act was based. It was felt the continuing influx of population and the emergence of new settlements made it unwise to establish a rigid unit of representation based on population.[111] Then adhering to the old principle of area and population, the Assembly made the final changes in the representation. York County was equated with Lincoln by its division into four single-member ridings, and the Huron Tract, being settled by the Canada Company, was erected into the county of Huron.[112]

The extension of representation by the Legislature of Upper Canada reflected an attempt to adjust representation in line with the spread of settlement. The number of constituencies rose steadily from 15 in 1792 to 21 in 1808, 23 in 1817, and 27 in 1821, declined to 26 in 1825 with the disappearance of the four ridings of Lincoln in favour of representation by the county at large, rose to 38 in 1835 with the redivision of Lincoln and York counties into ridings, and to 40 constituencies in 1836. This increase in constituencies had the advantage of reducing the disfranchisement caused by distance. Nevertheless, while the counties were being continually redesigned to place each resident within a day's journey of the county town, the Attorney General, H. J. Boulton, had to admit in 1832 that "every man should have the power of voting in his respective right, which it is impossible they can do at county elections where the county is as large as that of York. For an obvious reason, who would travel 40 or 50 miles to vote at an election."[113] And where the population required the junction of two counties for representative purposes the evil was only intensified.

Upper Canada never progressed beyond one place of polling, whereas Lower Canada had established two places of polling in a number of constituencies as early as 1800 and Nova Scotia had established the practice of adjourning the poll around the county by 1792. The disfranchisement caused by lack of dispersed polls was first brought to the attention of the Assembly in 1830 by complaints from the counties of Lincoln and York. These counties had been divided into four and two ridings respectively in 1792 and by 1809 each riding had been returning distinct representation. In 1820 the general representation act in allotting representation had assigned it to the counties and had made no mention of ridings. This feature had gone unnoticed until the general election of 1824, when the Attorney General, John Beverley Robinson, expressed the opinion that separate representation accorded each riding had been superseded by representation for the county at large.[114] As a result the four members for Lincoln were returned by the county at large and the electors had to vote at one poll rather than at four polls as formerly. The returning officer, on returning the writ of election for the general election of 1830, took

the liberty to suggest for His Excellency the Lieutenant Governor's consideration the extreme inconvenience and disadvantage attending the elections, now substituted for the elections in this district, in consequence of the distance electors are obliged to travel to give their votes. At the three last elections that I have presided as returning officer for the county, not more than one third of the freeholders at each election have given in their votes at the county elections. I have found the three last elections strongly liable to the objections I have stated, wheres at the ridings, the freeholders generally make choice of a person known to them in their own riding, and little inconvenience attends going to the place of election at any season of the year.[115]

While the abolition of riding representation for Lincoln and York should have brought the broader question of the general disfranchisement occasioned by the sparsity of polls to the attention of the House, it was not until the Reform defeat in the election of 1830 that serious thought was given to the matter. In the new Parliament the question was raised in Mackenzie's select committee on representation and, but for prorogation, it contemplated recommending that "in order to lessen the distance to the voters in large counties.... two, three or more central places should be fixed by statute."[116] The solution offered by the Reform party was not the subdivision of the larger constituencies into single-member ridings, for they believed the latter were more liable to fall under the undue influence of men of wealth and position; but taking their remedy from the English Reform Bill they wished to retain the large constituencies and subdivide them into polling subdivisions, or failing that to adopt the circulating poll.

This reform assumed some urgency to the Reformers following the repeated elections for Leeds County in 1834-5. The general election and a by-election for this populous county closed in riots as the Irish supporters of the Tory party, urged on by the Attorney General, Robert Jameson, and the Grand Master of the Orange Order, Robert Ogle Gowan, stormed and held the one central poll for the Tory candidates. These incidents might have produced reform if it had not been the misfortune of the Reform party to have passed from the able, moderate leadership of Marshall Spring Bidwell to the intemperate leadership of Mackenzie. Mackenzie, however, had so abused the Legislative Council that they had become irrationally opposed to all suggestions of reform emanating from the Reform party, and they repeatedly rejected all bills to establish better polling facilities.[117]

When the Reformers lost control of the Assembly in the general election of 1836, the advocacy to establish polling subdivisions passed to Edward William Thomson, the Conservative who had defeated Mackenzie in the second riding of York. He piloted the reform through the House for two sessions to have it perish in the emotional cross-currents of the Assembly.[118] The lustre had been rubbed off the reform by its association with Mackenzie, it affronted the traditionalists, and it was opposed by those who feared that polling subdivisions unless accompanied by the voters' register would create a class of "saddle bag" voters who would ride from poll to poll. The life of Upper Canada closed without the provision of more than one poll for each constituency. Save for the redeeming feature of smaller constituencies Upper Canada might be said to have made but slight progress in overcoming territorial disfranchisement and thereby liberalizing the franchise.

CHAPTER SEVEN

THE PROVINCE OF CANADA: ITS FORMATIVE YEARS

THE REBELLIONS in the Canadas resulted in the suspension of the Legislative Assembly of Lower Canada, the substitution of an appointive Special Council, and the appointment of the Durham Commission to investigate the Canadian impasse. The Imperial authorities were anxious that a workable political settlement should be devised which would be productive of a loyal and well-affected Canadian peoples. When the Commission came to recommend a legislative union, which was in the tradition of the abortive union bill of 1822 and of several previous attempts to secure an English hegemony in Lower Canada, the recommendation was readily incorporated into an Act of Union.[1] It is the electoral provisions of this act, the reasons for the provisions and the attempts made to rectify some of the wrongs issuing from them that will here be considered.

The Act of Union did not modify the franchise. Durham made no recommendation concerning it, and the Colonial Office, because the franchise prescribed by the Constitutional Act had never been a bone of contention, did not contemplate a change, as evidenced in the many draft bills prepared prior to the passage of the act. Nor did Colborne and Poulett Thomson, to whom, as governors of Canada, the draft bills were submitted for comment, suggest a change.[2] Nevertheless representations to the Colonial Office for changes in the franchise were not wanting. These suggestions emanated from two sources, the North American Colonial Association and the Constitutional Association of Montreal, representative groups of English-speaking merchants.[3] If the tenure were freehold, both associations were agreeable to a continuation of the existing county franchise; but if the tenure were seigniorial the qualification was to be raised to £10 clear yearly value. Both organizations advocated the extension of the franchise to a new rural class, tenants, who paid an annual rent of £20. In towns the North American Colonial Association was prepared to allow the existing qualification, ownership of property of a clear yearly value of £5, to continue for those possessed of a freehold tenure, but would have raised the qualification to £10 clear yearly value for those possessed of seigniorial tenure. The Constitutional Association would have raised the qualification to the same amount for both tenures. Neither association recommended any change in the urban tenancy qualification of twelve months' occupancy of premises whose rental was £10. As freehold tenure was limited in Lower Canada to the Eastern Townships and the townships along the middle and upper Ottawa, the racial discrimination inherent in the higher qualifications desired for those possessed of seigniorial tenure is at once apparent.

The above restraints were not adopted, nor do they seem to have been strongly urged. This fact is surprising in view of the repeated attempts made by the Montreal commercial interests in the late 1830's to secure a higher urban franchise for Lower Canada. While the agent of the Montreal Constitutional Association did press for an increase in the urban franchise,[4] the hostility of British opinion, fresh from the first Reform Bill, to any restriction of an established franchise soon led him to realize the disfranchisement of the French Canadians would have to be achieved under another guise. The English Canadians turned to seek their objective in the establishment of a stiff property qualification for members of the Assembly, in the distortion of the representation, in the control of the election machinery, and in the intimidation of the electorate and the employees of the Crown.

The establishment of a property qualification for members was an innovation of the Act of Union. The Constitutional Act had not specified a property qualification but merely gave the colonial legislatures permissive power to establish such a qualification. Upper Canada had been the only legislature to avail itself of this power and had established a real property qualification of £80.[5] Following precedent, the draft union bills that reached Canada from the Colonial Office in 1839 continued this policy and left the question of the qualification of members to the new legislature. However, the Constitutional Association of Montreal, the North American Colonial Association, the Assembly of Upper Canada, and the Governor General all recommended that the Act of Union should incorporate a property qualification for members. The Constitutional Association recommended a substantial qualification, ownership of £2,000 real or personal property; the North American Colonial Association recommended ownership of five hundred acres of land or £2,000 real or personal property; and the Governor General recommended ownership of real property in freehold or seigniorial tenure to the value of £500.[6] The Imperial Parliament adopted the latter recommendation, for it was in harmony with current British practice and with the 1822 union bill where ownership of £500 real property was to have been required.[7] The incorporation in the Act of Union of the requirement that all candidates for membership in the Assembly must possess real estate to the actual value of £500 above all encumbrances was designed to cripple the radical and republican elements and to reduce substantially the number of French Canadians able to stand for election. In the words of the Secretary of the North American Colonial Association, "the object which the Committee is anxious to attain, and without which they are satisfied that all attempts to govern the Canadas must ultimately fail, is that in framing a new constitution for these provinces, a preponderance should be given to the opinions and interest of the loyal British population. . . ."[8]

The main disfranchisement of French Canada was to be achieved, however, by a distortion in representation. Durham had had considerable to say on this issue. He had recommended that the representation assigned the two provinces in the joint legislature should be on the basis of population, because he was opposed "to every one of those plans which propose to make the English minority an electoral majority by means of new and strange modes of voting or unfair divisions of the country"; he had felt that if Canadians were to be deprived of representative government, "it would be better to do it in a straightforward way than to attempt to establish a permanent system of government on the basis of what all mankind would regard as mere electoral frauds."[9] Durham had opposed giving an equal number of members to the two provinces in order to attain the temporary end of out-numbering the French, because he believed that "the same object [would] be obtained without any violation of the principles of representation, and without any such appearance of injustice in the scheme as would set public opinion, both in England and America, strongly against it."[10] He had specifically rejected equal representation in favour of representation based on population despite his avowed object "to establish an English population, with English laws and language, in this province, and to trust its government to none but a decidedly English Legislature."[11] He had done so on the conviction that political ascendance could be secured for the English on the basis of the current population. He estimated the joint English population of the two provinces at 550,000 and the French population at 450,000, and he believed future immigration would swing the racial balance more strongly in favour of the English.

Durham's recommendation was blatantly ignored, for the Act of Union assigned equal representation to the two provinces. It appears that the Imperial Cabinet decided on equal representation as soon as they decided on union.[12] The two draft union bills referred to Colborne in the summer of 1839 gave equal representation to the two provinces;[13] and Sydenham, in bringing the proposals for union before the Assembly of Upper Canada, stated the union was to be on the basis of equal representation.[14] This decision conformed to current practice and opinion. Durham's decision in favour of representation by population did not. The representation of Scotland and Ireland in the Parliament of the United Kingdom was not based on population; the Canada union bill of 1822 had provided that representation in the joint legislature should work towards an equality of sixty members each; the Upper Canada Assembly on March 27, 1839, had requested a majority of the joint membership be assigned the upper province; the draft bills prepared by the North American Colonial Association and the Montreal Constitutional Association had espoused equal representation. The opposition to equal representation, which came from such sources as *Le Canadien* and John Neilson, was discredited from their authors' past association with Papineau, and the Lower Canada petition of 39,000 signatures was disregarded because it was opposed to union, a principle on which the Imperial Parliament was irrevocably determined.

The equal representation clauses of the Union Act passed the Imperial Parliament with ease, despite opposition from O'Connell and Lord Ellenborough, and the admonition in the Durham report that "it is not in North America that men can be cheated by an unreal semblance of representative government, or persuaded that they are outvoted, when, in fact, they are disfranchised."[15] It must be remembered that the whole object of union was to establish English dominance, and the abandonment of representation based on population for equal representation of the two provinces was but the sacrifice of a lesser recommendation of Durham's in order to more quickly and surely attain his main intent. That equal representation was a modification but not a violation of Durham's recommendation accounts for the ready acceptance of the principle and for the fact that Colborne and Sydenham, in face of their estimates that the united provinces would possess an English majority, did not therefore urge a return to representation by population.[16]

The principle of equal representation, as incorporated in the Act of Union, acquired an entrenched position. Whereas the draft union bills dispatched to Colborne merely required bills modifying the representation to be reserved for royal assent, the Act of Union required that all bills adjusting the representation must secure a two-thirds majority on second and third readings. This stringent requirement had been a feature of the union bill of 1822 and of the draft bills forwarded to the Colonial Office by the Montreal Constitutional Association, by Chief Justice John Beverley Robinson, and by Sydenham. This clause was sponsored by the Canadian Tories because they suspected republican sentiments in part of the English population. They feared the disaffected French and republican English members might form common cause to disrupt the equality of representation. It was with this fear in mind that Robert Gillespie, agent of the Montreal Constitutional Association, wrote to Russell that:

if the division of the representation proposed by your Lordship be persevered in, that is thirty-nine members to each province, and if only so small a number of members favourable to the British Government and British interests can be counted upon out of the thirty-nine representatives of the Lower Province and considering at the same time that several if not many will be returned for the Upper Province unfavourable to the same Government and interests it certainly is not too much to predict that a joint legislature would not answer the purpose intended but what is more to be deprecated it would place in the hands of the enemies of the British connection a sort of legal power to dissolve it.[17]

The Tory commercial interests working on the Colonial Office through Gillespie and Chief Justice Robinson in London, and on Sydenham through Badgley and Chief Justice Stuart in Montreal, entrenched the representation clause. The merchants, avid for immediate security, showed a further lack of political foresight. They would not trust their countrymen's numerical majority to produce a reliable political majority, nor would they wait for the increasing security that immigration would inevitably bring. They adopted the very electoral arrangements that Durham prophesied would "defeat the purposes of union and perpetuate the idea of disunion."[18]

Durham's prophecy was to prove true. The equality of representation accorded the two sections of the united province had the effect of distorting the franchise and heightening racial and political friction. By giving the minority section (originally Canada West, later Canada East) equality of representation, it in effect raised the franchise for the more populous section of the united province. The forty-two representatives given in 1841 to Canada East with an estimated population of 650,000 were matched by a similar number from Canada West representing a population of 465,357 as determined by the census of that year. As forecast by Durham the pendulum soon swung and by 1849 it was estimated that the two provinces reached equality and thenceforth the population of Canada West was in excess of that of Canada East (by 62,000 in 1851, by 285,000 in 1861, and by nearly 400,000 at Confederation). It might, therefore, be said that from 1851 an elector voting in Canada West did not exercise equal political influence with his compatriot in Canada East.

While no remedy was ever found for this disequilibrium within the framework of the united province, it is nevertheless necessary to consider briefly the tortuous struggle for an adjustment of the representation. The problem first claimed serious attention in 1849 when Lafontaine proposed to increase the representation from each section to seventy-five. The phenomenal increase in population (that of Canada West rose by more than 100 per cent in the decade 1841 to 1851) made the distribution of representation obsolete and the Lafontaine legislation would have erected ridings where there had been but wilderness a short ten years before. The measure accorded rough justice; the population of the two sections was near equality, the new settlements were to be given representation, and the old settlements were not to be disturbed. The measure, three times presented by Lafontaine to the Assembly, three times secured an ample majority but three times failed to secure the two-thirds majority demanded by the Act of Union.[19] Defeated by a small group of members from Canada West led by Boulton of Toronto City, the measure perished on their desire to secure a graduated formula that would allow the representation of any riding or any section to grow with

D*

population. From a condition of equality of population with Canada East, these members insisted on a plan which would give them for the future the political advantage of their more rapidly increasing numbers. Not for them the principle of equality that had been foisted a scant decade earlier on their French Canadian compatriots when the latter possessed the numerical majority.

The roots of the political deadlock of the next twenty years were laid at this time between those who demanded representation by population and those who were determined to maintain the *status quo*. They who had sown the wind were now to reap the whirlwind, for the French Canadian population had become, in the words of the *Journal de Trois Rivières*, "the masters of those for whose benefit the union was designed."[20] Lafontaine, in the circumstances, had shown the only possible remedy for the maladjustment in representation, that of an equal increase in representation to both sides.

The population growth of Canada West forced in 1851 a reorganization of the county structure for municipal and judicial purposes.[21] The resulting anomaly of one county structure for municipal purposes and another for parliamentary purposes enabled the Hincks-Morin ministry to secure a readjustment in the representation. In 1853 Morin introduced and carried a bill which increased the representation accorded each section from forty-two to sixty-five members.[22]

During the passage of the bill, George Brown espoused the cause of representation by population. Henceforth he and his followers sponsored this reform in season and out of season. It was adopted as the foremost plank in the Reform platform at the great convention of January 8, 1857; it was moved by resolution and by bill in the House; it broke up political parties; it brought down governments. The issue bedevilled the whole life of the Province of Canada. The plight of the English Canadians might warrant little sympathy, for they were reaping the fruits of their own planting, yet the injustice could not endure forever.

The maladjustment in sectional representation compounded as it was by racial, sectional, and political interests obscured the growing inequalities between constituencies within each section. By 1861 the inequalities within Canada West were as great and as objectionable as the inequalities between Canada West and Canada East. Ridings like Huron-Bruce with 80,000 population, Grey with 38,000, Perth with 38,000, were represented on the same basis as Russell with 7,000, Dundas with 19,000, Brockville with 4,100, and Niagara with 4,500. The Hincks-Morin representation act of 1853 had made no attempt to overcome the maladjustments within each section. In fact the two-thirds majority required to secure the passage of the legislation had made it impossible to offend any riding.[23] These distortions in representation were as effective in restricting equality in the exercise of the suffrage as specific restraints on the franchise itself. As the political climate stood, this wrong inflicted on the Province of Canada by the Act of Union was never rectified during the life of that province. The remedy was to involve termination of the legislative union and the achievement of Confederation.

While the Colonial Secretary, Lord John Russell, did reduce the political power of the French Canadian people by distorting the representation, he rejected other suggestions which would have increased this distortion. He refused to suspend the representation of the district of Montreal and he refused to allot special representation to those possessed of freehold tenure in Lower Canada. The commercial interests had urged that ten counties in the Montreal district, where acts of insurrection had taken place during the Papineau rebellion, should be disfranchised for a period of from five to ten years.[24] The same interests had also urged that, of the two representatives assigned to each county, one member should be returned by those possessed of property in freehold tenure and the other member by those possessed of seigniorial tenure. Although the advocates of this scheme would have required that each county or electoral division possess at least two hundred electors of either category before the representation would be split, this scheme would have secured representation for the English minority in overwhelmingly French counties.

There remains one limited distortion in representation which Russell did not prevent. The commercial interests had insisted that the representation of Montreal and Quebec should be placed at their disposal. In the past, these proud men had been humiliated to see the chief commercial centres of Canada represented by such men as Papineau, Nelson, and Berthelot. When they had been unable to secure a higher urban franchise, they had turned through their agent Gillespie to urge a reduction in the size of the constituencies of Montreal and Quebec to the area encompassed by the old city walls. It was their belief that the exclusion of the residents of the suburbs would ensure them political control of the cities through their property holdings therein.[25] In writing to Russell on May 27, 1840, Gillespie argued that by "transferring part of the voters of both races from the towns to the counties," Russell would be "making the returns of English members for the towns more certain and numerous."[26] Russell sidestepped the pressure and passed it on to the Governor General by granting in the act power to the Governor to define by letters patent the boundaries of representative towns and cities.

Sydenham was annoyed at this concession to the representations of the Canadian merchants, not because he was hostile to their aspirations, but because he was convinced that their interference had only further convinced the French Canadians that the Act of Union was designed to destroy them as a political force.[27] The constriction of these two electoral divisions was rendered more odious because it involved the adjustment of municipal boundaries that had stood unchanged since 1792 and because the Imperial Parliament had assigned two representatives rather than one to these shrunken boroughs. Sydenham felt, however, that the inclusion of this provision in the Act of Union was tantamount to a command; and following the proclamation of union, the boundaries of the constituencies of Montreal and Quebec were contracted. This action was rendered even more obnoxious when it became know that the boundaries of the representative towns in the upper province were left undisturbed.[28] "The sole object of this measure" as seen by the *Montreal Herald* on February 27, 1841, was "to secure two members to represent this city, who will strenuously advocate the views of the old country residents in the suburbs and if that object is attained by their own virtual disfranchisement, all they wish for is gained and they will rejoice at the result."

The object was attained and the cities of Montreal and Quebec returned a complete slate of English members in the first general election. This contraction of boundaries had not merely transferred voters from the city to the county, it had disfranchised many former electors. The propertied electors of the two cities had possessed votes in both city and county elections, as the cities had always been within the limits of their counties for electoral purposes. The owners of property placed outside the city by the Governor's proclamation were reduced to a single vote, while tenants similarly situated were entirely disfranchised as the tenancy franchise was confined to the city and did not extend to the county. The net result was an estimated two-thirds reduction in the electorate of Montreal and Quebec.

The anomaly of cities with one set of limits for the purposes of taxation and municipal government and another for parliamentary representation was keenly felt. A petition, signed by 2,450 electors, reached the first session of the first Parliament from the city of Quebec. The Assembly referred it to a select committee of five including John Neilson, member for the city, and in the last days of the session the committee tabled a blistering condemnation both of equal representation and the disfranchisement of Montreal and Quebec.[29] In the concluding words of the report: "Your committee hopes that more liberal, more just, and more honourable views will be entertained hereafter by the Government, and that no distinction whatever will be made or recognized between the treatment of any class of Her Majesty's subjects. It is only by an honest and fair policy that this great colony can be satisfactorily governed, and it is only by granting equal rights to all, that all shall equally from their heart respond to the call of loyalty to the Crown and affection for the Mother Country, and British connection." In the next session with a Reform administration under Baldwin and Lafontaine in power, and a new Governor, a measure was passed restoring for all future elections the old boundaries of Montreal and Quebec.[30] This was the first step taken to remedy a distortion in the representation and franchise occasioned by a provision of the Act of Union.

In addition to the property qualification established for members and the distortion in the representation occasioned by the Act of Union, the control of the election machinery granted the Governor by the Act of Union was used to enhance the influence of the English electors. Closely bound up with this control was intimidation of the electors.

Sydenham, as authorized by the Act, had to issue the election writs designating the time and place of election. By law the Upper Canada electoral districts had confined voting to a single poll and a six-day period; in Lower Canada a majority of the electoral districts had had two polling places and the duration of the election had been unlimited save for the date of return set by the writ, or by the exhaustion of the electors, or by agreement among the candidates. Sydenham was not permitted by the Act of Union to determine the duration of the election but he made use of his power to designate the places of election.

As Sydenham was desirious to secure an assembly which would endorse the union and remove any stigma attaching to the manner in which he secured *carte blanche* permission from the governing bodies of the two provinces to proceed with the union, the success of the pro-union forces in the general election was essential to him. He utilized his powers under the act to abandon the dual polls in Lower Canada and to revert to a single poll for each constituency. To intensify the resultant territorial disfranchisement, he located the polling place in the extremity of many counties, far removed from the centres of population. In Terrebonne, the poll was located at New Glasgow, a small Irish and Scottish settlement in the northern extremity of the county, several days' journey from the populous French settlements on the Isle Jesus; in Ottawa County, the poll was moved to Aylmer far from the siegniory of Le Petit Nation; in Chambly the poll was located at St. John in the southern extremity of the county; and in Berthier, the poll was placed at Ste Elizabeth in the northern reaches of the county.[31]

Not content with the above steps, Sydenham threw the whole voting power of the servants of the Crown on the side of the English or administration party. Where that was of no avail, force and bludgeons in the hands of hired bullies were used to persuade or deter the electorate. Sydenham participated so actively in these events that Lafontaine was able to charge him with substituting the "law of the bludgeons" for the law of elections. In Quebec City, Henry Black, Judge in Admiralty, was returned by the votes of the Crown employees in opposition to the French vote.[32] The near unanimity of the servants of the Government was influenced by an incident which had occurred at Hamilton in the first stages of the general election. Sydenham had dismissed a Robert Berrie from his office of Clerk of the Peace for the district of Gore, after Berrie had declared publicly his support for Sir Allan MacNab in opposition to the candidature of the Provincial Secretary for Canada West, S. B. Harrison.[33] In the words of Harrison, "Every man's opinions are entitled to respect, and everyone should have the fullest opportunity of exercising unbiased his political franchise of voting for such a representative as he thinks most fit. On the other hand, however, the government has the undoubted right to expect that its servants should not act at variance with the policy it is pursuing. When that policy militates with the opinions entertained by any person in such a situation, there is an obvious option open to him to avoid the difficulty."[34] When Berrie did not avail himself of the option of resignation, Sydenham promptly dismissed him, and the dismissal coming in the midst of the election campaign was judiciously timed to accomplish the Governor's purpose.

In six counties of the district of Montreal, the elections were marred by riots, and in a seventh, Terrebonne, a riot was averted only by the withdrawal of Lafontaine, the French candidate. All of these counties but one returned members in support of the administration and in all but one of the counties the French Canadians constituted the great bulk of the population.[35] The relations of the two races in the district of Montreal were bad. The French deeply resented the injustice of their disfranchisement and the threats to their racial survival in the union. The English were determined to secure from their political power in the United Legislature the public works which had been denied by the Lower Canada Assembly, and which they deemed necessary to their commercial progress. As a result, the initiation of the riots was not the prerogative of one party; but it must be said the English party were quick to utilize the antipathy between French and Irish. The Irish, whether Orangemen or shantymen, were the bully boys. The experience in the county of Terrebonne may give some indication of the extent of the preparations. Some 250 Irish labourers who had been breaking rock to construct roads in Montreal under trustees appointed by the Governor were engaged at 2/6 per day and expenses and sent to Terebonne "where they were told that they were wanted by the government to break stones."[36] But the *Montreal Herald* of March 13 revealed the real purpose: "from the known character of the majority of the electors of the county of Terrebonne, we doubt not Lafontaine would be returned, if all the votes were polled, but it must be the duty of the loyalists to muster their strength and keep the poll."[37] In case the Irishmen should have proved ineffectual, the English party had Highlanders marching for Terrebonne from the county of Glengarry. They were not needed.

In the county of Montreal, the poll was closed by a riot on the opening day, when the French Canadians proved too strong and placed their candidate in the lead despite the presence of help from Canada West for the English party. On the following morning the English party gathered 1,000 to 1,500 men at the Place d'Armes and sent them out to the poll at St. Laurent. When their opponents had been scattered and their

candidate placed in a majority, the English party had the election terminated although from a population in excess of 60,000 fewer than a hundred electors had been
polled.[38] The cumulative effect of these assaults on the electorate was that electoral
districts possessing an English majority returned none but English members, and
twelve electoral districts in which the French possessed a majority returned English
members.[39] Under a constitution which Sydenham described as providing "adequate
representation" and "equal justice to all classes," the French Canadians elected but
nineteen members in an Assembly whose total membership was eighty-four.

The extent and severity of the rioting in Canada East was blamed on Sydenham.
He was accused of discouraging the restoration of peaceful elections by neglecting to
dispatch military detachments when it was to his party's advantage to do so, but being
prompt with the military when the riot was going against his partisans. He certainly
refused to honour the returning officer's request for a military force for the county of
Montreal although the first day's polling had ended in riot and deaths, while he dispatched troops with haste to the counties of St. Maurice, Rouville, and Berthier.

Sydenham was also accused of financing the election for the English party. The
charge was generally believed and certainly much money was spent by the English
party on entertainment and the conveyance of bully gangs. Whether the charge be
true or not, it is known that Sydenham had a vain pride in his power to buy men, and
that he wrote privately to Russell to secure the cancellation of an order that his Military Secretary, Major T. E. Campbell, should rejoin his regiment because Campbell
was politically useful to him. For in Sydenham's own words, "he is the *only* officer
in these regions who can be of the least use to me because he is the *only one* who has
taken any pains to know the people and the country, and at this juncture [January 29,
1841] his loss would be most disastrous to me, as he manages the *members* for me,
both as to their elections and their votes, and is the sole reliance I have. . . . But spare
him till I have met my Parlt. I cannot."[40]

Turbulence in the elections was not confined to Canada East, although it was there
found in its most severe form. There were disturbances at the poll held for Hastings
County and for the second riding of York, while Toronto City had a riot subsequent
to the election, on the occasion of the victory parade of the winning candidates.
These disturbances, while often immediately caused by the natural pugnacity of the
Irish and by the entertainment provided by each candidate, were in larger measure
due to the crowds congregating at the single poll for each riding. The Reformers perceived this fact and in the first session of the United Legislature revived their programme to create multiple polling subdivisions in each constituency.

In the Assembly of Upper Canada, this reform had always met defeat because the
Conservatives had insisted that the creation of multiple polling subdivisions should be
accompanied by a voters' register in order to avoid fraud as electors moved from
poll to poll to engage in multiple voting. The same political cleavage was now revived. When Baldwin, as leader of the Reformers, introduced a bill to establish a
poll for each township and parish, the Provincial Secretary, Harrison, introduced a
Government measure to provide for multiple polls and a voters' register. On reference
to a select committee, it was decided to press both bills. Baldwin's bill was left essentially unchanged but Harrison's bill was reduced to its registration clauses, and the
voters' register was made applicable only to Canada West and to the cities and townships of Canada East.[41] It was on the insistence of the members from Canada East
that the select committe had decided the registry should not be applied to the seignio-

ries. Neilson had claimed the French were hostile to any registry and their settled population, less fluid than the English, made a registry less necessary.

While the Reform element on the committee had been hostile to the voters' register on the grounds it would place more patronage at the disposal of the Executive, they had to accept the voters' register in order to secure the passage of the multiple polling bill. On this understanding Baldwin's poll bill rapidly cleared the Assembly and the Legislative Council, but the registry bill was allowed to stagnate as the Government was displeased that it was not applicable to all Canada East. It was not until the last days of the session when many French members had departed Kingston that Harrison revived the bill, moved it into committee of the whole, and moved an amendment to make the registry applicable to all of Canada East. The manœuvre failed, the amendment was defeated, and the registry bill cleared the Assembly to be allowed to perish in the Legislative Council.

The Government had looked on the poll bill as the price paid to secure a voters' registry. When the latter failed to pass, Sydenham ordered the poll bill reserved. In transmitting the bill to the Colonial Office, he advised the Colonial Secretary that Her Majesty's decision on the bill should be suspended in order to allow the Legislature to reconsider its conduct.[42] The belief that the Assembly would see the necessity for passing a registry bill at its next session was ill-founded. The Assembly was more determined that a multiple polling bill should pass devoid of a voters' register. Baldwin reintroduced the polling bill and the Reformers, despite the fact that Baldwin vacated his seat on appointment as Attorney General, carried the bill through the Assembly, In face of the Assembly's second passage of the poll bill, its indisposition to entertain the voters' register, and the violence at a by-election in Hastings, Sydenham's successor felt obliged to give his assent to the bill.[43]

The act[44] established distinct polls under the jurisdiction of a deputy returning officer in each township, parish, or ward into which a county, riding, or city might be divided. If a township or parish was united with an adjacent township or parish for municipal purposes because of the sparsity of population, the united townships and parishes were to be serviced by one poll. The polls were to be held at the same place as the annual election for parish or township officers. Towns and cities lacking a division into wards were to be divided into wards for electoral purposes by the returning officers and a poll was to be located in a central place in each ward. The electors were required under a penalty of £10 to vote at the poll in that township or parish in which the property, by right of which they voted, was situated. To prevent multiple voting, the polling was to be simultaneous throughout each electoral division and was to be limited to two days. To ensure further that multiple voting was eliminated, any candidate was privileged to require any elector to take an oath that he had not previously voted. With this legislation the second step had been taken in remedying electoral evils occasioned by the Act of Union.

By reducing the crowds at each poll, the increase in polling places was to reduce disorder. A similar result was to follow from a change in the manner of conducting the election prescribed by the new legislation. The day of nomination was, for the first time in the Canadas, to be separated from the days of polling. The returning officers had formerly proceeded directly from nominations to polling, and the electors, intoxicated with the orations and hospitality of the candidates, were easily inflamed to violence. The returning officers were now to be required to hold a distinct nomination at a central point in each electoral division and the polling was to commence later within a minimum of four and a maximum of eight days. The fumes of oratory and hospitality were unlikely to sustain martial spirits over such an interval of time, although as events transpired the candidates found it judicious to provide houses of entertainment at each poll and the martial spirit was on occasions revived. The reduction in time of polling to two days was similarly helpful when contrasted with the six days' polling which had been permissive in Upper Canada or the polling in Lower Canada which had been limited only by the date of the return of the writ.[45]

The act took other steps to reduce violence. The returning officer was entrusted with the powers of a conservator of the peace with authority to swear in special constables or summon the militia to maintain order. Party colours, labels, flags, and the carrying of offensive weapons such as firearms and bludgeons were banned. It was made an offence to engage in assault and battery within two miles of a poll, to bribe or treat electors. Many of these practices, such as the wearing of party favours, had been illegal under the Lower Canada act of 1825 but in Upper Canada they had never been a statutory offence. These innovations so annoyed the *Toronto Patriot* that on October 21, 1842, it wrote:

this law also prohibits, under penalties of fines of fifty pounds and imprisonment for six months, or both, the exhibiting of any ensign, standard, color, flag, ribbon, label, or favor whatever, or for any reason whatsoever at any election, on any election day, or within a fortnight before or after such a day! So that any body of honest electors who for a fortnight before or a fortnight after any election (being a period of one month) shall dare to hoist the Union Jack of Old England, or wear a green or blue ribbon in the buttonhole, shall be fined fifty pounds or imprisoned six months or both under Mr. Baldwin's election bill! We defy the whole world to match this bill for ridiculous enactments and for grinding and unsupportable tyranny. . . . Verily, Messrs. Lafontaine and Baldwin, ye use your victory over the poor, loyal serfs of Canada with most honourable moderation. . . . How long this Algerine Act will be allowed to pollute our statute book remains yet to be seen.

The *Patriot* need not have been disturbed. There was little will among Canadian politicians to enforce the statute, and many a day was to pass before villainy, violence, and hospitality disappeared from the Canadian electoral scene.

While the Baldwin act did end executive control of the location of the polls and by increasing their number reduced their inaccessibility, adjustments remained to be made. The 1844 election illustrated the inadequacy of a single poll for each ward of the city of Montreal. In the two days of polling allowed by law, the polls were found inadequate to handle the number of electors in the three most populous wards and the election closed, it was asserted, with a majority of the electors unpolled.[46] The result was to give the election to the English party, for the three English wards were fully polled. The Reform leader of Canada East, Lafontaine, made several attempts to overcome this disfranchisement. When he sought to remedy this defect by an extension of the days of polling, the Conservative ministry criticized and defeated the bills on the grounds they would facilitate violence as well as polling.[47] The Conservatives suggested the better remedy lay in the erection of more polls, but they took no steps to implement their remedy. It was left until Lafontaine's return to office, when, as member for Montreal and Attorney General of Canada East, he introduced and carried into law a bill which, while consolidating the election law, augmented from one to three the polls in the more populous wards of Montreal and Quebec.[48]

This increase in polling facilities soon proved inadequate in the larger cities for on April 15, 1859, the *Globe* had to report that the populous wards of Griffintown in Montreal and St. John and St. James in Toronto had never been polled out. The difficulty was not confined to the cities, for as settlement intensified, many townships and parishes found a single poll and two-day polling inadequate. But it was not until the last year of the Province of Canada that John A. Macdonald passed a bill to authorize municipal councils to divide any township, parish, or ward into additional polling subdivisions.[49] They were authorized to create an additional polling subdivision for every four hundred voters in excess of the first six hundred. This legislation was the meagre result of agitation begun by William Lyon Mackenzie in 1854 and carried on by Dorion to secure single-day polling and simultaneous province-wide elections.[50] These reforms failed to win the support of Conservative ministries who were not willing to secure electoral quiet by sacrificing the right to precipitate eletoral contests timed to give the right partisan fillip to the electorate; nor to sacrifice the freedom of moving a defeated candidate to fresh political pastures.

The Lafontaine legislation in 1849 had also taken steps to remove election officers from Executive influence. During the separate life of Upper and Lower Canada, their governors had possessed the power to appoint returning officers and this power had been continued by the Act of Union. There had been murmurings against Sydenham's exercise of this power; the institution of alternative voting in the general election of 1844 for Montreal City had been blamed on the partisan leanings of the returning officer, and in the 1848 general election the returning officers for the counties of Carleton and Huron had appointed deputies and poll clerks specified by the Conservative candidates.[51] In the first three general elections twenty-one disputed elections had complained of the conduct of the election officers. While the misconduct of the officers in some cases may have been due to inexperience or neglect,[52] the Reformers were hard pressed to believe there was no partisan malice when the Conservatives had suffered in only two of the twenty-one occasions. As the concession of responsible government would ensure that the power of appointment would for the future be exercised by the Governor on the advice of a partisan ministry, the Lafontaine legislation sought to limit ministerial discretion.

The legislation was to achieve this goal by entrusting the conduct of elections to the occupants of designated offices. The sheriff or registrar of deeds for each county was to be the returning officer. In the event they could not serve, the Governor was to continue to make the appointment subject to a proviso; he could appoint no one who was not an elector, nor twelve months resident in the riding, nor could he appoint any clergyman, Executive or Legislative Councillor, nor a member of the past or a previous Assembly.[53] In Canada West the returning officers were obliged to appoint the township clerks, assessors, or collectors as their deputies but because of the unsatisfactory condition of the municipal administration in Canada East the returning officers retained their discretionary power to select deputies.

The requirement that returning officers should be employees of the Crown was criticized as unlikely to create a corps of impartial electoral officials. Substance was lent to this criticism by the dismissal during the same session of the Inspector of Licences for the Brock District. The Inspector had been the returning officer at the late election for Oxford County in which he had ruled invalid Hincks's declaration of qualification. This action had become the subject of adjudication before a controverted election committee. When it found Hincks's declaration valid, the Assembly had on a partisan vote ordered the Inspector dismissed.[54] The Conservative Opposition claimed this incident would ensure all election officials would be partial to the party in office, but the Reformers claimed it would serve as an object lesson and ensure impartiality; for the office of sheriff and registrar of deeds were in practice life appointments and their incumbents would not be inclined in jeopardize their positions by partiality.

The creation of one or more polls for each township and ward and the designation of the returning officers and their deputies were to curb any repetition of the Sydenham technique of influencing the election by a judicious location of the county poll or by a partisan selection of election officers. The multiple polls were as well to reduce the intimidation to which the electorate had been subjected at the hands of bully gangs.

There remains to consider the action taken to reduce the consequences of the political intimidation of Crown employees. The answer to this problem was to be found in disfranchising them rather than in a removal of Executive intimidation. On first assuming office in 1843 Lafontaine excluded the incumbents of many political offices from the exercise of the franchise. He disfranchised all judges, the Vice Chancellor of Upper Canada, the commissioners of bankrupts, the officers of the Probate Court, the recorders of cities, custom officers, and the Imperial excise officers.[55] These officials were placed in the same category as the clergy and paid election agents, the latter having been disfranchised for different reasons the previous year.[56] The disfranchisement of the clergy proved to be of short duration but the ranks of the politically neutralized were augmented over the years. For the ten-year duration of the election act of 1849, civil and military officers occupying rent-free premises provided by the Crown or by any incorporated society or company were disfranchised; in 1857 the Chancellor of Upper Canada, the clerks of the Peace, the registrars, the sheriffs, the deputy sheriffs, the deputy clerks of the Crown, the agents for Crown lands were all added to the ranks of the disfranchised;[57] and in the following year the process was completed with the exclusion of all returning officers, deputy returning officers, election and poll clerks.[58] The creation of a caste of disfranchised officers was not common practice in British North America; Prince Edward Island, Vancouver Island, and Canada were the sole exceptions. Prince Edward Island disfranchised the members of the Legislative Council from 1806 until after Confederation;[59] and Vancouver Island disfranchised by statute in 1859 all those disqualified from voting under the laws of Great Britain.[60] In all cases, the motive seems to have been to reduce the political influence of the administration rather than assert the political neutrality of the particular offices. In Canada, the general election of 1841 had been an object lesson in the necessity for such legislation, and subsequent elections continued to confirm the need.

CHAPTER EIGHT

THE PROVINCE OF CANADA: THE YEARS OF TURBULENCE

THE QUARTER CENTURY between the Act of Union and Confederation was a period of political instability and turbulence for the Province of Canada. The political parties lacked coherence and the retirement of Baldwin and Lafontaine from politics in 1851 intensified the instability. Their departure fragmented the Reform party and left a political void which neither Reformer nor Conservative was able to fill effectively. It was only after long and rancorous partisan warfare that the Macdonald-Cartier dyarchy emerged and stability was partially restored. The change and confusion which characterized Canada's political administration was reflected in hasty and disordered changes in the franchise. Lafontaine's prosaic consolidation of the franchise laws of Lower and Upper Canada in 1849 was followed by the Hincks-Morin adventure into an assessment franchise and a voters' register in 1853. The displacement of this ministry by the MacNab-Morin ministry brought the abolition of the voters' register in 1855 and the establishment of a dual freehold and assessment franchise. The public outrage at the excesses of the general election of 1858 forced the Macdonald-Cartier ministry to abolish the dual franchise and to re-establish the voters' register to accompany an assessment franchise. While these changes in the franchise did extend the suffrage, the extension originated less in democratic sentiment than in the turbulent rivalry of the political factions.

The first legislation to deal with the franchise came in 1849 when Lafontaine sponsored a bill to amend and consolidate the election laws of Lower and Upper Canada into a uniform law for the united province. The consolidated act continued the existing suffrage to male British subjects of twenty-one years who possessed property on seigniorial or freehold tenure having the clear yearly value of 40s. sterling (£44/5/1 local currency) in counties, or in towns possessed a dwelling house and lot of the clear yearly value of £5 sterling (£5/11/1/1 local currency), or being an urban tenant had been twelve months resident in the town and had paid an annual rent of £10 sterling (£11/2/2/2 local currency) on a dwelling house.[1]

Lafontaine introduced one innovation into the franchise with this consolidation. Tenure secured by a promise of sale (*promisse de vente*) was equated, for purposes of the franchise, with seigniorial and freehold tenure. This provision was designed to enfranchise settlers on the lands of the British American Land Company and was of especial benefit to Lewis T. Drummond, the Solicitor General, in whose riding the British American Land Company possessed substantial holdings.[2] The company, unable to secure British immigrants, had turned to attract settlers from the seigniories and these settlers were given occupancy of company lands on a promise of sale. The promise of sale required no downpayment from the recipient but rather the entrance into an obligation to pay the interest on the value of the land for ten years at the end of which the principal was to fall due in four equal annual instalments. The enfranchisement of persons holding land on such a tenure was a departure from the principle that no man should vote in county elections who did not possess an absolute right to his property. However, the tenure of these settlers was relatively secure for under the civil code neither party could withdraw from such an agreement without forfeiting *un arrhes* or a sum of money to the other.

Nevertheless the denial of the same privilege to purchasers of Crown lands who entered into their holdings with a similar status, and to tenants on the Huron Tract of the Canada Company whose ten-year leases contained an option of purchase, was viewed as racial and partisan legislation. The Conservative Opposition regarded this change in the franchise as a move to introduce French votes into the Eastern Townships, and to secure those townships for the Reform party. The *Montreal Gazette* of May 15, 1849, stated: "The election bill which the Ministry are now urging through Parliament offers proof in point. The Ministry, being supported by every French Canadian elector in Lower Canada, have embodied a clause in that bill which gives to the French Canadian squatter upon another man's land, the right to vote in Lower Canada; because these squatters, being found only in the Anglo-Saxon counties, may be able to wrest the elections from the English in favour of the [Reform] party." The Reform party was not unanimous in support of this change. The Commissioner of the British American Land Company, A. T. Galt, who was elected for Sherbrooke County in a by-election at this time, was opposed to the enfranchisement of possessors of promises of sale who might never secure the title to their property.[3] Baldwin, co-head of the ministry, was opposed to any person voting on a tenure less than freehold, but in this regard as in a second provision of the bill, Baldwin was overborne by Lafontaine. Baldwin had sought to reduce the influence of property by denying owners the right to vote in any riding but the one in which they resided. The Conservatives and the Reformers of Canada East led by Lafontaine voted to retain the multiple votes of property holders.[4]

The Lafontaine consolidation of the franchise can only be construed in a limited sense and in a limited area as an extension of the franchise. In this respect, it does not bear comparison with Baldwin's election act of 1842 which, although concerned with the provision of better polling facilities, did in effect extend the franchise. The better polling facilities, it would appear from the scattering of returns in the newspapers, had increased the 1844 electorate approximately 40 per cent over the electorate of 1841.[5] It was unfortunate Lafontaine did not take advantage of the consolidation to make a general extension of the franchise, for the cessation of free Crown land grants had by 1849 created a sizeable class of non-freeholders. This class was primarily drawn from the new immigrants; the surplus holdings of the older settlers and the outstanding claims on the Crown of military settlers and of the descendants of loyalists permitted a large part of the native born to become freeholders.

The number of tenants and occupant-purchasers was already numerous in certain parts of the country as early as 1841. For instance in Huron County in the general election of that year only 308 votes were polled out of a population near 6,000. The vote was kept low by the action of James McGill Strachan, candidate and solicitor to the Canada Company, who stationed an officer at the poll with a list of the title deeds issued by the Company in order to prevent tenants and occupant-purchasers on lands of the Canada Company from voting.[6] The problem had only been rendered more acute by the heavy immigration of the forties. In that decade the population of

Canada West doubled and the increase was substantially greater in the fronter districts; for instance, the population on the Huron Tract increased fivefold.[7]

A freehold franchise which was becoming more restrictive with each season's immigration, its extension to the residents of Canada East possessed of promises of sale, and the precedent set by the first English Reform Bill might have been expected to have aroused interest among the politicians in an extension of the suffrage. In fact, the Conservative and Reform leaders showed remarkably little interest. The reason for this indifference may, as one critic stated, have been an uncertainty as to the political inclinations of the new settlers; but the main reason would seem to have be a latent hostility among the old settlers to the new immigrants and a pervading conservative sentiment among the Canadian people and politicians. The politicians were most fearful that the abandonment of the freehold franchise would inevitably lead to manhood suffrage, to anarchy, and to republicanism.

As might be expected it was the radical parties that espoused an extension of the suffrage. The Clear Grits, at their Markham convention in 1850, adopted a platform which favoured extending the franchise to householders and rural leaseholders.[8] In Canada East the Parti Rouge advocated universal suffrage.[9] Franchise reform would have remained the concern of none but the radical parties had not Baldwin and Lafontaine retired from public life in 1851. They bequeathed to their successors, Hincks and Morin, a splintered Reform party. Faced with an imminent election, Hincks was forced to construct both a ministry and a party to support it, and these circumstances led him to effect an alliance with the Clear Grits.

The alliance was consummated when Rolph and Cameron, leading members of the Clear Grit party, joined the Hincks-Morin ministry. The price of coalition was the adoption by the ministry of several planks of the Clear Grit platform, of which the extension of the suffrage was one. When the ministry successfully carried the election, Hincks honoured the compact and in the first session of the new Parliament he introduced a measure to modify the franchise. Political necessity was thus the father of Canada's first venture into an assessment franchise and a voters' register.

The new franchise extended the vote to all British males of twenty-one years, who were assessed on the last assessment roll as owners, tenants, or occupants of real property in any county of £50 currency actual value or £5 currency yearly value.[10] In the towns and cities entitled to representation those entered on the assessment roll as owners, tenants, or occupants of real property of the yearly value of £7/10 currency were given the vote. This extension of the suffrage was accompanied, as the 1832 extension of the English suffrage had been, by the adoption of the voters' register. The municipal clerks were charged with preparing the voters' registers from the assessment rolls, and provision was made for the revision of the voters' registers in the same manner and by the same bodies as revised the assessment rolls. From this revision a right of appeal lay to a judge of the county or circuit courts. It was Hinks's regret that the same municipal council that revised the assessment rolls also revised the voters' register but it was felt to be financially impossible to adopt the system of revision by barristers that prevailed in England.

The above franchise, by qualifying tenants and occupants of real property in the country districts, extended the suffrage to the purchasers of Crown lands who occupied their farms but until the last instalment was paid would not receive their title deeds, and to the tenant-immigrants who leased lands from the Crown, the Canada Company, or private landlords. To avoid the danger that these qualifications would enfranchise mere squatters, the act declared no tenant or occupant of Crown lands would possess the franchise unless he held the lands by consent of the Crown and had paid to the Crown all rents or instalments due on the purchase price. This restriction did not apply to tenants or occupants of private lands, the self-interest of the private landlords being considered to be sufficient safeguard.[11] To ensure no squatter, tenant, or occupant indebted to the Crown was placed on the voters' registers, the Crown Land Office was required to transmit annually to each municipal secretary-treasurer a list of all Crown lands within the municipality which had been granted, leased, or held by licence of occupation, a list of all ungranted lands on which no person had permission to take possession, and a list of all lands on which any instalment or rent was overdue.

The capacity of the Canadian municipal system was to determine whether the new franchise was or was not to be effectual, for on the municipalities rested the preparation of the assessment rolls and the voters' registers. The Government realized this fact and for that reason the assessment franchise and the voters' register were made the sole and compulsory suffrage for Canada West and the cities of Quebec and Montreal only. For Canada East outside those two cities the new suffrage was made optional. If the rural municipalities of Canada East possessed an assessment roll, they might by preparing a voters' register adopt the new franchise, but whether they did or did not, the traditional 40s. freehold franchise was to remain operative.

Before the assessment franchise and the voters' register was scheduled to come into effect, the municipal system revealed its incapacity to discharge the tasks imposed upon it. The municipalities found themselves unable to provide satisfactory assessment rolls, partly because the assessors lacked experience with a new method of assessment introduced into Canada West three years previously, and partly because the assessment rolls and voters' registers had to be prepared during a general election.[12] The old mechanical method of assessment in which all forms of property without regard to location or quality received a fixed valuation prescribed by statute had been replaced by a system which required the assessors to assess property according to its real value. Unaccustomed to their new discretionary power, the assessors were subjected to the partisan knowledge that they might enfranchise or disfranchise a citizen by a slight variation in valuation; and the municipal councils, having revised and affirmed the assessment rolls for tax purposes, were provided with the partisan opportunity of revising the same rolls to constitute the voters' register. The partisan pressures on the assessors and municipal councils were particularly distressing as the defeat of the Hinks-Morin ministry in June, 1854, forced the preparations for the first assessment franchise to proceed during the heat of an election campaign. The confusion surrounding the preparation of the voters' register was accentuated by the belief in some quarters that the extended franchise and voters' register were to apply to the general election. The 1853 act extending the franchise had come into effect on January 1, 1854, although the voters' registers prepared under it were not to become effective until January 1, 1855. In some counties and towns the municipal councils proceeded in haste to prepare the registers in the belief they were required for the general election; others realized that the traditional 40s. franchise prescribed by the consolidation act of 1849 remained operative to January 1, 1855, and neglected the preparation of the registers.[13]

When in the first days of the new Parliament the MacNab-Morin ministry was formed, the new Government found the voters' registers non-existent in Canada

East and few completed in Canada West. As the new franchise was scheduled to come into full effect in a matter of weeks, the Attorney-General West, John A. Macdonald, was forced to secure a temporary act to delay the operation of the voters' registers for a year, that is until January 1, 1856.[14] The temporary act, however, allowed the assessment franchise to come into effect as scheduled by the Hincks act, and as a result during the interim year two franchises, the traditional 40s. freehold and the assessment franchises, were to operate. In the interim the franchise was to be secured from abuse by the application of appropriate oaths to prospective electors at the polls. The optional franchise the Hincks act had prescribed for Canada East was in fact extended to the whole Province of Canada.

The year's delay was to allow the assessment rolls and the voters' register to be prepared unaccompanied by the distraction of a general election. But the preparation of the voters' registers during the course of the year revealed an unexpected flaw in the assessment franchise. Electors long privileged to vote under the 40s. freehold franchise might not be assessed for £50; and the municipal clerks, required to prepare the voters' registers by transferring from the assessment roll the names of all owners, occupants, and tenants who possessed rural estates of £50 actual value of £5 yearly value, were obliged to omit citizens who had possessed the franchise since the inception of representative government in the Canadas. It also became apparent that the voters' registers remained in administrative difficulties in many municipalities. In this regard there seems reason to agree with the *Globe* that the difficulties in which the voters' registers floundered were as much due to the failure of the Government to inform adequately and forcefully the municipal officers of their new responsibilities as to the negligence of those officers.[15]

The realization that the voters' registers were not everywhere satisfactorily prepared, and that the assessment franchise proclaimed as an extension of the suffrage was to present the anomaly of disfranchising some traditional electors, forced the Government to view with misgivings the prospect of the assessment franchise and the voters' register becoming as of 1856 the sole avenue to the polls for Canada West and the cities of Montreal and Quebec. It might have been possible to retain the voters' register and not disfranchise the traditional electors by reducing the assessment conferring the franchise on all electors, freeholders, tenants, and occupants, or by reducing the assessment for freeholders only.[16] But the Government, exhausted by a protracted and contentious session, gave the problem little attention. It decided to abandon the voters' register and to make permanent the temporary act of 1854. The resultant franchise preserved the traditional franchise as defined in Lafontaine's consolidation of 1849 and maintained the extension envisaged by Hincks in 1853.[17] These multiple qualifications may have pleased Macdonald's professed preference for a fancy franchise but the impression subsists that the complexity was due rather to Macdonald's lethargy. Unwilling to muster the political courage or foresight to go back to a freehold franchise or to go forward to a wider suffrage, the Government allowed the franchise to sink into a morass of complexities.

To ensure the complexities would not serve as loopholes through which the non-qualified might exert the suffrage, the Government substituted a multitude of oaths to replace the voters' register. This reliance on the efficacy of oaths had little to recommend it, and incidents in the previous general election should have given the Government no assurance that it would. In that election, the counties of Saguenay and Kamouraska recorded more votes in many parishes than the parishes possessed population. In Saguenay itself 14,319 votes were polled from a population set at 12,965 by the census of three years previous. The Assembly was, nevertheless, surprisingly uncritical of the Government's abolition of the voters' register and the retention of a dual franchise.[18] The Assembly and the Government were both to be rudely jolted out of their complacency when the next general election produced a staggering 88 per cent increase in the votes polled.[19] As might have been expected from the destination of the recent immigration, the percentage increase was substantially higher for Canada West than Canada East, being 117 per cent in Canada West and 52 per cent in Canada East. Likewise within Canada West the increase varied from an increase of 330 per cent in the newly settled riding of Huron-Bruce to an increase of 27 per cent in the older settled riding of Leeds-Grenville North, a reflection of the prevalence of freeholders in the older counties and of occupants and tenants in the new counties. Needful as the extension undoubtedly was, the Assembly had reason to believe that the actual increase in the electorate was much larger than the new qualifications warranted.

There were glaring examples of fraudulent voting in three ridings in Canada West and nine ridings in Canada East, of which Quebec City was the most notorious. In the words of a contemporary report

upwards of three times as many votes appear to have been polled as there are qualified voters in the city. In one ward containing about 300 voters, 1,500 appear to have been polled. In another containing about as many, 1,300 or thereabouts were recorded on the poll book. The ministerial candidates invented an easy process. They obtained the votes of Lord Palmerston and other European notables, D'Arcy McGee voted several times, James F. Bradshaw, banker, appears to have voted, his representative being a squalid unshaven Hibernian in rags.[20]

In addition to this brazen perjury, there was perjury of a less offensive nature by which citizens secured a vote as tenants or occupants. The legislation had not specified that a tenant possess a written lease nor that an occupant be resident on his property. As a result many voted and took the oath who were neither tenants nor occupants as contemplated by the legislation. Young men living with their parents had voted as occupants or tenants; occupants of shanties on public lands, lines of railways, and canals voted as occupants though they never intended nor expected to become the owners of the property on which they voted. The *Globe* of February 22, 1858, declared that

in a hundred ways the law has been evaded by unscrupulous persons, while the honest and conscientious occupying a similar position have refused to avail themselves of loopholes in the law. Universal suffrage would be infinitely preferable to the present system. The most ignorant and the most dependent classes are admitted to the franchise or, at all events, exercise the right under the present law, while thousands of intelligent young men such as clerks, journeymen, etc., are excluded. If this class were admitted, we should have an element to counterbalance the degraded occupants of hovels and shanties, who are ready to sell their votes for a glass of whiskey or the promise of some petty favour.

The public conscience was roused. Chief Justice Lafontaine chose to deliver himself of a lecture to the Grand Jury of Montreal against election frauds.[21] The Administrator of the Archdiocese of Quebec, Bishop Baillargeon, issued a directive to the clergy of the archdiocese to petition the Assembly against "the continuation of a system, which offensive to the right of electors, contributes to the profound demoralization of our people."[22] The main Conservative organ in Toronto editorially condemned the gross frauds and claimed that "there is a general agreement among all parties that some step should be taken to prevent a recurrence of these illegal proceedings at future elections. A registration of votes is the remedy which appears to be most generally accepted."[23] Perhaps the *Globe* of February 22, 1858, best reflected the feelings of the well informed.

It is universally admitted that the crop of frauds and perjuries produced at the last general election exceeded all former example. Morality was shocked, and religion outraged, by the degrading spectacle which the polling booths too often presented. The evil was not limited to one class of voters, nor to one political party. . . . Spurious votes have been recorded on both sides, and the lax provisions of the law have been taken advantage of by both. This is proved by the fact that an amendment of the law is demanded by all parties, and from both sections of the province. . . . There are two things which a new law ought to secure. First, that every man's right to the franchise should be ascertained and settled before the day of election. The polling booth is not the proper place for a trial, nor is the deputy returning officer the proper person to preside as judge.

When the first session of the new Parliament assembled, it was informed in the Speech from the Throne that the Government was determined to secure the proper registration and protection of all qualified voters.[24] There was ready agreement on this reform. Private members from Canada East were now anxious to sponsor the legislation.[25] The Reform party had already adopted the voters' register as a plank in their platform at the Reform convention of January, 1857, and in the last session of the previous Parliament George Brown had gone so far as to secure the establishment of a select committee to devise an economical system of registration.[26] The Conservatives, who had not hesitated to jettison the voters' register in 1855 when confronted by its administrative difficulties, recalled that they had espoused a registration of voters as long ago as the last sessions of the Assembly of Upper Canada.[27] Galvanized into action by an aroused public opinion the politicians dismissed their late misgivings and hastened to enact a voters' register into law.[28]

The legislation, as introduced by the Attorney General West, John A. Macdonald, and passed by the Assembly, established a voters' register on much the same lines as in the Hincks Act of 1853 except that the voters' register was to be applicable to Canada East as well as Canada West. The clerk of each municipality was to be required to prepare from the last revised and corrected assessment roll an alphabetical list of all persons entitled to vote in parliamentary elections and a description of their property. In Canada West this list, to be completed by October 1 each year and certified before a county judge (or two justices of the peace), was the voters' register. The Government felt that the assessment procedure in Canada West had reached a degree of perfection that made it unnecessary as under the Hincks Act to have the municipal council revise the assessment roll on two occasions, once for taxation purposes and then via the voters' register for parliamentary purposes. In Canada East because of the less robust state of the municipal institutions a dual revision was maintained. The secretary-treasurer of each municipality was to prepare a provisional voters' list from the raw assessment rolls. After public exhibition of the list any person who felt his name or the name of another had been wrongly inserted or omitted could appeal to the municipal council sitting as a court of revision, with the right of a further appeal to a judge of the Superior or Circuit Court. On completion of the revision the provisional voters' list became the voters' register and was to serve as the sole avenue to the franchise until such times as a new voters' register was prepared.

The readoption of the voters' register was open to certain risks and criticisms. As previously the great risk was the capacity of the municipal officers, assessors, clerks, and secretary-treasurers, to discharge the administrative burdens placed upon them. Was there any reason to believe that there would be success in 1858 where there had been failure in 1855? The politicians thought there was, and their reasoning was not without foundation. The excesses of the 1858 general election had brought about a fundamental change in public opinion. The public were now convinced that a voters' register was essential to the freedom of elections. In the words of the Toronto *Leader* of January 15, 1858, the circumstances necessitating the repeal of the previous voters' registration law was not now decisive of the question because "it came suddenly into operation, when people were not prepared for it. Public attention had not been generally fixed upon the question; and the necessity of such a law was only very partially felt. The illegal proceedings which have occurred in many places during the late election have directed public attention to the subject, till the necessity of having the qualified voters registered has come to be generally admitted."

Aside from the change in the attitude of the public, there were other changes that augured well for the success of the voters' register. There was to be a single uniform franchise and a similar voters' register applicable to all Canada. The success of the new departure was not to be bedevilled by the carping criticism that there was one franchise and one procedure applicable for the elections of Canada West and another franchise and procedure applicable to Canada East. The traditional 40s. freehold franchise was abolished and a single assessment franchise identical with that set forth in the act of 1855 was to apply to the whole province.

Had any changes occurred which were likely to have improved the capacity of the municipalities to discharge their responsibilities? In Canada West several years' experience with the new assessment procedure should have overcome difficulties which plagued the preparation of the first voters' register, and the severe penalties incorporated in the new legislation should have forestalled any disposition towards partisan manipulations in the preparation of the second. In Canada East the municipal system had been reorganized in 1855. Where the parishioners had failed to avail themselves of municipal machinery, the Governor General had been specifically empowered by the reorganization act to appoint councillors, assessors, and other municipal officers.[29] In consequence the Government could now only blame itself if municipal institutions were absent in any riding in Canada East. The reorganization act, however, had only required the municipalities of Canada East to assess property every five years; as a result the new election act did not require the annual preparation of a voters' register for Canada East as it did for Canada West. Each register in Canada East was to remain in effect until a new one had been prepared following each municipal assessment. In the event that the public came to consider the existing register obsolete, the municipal council (the county registrar, or any two proprietors) could so inform the Governor General who in such circumstances was authorized to appoint special assessors and municipal clerks to reassess the municipality and to prepare a new and special voters' register.

The ultimate test of the public's determination to have, and of the municipalities' capacity to provide, a voters' register was supplied by the general election of 1861. That election showed the registers to be in surprisingly good condition for their first trial. In only three counties was extensive padding revealed. These counties were in the Montreal district, notorious for its electoral corruption, and the padding could have been corrected if the voters' list had been revised. In some cases, deputy returning officers had refused to deny the vote to persons not on the voters' register, and in Canada West some deputy returning officers had used the 1860 voters' registers and others the 1861 voters' registers, although the latter were not officially operative until October 1, some ten weeks after the election. While these failings were to produce a spate of measures to improve the voters' register, the absence of demands for its abolition may be taken as conclusive evidence that the public and the politicians considered the voters' register a considerable advance on former electoral procedure.

Various corrective steps were taken. To prevent a repetition of the padding which had occurred in the three counties of Canada East because the municipal councils had failed to revise the lists prepared by their municipal clerks, the judges of the Superior Court were given the authority to adjudicate complaints against the voters' registers. If after their preparation, any municipal council in Canada East should fail to revise their voters' register, the judges were to entertain the complaints *ab origine* rather than wait until appeals could be launched from the revision of a municipal council.[30] Formerly such appeals had been the sole occasion on which the judges might intervene; for the future they were still to continue as the usual method of invoking judicial review. The defects in the voters' registers of Canada East occasioned by the long periods between assessments were partially remedied in 1863 when the Governor General was empowered in cases of neglect to appoint assessors to revise annually the assessment rolls of a municipality in order to allow the annual preparation of the voters' register.[31] As an adjunct to the register's annual preparation, the Governor General was no longer to be obliged to wait for the receipt of a complaint from a locality before he could invoke his powers to appoint *ad hoc* assessors and municipal clerks. For the future all governments were to possess the authority and power to ensure each parish of Canada East had a voters' register annually prepared and revised.

The corrective measures for Canada West were primarily concerned with the lethargy of the municipal clerks and the need to ensure the annual preparation of the voters' register. The remedies devised took the form of subjecting the dilatory clerks to punitory discipline.[32] There was, however, one prime defect that the Legislature did not correct. No provision had been made in Canada West for a revision of the registers compiled by the municipal clerks from the revised assessment rolls. George Brown had, at the beginning, pointed out that the assessors assessed persons without regard to age or nationality and that such persons would, if possessed of an adequate assessment, be transcribed to the voters' register by the municipal clerks. John A. Macdonald had admitted this danger as well as the further possibility that squatters might be assessed as occupants or tenants and if they escaped detection when the assessment rolls were revised they would be put on the voters' register. But Macdonald was content to rely on the revision of the assessment rolls by the municipal councils for the elimination of the squatters and on the single oath applicable to each elector for the prevention of such minors and aliens as were on the voters' registers from exercising the franchise.[33] In consequence no provision was ever made for a revision of the municipal clerks' compilation of the eligible voters; the zeal of partisans on municipal councils and of scrutineers on the hustings of Canada West had to be relied upon to exclude the ineligible from the suffrage.

As has been stated, the traditional 40s. freehold franchise was abolished and the suffrage was confined to an assessment franchise. This franchise was to limit the vote to British males of twenty-one years who within a parish, township, town, or village possessed as owner, tenant, or occupant real property to the assessed value of $200 or the yearly assessed value of $20, or who within any city or town entitled to distinct representation possessed as owner, tenant, or occupant real property to the assessed value of $300 or of the yearly assessed value of $30. The assessment values conferring the franchise were identical to those set forth in the act of 1855, transcribed into dollars at the rate specified by the currency act of 1853.[34] There was some fear that the assessment franchise would disqualify many freeholders who had voted under the 40s. qualification. Macdonald sought to allay this fear by arguing that property valued at $200 approached so near to the annual value of 40s. sterling as to make the change of little moment. Many members from Canada East considered Macdonald's argument specious and were by no means convinced that the assessment franchise would not disfranchise some of the traditional electors.[35]

The establishment of the assessment franchise as the sole qualification brought to an end the 40s. franchise that had prevailed in the Canadas since 1791. This franchise had produced near manhood suffrage as long as Crown grants were freely available. The approximation to manhood suffrage was aided by certain latitudes that had grown up. For instance, although this franchise would appear to have required that the property be productive, it was customary in Upper Canada to allow those possessed of unimproved and non-productive lands to vote if the actual value of the land was equivalent to the capitalized value of 40s.[36] This custom appears to have been less universally adopted in Lower Canada where settlement was more general. In towns the traditional franchise had required the resident voters to be possessed of a dwelling house and lot to the yearly value of £5, or to be a tenant paying at the rate of £10 per annum. The former qualification had led to a diversity of practices. In the case of towns composing part of a county for representation purposes it was customary for a resident of the town to vote under the 40s. freehold provision or the £5 dwelling and lot provision depending under which he qualified. In the case of cities and town possessing distinct representation, the 40s. freehold qualification did not apply and the franchise was confined to tenants and owners of dwelling houses and lots. As the owner of a vacant town lot was not qualified, it had become customary in Lower Canada for these individuals to vote in the election for the adjacent county. With the passage of time, this custom was extended to those possessed of built-up lots, and the latter came to possess a dual vote in town and county.

As towns with distinct representation did not emerge in Upper Canada until 1821, the Lower Canada custom was slower in arising there. It does not appear to have been generally adopted in Upper Canada until after the union, and for some time the owners of vacant lots in such towns in the upper province appear to have been disfranchised.[37] Upper Canada had, however, not been lacking in ingenuity. Methods had been improvised to restore to these freeholders the franchise which had been lost when their town became an urban riding. Enterprising candidates had conceived the idea of enfranchising the owners of vacant lots by promptly building shanties on the property thereby fulfilling the technical requirement of a dwelling house and lot of land. In the general election of 1841 electors for the town of Niagara had complained that the winning candidate had "erected at his own expense, costs and charges, and after the teste of the said writ of election for this town in and upon divers vacant plots of ground . . . held, or pretended to be held by certain conveyances, divers small moveable buildings intended to be represented as dwelling houses, in order that the persons holding or pretending to hold, by virtue of such conveyance, the said plots of ground, wherever the same were placed, might vote at the election for the said Edward Clarke Campbell under colour of such buildings being their dwelling houses."[38] While only Niagara and Cornwall appear to have used this device, the practice of residents of enfranchised towns voting in the adjacent county seems to have become general after 1845. In that year it received tacit approval with the defeat of a bill, sponsored by Macdonnell of Glengarry, to declare proprietors possessing votes in the towns of Canada West should not vote in the adjacent county.[39] The defeat was secured by the narrow margin of one vote, after Henry Sherwood, the Solicitor General and member for Toronto City, had exuded clouds of legalistic confusion to the effect that the Act of Union allowed the provincial Parliament to repeal the franchise clauses of the Constitutional Act but not to declare their meaning.

The assessment franchise and the voters' register had their first trial in the general election of 1861. While many members had advocated the lowering of the assessment franchise to avoid any possible disfranchisement of the traditional voters, the election gave inconclusive evidence as to the effect of the abolition of the 40s. franchise. There was a falling off in the vote from the previous election in Canada East of 24 per cent as compared with a drop of less than one per cent in the vote in Canada West.[40] The drop in Canada East may have been due more to the presence of the voters' register and the cessation of fraudulent voting than to a decline in the number of enfranchised citizens. Certainly the relation of the voting public to the total population was identical in each province, 13·15 per cent of the population of Canada East being on the voters' register and 13·9 per cent of the population of Canada West, while 67·4 per cent of those on the voters' register in Canada East voted as compared with 74·8 per cent in Canada West. It would seem that the franchise was not constricted since there was no agitation in the years immediately following for its extension.

The smaller holdings in Canada East might have been expected to make it more susceptible to any contraction of the voting public on the abolition of the 40s. qualification. Certainly Sicotte, the Commissioner of Crown Lands, was of the opinion a farm producing a revenue of 40s. might not be assessed at $200. Agitation in Canada East against this franchise may, however, have been forestalled by an ingenious change in the assessment procedure prior to the general election. By law the assessors of Canada West had been required to assess real property in the counties at its actual value but real property in the villages, towns, and cities had to be assessed at its annual value; in Canada East real property was assessed in all cases at its actual value. The 1858 franchise act had specified that owners, occupants, and tenants of real property assessed for a specified actual or annual value possessed the franchise. As a result the electors of Canada East and the rural electors of Canada West were enfranchised on the actual value of their property, while the urban electors of Canada West were enfranchised on the annual value of their property. In 1859 Macdonald and Cartier sponsored an amendment to the franchise act which required the assessors in Canada East to specify the annual value as well as the actual value of all property.[41] This double assessment would allow any rural owner, occupant, or tenant to receive a vote if his property was assessed for an annual value of $20 although assessed for less than $200 actual value. Since taxation was only imposed on the actual value the legislation opened an avenue to extend the franchise. The Assembly, in no mood to circumscribe those political possibilities, rejected an attempt by Dorion and Brown to confine the preparation of the voters' register to that valuation on which taxes were levied.[42] It would appear, and John Sandfield Macdonald was of this opinion, that this amendment extended the franchise in Canada East and placed it upon a different footing than that upon which it stood in Canada West.[43]

When the John Sandfield Macdonald–Dorion ministry came into office following the general election of 1861 and the defeat of the John A. Macdonald-Cartier ministry on the militia bill, the flexible interpretation of the franchise in Canada East possible under the act of 1859 was brought to an end. Sponsored by a private member (Bellerose, M.P.P. Laval) legislation was passed which declared the assessed actual value of property was to determine the franchise for property owners and the assessed annual value was to determine the franchise for occupants and tenants.[44] While the legislation limited the opportunities to qualify, it did not limit these possibilities as much as some members of the Rouge party desired. They would have preferred that the franchise be bestowed only on the value on which taxes were levied.[45]

The above adjustment was the last change in the franchise for Canada East; but in Canada West dissatisfaction with the method of assessing urban property on its annual value and the breadth of the municipal franchise produced a change in the parliamentary franchise for that section. The municipal act had prescribed that the municipal electors of Canada West should, in the rural municipalities and police villages, be all freeholders and householders whose names appeared on the assessment roll without regard to the amount of the assessment, while in the incorporated villages, towns, and cities, the municipal electors should be assessed for property to the annual value of $12, $20, and $30 respectively.[46] When the urban depression following the cessation of the American Civil War made the property holders sensitive to municipal tax rates, it was believed that the prevalent high rates stemmed from the breadth of the municipal franchise. Many public men, including such Reformers as George Brown, came to the conclusion that property had to be better protected in the municipal councils. As a result the Legislature in 1866 abolished the old method of urban assessment and required all property to be assessed at its actual value, and at the same time raised the municipal franchise.[47] The municipal suffrage was to be confined to those who possessed leasehold or freehold property to the value in cities of $600, in towns of $400, in incorporated villages of $300, in townships and police villages of $100. On the passage of the bill through committee a rider was added changing the parliamentary franchise for Canada West to coincide with the municipal franchise. The parliamentary franchise was to be confined to owners and occupants of real property assessed at an actual value in cities of $600, in towns of $400, in incorporated villages of $300, and in townships of $200.[48] This new franchise was higher than that prevailing in the case of cities, towns, and villages but was unchanged for rural residents.

The motives for this change are not clear. One thing is certain, the increased qualifications received the support of all parties. A motion to give the bill the six months' hoist, introduced by John Carling because he claimed the rider would disfranchise a quarter of his London electorate, was only able to muster the support of seven members.[49] The change appears to have been in part a manifestation of an agrarian conservatism which felt some concern at the political influence the shiftless urban labourers had acquired in the United States and might acquire in Canada. The changed franchise was also in part a reassertion of a basic Canadian conservatism which had been frequently submerged during the previous turbulent decades when each political faction had had to grapple for every cross-current of public favour. This conservatism was now released by the knowledge that the existing political institutions were coming to an end, and that the new franchise would not be in effect until after Confederation, when in the changed milieu the public would find difficulty assigning responsibility for the disfranchisement. Whatever the motive may have been, it resulted in Ontario and Quebec entering into existence with distinct franchises, thereby ending a similarity that had commenced with the Constitutional Act in 1791.

CHAPTER NINE

VANCOUVER ISLAND AND BRITISH COLUMBIA

ALTHOUGH THE COLONIES of Vancouver Island and British Columbia had been united by the time British Columbia entered Confederation, they had separate beginnings. Vancouver became a colony on July 16, 1849, when Richard Blanshard was commissioned Governor and continued its separate existence until 1866 when an Imperial statute united it with the colony of British Columbia. British Columbia was created a colony by Imperial statute in 1858 and remained under the supervision of the Colonial Office until Confederation in 1871.

I

Governor Blanshard brought with him to Vancouver Island Instructions to appoint a council, to summon a general assembly of freeholders, to proclaim the number of representatives, to divide the Island into counties or townships, to appoint the returning officers, and to issue the writs of election.[1] His Commission was more specific when it came to defining the franchise. It required Blanshard "to summon and call General Assemblies of the inhabitants owning twenty or more acres of freehold land within the said Island."[2] Yet, the Governor did not follow these directives. He found the European population of Vancouver so small (they were chiefly employees of the Hudson's Bay Company or its affiliate the Puget Sound Agricultural Company) that he was forced to postpone not merely the calling of an assembly but the appointment of a council.[3]

There were few settlers because Vancouver Island was far removed from the main stream of European immigration to North America; the cheaper land available in the United States attracted settlers there; and the gold rush of 1848 had lured settler and immigrant alike to California. The Hudson's Bay Company, which had been granted the Island by letters patent on January 13, 1849, on condition it settle the Island with British subjects, had determined to sell the land at £1 sterling per acre.[4] In the United States land was selling for $1 an acre, and in Oregon land was being given away free under the donation law of 1850.[5] Further, the Hudson's Bay Company refused to sell land in blocks of less than twenty acres, and for each hundred acres purchased the purchaser had to bring out five single men or three married couples as settlers. The minimum block of land purchasable would have proved sufficient to meet the franchise suggested by the Commission to Blanshard, but the cost of the land and the cost of passage to Vancouver Island set a high price on the privilege of being an elector.

Discouraged by the colony's prospects, Blanshard resigned the Governorship on November 18, 1850. Prior to his departure he appointed a provisional council of three to administer the affairs of the Island, and the senior member of this Council, James Douglas, was subsequently appointed Governor.[6] Douglas, the Chief Factor of the Hudson's Bay Company at Victoria, and the Provisional Council administered Vancouver Island for a further period of three years without the aid of an assembly. Douglas (like Blanshard) was of opinion that there were insufficient persons of education and intelligence in the colony to constitute an Assembly.[7] This autocratic régime was brought to an end in 1854 when the Law Officers of the Crown invalidated an ordinance establishing judicial machinery for the Island because the power of legislation had been vested by Royal Instruction in a governor, council, and assembly.[8] As in Nova Scotia and Prince Edward Island the questionable validity of the ordinances of a governor and council were to force the erection of an assembly.

The ruling perplexed the Colonial Office, which had been left in doubt by Douglas' dispatches whether there were a sufficient number of freeholders resident in the colony to allow the formation of an assembly.[9] The Hudson's Bay Company officials in London, however, reassured the Colonial Office. Their assurances were not without motive. The Company feared that their grant of Vancouver Island might be revoked because of their failure to colonize it, and they foresaw that an assembly could serve as a tangible proof of settlement and a refutation of their critics. Colville, Governor of the Company, therefore urged the Colonial Office to summon a seven-man assembly; and because of the small number of freeholders, which he estimated to be somewhat in excess of forty, he urged that the members be returned by the freehold population at large.[10] The Colonial Office after some hesitation accepted the advice of Colville and ordered Douglas to call an assembly.[11]

With some diffidence Douglas and his Council set about summoning the first Assembly. On June 16, 1856, a proclamation was issued dividing the inhabited portion of the Island into four electoral districts, each possessing one poll and returning a total of seven members.[12] As defined in the Governor's Commission the franchise was extended to all freeholders possessed of twenty or more acres of land. To increase an insignificant electorate, absentee proprietors were allowed to vote through their resident agents. This novel feature, proxy voting, seems to have been inspired by the example of British Guiana where Douglas' father had possessed this privilege as a sugar planter. Douglas and the Council also adopted a practice of the English boroughs and required each member to be possessed of a freehold estate worth £300.[13] These two features, proxy voting and a high property qualification for members, were to enhance the political power of the Hudson's Bay Company. Few citizens other than its officers possessed the amount of property required to qualify as a member and the proxy voting was of benefit to few but absentee officers of the Company. Hence six members of the first Assembly were in the service of the Hudson's Bay Company or the Puget Sound Agricultural Company, and the seventh member was the Company's nominee.[14]

When the forty or so freeholders had exercised their franchise, the smallest Assembly ever constituted in British North America met for business on August 12, 1856. The whole procedure had the staging of a comic opera. The electors were so few in number that in all districts but Victoria the elections were mere nominations. In Nanaimo the single elector personally appointed his member, an incident that prompted the *British Colonist* of July 1, 1859, on the occasion of a subsequent by-election to declare, "this caps the climax of all the elections that were ever heard of where the Anglo-Saxon language is spoken." When the Assembly convened for business and found the

E

eligibility of three of its seven members challenged, it was embarrassed to find too few members available to constitute a committee of enquiry.[15] The Assembly was only rescued from the dilemma by the failure of one petitioner to press his charges.

Vancouver Island in subsequent years made efforts to increase the electors and the number in the Assembly. In the first Assembly the two members for Victoria District introduced a bill to extend the franchise within the town to British subjects of mature age who were literate and possessed a freehold in buildings to the value of £50.[16] This legislation passed the Assembly with the literacy requirement removed and the franchise farther extended to include all tenants who for a twelve-month period had rented a house at £10 per annum.[17] The bill was forwarded to Douglas, but he did not bring the bill to the attention of his Council until some twenty-two months later, when it provoked a dispute in Council over the preponderant influence of town and country in the Assembly and the definition of a British subject.[18] The Council was uncertain whether the requirement would not exclude persons, British-born, who, to secure lands in the United States, had been obliged to make a declaration of their intention to become American citizens.

In the interval one of the members for Victoria District, despairing that the Council would ever consider the bill, had introduced a new franchise bill into the Assembly. This bill was of general application and was not as its predecessor confined to the town of Victoria.[19] It recognized that the colony had changed greatly since the Assembly passed the first franchise bill in June of 1857. The discovery of gold on the Fraser had brought a sudden increase in population to the Island. The increase was not merely reflected in the few urban centres but also in the extension of agricultural settlement to meet the new demands for produce. Although the bill was unacceptable to the Assembly it led to the establishment of a select committee to draft the requisite legislation. The result of the Assembly's deliberation was a composite measure to increase the representation, to extend the franchise, and to establish a voters' register.[20] The measure was subsequently extensively amended in the Council from whence it emerged as three distinct pieces of legislation.

The acts extending the representation and the franchise alleviated the embarrassments and absurdities occasioned by the scarcity of members and of electors.[21] The membership was increased from seven to thirteen to facilitate the running of a parliamentary institution and a diversified rather than a single uniform franchise was adopted to create an electorate of respectable size. While the adoption of manhood suffrage, current in the Australian colonies, would have achieved the same result, Vancouver Island's proximity to the flotsam and jetsam of the gold diggings on the Fraser inclined the legislators to a more conservative franchise. The franchise was extended to all British males of full age who had resided on Vancouver Island four calendar months and who possessed any one of five other qualifications; these were, to be owner of twenty acres, or owner of real estate valued at £50 and held for three months, or occupant for six months of real estate whose rental was £12 per year, or sharecropper for twelve months on a farm of which twenty acres were under cultivation and from which he received one-quarter of the product, or, lastly, a surgeon, physician, barrister, or graduate of any chartered university or college of Great Britain or her colonies.

This legislation had initially been less liberal but expressions of public opinion as the bill worked its way through the Assembly had led the legislators to greater liberality. The editor of the *British Colonist*, Amor de Cosmos, had continually criticized the bill during its passage and his criticism had led the citizens of Victoria to hold a public meeting of protest.[22] While both parties had rejected manhood suffrage as it would "not suit the age or the colony," De Cosmos had, after having toyed with the idea of a resident householder qualification, endorsed a taxpaying franchise, and the citizens' choice fell on qualifications which could be equated with the existing qualification (ownership of twenty acres of land).[23] A taxpaying franchise was inappropriate to a colony which as yet paid no direct taxes. The suggestions of the citizens' meeting were more realistic. Since the Hudson's Bay Company sold land at £1 an acre, the citizenry of Victoria had resolved that ownership of real estate worth £20, or tenancy of real property at an annual rental of £12 should be adopted as equivalent. As the Hudson's Bay Company had been selling town and suburban lots for £20 and £25 sterling respectively the owners or occupants of premises built on these lots would have been enfranchised by the adoption of these suggestion.[24] The Assembly in a last flurry of amendments tried to incorporate them into the franchise bill but the Council had objected and the legislation previously mentioned was the compromise.

The two qualifications which bestowed the franchise on sharecroppers and university graduates reflected the personal interests and associations of the legislators. Thomas Skinner, member for Esquimalt, was manager of a farm for the Puget Sound Agricultural Company. This company possessed four large farms on the Island staffed by indentured servants and under the management of "gentlemen bailiffs" who received for their services a residence, a small honorarium, and a share of the profits.[25] Helmcken, resident doctor to the Hudson's Bay Company, and Pemberton, Surveyor General and a graduate of Trinity College, Dublin, sponsored the clause to enfranchise all professional men and university graduates on the Island. These provisions indicate the personal exertions made by the legislators to extend the franchise and yet retain respectability in an electorate which was endangered from the riffraff of a gold mining boom.

This fear of the transient mining population which had led De Cosmos, the citizens of Victoria, and the legislators to stop short of manhood suffrage and the maximization of the electorate, accounts for the insistence of the legislators on a period of residence, on property ownership, and on the establishment of a voters' register. It is true a voters' register was in use in Great Britain, Canada, and New Brunswick and had been suggested to Douglas by Merivale, the Colonial Under-Secretary, when the establishment of representative government in Vancouver Island was under consideration; but if fear had not overridden economy, the administrative difficulties and the costs of preparing a voters' register as experienced by Canada and New Brunswick should have deterred its adoption in Vancouver Island.[26] The Assembly would not extend the franchise without the safeguard of a voters' register, for in the words of the Speaker, "God made the country, but the devil made the town."[27]

The voters' registry act[28] authorized the Sheriff of Vancouver Island to post notices in conspicuous places in each electoral district, requiring all citizens entitled to vote to transmit to him within a period of two weeks their claim to vote. The claim was to contain, besides the name of the claimant, his place of residence, the nature of his qualification, and its location. The Sheriff within a week from the final date for the deposit of claims was to prepare an alphabetical list of claimants containing not only their names but the nature and location of these qualifications. These lists were to be posted in conspicuous places in the electoral district to which each list was applicable. During a two-week period following, any elector or the Sheriff might object to the preliminary lists, and objections were to be prepared and posted in each electoral district by the Sheriff. After a further ten days, the Sheriff was to transfer the list of voters and the list of objections to the Revisor of the voters' lists. The Revisor, a single officer appointed by the Governor to service all electoral districts, was to fix the time and places for holding his revision court for each district. At this court the Revisor, with full power to summon and examine documents and witnesses, was to determine the validity of each objection or claim. His decisions, subject to appeal to the Supreme Court on points of law but not of fact, were to complete the voters' register. This official register was to be the sole entree to the polling booth, for no elector regardless of qualification was to vote unless his name was on the register.

The voters' register was not merely an assurance that transients would be excluded from the Island electorate, it was a positive restraint on the franchise itself. The Legislature, in order to finance the preparation of the voters' lists, had had to impose a fee or tax on each claimant for the vote. Each claim had to be accompanied by 4/2 to defray the costs of preparation. The fee reduced the voting population below that qualified by law, for as the *British Colonist* reported on November 16, 1859, "All the old settlers of the Colony and nearly all the new, complain justly at being compelled to pay a dollar [4/2] in order to register a vote with the sheriff. It is a matter conceded on all sides that the tax is exorbitant, that it is unjust and intended to deter many from voting if possible." While the preparation of the first voters' register was known to precede a general election, the number of the electorate disfranchised by the fee must have increased in subsequent years when the preparation of the voters' register was not known to precede an election.[29] The fee must also have discouraged the multiple exercise of the franchise by citizens qualified by property to vote in several electoral districts. Thus a criticism of the franchise, that its basis was property and not persons, was overcome in part by the fee.

Apart from the question of fees, the voters' register came under further criticism. As all demands to have one's name entered on the voters' register had to be made to the Sheriff at Victoria by post or in person, the two-week registration period was found too short. The electoral district of Salt Spring Island and Chemainus had found the period reduced to three days when the Sheriff's notice of registration did not reach the district until eleven days after it was first posted in Victoria. The resultant disfranchisement provoked considerable protest and the register was clandestinely reopened for this and other districts.[30] The register came under a second attack when a controverted election committee for Victoria Town ruled that the presence of a person's name on the voters' register was indisputable evidence of his right to vote. This decision was made in the face of the prohibition on the Revisor against entertaining claims to vote, or objections to claims, unless they had been made to the Sheriff. The Revisor could not act on his own initiative to strike out claims which were known to be objectionable.[31] The third complaint concerned the failure of the act to indicate the length of time the voters' register prepared in the autumn of 1859 was to apply, and the failure to provide for periodic revision or preparation of a new voters' register. On the edge of the gold fever the population of Vancouver Island was sufficiently fluid that a voters' register became rapidly obsolete.

A by-election for Esquimalt Town in August, 1860, brought this defect in the legislation before a controverted election committee. The by-election had been disputed because many persons legally qualified to vote had been denied the vote when the returning officer on the instruction of the Secretary for the Colony, W. A. G. Young, had allowed only those on the 1859 voters' list to vote. The select committee voided the election on the grounds that the voters' register prepared for the general election of 1860 was not applicable to a by-election seven months later.[32] Although the Assembly reversed the ruling, it did accept a subsequent bill sent down by the Council which authorized the machinery set up by the act of 1859 to prepare annually a new voters' register.[33] The act did not correct the other faults of its predecessor, and complaints continued to be made against the voters' register.

The representation and franchise acts were also not free from criticism. The mercantile interests of Victoria claimed the agricultural interests had representation out of all proportion to the revenue they contributed to the colonial treasury. The outsettlers claimed that the property franchise and the privilege accorded property owners to vote in every electoral district in which they held property had given the residents of Victoria undue political influence. The five years of independent existence that remained to the Legislature of Vancouver Island was taken up by this rural-urban bickering.

By 1862 the unequal distribution of representation had become a subject of heated complaint. The *British Colonist* of June 12, 1862, pointed out that Victoria returned two members out of a total of thirteen, although Victoria had 446 registered voters, whereas Victoria County with 116 registered voters, Nanaimo with 29, and Sooke with 16 returned a total of five members.[34] The merchants were able to bring sufficient pressure to secure the incorporation of Victoria and the increase of its representation to four.[35] The agriculturalists protested and entered a counter claim that agricultural settlements existed which were outside the limits of any electoral districts and whose residents were in consequence totally disfranchised.[36] The upshot was the granting of representation to the districts of Cowichan, Comox, and Alberni.[37]

The voters' register of 1864 revealed that residents of Victoria were indeed unduly favoured. It set the total electorate at 1,213 but as many residents of Victoria held land for speculative purposes in the outsettlements, the actual electors were less than three-quarters of the nominal list. The number of eligible voters outside Victoria Town and County was approximately 367 but the voters resident in the outdistricts numbered a mere 141.[38] Since the elections were not held simultaneously throughout the colony the residents of Victoria could with some physical exertion have returned the representation of each outsettlement. This condition and the more liberal franchise prevailing in the adjacent colony of British Columbia led to determined efforts being made in 1865 and 1866 to modify the franchise.

The agitators sought to abolish the privilege of multiple voting by limiting the elector to a vote in the district in which he resided, to abolish the vote accorded professional men and university graduates, and to extend the franchise.[39] The period of residence on the Island was to be reduced in all cases to three months, the rental qualification was to be reduced from £12 to £8 per annum, and all pre-emptors and taxpayers under the Salary Act were to be enfranchised. The two latter qualifications would have extended the vote to all *bona fide* settlers who had acquired land by the simple process of occupying unreserved Crown lands and recording their claim at the Surveyor General's Office, and to all who paid the 1 per cent tax on incomes over $727.50 per annum.[40] This franchise, which was to have been accompanied by the abolition of the £300 property qualification for members, would have placed the voting power and membership in the Assembly in the hands of the general populace of British nationality. Governor Kennedy was appalled at the prospect. He considered the quality of the Assembly to be already decidedly low and he believed this franchise would further reduce the calibre of the members. He feared that it would increase the influence of American democratic ideas in the Assembly and lead to a premature demand for responsible government.[41] The hostility of the Governor and the prospect of imminent union with British Columbia led the Council to shelve the legislation.

The failure of the Assembly to extend the franchise meant that the independent political life of Vancouver Island closed with the 1859 franchise still in operation. But although there had been no legal change in the franchise, it had been gradually extended through changes in the terms governing sales of land. The Hudson's Bay Company had been forced to liberalize the terms of sales on account of the land policy of the United States. In 1858 the Company sold considerable amounts of land in the Saanich and Cowitchin districts on the instalment basis of 25 per cent down and the remainder in three equal annual instalments.[42] In 1859 the price of inferior land was reduced from the uniform rate of £1 per acre to 4/2 ($1), and in 1860 the lower rate was made applicable to all lands.[43] In the same year settlers were given the right to pre-empt 150 acres of Crown land by entering into occupancy and by registering their claim with the Surveyor General, no payment to be made until the land was surveyed.[44] The reduction in the cost of land and the ruling of the Attorney General[45] that lands purchased on instalments were in the full legal possession of the purchaser meant the franchise was gradually extended without any positive enactment to that effect.

While the greater ease in securing land had extended the franchise, the requirement that electors be British subjects had denied it to an increasing number of settlers. Aliens had been excluded from the franchise in 1856 because the electorate was restricted to freeholders and aliens could not acquire land in Vancouver Island. When the franchise was extended to tenants in 1859, the vote was restricted to British subjects by positive enactment. The severity of the restriction was alleviated by a provision that British-born settlers who had taken the oath of allegiance to the United States in order to secure land could regain their British citizenship by taking an oath of allegiance to Her Majesty before the Chief Justice of the Island.[46] This provision did not facilitate the naturalization of the foreign born, and it was not until 1861 that the Legislature passed a general naturalization law which allowed aliens to become naturalized subjects after three years' residence in the colony and subscription to the oath of allegiance.[47] Aside from negroes, few Americans availed themselves of this privilege.[48] A feeling of impermanency among the settlers and a certain pan-Americanism combined to reduce the number who sought naturalization. As a consequence the Governor was forced to report in 1865 that the 2,000 British males constituted about a third of the population.[49]

If the union had not intervened, it is likely the Assembly of Vancouver Island would ultimately have given the franchise to aliens or at least to American aliens. The American residents wielded considerable influence. In 1865 the desire to induce them to invest capital and take up permanent residence in the colony lead Helmcken, Speaker of the Assembly, to sponsor a motion to extend the franchise to them.[50] There was no intention to extend it to all aliens, such as the Chinese who were numerous in the mining camps, for the relaxation was to be accompanied by a requirement that the electors be able to read and write English. The move was defeated, for too many members were afraid that such action might deliver the colony into the hands of the

Americans. The pressure was strong, however, and the Assembly did approve the extension of the municipal franchise of Victoria to aliens.[51]

II

In the years following the establishment of representative institutions on Vancouver Island, the colony of British Columbia had grown up across the Gulf of Georgia. The Imperial Parliament had erected a civil administration over the British territory on the mainland in 1858 following the discovery of gold on the Fraser. The legislation had authorized the Crown by Order in Council to appoint a governor, council, and assembly to govern the colony.[52] In the first instance the Crown had entrusted the administration to Douglas, the Governor of Vancouver Island, and had delayed representative institutions until growth of a fixed population would provide the necessary materials.[53]

The lack of a British and fixed population "established on the soil" led Douglas to approve of the delay. The migratory nature of the mining population and the great preponderance of foreigners, American and Chinese, left New Westminster as the only centre with a resident British population.[54] But pressure from the Colonial Office and a desire to ease his own administrative burden ultimately led Douglas to establish a municipal council at New Westminster.[55] This concession served to whet the appetite of the British residents of British Columbia for a resident governor and a representative assembly. In 1860 a memorial from 433 British subjects petitioned the Colonial Secretary for an assembly; in 1861 a convention of delegates elected from the districts of New Westminster, Hope, and Douglas assembled at New Westminster and petitioned the Colonial Secretary to the same purpose; and in the autumn of the same year the convention reassembled at Hope and renewed its demand.[56] When the Municipal Council of New Westminster in the following year added its memorial to the chorus in favour of representative government, Douglas conceded that representative institutions in some form would have to be granted.[57]

The rough migratory mining population and the small, scattered numbers of settled British subjects led Douglas to recommend a unicameral legislature. To secure stability and British suzerainty over this turbulent colony Douglas suggested one-third of the legislature should be nominated by the Crown and two-thirds elected by the people. The Colonial Office had in 1856 suggested this form of government for Vancouver Island, and it had been successfully implemented in Newfoundland and Ceylon. As Elliott, the Assistant Under Secretary of the Colonial Office, had already been contemplating this form of government for British Columbia, Douglas' recommendation was readily adopted. By Imperial Order in Council dated June 11, 1863, the governing of British Columbia was entrusted to a governor and a legislative council.

The Council was to consist of fifteen nominated members, of whom two-thirds were to be colonial officials and the remaining one-third, while nominees of the Crown, were to be designated by the people of the colony.[58] The Colonial Secretary left Douglas to decide how the populace was to designate its nominees, but he indicated a wide latitude might be allowed. He did suggest the Governor might informally ascertain the sense of the local residents, or he might accept the nominees of public meetings or of corporate bodies. Douglas did little to formalize the manner in which these quasi-representatives were to be chosen; he conferred the status of electoral districts on the gold districts into which British Columbia was divided and left the manner of selection to be determined by the residents of each district.

The gold districts had previously been created by Douglas for the purpose of administration and maintenance of law and order. Each district was under the superintendency of a gold commissioner who served both as a registrar of mining claims and as a stipendiary magistrate. While the limits of the gold districts were never clearly defined and they shifted annually with the arise of new gold fields, they did cover all the mining sites. These districts were now either singly or in combination to select a nominee. Douglas instructed each magistrate to request the people to select and forward for his approval the name of a person of good character and proved loyalty to represent its interests in the Legislative Council.[59] He did not prescribe the mode of election or fix the qualification of electors or nominees but left the magistrates and the residents of each gold district freedom of choice.

Douglas' failure to erect barriers to the exercise of the franchise is surprising in view of his former insistence that an assembly could not be called because of the inadequate numbers of British subjects and resident settlers. When he had first suggested a unicameral legislature, he had indicated the electors should possess real estate to the value of £100 and members to the value of £500.[60] The change in Douglas' attitude may be attributed to four factors: first, the Legislative Council was to contain not a majority but a minority of popular members; second, the popular members while selected by the public owed their appointments to the Governor and the appointment of an obstreperous member could always be revoked; third, the Colonial Office, in the light of prevailing conditions in British Columbia, was hostile to the creation of any distinction between British and non-British, migratory and non-migratory residents; and fourth, administrative machinery to establish and enforce a selective franchise was lacking.

Left to its own devices, the public revealed a surprisingly conservative nature. The citizens of New Westminster requested Douglas to establish a propertied franchise. When he refused, the citizens at a public meeting fixed the qualifications for their district at British citizenship, three months' residence in the district, and possession of freehold property to the value of £20, or leasehold property to the annual value of £12, or of land to the value of £20 held in freehold or by pre-emption.[61] Public meetings at Douglas, Pemberton, and Lillooet in the electoral district of Douglas and Lillooet adopted the New Westminster franchise.[62] In the ensuing election the resident magistrates enforced this franchise at Douglas and Pemberton, but at Lillooet the resident magistrate allowed all comers to vote. In the other and more remote districts no attempt was made to limit the franchise and all voted who cared to vote. The *British Columbian* of November 11, 1865, describing the elections of 1864, stated: "In the interior districts not only were the elections characterized by the total absence of any franchise whatever and of anything like system or order, but Europeans were permitted to vote without the slightest reference either to nationality or to the boundaries of different electoral districts; and not only so, but Asiatics, on the way down from the mines, many of them doubtless en route to China, were dragged up to the so-called polling booth and taught to list the name of the ambitious candidate for legislative honors!"

The British Columbia franchise remained at this universal extent when the colony was united with Vancouver Island by Imperial enactment in 1866.[63] The union had always been desired by the Colonial Office, and the economic distress in the two colonies attendant on the decline of the gold fields made it desirable on grounds of economy. When the Assembly of Vancouver Island had approved resolutions in favour of union and the public had sustained the advocates of union in by-elections, the Colonial Office acted.[64]

The Colonial Office had to determine the form of government to be bestowed on the united colonies. Would the replica of Parliament possessed by Vancouver Island or the more rudimentary Legislative Council possessed by British Columbia be extended to the united colony? The problem confronting the Colonial Office was considerably eased by the agreement of the governors of the respective colonies. Kennedy of Vancouver Island, who had a poor opinion of the competence and capacity of his Legislative Assembly, felt the united colony would be too circumscribed in numbers and intelligence to carry a mature governmental structure and recommended a legislative council similar to that possessed by British Columbia.[65] Seymour of British Columbia was of the same opinion.[66] He believed the erection of an assembly would necessitate the establishment of a franchise which, if reserved to British subjects, would in his opinion exclude the majority of the population of the mainland and create a dangerous cleavage in the colony. It would throw the government of the colony into the hands of a small urban official and commercial class and would enable Vancouver Island politicians to extend their control over the mainland. Seymour felt such political dangers could be avoided by a continuance of the present nominated council whose majority of official members would be a safeguard against any dangerous ferment arising from universal suffrage. The Colonial Office accepted the advice of the governors. The Legislative Assembly of Vancouver Island was abolished and the Legislative Council of British Columbia was extended to the Island.

III

The union of Vancouver Island and British Columbia came into being by proclamation on November 18, 1866, and Seymour, Governor of British Columbia, was retained to be Governor of the united colony. It was his task to fuse the two governments. While the Act of Union had stated there would be a Legislative Council of twenty-three members, it had not indicated what proportion were to be popularly selected, nor had it indicated how the popular nominees were to be apportioned between Vancouver Island and the mainland. In consequence, Seymour arbitrarily allotted fourteen seats to government officers and magistrates and left nine to be filled on the recommendation of the people, of which number he allotted five to the mainland and four to the Island.[67]

The Act of Union, having authorized the laws of each colony to remain in effect until appealed or amended by the new Legislative Council, continued the franchise laws of Vancouver Island. When Seymour by proclamation on December 6, 1866, converted the nine electoral districts on the Island into three, he specified the Island electors would be those listed on the latest voters' register.[68] Whereas the electors of Vancouver Island were confined to British males of full age who were university graduates, or occupants paying £12 annual rent, or owners of twenty acres of land, or owners of real estate worth £50, the electors on the mainland were confined by no statutory restraint. New Westminster on its own initiative again established its own franchise, but the qualifications were fewer than in 1863. No property or nationality

B*

qualification was established, the electors being required only to be three months resident in the electoral district and to be neither Chinese nor Indians.[69] In the remaining mainland districts there were no limits on the franchise; all who desired to vote were free to present themselves at the time and place stipulated by the resident stipendiary magistrate.[70]

Governor Seymour, on accepting the popular choices, appointed them to the Legislative Council for a period of two years. When their tenure came to a close in 1868, he had to call new elections. He made no change in the numbers, distribution, or constituencies of the popular nominees but he was forced to make an adjustment in the franchise of Vancouver Island. As the annual preparation of the voters' register had fallen into abeyance, and as by law no one could vote unless his name was on the voters' register, Seymour was faced with the problem of violating the law or abiding by the law and disfranchising the Island. He decided to ignore the law and ordered the High Sheriff to apply the franchise of the mainland to the Island. Thereupon the High Sheriff adopted the New Westminster suffrage and gave notice that he would accept the votes of all three-month residents on the Island save Chinese and Indians.[71] The liberality was not entirely appreciated by the Islanders. The *British Colonist* of November 4, 1868, denounced on the occasion of the election:

several noticeable features in this poll, amongst others, the absurdity of allowing indiscriminate voting so that many persons were allowed to come up and record their votes who have neither residence or place of business in the city; then again Kanakas and half-breeds, who were tutored to pronounce something approaching to the names of Helmcken and Drake, and De Cosmos and Powell, were allowed to record their votes, and the absurdity of the arrangement under which these enlightened inhabitants were allowed to exercise the right of franchise, reached its climax when the intended voters were unable to articulate any names at all.

The protests from the newspaper and citizens of Vancouver Island against the universality of the franchise had little effect.[72] The franchise was to be restricted, but the motivation was to come from another source and from the desire to bring British Columbia into Confederation. The immediate occasion for the change was the passage by the Imperial Parliament of an act to amend the constitution of the Legislative Council.[73] This legislation was due to the Colonial Office's desire to have the request for Confederation come from the British Columbia Legislative Council and the necessity under the Colonial Laws Validity Act[74] that a colonial legislature must possess a majority of popularly elected members before it could alter its own constitution. The legislation authorized the Queen in Council to reconstitute the Legislative Council, to determine the qualification of electors and elected members, to divide the colony into convenient electoral districts, to provide a voters' register, to appoint returning officers, to issue writs, and to determine the validity of disputed returns.

The Imperial Order in Council, when it was issued from Osborne on August 9, 1870, retained the nine elected members but reduced the fourteen official members to six, confirmed the existing electoral districts, and established a franchise which allowed every literate British male of twenty-one years to vote.[75] The franchise was basically that recommended to the Colonial Office by Governor Musgrave.[76] Having felt it would be impossible to establish a franchise fundamentally different from that in existence, he had merely suggested that aliens should be excluded, for he feared the American vote might defeat the advocates of Confederation in the election that was to be called on the issue of union with Canada. The requirement that the electors be able to read English was added by the Imperial Privy Council in order to exclude the Indian population, being British subjects, from the exercise of the franchise.

While the Imperial Order in Council had specified the electoral districts and the franchise, it had authorized the Governor to rearrange the electoral districts further or to alter the franchise if he chose, and had passed on to him the responsibility for establishing a voters' register, appointing the returning officers, and issuing the writs of election. These anomalous instructions were occasioned by the anxiety of the Imperial authorities to precipitate a general election on the issue of Confederation before they had had adequate time to engage in the customary exchange of correspondence. Musgrave, no less anxious to secure a Legislative Council with a fresh mandate did not delay to establish a voters' register or to adjust the electoral districts but promptly issued the writs of election.[77] He allowed the electors to go to the polls on the franchise specified by the Imperial Order in Council with the additional proviso that each elector should have resided three months in the electoral district before he might vote. The election was carried by the pro-Confederation interests and in January, 1871, the new Legislative Council passed an Address to the Crown in favour of union with Canada.

The above franchise, open to all literate British adult males, was altered before British Columbia became a Canadian province. In the last months of the colony's life the franchise and the entire constitution of British Columbia was remodelled. While Musgrave did not believe British Columbia was ready for responsible government and would have preferred to retain the existing Legislative Council, he knew that the grant of responsible government to Manitoba the previous year had made its denial to British Columbia impossible. Musgrave, therefore, felt that it would be wiser to allow responsible government and Confederation to come simultaneously to British Columbia, and to secure the concomitant legislation while he possessed a legislature which he could influence.[78] With this object in view he sent down to the Legislative Council bills to establish a franchise, a voters' register, and the machinery of election, to define the extent of and the penalties for corrupt practices, and to determine the manner in which disputed elections should be settled. The Legislative Council complied and the bills passed into law.[79]

The franchise established by the Legislative Council for the new province was surprisingly complex. The suffrage was to be restricted to British males of twenty-one years who were able to read English and had resided six months in the colony and who possessed a freehold estate of $250 clear value or a leasehold estate of $40 clear annual value, or as householder occupied premises worth $40 clear annual value, or possessed a recorded pre-emption claim on a hundred acres, or a free mining licence on which a claim had been duly recorded, or paid the annual sum of $40 for lodgings or $200 for board and lodgings.[80] In addition, the possessor of the above qualifications had to be duly registered on the voters' list and to have paid all provincial taxes. Aside from the lodgers' and miners' clause the franchise adopted bore a strong resemblance to the franchise the Legislative Assembly of Vancouver Island had tried to establish in 1866. The miners' clause was especially appropriate to Birtish Columbia and together with the lodgers' clause brought the franchise as close to manhood suffrage as it was possible to bring it without adopting that suffrage itself.

When Musgrave had advised simplicity it may be wondered why a complex franchise was adopted. The answer appears to lie in the Legislative Council's desire to avoid committing the prospective Assembly to manood suffrage. It was realized that its concession at the province's inception would subsequently prevent the Assembly withdrawing it.[81] While political strategy was uppermost in the minds of the legislative councillors they were also influenced by a yearning for respectability. On the Pacific Coast British feelings had always been distressed to see democracy exposed to the physical and moral excesses of the mining camps.[82] They would have preferred the comfortable respectability of a propertied franchise exercised by British subjects, had the scarcity of propertied citizens and the danger inherent in a large alien population not made it politically necessary to conciliate. The declining mining population and the prospect of Confederation now gave that increased feeling of security which allowed the Legislative Council to draw back from manhood suffrage. Not only did the new qualifications assuage the yearning for respectability but through its multitudinous clauses the suffrage was less constricted than it appeared and serious offence to the former electorate was also avoided.

Whereas Vancouver Island had employed a limited franchise, British Columbia, because it lacked a hard core of British subjects and was deluged with a transient mining population of many races and tongues, had been forced to pursue a more liberal policy. The colonial authorities had thought it wise to float with the tide and to accord to all the privileges of British subjects, for by appeasement British Columbia sought to escape the fate of Texas and of Oregon where appeals from American citizens for the protection of life and property had brought an extension of American suzerainty. The tenuous hold that the Crown possessed over British Columbia explains the difference between a propertied franchise and a popular assembly in Vancouver Island and manhood suffrage and a nominated legislative council in British Columbia. Insecurity explains and justifies the discrepancy in practices not merely between Vancouver Island and British Columbia but between British Columbia and the British colonies on the Atlantic.

CHAPTER TEN

RELIGIOUS DISQUALIFICATIONS IN THE FRANCHISE: ROMAN CATHOLICS

THE FRANCHISE in the British North American colonies was not free from the religious restraints that had plagued the suffrage in Great Britain. These retraints especially concerned Roman Catholics, Jews, and Quakers. As a corollary, clergymen were on occasions disfranchised for no other reason than their clerical calling. Because of the numerical size of its adherents, the political restraints on the Roman Catholic faith were by far the more important.

I

In 1755 when the Board of Trade ordered Governor Lawrence to call the first Assembly in Nova Scotia and to formulate with his Council the composition and size of the electorate and the Assembly, the penal laws against the Roman Catholics were in full force in England. The Roman Catholics were excluded from sitting in Parliament, from voting at elections, and from purchasing or inheriting estates.[1] The legislation applied literally only to England and Wales and the Instructions to Lawrence did not specifically authorize its application to the new Royal colony. Lawrence and his Council applied these restraints in Nova Scotia, however, and they had a legitimate basis for doing so. The Commission to Lawrence specified that the Council and Assembly were to pass laws for the public peace, welfare, and good government of the province, such laws "not to be repugnant but as near as may be agreeable to the laws and statutes of this Our Kingdom of Great Britain," and that the Governor was to require the members of Council and Assembly to subscribe to the oaths set forth in 1714, "An Act for the further security of His Majesty's Person and Government, and the succession of the Crown in the Heirs of the late Princess Sophia, being Protestants; and for extinguishing the hopes of the pretended Prince of Wales and his open and secret Abettors," as well as the declaration set forth in 1672, "An Act for preventing Dangers which may happen from Popish Recusants."[2]

The Governor and Council of Nova Scotia were also aware that it was colonial practice to exclude Roman Catholics from the exercise of the franchise. In the thirteen American colonies, it was the general rule to exclude them from all civil rights. This exclusive spirit was so pervasive that even Maryland, founded by Lord Baltimore as a sanctuary for English Roman Catholics suffering persecution at home, had succumbed.[3] Following the Whig Revolution, the Protestants in Maryland had used their growing numbers to modify the franchise and by 1717 they had succeeded in securing an act to deny Roman Catholics the right to vote. This religious restraint remained until the War of Independence.

Against this background of religious exclusiveness in the British and colonial franchises, Governor Lawrence and Council drew up the requirements for the first Nova Scotian electors. The Council resolved that no one should vote or be a member of the Assembly who was under the age of twenty-one years, a non-freeholder, or was a popish recusant.[4] To reinforce the denial, the Council resolved that if any candidate so required, the electors must take the State Oaths and the Declaration against Transubstantiation. These resolutions along with others detailing the manner of representation and election were submitted to the Board of Trade, and the Board by dispatch of February 7, 1758, approved the resolutions and ordered the Governor to call an Assembly. The Board of Trade, it is true, had never issued a directive as to religious restraints on the franchise but it did not demur at their inclusion.

The first Assembly was elected on a Protestant suffrage. It was no great hardship to the settlement. The number of Roman Catholics in the colony must have been small, a few Swiss Catholics who had inadvertently been shipped out with the Lunenburg settlers, a few disbanded Irish soldiers, and those Acadians who had escaped the expulsion of 1755. The first Assembly nevertheless enacted several of the penal restraints then common in England. They ordered "every popish priest" to leave the province by March 25, 1759, or suffer perpetual imprisonment;[5] they denied the right to Roman Catholics to hold or acquire land except by grant from the Crown, while those who possessed or should acquire land by inheritance were to forfeit the same to the Crown.[6] These penal laws against Roman Catholics did not directly extend to the franchise. The franchise continued to rest on executive resolution. On the dissolution of the first General Assembly in 1759, the Council in a Minute dated August 22, 1759, reaffirmed the exclusion of "Popish recusants" from the exercise of the franchise. When the Assembly in 1775 tried to remove elections and electoral matters from executive discretion, the bill introduced into the Assembly contained a clause denying the franchise to Roman Catholics and requiring the electors to take the State Oaths and the Declaration against Transubstantiation.[7]

In Prince Edward Island, the only other colony with a separate representative government prior to the American Revolution, Walter Patterson on the advice of his Council had called an Assembly elected by all residents of the Island who were Protestants.[8] While Patterson and his Council had followed the pattern established by Nova Scotia, they had ample evidence that the Imperial authorities desired this pattern to be followed. The Island's proprietors had been authorized to settle their grants with foreign Protestants only and Patterson's own Instructions as Governor had been to grant liberty of conscience to all but papists.[9]

When in 1780 the Island Assembly passed an act regulating elections, the vote was restricted to Protestants.[10] As the Act contravened an instruction from the Board of Trade which denied colonial legislatures the right to pass laws dealing with the franchise without prior approval from the Colonial Secretary, the Board felt obliged to take disciplinary action and the act was disallowed. Nevertheless the franchise remained confined to Protestants on the basis of the Minute of Executive Council. Thereby the two colonies which possessed representative assemblies and remained loyal to the Crown at the conclusion of the American Revolutionary War both denied Roman Catholics the right to vote or hold public office.

II

The status of the Roman Catholics in Nova Scotia and Prince Edward Island was in sharp contrast with their position in the colony of Quebec. In the Instructions issued to Guy Carleton as Governor on January 3, 1775, Roman Catholics were appointed to the Council of Quebec. Carleton and the Protestant councillors were required by the Commission to take the State Oaths and the Declaration against Transubstantiation, but all councillors and officers of state who were Roman Catholics were only required to take the oath of allegiance as set forth in the Quebec Act.[11] This oath was not offensive to the religious scruples of Roman Catholics.

This concession to Roman Catholic religious belief had not been granted without much consideration and hesitation. By the definitive treaty of peace which ended the Seven Years' War, His Majesty had guaranteed to the Crown of France that the former French subjects who remained as inhabitants of Quebec should be granted liberty to practise the Roman Catholic religion. This concession had been hedged by the proviso that the "new Roman Catholic subjects may profess the worship of their religion according to the rites of the Romish Church, as far as the laws of Great Britain permit."[12] As Great Britain by law did not tolerate the Roman Catholic religion at that time, the treaty in fact was to the Canadians no guarantee of religious freedom. This construction of the Treaty of Paris was borne out by the Commission to Murray as first Governor of Quebec. The Commission gave no indication that any exception was to be made for the Roman Catholics in Quebec. It excluded Roman Catholics from official positions by requiring the members of Council and Assembly, if and when the latter should arise, to take the usual State Oaths and the Declaration against Transubstantiation.[13] The only concession to the religion of the new subjects was to be found in Murray's Instructions, where the Canadians on being required to swear allegiance to the Crown had to take only the State Oaths but were not required to subscribe to the Declaration against Transubstantiation.[14]

This concession by the Imperial authorities had been granted on the basis of necessity. To have required the Canadians to renounce their religion as the price of allegiance would have met with mass refusal and resistance. The experience with the Acadians was too recent and too painful to be soon forgotten by the officials in Whitehall. Governor Murray was, moreover, anxious to make concessions to the religion of the Canadians in order to gain their affection and he pressed his point of view upon the Lords of Trade.[15] The English commercial interests in Quebec shared Murray's views and were willing to allow them the vote provided membership in the Assembly was confined to Protestants.[16]

On being advised to pursue a policy of toleration by the Governor and traders of Quebec, the Board of Trade in 1765 asked the advice of the Attorney General and the Solicitor General, if the English penal laws against Roman Catholics extended to His Majesty's American colonies. The Law Officers replied that "we . . . are humbly of opinion, that His Majesty's Roman Catholic subjects residing in the countries, ceded to His Majesty in America, by the definitive Treaty of Paris, are not subject in those colonies, to the incapacities, disabilities, and penalties, to which Roman Catholics, in this Kingdom, are subject by the Laws thereof."[17]

On the basis of this decision the Lords of Trade advised the King to create an assembly in Quebec for which Roman Catholics might be electors but, owing to the terms of His Majesty's Commission to the Governor, could not be eligible for election as representatives.[18] Their advice was supported by Maseres, the Attorney General of Quebec, who in a pamphlet issued in London in the following year argued that justice and political wisdom demanded that Roman Catholics should be admitted to full citizenship with freedom to vote and be members of the assembly. He argued that if it was considered premature to grant legislative powers to the new subjects, it would be better not to grant an assembly than to grant one from which Catholics would be excluded.[19] The Crown deferred a decision on an assembly; but in the first Instructions to the new Governor, Sir Guy Carleton, Roman Catholics continued to be excluded from all official posts.[20]

During this time the Lords of Trade were concerned with the same problem in Grenada. In 1764 the Governor of Grenada had been instructed to erect an assembly but the bulk of the inhabitants being Roman Catholics were to be excluded from membership. The populace resented the policy of religious exclusion and petitioned the Crown for admission of Roman Catholics to both the Council and Assembly. Their petition was referred to the Attorney General who replied that it was a "matter of political judgment whether His Majesty will require it [The Declaration against Transubstantiation] to be taken by all persons who may become members of the Assembly or Council."[21] As a result of this advice the Governor of Grenada was instructed to admit two Roman Catholics to the Council and three to the Assembly.[22]

The precedent set in Grenada was followed by the Lords of Trade when in 1769 they advised for a second time the erection of an assembly in Quebec. The Roman Catholics were to be admitted to the vote, five Roman Catholics out of a total of fifteen members were to be admitted to the Council, and a maximum of thirteen out of an assembly of twenty-seven might be Roman Catholics.[23] The Quebec Assembly did not materialize for the Grenada experiment proved a failure. The Roman Catholic population so resented electing a majority of Protestants to the Assembly that the political situation deteriorated to a state of civil anarchy. As a result when the Crown in 1772 again referred the question of a representative government for Quebec to the Solicitor General, Wedderburn reported against its immediate creation. He felt it would be impossible to exclude the French Canadians from the franchise and it would be oppressive to require them to elect Protestants. He also felt that to allow them to elect their own kind to the Assembly "would be a dangerous experiment with new subjects, who should be taught to obey as well as to love this country and, if possible, to cherish their dependence upon it."[24] Until such time as the French Canadians could be given full rights as citizens, Wedderburn advised that an assembly should be withheld from Quebec.

On this advice, the Quebec Act, formulating the government of the colony, was passed in 1774. The act declared it was inexpedient to call an assembly at that time and established a Council with the power to pass ordinances. To this Council, Roman Catholics might be appointed, for whom the act decreed a new oath of allegiance.[25]

The Quebec Act paved the way for the full concession of political rights to Roman Catholics within the British Empire. By this act the British Parliament acquiesced in the extension of political toleration; its endorsement had not been given to the political rights granted Roman Catholics in Grenada where the concession had been by Royal Instruction. The Protestant population of Quebec accepted this concession, and in all petitions that emanated from Quebec for an assembly between 1774 and 1791, none desired Roman Catholics excluded from full political partnership.[26] As a result when the Imperial authorities decided to concede representative institutions to Quebec, the Constitutional Act granted the right of franchise and of election to all citizens in the newly created colonies of Lower and Upper Canada regardless of religious persuasion.[27] Not merely the letter but the spirit of the law was observed when in the first elections under the Constitutional Act, Antoine Panet and John Macdonnell, both Roman Catholics, were selected as Speaker of the Lower and Upper Canada Assembly respectively.

The concession granted by the Constitutional Act reflected the toleration movement in England. In 1778 the Imperial Parliament had passed the first English Relief Act which had allowed Roman Catholics to hold and purchase land and which had ended the persecution of their clergy; in 1791 the relief was extended to allow them to worship in public.[28] The Imperial Parliament had therefore granted political liberties to Roman Catholics in the Canadas at a time when it had lifted the penal laws in civil matters against their co-religionists at home, but had not extended to them the right to vote or to membership in Parliament.

Why had Canadian Roman Catholics been allowed political liberties? There were factors in England and Ireland as well as Canada that influenced the Imperial Parliament. The Canadian Roman Catholics were fortunate that there were important leaders of the British House of Commons, such as Pitt, Grenville, Fox, and Burke, who were favourable to Catholic relief when the problem of the political future of Quebec arose for settlement. Further, Pitt was faced at the same time with the task of confining the spread of the contagious liberalism of the French Revolution and he felt the need to allay all grounds for discontent in the colonies. This policy, made more imperative by the outbreak of war with France, forced Pitt in 1793 to order the Irish Parliament to concede political liberty to Irish Catholics.[29] The relief act passed by the Irish Parliament did not extend as many privileges to the Irish as the Constitutional Act did to the Canadians. The Irish Catholics, who formed three-quarters of the Irish population, were allowed to vote for members of the Irish Parliament but were denied the right to sit in that Parliament.[30] The foreign policy of England, the domestic problem of Ireland, and the realities in Quebec all combined to influence the concession of liberty to Canadians of the Roman Catholic faith.

These favourable elements, as well as the pro-Catholic sympathies of Grenville who presided at the Home Office and prepared the Constitutional Act, were augmented by the affection Sir Guy Carleton bore the French Canadian people. His agitation on their behalf and their loyalty in the late American Revolutionary War were the decisive factors. The loyalty of Quebec had left a marked impression on the minds of British politicians evident in a letter written by Edmund Burke in 1792 to a fellow member of Parliament:

It is true that some people, and amongst them one eminent Divine, predicted at that time that by this step [the Quebec Act] we should lose our dominions in America. He foretold that the Pope would send his indulgences hither; that the Canadians would fall in with France, would declare independence, and draw or force our colonies into the same design. The independence happened according to his prediction; but in directly the reverse order. All our English Protestant colonies revolted. They joined themselves to France; and it so happened that popish Canada was the only place which preserved its fidelity, the only place in which France got no footing, the only peopled colony which now remains to Great Britain.[31]

III

While Grenville was preparing the Constitutional Act for Quebec, Nova Scotia passed a franchise act which allowed Roman Catholics to vote in that colony.[32] The reason why Nova Scotia granted religious tolerance at this time is uncertain. Parr in his dispatch to the Secretary of State covering the transmission of the act gives no information; the Assembly Journals do not indicate the sponsor and although the bill was only carried on a third reading by a vote of sixteen to fifteen there is no indication that the opposition came because of the grant of the franchise to Roman Catholics.[33] The division recorded in the Assembly Journals shows all loyalist members voting against the measure and it may be that the pre-loyalist members enfranchised Roman Catholics to secure Acadian support against the loyalists.

It would appear that there was a movement towards toleration in Nova Scotia at this time for in 1782 Nova Scotia had passed its first Catholic relief act.[34] The act was disallowed but a modified version was passed the following year which allowed Roman Catholics the ownership of land and removed the penalties against their clergy.[35] This sentiment must have received a strong impetus from America where the new Constitution proclaimed religious liberty and where five states, including the old loyalist colony of New York, had removed religious restraints against Roman Catholics following the Revolutionary War. These influences, together with the knowledge that Great Britain had conceded the franchise to the Roman Catholics of Grenada in 1768, and that Royal Instructions had in 1775 appointed Roman Catholics to His Majesty's Council in Quebec, must have proved a strong stimulus for toleration among Nova Scotians. When they knew that with Pitt's return to office a ministry favourable to toleration was in power in England, the Nova Scotia Assembly may have been moved to action. The sympathy of the Secretary of State to the bill became obvious when he overlooked a gross breach of the Royal Instructions wherein the Governor had been obliged to pass no bill respecting the franchise unless it had received prior approval in draft form from the Secretary of State or incorporated a suspending clause. The Nova Scotia legislation fulfilled neither requirement, yet Grenville allowed it to stand although two years previous the Board of Trade had disallowed a franchise act of Prince Edward Island because it had similarly violated the Royal Instructions.

New Brunswick, being an integral part of Nova Scotia until 1784, had by the Nova Scotia act of 1783 opened to Roman Catholics the right to own, purchase, and inherit land within the colony. In consequence New Brunswick opened her history of separate existence with Protestants and Roman Catholics equally enjoying the privilege of holding property both personal and real. Against this background the first Governor of New Brunswick and his Council drew up the terms of New Brunswick's first franchise. The Governor was instructed, as were all governors, to require the State Oaths and the Declaration against Transubstantiation to be taken by all members of His Majesty's Council and of the Assembly, and as in the Instructions to Nova Scotia and Prince Edward Island no mention was made that these oaths were to be applicable to electors. On the basis of these Instructions, Governor Carleton and Council called an assembly and allowed all males to vote who were of full age and three months resident in the colony.[36] In the first New Brunswick elections, there being no religious requirements, both Protestants and Roman Catholics voted. Whether this concession was of conscious intent on the part of the Governor and Council, or whether they simply forgot the presence of a substantial Acadian vote in some counties, is uncertain. Whatever may have been the reason, the Assembly had no such feelings of liberality. When a candidate was defeated in Westmorland County by the Acadian vote, the Attorney General and member for the city and county of St. John, Jonathan Bliss, brought the matter to the attention of the House. As a result the House in Committee of the Whole resolved that the French vote was illegal, being contrary to the laws of England.[37] They then unseated the winning candidate and seated his defeated opponent.

The House, which had just disfranchised Roman Catholics by resolution, then set about on specific instructions from the Secretary of State to draw up a law regulating elections. The resultant act did not specifically disfranchise Roman Catholics but it allowed the Sheriff to reject the votes of all electors who refused to take the State Oaths. This act was disallowed in 1790 because of a technical error and the Assembly again passed it in 1791.[38] As the bill was not given royal approval until 1795, the first two elections in New Brunswick were conducted on the suffrage determined by the Executive Council in 1785 which, modified by the resolution of the House of Assembly in 1786, declared Roman Catholic votes illegal since they were excluded by the laws of England.

The election act of 1791 was first used for the general election of August, 1795. While this act required the electors to take the State Oaths, it did not require them to take the Declaration against Transubstantiation. The latter declaration would have positively excluded all Roman Catholics as it denied a major tenet of their faith, but the Oath of Supremacy might have been taken by them as was done in Grenada when they acquired the franchise in that colony. While the Oath of Supremacy could have excluded Roman Catholics of a devout and tender conscience, it was an even more effective barrier through its misrepresentation to the public. In the first session subsequent to the general election of 1795, a petition reached the Assembly from twenty Acadians to the effect that they were prevented from giving their votes at the late election for the county of York by the "improper representations being made to them respecting the oaths required by law to be taken."[39]

This restraint on Roman Catholics voting was attacked on several occasions by members of the Assembly. In 1791, the year in which the election act was passed, Elias Hardy, member for Northumberland where the largest number of Acadians in the province resided, introduced a bill to allow Roman Catholics to vote at elections. The bill was passed through two readings and was favourably reported to the House from the Committee of the Whole when it was given the six months' hoist.[40] New Brunswick was not willing to follow the lead given by the passage of the Constitutional Act for Quebec. Again in 1795 the Assembly rejected a bill introduced by James Glenie, the Jacobin member for Sunbury County; this bill declared in one of its many clauses that all laws against recusants and non-conformists which emanated from the Parliament at Westminster were inapplicable to New Brunswick. It was defeated by the Assembly not on religious grounds but because the bill in its manifold clauses denied the supremacy of the Imperial Parliament.[41] One reason for New Brunswick opposition to emancipation when Nova Scotia and the Canadas had already given the vote to Roman Catholics may have been the influence of the Governor, Sir Thomas Carleton, and the leading loyalists whose autocratic concepts and Episcopalian beliefs may have defeated the measure. This may explain the defeat of Hardy's measure of 1791 on the third reading and the measure of 1795, both of whose sponsors were inveterate enemies of the official circle.

The departure of Carleton in 1803, the death of the leading members of the official circle, and the rout of the remainder in the election of 1809 led, in the first session of the new Assembly, to the introduction of a relief measure. In 1810, Peter Fraser, member for the extensive county of York which included the Acadian settlement of Madawaska, introduced a Catholic relief bill as an amendment to the election act of 1791. Supported by the increasing dissenter influence in the province, it passed both the Assembly and Council. The act abolished the requirement that electors should take the State Oaths before being allowed to vote, and substituted in their place a simple oath of allegiance.[42]

On the passage of the New Brunswick act, all British colonies in America except Prince Edward Island had allowed Roman Catholics the vote. Yet of the three Maritime colonies, Prince Edward Island had the largest proportion of Catholics. In 1789 John Inglis, Anglican Bishop of Halifax, estimated that one-third of the Island population was Catholic, and the main Highland Catholic immigration did not commence until the following year.[43] In 1790 Father Aeneas McEachern led the vanguard of a long line of Highland Catholic immigrants into Prince Edward Island. In 1790 he found forty Highland Catholic families but by 1818 he reported six hundred, in addition to the three hundred Acadian families under his pastoral care. The situation was such that in 1814 the Lieutenant Governor was prompted to report that the Island must be considered as a Roman Catholic country.[44]

The franchise in Prince Edward Island had been determined by Minute of Executive Council on February 17, 1773, when there was still some hope that the proprietors might people their estates with foreign Protestants, a condition on which they had received their lands. The minute as a result had required the electors to be Protestants and this religious restraint had been continued in the first election act of 1780 which was, as previously mentioned, disallowed. This religious exclusion was retained for the general elections of 1785, 1787, and 1790 on the basis of the former Minute of Council.[45] It is true that in 1786 Prince Edward Island by statute had allowed Roman Catholics to hold land; but aside from imitating Imperial and Nova Scotian examples, this act seems to have been motivated by the desire to secure settlers. The Island had been disappointed in the number of loyalists that had settled on the Island, and this act may have been passed to remove a deterrent to immigration. Certainly the Island showed no desire to allow Roman Catholics political privileges. The only act introduced to grant them political relief had been withdrawn by its sponsor after first reading, ostensibly to allow the members to inquire into the matter during the recess.[46]

When in 1801 the Island Legislature for the first time succeeded in getting an act on the statute books to regulate elections, the electors were required to be Protestants and this qualification was retained by the election act of 1806.[47] The reason for the continued disfranchisement appears to have been an aspect of the proprietor-tenant struggle. The Council and Assembly were mainly composed of proprietors or proprietors' agents; the Catholics were virtually all tenants and to have allowed them to vote would have added to the political support the escheat question was already receiving. A further reason for opposition was the very size and thriving growth of the Roman Catholic population itself; the Protestants saw themselves being rapidly reduced to a minority in what was intended to be a Protestant preserve. This fear led the Assembly unanimously to petition the Lieutenant Governor, in the very same year the first election act was passed, to curb the activity of Roman Catholic priests in the Island who were actively proselytizing, appearing in their habit, holding processions, erecting shrines, and subverting the Protestant religion established by law.[48]

The Roman Catholics could not be expected to suffer political isolation forever, especially as their co-religionists in the neighbouring colonies were exercising the franchise, and in the Canadas were even eligible for election to the Assembly. At the very moment that Nova Scotia was seeking ways despite Imperial opposition to grant the right of election of Catholics to her Assembly, the Roman Catholics of Prince Edward Island tabled a petition signed by nine hundred of their faith praying that the Assembly "would do its part towards removing all invidious and impolitic distinction, on account of their religious beliefs, and place them on a similar footing with their Protestant fellow subjects and thereby unite the inhabitants of this Island in mutual confidence."[49] Cameron of Queens piloted the petition in the Assembly and had it considered in Committee of the Whole, but due to the lateness of the session the final determination was deferred until the next session.

Because of the Lieutenant Governor's absence, the Assembly did not meet again for two years, but when it did, Cameron moved, on the second day of the session, that the House reopen consideration of the petition. He later moved a further resolution "that it is the opinion of this House, that the right of voting at elections of members to serve in General Assembly ought to be extended to H.M.'s subjects of the Roman Catholic religion within this Island; and that the election law should be altered conformable to this resolution."[50] The opposition was strong and based mainly on the argument that as the question had not been settled in England the Island should take no action on the matter. On this ground, a compromise amendment was moved "that a dutiful and humble address be prepared to His Majesty praying that this House may be permitted to so alter the law of this Island . . . that our fellow subjects of the Roman Catholic persuasion may be enabled to vote for the election of members of Assembly on the same terms, and under the like qualifications as their Protestant fellow subjects now do, or under any future law, may be required to do."[51] The amendment was defeated on a division of six to eight, Cameron, proponent of the Catholic cause, himself leading the opposition. On the main resolution the House divided equally and the Speaker, John Stewart, cast his vote against it on the grounds that the Island should wait until the issue had been decided in England.[52] The division on the resolution reflected party standing in the Legislature. Of those who voted for it, five represented Queens County and royalty with support from two members from Kings County; Queens County had been the main support of the "Loyal Electors," the escheat party and the forerunner of the Island Reform party. All the members present for Prince County and royalty voted against the measure; Prince County represented the Stewart faction whose land holdings were by now extensive.

In the following session when the Attorney General introduced a bill to amend the election act, the Reform members took the opportunity to introduce a resolution that the bill should be amended to remove the restraints against the Roman Catholic religion and to raise the qualifications for the electors. This resolution was defeated more decisively than the resolution of the previous session. The party, favouring toleration, remained steadfast but their strength had been depleted by death and non-attendance.[53] This incident is remarkable in showing the partisan aspect emancipation had acquired, and in foreshadowing the nature of the Imperial emancipation legislation of 1829. The Island resolution had coupled Catholic emancipation with a higher qualification for the franchise. This was to be the line adopted by Wellington's Government in 1829. When Wellington was forced by the O'Connell campaign and the rising temperature in Ireland to abandon his party's settled opposition to emancipation, he granted the Roman Catholics the vote; but he coupled it with an act which, while it applied solely to Ireland, disfranchised the 40s. freeholders and increased the freehold qualification to £10 a year.[54] The Island amendment had sought to disfranchise the same class as the Imperial legislation for since 1825 the British colonies in America had been deluged with pauper and near-pauper immigrants from Ireland.

In 1829 Prince Edward Island raised the franchise qualifications but continued nevertheless to restrict the franchise to Protestants.[55] The Colonial Office refused to confirm the bill; for on the day previous to its dispatch, the Secretary of State had written to the Lieutenant Governor, Colonel Ready, forwarding the English emancipation act and ordering him to secure an Island statute extending the Imperial privileges to Roman Catholics on the Island.[56] This instruction was dutifully obeyed and in the next Speech from the Throne the Island Legislature was asked to emancipate Roman Catholics. The Assembly passed a relief bill which, after being imperilled by diehards in the Council, was ultimately enacted into law.[57] The Island legislation not merely opened the franchise to Roman Catholics but it also opened to them all elective offices.

While Nova Scotia and New Brunswick in 1789 and 1810 respectively had opened the franchise to Roman Catholics, they had continued to follow the Royal Instructions and exclude them from the Assembly by requiring all members to take the State Oaths and the Declaration against Transubstantiation. As no franchise can be of value, regardless of its universality, until the voters can freely elect members to the Assembly of their own choice, so the religious restrictions on the free exercise of the franchise cannot be said to have been removed until the voters could elect members of their faith to the Assembly. This freedom had been in existence in Upper and Lower Canada since the creation of their representative institutions. New Brunswick Catholics never petitioned the Assembly for the right of election, for their possession of the vote had not proved an entirely happy boon. On the North Shore the Acadians, separated by forest and language from Fredericton, had found themselves ground between the powerful lumbering interests based on the Miramichi who outrageously intimidated them for their vote. As a result there was no local agitation to complete the process of emancipation until the Secretary of State ordered New Brunswick to conform to the emancipation granted in the United Kingdom.[58] Subsequently, the Assembly by an enabling act made the Imperial statute applicable in its totality to New Brunswick in 1830.[59] The bill did not pass the Legislature without opposition. In the Legislative Council Chief Justice Saunders, an old Virginian, refused to rest his opposition on an unrecorded vote and insisted on entering his protest on the Council's Journals. To Saunders loyalty meant acknowledgement of the King's supremacy in all matters; there could be no division of allegiance between temporal and spiritual sovereigns.[60] His protest was a last outcry from the Protestant ascendancy of the first Empire.

Nova Scotia, with the smallest Catholic population, was the first to pursue actively the principle of complete emancipation. When Cape Breton, largely peopled with Scottish and Acadian Catholics, was reunited to Nova Scotia by Royal Instruction in 1820, the Executive Council of Nova Scotia was ordered by Bathurst to issue writs for the election of two members for Cape Breton to the Nova Scotian Assembly.[61]

The Executive Council, because of the conflict between the Royal Instructions, the acts of Nova Scotia, and the condition of Cape Breton, decided that the Nova Scotia election laws were not applicable to Cape Breton. Instead the Council issued resolutions to regulate the new election. These resolutions placed no religious restrictions on the elector's choice of candidates, nor on the extent of the franchise itself.[62] In the ensuing election, Kavanaugh, a Roman Catholic, was elected as one of the members for Cape Breton. Kavanaugh's election brought the issue of complete political emancipation to a head, for the Lieutenant Governor by Royal Instruction was still required to administer the State Oaths and the Declaration against Transubstantiation to each member before the latter could take his seat. Kempt, the Lieutenant Governor, was sympathetic to Kavanaugh but determined to follow his Instructions.[63]

During the first session of the new Assembly, Kavanaugh did not appear to take his seat and Kempt took advantage of the respite to present the problem to the Secretary of State. The cautious Bathurst refused to make any decision in advance of Kavanaugh's presenting himself for admission to the Assembly. He hoped the occasion would not arise but if Kavanaugh did present himself, Kempt was to follow his Instructions and require that he take the State Oaths and Declaration. If Kavanaugh, refused, then and only then would Bathurst consider the problem, but he intimated that on such an occasion he would favour a dispensation in Kavanaugh's favour.[64] In 1822 Kavanaugh presented himself to take his seat in the Assembly; Kempt required the State Oaths and Declaration; Kavanaugh agreed to take all but the Declaration; and the Lieutenant Governor refused to allow him to take his seat.

The Assembly was sympathetic and Fraser of Windsor sponsored a bill to abolish the Declaration against Transubstantiation as a prerequisite for holding office in the Assembly or the Legislative Council if the aspirant would take the State Oaths.[65] The Assembly agreed but the Council demurred. The Council was not hostile to Catholic emancipation, but considered it unwise for the Legislature to pass a general bill in direct violation of Royal Instructions without first addressing His Majesty. The Council feared that by attempting too much in the first instance all might be lost and suggested a particular bill to admit Kavanaugh. This bill was to meet the current problem and allow time to sound out the Home Government on the general measure. The Assembly was determined to use Kavanaugh as a test case and by twenty-one to twelve defeated a motion for a particular bill. The Legislative Council refused to concur in the general measure and proposed a joint Address to the Crown for removal of the obnoxious Declaration. The Assembly in high dudgeon refused to be a party and the Legislative Council alone forwarded the Address.[66]

Kempt in a dispatch covering the Legislative Council's Address expressed his strong endorsement but Bathurst replied in his usual cautious manner.[67] He simply ordered the Lieutenant Governor to dispense with the Declaration against Transubstantiation in order to admit Kavanaugh, but he gave no opinion on the larger question of general relief.

At the next meeting of the Assembly, Kempt informed the Assembly of Bathurst's decision. The anti-Catholic forces led by Ritchie of Annapolis and Blair of Cumberland did not yield graciously to the order from Bathurst. They introduced a resolution that the Lieutenant Governor be required to table his Commission and Instructions, as well as Bathurst's dispatch, for consideration of the Assembly before the House should take any action on the Kavanaugh case. Uniacke, Kavanaugh's running mate for Cape Breton County and leader of the toleration forces, introduced an amendment that Kavanaugh be sworn in as authorized by the Lieutenant Governor's message. The House divided equally on the amendment eighteen to eighteen, the representatives from the evangelical counties of Annapolis, Kings, Hants, Cumberland, and Lunenburg being solidly opposed to the amendment, while Halifax, Queens, and Shelburne as solidly supported it. The Speaker, Simon Robie, member for Halifax County, announced he disapproved both of the resolution and the amendment; and if Uniacke would introduce a second amendment to admit not only the Catholic member from Cape Breton but all Roman Catholics who might in the future be elected to the Assembly, he would vote against the present amendment. Uniacke agreed, the amendment was defeated, and the House then passed the second amendment resolving that the Assembly of Nova Scotia would "in future permit Roman Catholics, who may be duly elected, and shall be qualified to hold a seat in this House to take such seat without making the Declaration against Property and Transubstantiation."[68]

This resolution of the Assembly, opening its membership to Roman Catholics, was of dubious legality. It was directly opposed to the Royal Instructions and while an act of the Legislature approved by the Colonial Secretary could contravene the Instructions, a resolution of the House subject to review by neither the Colonial Secretary, the Lieutenant Governor, nor the Legislative Council could not. Kempt, sympathetic to the resolution, made no comment either to the Assembly or the Colonial Office, and since no further Roman Catholics were elected, he did not have to resolve the problem.

The resolution indicated that a strong feeling of toleration continued to exist in Nova Scotia. This feeling was evident in the succeeding years. In 1826, the Legislature repealed those sections of 23 Geo. III, c. 9 (1783), which had required Roman Catholics to swear a special oath of allegiance and abjuration before they could purchase, inherit, or otherwise hold land.[69] This act did not extend privileges to Roman Catholics, it simply removed an oath which served to maintain an invidious distinction. In 1827 Uniacke presented to the Assembly a petition from a thousand Roman Catholics of Halifax asking the House to address the Crown for the removal of the Declaration against Transubstantiation. The petition wanted no more than a legal basis for the privilege already granted to Roman Catholics by resolution of the Assembly in 1823. This petition was the first overt political act of the Irish population of Halifax whose numbers were rapidly being augmented by immigration.[70] The Assembly unanimously passed the requested Address to the Crown. The opposition to Catholic emancipation shown in the Assembly in 1823 had disappeared; the general election of 1826 had powerfully stimulated the change of sentiment. Ritchie, the leader of the anti-Catholic forces, had fallen in the Baptist county of Annapolis before Haliburton who had been, as he himself said, returned on the votes of the three thousand Catholics of Clare; and Murdoch, representative for Halifax Township, supported the address because "a feeling of gratitude [to his Catholic electors] would not allow him to remain silent."[71]

The Colonial Office never acknowledged receipt of this Address. In England, the political atmosphere was charged with crisis. Three ministries had fallen during 1827 over the emancipation question. The crisis deepened until the anti-Catholic ministry of Wellington and Peel was forced to bow to the inevitable and the Catholic emancipation act was passed. When Murray, Secretary of State, ordered Nova Scotia to adopt the Imperial statute, the Address of the Assembly was in effect answered. The Assembly passed the relief act in 1830 and Roman Catholics obtained by law what the

Assembly had granted by resolution in 1823.[72] In Nova Scotia the full right of the franchise had been legally granted Catholics. To the technical freedom to vote, the Legislature had now joined complete freedom in selection of candidates.

IV

In all the British colonies in America political emancipation was completed in 1830. There remains, however, one aspect of Catholic emancipation that should be considered. The franchise was with one exception confined in all the colonies to freeholders. If Catholics were denied the right to hold lands in fee simple, they would be disfranchised without positive enactment to that effect. The act of the Assembly of Nova Scotia in 1758 was of that nature.[73] It denied them the right to hold lands except by grant from the Crown and specified further that lands then held or later acquired by inheritance were to be forfeited to the Crown. Thus no Roman Catholic could possess land unless he had received it by immediate grant from the Crown, and then the land would remain in his or his family's possession for the grantee's lifetime and no longer. If Crown grants were denied or, if given, not renewed with each generation, the Roman Catholics as a body would have become a landless people and would not have been in a position to exercise the franchise when the religious restraints on the right to vote were lifted.

The issue whether land should or should not be granted on a sectarian basis had to be considered from the commencement of government in Nova Scotia because of the Acadians. The first indication that the Crown would be non-sectarian in the distribution of land is to be found in the Instructions to Thomas Hopson on April 23, 1752, when the Governor was instructed to allow the French subjects to practise their religion and retain the property they then cultivated if, within three months from the time of a declaration to that effect from the Governor and Council, the Acadians took the oath of allegiance. This Instruction (no. 68) was never carried out, for the Acadians, determined on neutrality, would only take a qualified oath of allegiance that would exempt them from military service. Hopson's successor, Colonel Lawrence, demanded the oath of allegiance without qualification and the Acadians were expelled from their lands. The Crown, however, did not retreat from its non-sectarian land policy for on June 9, 1764, Halifax wrote to Governor Wilmot to settle the Acadian refugees on their taking the oath of allegiance.[74] As a consequence Lieutenant Governor Francklin in 1768 offered each Acadian family eighty acres of land for the head of the family and an additional forty acres for each of its members.[75] Francklin submitted his proposal to the Secretary of State Hillsborough who in reply stated:

It has been adjudged upon opinion of the best authority that the statutes of Great Britain, by which Papists are disabled from taking and enjoying lands by grant or purchase do not extend to the Plantations and therefore, as there is on one hand no legal obstruction to the granting of lands in fee to the Acadian subjects, and as on the other hand the expediency and policy of it cannot admit of doubt, there seems to be no reasonable objection to carrying into execution His Majesty's pleasure, that all such of His Acadian subjects as shall comply with the requisition contained in the Proclamation published by you in November last shall have grants in fee of lands in Nova Scotia in the proportions which you mention to have been recommended by the Council.[76]

It was on this approval that fifteen hundred to two thousand Acadians were settled on freehold grants in Clare Township, the Pubnicos, the Bay of Chaleur, Canso, and Isle Madame.

Hillsborough had given the general opinion that British penal statutes which prevented Roman Catholics from enjoying lands by grants or purchase did not extend to the colonies; but the specific order was applicable only to the Acadians. Governor Legge, in 1774, desired to clarify the issue and he wrote two dispatches to Dartmouth to ascertain if grants of land were to be given to all Roman Catholics without distinction and also to learn if His Majesty approved of Roman Catholics having the right to purchase lands although Nova Scotia law at the moment forbade such practice.[77] The reply from Dartmouth was less than satisfactory. He agreed with Hillsborough that British laws against Catholic ownership of land did not extend to the colonies but he offered no opinion regarding the freedom of Roman Catholics to purchase lands in the colonies, observing that the provincial law already precluded their purchase of land. Dartmouth then went on to restrict the freedom of the Governor in making grants of land to Roman Catholics by requiring him to refer each grant to the King for the prior expression of His Majesty's pleasure.[78] This requirement would have virtually prevented Crown grants of land to Roman Catholics, but the order never became effective, for Governor Legge had in the previous year by Royal Instruction been ordered to cease all Crown grants except to reduced military settlers, and when the ban was lifted in the following year the new Instructions authorized the disposal of land by sale only.[79] This Instruction and the Nova Scotia statute of 1758 which forbade the purchase of land by Catholics meant that up to the conclusion of the American Revolutionary War, Catholics were denied the right to acquire land in the colony. During this time, except for the Acadians and discharged soldiers who qualified for land grants under the proclamation of 1763, Roman Catholics in Nova Scotia were not in a position to qualify to exercise the franchise even if the State Oaths and the Declaration against Transubstantiation had not been required of electors.

The Nova Scotia Legislature made no attempt to release the Catholics from this burden. The restraint was irksome but of no great economic moment in a colony whose Catholic population was not large. Although the colony had the example of the Quebec Act which allowed people of all faiths to receive and hold lands, Nova Scotia at this time looked to New England whose puritanism had been imported into the colony with the pre-loyalist settlers from Massachusetts and New Hampshire This spirit maintained the penal laws against Roman Catholics in Nova Scotia, even though Great Britain by 1778 had repealed the limitations on Catholic civil liberties which had stood since 1700. It was only as the Revolutionary War progressed, and the New England sympathy prevalent at the beginning of the conflict began to yield before renewed loyalty to the Crown, that Nova Scotia followed the Imperial example.

In 1782 several Halifax Catholics petitioned Lieutenant Governor Hammond for the removal of the disabilities on their faith. The Lieutenant Governor referred the petition to the Legislative Council. A measure was consequently passed which would have allowed Roman Catholics to inherit, purchase, and hold lands without restraint, but the bill was not confirmed by the Crown on the grounds that it was more liberal than the English relief act of 1778.[80] In the following year the Nova Scotia Legislature passed a second relief bill which was a virtual copy of the English measure and the bill was approved by Order in Council on July 2, 1784. By this legislation all Roman Catholics were allowed to hold land by descent, gift, or purchase if on attaining their twenty-first birthday they took an oath of loyalty to the Protestant succession and abjured the temporal power of the Pope.[81]

The legal freedom given in Nova Scotia to Roman Catholics to hold and acquire land was applicable to New Brunswick and Cape Breton so that when they were later erected into colonies independent of Nova Scotia the Catholics there were free to hold and purchase land. The new administrations in these colonies allowed the privilege to remain. The same privilege did not apply to Prince Edward Island as it had been detached fron Nova Scotia in 1769. The Acadians had not there been given grants of land, as the Island proprietors had been required to settle their lands with Protestants or forfeit their grants. The Island Legislature, however, followed Nova Scotia example and in 1786 passed a measure which allowed Roman Catholics to hold lands by purchase, descent, or gift.[82] The important issue in Prince Edward Island was less the question of the right of ownership than of the right to hold lands by lease. This question the relief act of 1786 did not specifically settle although by inference it might be assumed that if Roman Catholics could hold land in fee simple, they might hold land on lease. In 1787 Lieutenant Governor Fanning acted on this assumption and granted licences of occupation to Acadians on lands belonging to two of the proprietors, Lords Townshend and Milton.[83] Prior to this action, Captain John Macdonald, Chieftain of Glenaladale, had purchased two townships and between 1770 and 1773 had settled on them three hundred Highland Catholic families, his former tenants, on 999 year leases; and subsequently another colony of Highland Catholics settled under the direction of Father McEachern.[84] This settlement of Roman Catholics on leases was contrary to the Instructions of the Board of Trade; but they were tolerated because of the difficulty in securing settlers for the Island. While technically these Roman Catholics were leaseholders by grace rather than by right, their tenure was not disturbed. The legal situation was brought into conformity with reality in 1818 when on July 28 Lieutenant Governor Smith on the authority of the Secretary of State issued a proclamation releasing the proprietors from the obligation to settle their grants with Protestants.[85] As religious restraints on the tenure of land never existed in Upper and Lower Canada, and as they were abolished in Nova Scotia in 1783 while Nova Scotia still encompassed what became the colony of New Brunswick, so with the proclamation of 1818 in Prince Edward Island, the last legal restraint on Catholic tenure of land was abolished. As a result Roman Catholics, once the franchise was conceded to them, possessed the property qualification to exercise it.

CHAPTER ELEVEN

RELIGIOUS DISQUALIFICATIONS IN THE FRANCHISE:
JEWS, QUAKERS, AND CLERICS

THE DISFRANCHISEMENT of the Jews in British North America was a collateral consequence of the struggle for Protestant supremacy. The State Oaths, and more particularly the Oath of Abjuration, which had been designed to exclude all Jacobites from public life, had the incidental effect of also excluding the Jews, for the Oath of Abjuration by requiring its recipients to swear "upon the true faith of a Christian" was repugnant to Jewish religious scruples. To the extent the State Oaths were required to be taken by electors, by members of the Legislature, or by incumbents of public office, to the same extent the franchise, the Legislature, and public office were closed to Jews.

Although Pennsylvania, Rhode Island, and New York were the sole colonies of the first Empire in which Jews were specifically excluded from the franchise,[1] the remaining colonies, which included Nova Scotia and Prince Edward Island, excluded them by the secondary effect of the above oath. They were excluded from the vote and from the Legislature in these colonies as in New Brunswick by the State Oaths which any candidate might oblige an elector to take before voting, and to which the Governor must require each member to subscribe before the member could take his seat in the Assembly. It was only in Lower and Upper Canada that the oaths prescribed for electors and members were inoffensive to the Jewish faith; the concessions made by the Constitutional Act to admit the Roman Catholic population into the political life of the Canadas incidentally conferred the same privilege on the Jewish population. This event foreshadowed the manner in which the Jews would be politically emancipated in the Maritime colonies where their deliverance was to be a sequel to Catholic emancipation.

During the pre-revolutionary period the Executive Council of Nova Scotia by Minute required all electors to take the State Oaths at the option of any candidate,[2] but in the abortive attempt of 1775 to regulate the franchise, the Nova Scotia Assembly would have dropped the Oath of Abjuration as a prerequisite to the vote.[3] This provision of the bill was designed for the sole benefit of the Jews since the bill, by retaining the Declaration against Transubstantiation, intended to continue to disfranchise Roman Catholics. The Assembly's singular interest in the Jews may have been a result of the disposition of the Halifax merchants and of Lieutenant Governor Francklin towards Joshua Mauger, a wealthy English Jew, a former resident of Halifax, and a business partner of Francklin. Mauger had gained their gratitude because he had been influential in securing the removal of Chief Justice Belcher as Administrator and Lieutenant Governor of Nova Scotia when that worthy gentleman had run afoul of the Halifax merchants by his refusal to prolong a moratorium on debts contracted abroad by Nova Scotians.[4] After the American Revolutionary War when the Assembly again moved to regulate the franchise it enfranchised the Roman Catholics by abolishing the State Oaths and the Declaration against Transubstantiation and thereby extended the franchise to Jews as well.[5]

In New Brunswick, Jews were able to vote at the first two general elections as the minutes of Executive Council regulating the franchise did not impose any religious restraint on the electors nor were they required to subscribe to the State Oaths.[6] But with the formulation of the first election laws, the Jews were excluded by the provision that an elector could be required to take the State Oaths.[7] They remained excluded at the discretion of the candidates' agents until 1810 when the State Oaths were abolished and a simple oath of allegiance was substituted.[8]

Leaving aside the exclusion arising from the application of the State Oaths, Prince Edward Island had the distinction of excluding the Jews from the exercise of the franchise by law. It is not to be assumed that the Island purposely intended or desired to disfranchise them, but the minutes of Council and the writs issued to the sheriffs for the first five general elections restricted the suffrage to resident Protestants.[9] When the Assembly passed an act to regulate elections in 1801, the act continued to restrict the franchise to Protestants as well as authorize the candidates to subject electors to the State Oaths.[10] These restrictions remained until 1830 when the Assembly of Prince Edward Island on instructions from the Colonial Office emancipated the Roman Catholics by abolishing the State Oaths and in doing so enfranchised the Jews.[11]

With the exception of the Canadas, the opening of the Legislature and public office to the Roman Catholics did not benefit the Jews. The State Oaths and the Declaration against Transubstantiation which were abolished for Catholic and non-Catholic electors alike, were not abolished for non-Catholic aspirants to a legislative seat. By royal instruction the State Oaths continued to be applicable to non-Catholic members of Assembly and Jews were thereby excluded from the legislatures of Nova Scotia, New Brunswick, and Prince Edward Island. The situation was too ludicrous to endure for long. Protestants were to be required to deny the temporal power of the Pope, to swear to maintain the Protestant succession, and to deny the mystery of the Mass in order to secure seats in the legislatures, after Roman Catholics had long been freed from such necessity. Nova Scotia finally undertook to end this anomaly.

On three occasions the Nova Scotia Assembly passed bills to abolish the State Oaths but in two instances these bills ran into opposition from the Legislative Council and in the third from the Lieutenant Governor. The former disapproved of the Assembly's refusal to "even require a person to profess the Christian religion" and the latter refused to assent to such a bill without prior instruction from the Crown. In consequence the Legislative Council and the Assembly addressed the Crown.[12] While the Legislative Council's desire to substitute one uniform oath applicable to all Christian denominations would have been unlikely to benefit the Jews, the Addresses did raise the question at the Colonial Office of the propriety and the legality of abolishing the State Oaths. The Colonial Office recognized the desirability of their abolition but the Law Officers of the Crown would not accommodate them with a suitable opinion. These officers reported to the Colonial Secretary:

. . . by the 6th of Geo. III c.54 [sic] s.2, the form of the Oath of Abjuration was fixed not only for Great Britain and Ireland but *for the rest of His Majesty's dominions*. The form has since been altered so far as relates to Roman Catholics, but not as to Protestants, and therefore, however reasonable may be the views of the Provincial Legislature, we are compelled to state it as our opinion that the act to which we have referred prevents Her Majesty from assenting to any proposal (not sanctioned by the Imperial Parliament) for altering the form of the oath.[13]

Subsequently a legislative delegation, while in England to discuss the problem of the Civil List, took the opportunity to press on Lord John Russell the desirability of abolishing the State Oaths; but the result was no better. The Colonial Office was agreeable but the Law Officers would not accommodate.[14]

Nova Scotian pleadings having proved futile, the matter might have been dropped but for a chance incident in Canada. Sydenham, anxious to bring Robert Baldwin into his Executive Council, had in 1841 dispensed with the Oath of Supremacy when Baldwin refused to take it as a prerequisite to his admission into the Executive Council and his assumption of the office of Solicitor General West.[15] Sydenham had taken this action on the advice of his Law Officers but without prior consultation with the Colonial Office.[16] Having been presented with a *fait accompli* the Colonial Office felt obliged to consult the Imperial Law Officers again. They were fortunate, for the incumbents of these offices having changed, the new law Officers were of the opinion that "it was not imperative on Lord Sydenham to administer the oath, but that he might omit to do so if he thought fit."[17]

The legal barrier having been breached, the Colonial Office readily complied when Nova Scotia in 1846, joined for the first time by New Brunswick, again petitioned the Crown to abolish the State Oaths.[18] Gladstone issued new Letters Patent to modify the commissions to colonial governors wherein the State Oaths were replaced by a single Oath of Allegiance.[19] With this executive act the obstacle to the admission of Jews to the legislatures of Nova Scotia, New Brunswick, and Prince Edward Island was removed. The emancipation of the Jews had been achieved; but it had been achieved not because of any public interest in the Jews *per se* but because the public had disliked the invidious distinction between Her Majesty's Protestant and Roman Catholic subjects maintained by the State Oaths.

The Constitutional Act had opened the franchise and the Assembly to Jews in the Canadas, yet in Lower Canada there occurred the only incidents where Jews were specifically excluded from the Assembly because of their religion. The first incident occurred in 1807 when Ezekiel Hart, a Jewish merchant, was returned in a by-election for the borough of Three Rivers. Hart came up to Quebec to take his seat in 1808 at a moment when the racial animosities in the Assembly were running high and when the relations between the French Canadian majority in the Assembly and the Governor General, Sir James Craig, were strained. Hart was tossed into the centre of this bitter struggle because he was a warm personal friend of Craig and was expected to augment the slender ranks of the English party in the Assembly. The leader of the French Canadian party, Pierre Bedard, was determined to thwart Craig on every occasion and he struck at Hart in order to attack Craig.[20] The attack was not in the beginning anti-Semitic but was an expression of the personal and racial animosities dividing Lower Canada.

The attack was launched on the legitimacy of Hart's oath as a member of the Assembly. The Assembly ascertained that Hart had taken the oath prescribed by the Constitutional Act on the Book of Moses with his head covered, whereas it was customary for members to take the oath on the New Testament with head uncovered. The latter practice was not decreed by law but had been sanctioned by usage. The oath had, moreover, been administered to Hart by commissioners appointed by the

Governor General and in the manner required by them.[21] As the colonial assemblies, like the Imperial House of Commons, did not possess the power to administer oaths to their own members on their admission to the Assembly, the determination of the requisite manner of administering the oaths was within the competence of the vice-regal commissioners.[22] The commissioners (and the Assembly had to admit the fact) had administered the oath to Hart in the manner practised in the courts of law when it was necessary to swear persons professing the Jewish religion.[23] This conformity and the opinion of V. Gibbs, the Attorney General of England, that he saw "no legal objection to the eligibility of a Jew who had been elected and seated in the House of Assembly, after having taken the oaths required," did not dissuade the Assembly.[24] On February 20, 1808, by a vote of 21 to 5, the Assembly resolved that Ezekiel Hart, being of the Jewish religion, could not take a seat nor sit nor vote in that House. During the long and acrimonious debate, the opposition had become increasingly anti-Semitic, and when after Hart's expulsion the Jews of Lower Canada petitioned the Assembly, the House refused to entertain their plea.[25]

The issue was not closed, for in the general election of 1808 Hart was again returned for Three Rivers. He was again sworn, and took his seat for several days, before his opponents began their attack. On this occasion Hart had taken the oath on the New Testament in the same manner as the other members. But it was argued that Hart, being a Jew, could not be bound by such an oath and that he had merely profaned a Christian practice. The result was the introduction by Bedard and Papineau, and its passage by a vote of eighteen to eight, of a resolution to the effect that those professing the Jewish religion could not sit nor vote in the House.[26]

The resolution had been opposed by the English minority on the grounds it was unconstitutional, as the Constitutional Act had specified that no person should be ineligible to be a member of the Assembly unless disqualified by "an Act of the Legislative Council and Assembly of the Province assented to by His Majesty."[27] While Bedard claimed that the Assembly alone was competent to rule on the eligibility of its members, there was sufficient uncertainty that Joseph Turgeon, one of Hart's chief antagonists, seconded the introduction of a bill to disqualify Jews from the Assembly.[28] The bill appears to have been designed by its sponsors to elicit Imperial opinion on the political rights of the Jews, but it never passed. As the session wore on, and the relations between Craig and the French Canadian majority deteriorated over the latter's attempt to exclude the judges from the Assembly, Bedard had the Jewish disabilities bill rejected on a motion to refer it to a select committee.[29] The claim of the majority in the Assembly was subsequently upheld when Castlereagh in a private dispatch to Craig stated: "With regard to the endeavours to expel Mr. Hart for being a Jew, it was obvious that a real Jew could not sit in the Assembly, as he could not take an oath upon the Gospels, it was therefore competent to the Assembly to enquire whether Mr. Hart had complied with all such requisites as might be legally necessary to prove his bona fide conversion to Christianity and that he took the oaths without mental reservation."[30]

The Hart case settled the political fate of the Jews in Lower Canada for two decades. It denied them the right to take the oath for admission to the Assembly on the Old Testament and declared that an oath taken by them on the New Testament was invalid. This principle could have been extended from a denial to seat Jews in the Assembly to a denial of the franchise to Jews, for any elector could be required by a candidate to take an oath of qualification before voting. There is no evidence that this extension ever took place. The Jews were probably spared this further indignity because their small numbers ensured their vote had no significance in any riding.[31]

The issue was not revived until 1831 when two petitions from Jewish citizens requesting full civil and political rights were presented to the Assembly.[32] These petitions were submitted by a powerful sponsor at an opportune time. John Neilson, member for Quebec City and close associate of Papineau, Speaker and leader of the French Canadian majority in the Assembly, presented the petitions; and their presentation coincided with the feverish efforts of the Assembly to gather all possible grievances to belabour the Executive. The second petition, which had complained that the Executive Council and the provincial Law Officers had denied the office of magistrate to Samuel Hart of Three Rivers, when the latter had been nominated to that office by Governor Kempt, being adaptable to the majority's designs, was at once ordered printed and referred to the Committee on Grievances.

The Jewish question was then resolved by legislation. Neilson introduced, and the Assembly passed without a division, a bill to grant to Jews who were natural-born British subjects all the rights and privileges of His Majesty's other subjects without restraint as to office or trust.[33] When in the following year His Majesty in Council approved the bill, it became possible for Jews to be elected to and take their seats in the Assembly of Lower Canada. Throughout this unedifying controversy the Assembly of Lower Canada was guided not by principle but by spite. The Jews were debarred from and readmitted to the Assembly because they had been sufficiently unfortunate to become pawns in the contentious struggle between Governor and Assembly, between English and French Canadian.

II

The third group of subjects prevented from voting and sitting in the Assembly because of their religious beliefs were the members of the Society of Friends (Quakers), Moravians, and allied sects. These sects refused to swear an oath because they believed all who possessed the spirit of Christ would speak the truth on all occasions in love for Him and in obedience to His command "Swear not at all."[34] The refusal to take the oath of allegiance was to the Quakers an essential part of their loyalty to Christ. The Quakers would affirm their loyalty to the Crown and their denial of the Pope in as ample terms as those in the oaths but they would not swear. For this belief the Quakers had endured great persecution by individuals and by the state in Restoration England. They had been barred during the mid-seventeenth century from the franchise and from all elective and appointive offices both in England and the American colonies with the single exception of Rhode Island.[35]

The height of the persecution had long passed when the first Assembly met in Nova Scotia. In America, the colonies of Maryland, New Jersey, North Carolina, and Pennsylvania had opened the franchise to them and in certain cases public office.[36] In England, the Quakers had by 1696 been allowed to make an affirmation in place of an oath, and except for the right to hold an office of profit under the Crown, to serve on juries, and to give evidence in criminal cases had been accorded full civil liberties.[37] The extent of the privilege of affirmation initially remained in doubt, doubt as to whether the privilege extended to all cases where the law prescribed an oath, or only to those cases where the law specifically designated it as an alternative to an oath. In 1749 Parliament in a declaratory act resolved the question to the effect that an affirmation might be substituted for an oath unless it was specifically forbidden.[38] Thus the first Assembly in British North America came into being at a time when Quakers in England could vote in elections and be members of Parliament but could not hold an office of profit under the Crown, serve on juries, or testify in criminal cases.

In the new era of liberality that had dawned for the Quakers, the assemblies of Nova Scotia, New Brunswick, and Lower Canada early passed legislation which allowed an affirmation to be substituted for an oath and thereby opened the franchise and the legislatures to Quakers.[39] In Prince Edward Island the consciences of the Quakers were not immediately relieved. Although the first Assembly passed a bill to allow affirmations, the bill appears to have displeased the Board of Trade and was never confirmed. It was therefore not until 1785 that the Island passed a statute which enfranchised the Quakers and admitted them to the Assembly.[40]

It is doubtful if many citizens were benefited in either New Brunswick or Lower Canada by the relieving legislation as there are no records of sizable numbers of Quakers in those colonies. In Nova Scotia and Prince Edward Island, however, there were Quaker communities. In Nova Scotia Quaker settlements arose at Barrington in 1762 and at Dartmouth in 1785.[41] From the latter settlement the first Quaker, Lawrence Hartshorne, was elected to the Assembly for the county of Halifax in 1793.[42] In Prince Edward Island the failure of the Board of Trade to approve the first Quaker relief bill caused some concern to the local administration as two of the Island's proprietors, John Cambridge and Robert Clark, were Quakers and were expected to people their holdings with Friends.[43] While it may be agreed that the Quakers were never numerous in these two colonies, they were nevertheless excluded from the vote and from the Legislature for the first Assembly of Nova Scotia and the first five assemblies of Prince Edward Island.

In Upper Canada, where the Quakers were more numerous, they in company with the Mennonites, Tunkers, and Moravians were excluded from the Assembly and the franchise. The Attorney General of Upper Canada was to inform the Colonial Secretary in 1822 that "Quakers have always enjoyed and exercised the privilege of voting in the election of representatives in Upper Canada as fully as any other person,"[44] but this freedom was dependent upon the returning officers, candidates, and electors abstaining from demanding that electors be sworn. If the Quakers had doubted that the absence of any provision for an affirmation limited their electoral rights, the action of the Legislature soon dispelled their doubts. A Quaker, Philip Dorland, was returned to the first Assembly from the Quaker settlement of Prince Edward and Adolphustown. The Speaker refused to accept his affirmation as an alternative to the prescribed oath. The Assembly agreed that an affirmation was contrary to law and thereupon issued a writ for a new election in Prince Edward and Adolphustown.[45]

Simcoe, subsequently, solicited the opinion of Dundas, the Home Secretary, on the position of Quakers in Upper Canada.[46] Anxious to encourage Quaker immigration, Simcoe had urged that they should be given their religious freedom, that their affirmations should have legal status equivalent to an oath, and that they should be exempt from military duties and military taxation. In reply Dundas doubted "whether the oath prescribed by the late Canada Act to be taken by all members of the Legislative Council and of the Assembly can be dispensed with in favor of any person"; he was

F

also dubious if an affirmation, in the same tenor as the oath, would be acceptable to a Quaker, because it would require him "to defend His Majesty to the utmost of his power against all traitorous conspiracies and attempts, etc. . . . whereas the principles of persons of his persuasion extend only to their being obedient to the King and the Government, and not to the bearing of arms in their defence."[47] While Dundas was in error when he stated that no legal provision existed which allowed an affirmation to take the place of the oath prescribed by the Constitutional Act, his opinion had sufficient authority to prevent Simcoe and his Council sponsoring legislation to relieve Quakers of their civil and political disabilities.

The members of the Assembly on several occasions over the next four decades introduced legislation to allow Quakers and similar sects the right to make affirmations, but the bills never cleared the Legislative Council. The High Church Anglican and Roman Catholic members formed common cause to defeat the relief measures; when they failed to block the measures in the Assembly, they achieved success in the Legislative Council.[48] The issue remained unsettled until Mackenzie brought the plight of these sects to the attention of the Colonial Office in his memorial of grievances in 1832.[49] Goderich thereupon ordered Colborne and the Upper Canadian Law Officers to report if there were any objections to the removal of the disabilities. If there were none, it was his intention to have the Constitutional Act amended.[50] Before Goderich's intention could be brought to fruition, a British general election had returned a Quaker, John Pease, to the House of Commons. After an enquiry the House had seated Pease and passed legislation which allowed Quakers and similar sects to take an affirmation on every occasion that an oath might be required. This general act[51] obviated the need to amend the Constitutional Act specifically, and full freedom to vote and sit in the Assembly was conferred upon the Quakers, Mennonites, Tunkers, and Moravians in Upper Canada. The privilege was continued in 1840 by the Act of Union.

III

Apart from those disfranchised because of their religious beliefs, some men were disfranchised because religion was their calling. For a limited time clergymen were disqualified from voting in the Province of Canada, and for a much longer period were disqualified from sitting in the assemblies of Upper and Lower Canada and of New Brunswick.

The disfranchisement of the Canadian clergy was occasioned by the sponsorship by the Baldwin-Lafontaine ministry of a bill to ensure the independence of the Legislature from Executive influence through the exclusion of office holders from the Assembly. The Reform members of the Legislative Council took the opportunity to add a rider to this bill to disfranchise clergymen.[52] The reasons for the disfranchisement were many, but primarily the members were tired of the bedevilment of the elections by religious issues. It was the same spirit of exasperation which had led them earlier in the session to pass the Secret Societies Bill. By banning the Orange Order the latter bill was expected to reduce the strife between Catholic and Protestant that had produced riots and bloodshed at the late election. The rider was agreeable to those Reformers, such as Baldwin, who believed in a separation of church and state; and it was agreeable to Lafontaine who felt the disfranchisement of the Roman Catholic clergy and their Protestant counterparts would be politically advantageous in countering criticism of the Government's ban on the Orange Order. The Governor General, Sir Charles Metcalfe, equally approved of the disfranchisement of the clergy as he hoped it might diminish their inclination to enter into political contests.[53] The Colonial Secretary strongly disapproved, but he felt obliged to defer to the judgment of the Canadian Legislature and the bill was confirmed.[54] The act was brought into force by proclamation on May 25, 1844, in sufficient time for the general election of that year.

The ban was not well publicized and many clergy voted in spite of their disqualification. The Assembly consequently received petitions from Presbyterian bodies in Montreal and the Eastern Townships, and from the Anglican diocese of Quebec, asking that their clergy be relieved of the penalty which they had incurred by voting through ignorance of the law.[55] These petitions, the disallowance of the Secret Societies Bill, and the Colonial Secretary's expression of disapproval led the Assembly to reverse itself and restore the right to vote to the clergy.[56] The restoration was carried over the strenuous opposition of the anti-clericals. After they had been defeated on the principle of clerical disfranchisement, they sought to achieve the same end by denying the clergy the right to vote on any property which the latter might occupy or hold on account of their clerical office.[57] With property the entree to the franchise such a limitation would have maintained the disfranchisement of the bulk of the clergy. The anti-clericals failed to secure their objection and the only occasion when clergymen were disfranchised in British North America was ended.

Whereas the disfranchisement of the clergy in the Province of Canada must be assigned to local circumstances, the barring of the clergy from seats in the assemblies of Upper and Lower Canada and of New Brunswick may be attributed to Imperial example. Although clergymen had not been denied entrance to the House of Commons by statute until 1801, a convention to that effect had long been established in Great Britain.[58] This convention was incorporated by the Imperial Parliament into the Constitutional Act and the assemblies of Upper and Lower Canadas were thereby closed to clergymen.[59] When the Canadas were united into the Province of Canada, the Imperial Parliament dropped the exclusion clause from the Act of Union; but the incorporation of a property qualification of £500 sterling for members of Assembly was a barrier few clergymen would be able to hurdle.

The exclusion of the clergy from the Assembly of New Brunswick was not due to an enactment of the Imperial Parliament as it had been in the Canadas, although their statutory exclusion from the Imperial Parliament in 1801 undoubtedly did advance the cause of exclusion in New Brunswick. It was not until the Episcopalians became alarmed a decade and a half later at the growing dissenter influence in the colony and at the zeal of their preachers and evangelists that legislative steps were taken to exclude clergymen from the New Brunswick Assembly.[60] While the act excluded all clergymen, the influence of the Church of England in the Legislature was expected to be maintained by the legislative councillors who were Episcopalian, and among whom the Bishop of Nova Scotia might be counted an absentee member. The legislation was designed to deny the dissenting clergy a public forum from which they might advance their views against the temporal and spiritual privileges and perquisites of the Church of England.[61] The exclusion of clergymen from the New Brunswick Assembly which began in 1821 continued until 1944 when the provision was quietly dropped from the revised statutes of that year.

CHAPTER TWELVE

MINORS, WOMEN, AND INDIANS

I

ONE CONVENTION respecting the franchise was recognized and adhered to by all the British North American colonies: minors were ineligible to exercise the franchise. This convention had been appropriated from the Imperial Parliament where minors could neither vote at elections nor sit in the House of Commons.[1] While there was universal recognition in the British North American colonies that minors should not vote, there was initial disagreement as to the age at which one became an adult. The age of majority varied, being dependent on whether the basis of the civil law was Roman or Common Law. The Common Law set the age of majority at twenty-one years, but the Roman Law set it at twenty-five, which might be reduced to eighteen by the securing of Letters of Emancipation from the civil authorities.[2] The Common Law prevailed in all British colonies except Lower Canada, where the Roman Law formed the basis of its civil law and civil institutions.

In the years following the conquest attempts had been made to introduce the Common Law into Quebec, but without success. Nevertheless Governor Murray was successful in extending the Common Law practice regarding the age of majority to the colony of Quebec by ordinance dated November 6, 1764. In consequence the age of majority was uniform throughout British North America when the Colonial Office determined upon the erection of representative institutions in Quebec.

The acceptance of the age of majority as twenty-one years and the equally general acceptance of the convention that minors could not exercise the franchise may account for the laxity of the colonial assemblies in defining in law the age at which citizens might acquire the franchise. In Nova Scotia, as long as the requirements were set by the Executive Council the electors were required to be twenty-one years, but after the franchise passed under the control of the Assembly the law did not restrict the franchise to any age group, and this legal oversight was not remedied until 1851.[3] The oversight does not appear to have occasioned any rush of minors to the polls for in the period from 1789 to 1851 there was only one election petition which charged the returning officer with allowing minors to vote and that election was set aside by the House of Assembly.[4] The reason was, as Beamish Murdoch states, because Nova Scotians believed that the laws and conventions of England erected prior to the establishment of their Assembly were part of the law of their colony. This belief is illustrated by the behaviour of the Executive Council on the annexation of Cape Breton to Nova Scotia. At that time the Executive Council, in its directive to the Provost Marshal to hold the first Cape Breton elections, stated that the electors must among other qualifications be twenty-one years of age.[5]

Prince Edward Island pursued a course similar to that of Nova Scotia. The age of the electors was not defined by statute until 1836 although as early as 1806 the elector's oath, applicable at the option of the candidates, required an elector to swear that he was twenty-one years.[6] The earlier elections, having been conducted under writs which required the Sheriff to conform to the "laws of our Kingdom of Great Britain and in such manner and form as our Sheriffs for our counties in England do usually practice and make use of upon election for Knights of Shires to serve in our Parliament in England,"[7] may account for the fact that no election petition in Prince Edward Island ever protested against the acceptance of the votes of minors.

In the colonies of New Brunswick and the Canadas, there was never such legal laxity. In New Brunswick, the Executive Council required that all electors be twenty-one years of age for the first two elections and for all subsequent elections the act of 1791 established the same condition.[8] In the Canadas the Constitutional Act had stipulated twenty-one years as the minimum age for voting. After the Union there were some doubts that the Canadian electors were still required to be twenty-one years. The Act of Union had repealed the Constitutional Act and while it had provided that all the colonial acts dealing with the qualification and disqualification of electors should continue in force it did not continue the franchise qualifications set forth in the Constitutional Act itself.[9] The disqualification of minors rested in this uncertain state until 1853 when the House was prompted to legislate because of occurrences at an election in Megantic County where the electors petitioned against the return of a Mr. Clapham on the grounds that over two hundred votes were invalid because they were cast by minors and other unqualified persons.[10] While the disputed election was never resolved owing to the sudden dissolution of the Assembly, it led to the insertion of a twenty-one-year age limit into the franchise law which was passed during that session.[11]

There was no part of the English franchise save possibly freehold tenure that was more readily accepted as a basic tenet of the colonial franchise than the twenty-one-year age requirement. It was no doubt violated on occasion. The 1824 elections in the counties of Richelieu and Durham in Lower and Upper Canada give evidence in this regard, but such occasions were always recognized as breaches of the law.

II

There was one substantial group of adult British subjects who were universally disfranchised by law at the end of the colonial period, namely women. Women were first disqualified by law in Lower Canada, where the abortive controverted election act of 1834 specifically disqualified them. They were disfranchised by law in Prince Edward Island in 1836, in New Brunswick in 1843, in the Province of Canada in 1849, in Nova Scotia in 1851.[12] In one colony only, Upper Canada, was the franchise never legally closed to women. The spate of legal restrictions which followed the Lower Canada controverted election act of 1834 was occasioned, firstly, by the appearance of women at the polls, and secondly, by the Imperial Reform Act of 1832. This act had for the first time formally restricted the Imperial franchise to males, although it must be mentioned that the denial of the vote to women was extended only to the classes newly enfranchised by the act, and did not technically extend to those formerly privileged to vote.[13]

The above omission was not an oversight nor had the Reform Bill established any new restraint on the franchise, for women had not exercised the franchise in Great Britain for centuries despite the lack of a formal legal restraint. Edward Coke, the famous seventeenth-century jurist, states that already in his day women were not entitled to vote, irrespective of their propertied status.[14] In 1868 a test case before the Court of Common Pleas was to confirm this convention when a Mr. Justice Byles declared that "Women for centuries have always been considered legally incapable of voting for members of Parliament; as much so as of being themselves elected to serve as members."[15] The disfranchisement of women in England by convention and the Common Law had been accepted by the colonies as part of their legal heritage. Even the Thirteen Colonies had accepted this restraint as an integral part of their franchise and where convention proved an insufficient barrier against the drive of the frontier woman, they had supplemented the convention by statute as in Virginia in 1699.[16]

The British North American colonies of the Second Empire did not depart from this precedent. Women were not allowed to vote although they were disfranchised neither by statute nor executive decree. New Brunswick alone of the colonies specifically disfranchised women. The Executive Council at the inaugural election restricted the franchise to "all males of full age" but the ban was not incorporated in New Brunswick's first franchise law of 1791.[17]

New Brunswick and Prince Edward Island, the first of the Maritime colonies to disfranchise women by statute, provide no record of women voting; whereas Nova Scotia, the last Maritime colony to disfranchise them, provides two recorded incidents. The first incident involved a disputed election for Amherst Township where the defeated candidate refused to press his petition when the Assembly decided to test the validity of the election on the property qualification of the member-elect and not on the women voters polled.[18] The second incident is amusingly recorded in the *Nova-scotian* of December 3, 1840, where a contemporary relates his experience in Annapolis County during the general election of that year.

I rode down to Annapolis Town to see what was going forward in the enemy's camp, and lo and behold, what did I find the Tories there up to. Getting all the old women and old maids, and everything in the shape of petticoats to be carried up to the hustings the next and last day to vote for Whitman. As it was 9 o'clock in the evening no time was to be lost. I gave my horse an extra feed of oats, and after a long, cold and muddy ride and weary from fatigue, and had only eaten one dinner in seven days, I had to post off through the country to inform our good folks what was to be expected. I rode all Tuesday night, and roused up every farmer; and what was the result, they harnessed up their horses, went off, and each one by 10 of the clock, was back with a widow or a fair young fatherless maid, to vote against the Tory women from Annapolis Royal. We mustered by women more than the Tories. They found out we should outnumber them, and at last we had the satisfaction of seeing them return to Annapolis without voting. I believe they numbered twenty-six and our party nearly forty. This manœuvre on their side was kept very sly but am happy to say we outgeneralled them.

The heat of partisan warfare and a desire to save a Tory riding from a Reform landslide doubtless inspired the Tory politicians to gamble on the vote of their womenfolk. The inspiration for this desperate toss of the political dice they may have gleaned from Lower Canada, for in Nova Scotia itself, Murdoch says, it had never "been agitated whether females may vote or sit."[19]

It was in Lower Canada that women exercised the right to vote most widely. The Constitutional Act had made no specific mention of the sex of the electors although it had been inspired by petitions from the inhabitants of Quebec, at least one of which was accompanied by a plan for an Assembly to be elected by "none but males."[20] In face of the silence of the Constitutional Act and the lesser influence of convention and the Common Law, it is not surprising that this colony gives repeated examples of women voting. The first recorded incident occurred in the bitter general election of 1809 when Joseph Papineau came out of retirement to lead the French Canadian radicals against the tyranny of Sir James Craig. In the East Ward of Montreal Mme Papineau came forward to the poll and when asked for whom she wished to vote replied: "For my son M. Joseph Papineau, for I believe that he is a good and faithful subject."[21] Practised by such a respected personage as Mme Papineau, female voting spread and in the general election of 1820 women voted in Bedford County and in the borough of Three Rivers. Of the latter election Judge Pierre Bedard writing to John Neilson stated that "Mr. Ogden et M. Badeau ont été élus par les hommes et les femmes des T. Rivieres. Car il faut que vous sachez qu'ici les femmes votent comme les hommes indistinctement. Il n'y a que le cas ou elles sont mariées et ou le mari est vivant; alors c'est lui qui parte la voie comme chef de la communauté. Lorsque le mari n'a pas de bien et qui la femme en a eut le femme qui vote."[22] This letter explains why in Lower Canada the emphasis was on widows voting. It was not because widows were favoured with the franchise over married or unmarried women, it was rather because they were more likely to possess the necessary property qualifications for exercising the franchise.

It was the election for Bedford County that first brought the issue of women voting before the Assembly. The elections in Bedford were especially bitter because it was a marginal county in which the races were evenly matched. The victorious candidate on this occasion was charged by his opponent with the receipt of many illegal votes based on Crown and Clergy Reserves to which the electors did not have title and with receiving the votes of "Femes Covert" (sic).[23] The evidence produced before the House revealed that twenty-two married women had voted on the same properties for which their husbands had exercised their right to vote.[24] The Assembly thereupon voided the election and at the same time resolved "that married women voted at the said election and that in the opinion of this House, such votes are illegal."[25] A suspicion, however, exists that the resolution was prompted less by a hostility to women voting than by racial antagonism, for the women's votes had returned the English-speaking candidate at the expense of the French-speaking former representative.

The suspicion that there was no strong antipathy to women voting is borne out by a petition that was forwarded to the Assembly some eight years later protesting the refusal of the returning officer for Quebec Upper Town to accept the vote of a widow.[26] The returning officer, an English-speaking Canadian, had refused to accept a widow's vote for Amable Berthelot, the vindictive deputy leader of the radical party, and upon this as well as other points the re-election of Andrew Stuart was disputed. The petitioners, after claiming that the returning officer "had no discretion to exercise, that he was bound to follow the letter of the law [and] that he was not to sit as judge of the law," declared that women were not disfranchised by law and were therefore entitled to exercise the right to vote. For

the only questions are whether women could exercise that right well and advantageously for the state, and whether they are entitled to it. That the petitioners have not learned that there exist any imperfections in the minds of women which place them lower than men in intellectual power, or which would make it more dangerous to entrust them with the exercise of the elective franchise than with the exercise of the numerous other rights which the law has already given them. That, in point of fact, women duly qualified have hitherto been allowed to exercise the right in question. That the petitioners conceive that women are fairly entitled to the right, if they can exercise it well. That property and not persons is the basis of representation in the English government. . . . It may be alleged that nature has only fitted her for domestic life, yet the English consistitution allows a woman to set on the Throne, and one of its brightest ornaments has been a woman. That it would be impolitic and tyrannical to circumscribe her efforts in society, to say that she shall not have the strongest interest in the fate of her county, and the security of her common rights.

The French Canadian party was in a position to benefit from sustaining the theme of the above petition, for in addition to Quebec Upper Town, there was the disputed return of Wolfred Nelson from the borough of William Henry. Nelson, an English supporter of the French Canadian party, had defeated the Attorney General by four votes but had had his election protested on the grounds that he had received "the votes of women, married, unmarried, and in a state of widowhood."[27] Should the Assembly have decided to stand by the resolution of 1820, the French Canadian party would have lost two seats. They would have had to unseat Nelson for William Henry and to confirm Berthelot's defeat in Quebec Upper Town. Unable to make up their minds to stand by precedent and lose seats or reverse themselves and gain seats, they made no decision at all. The two election cases were adjourned repeatedly until the end of the session, and although referred to the next they were never taken up again. The procrastination reflected a division of opinion among the French Canadian majority. The more radical leaders such as Louis J. Papineau, Denis Viger, and Louis Bourdages were favourable to women voting, but the traditionalists led by Vallières de St. Real were hostile.[28] The future was to be with the traditionalists, for Lower Canadian opinion was soon to be subjected to the orthodoxy of ultramontanism.

In 1832 a violent by-election in Montreal West, Papineau's riding, decided the question. In this election which lasted over three weeks and which ended with a riot and the deaths of three citizens, men and women had been equally subjected to bribery and intimidation. This venal display so changed Papineau's views that, when John Neilson towards the end of the same Parliament moved to consider the expediency of amending the election law and of settling the question of women voting, Papineau was vehemently in favour of their disfranchisement. "As to allowing women to vote," he stated, "it was just that it should be annulled, it was ridiculous and odious to see them drawn to the hustings by their husbands of their guardians, often against their wills. The public interest, decency, and the natural modesty of the sex required that such scenes should not be again witnessed."[29] The upshot was the addition of a rider to an act on controverted elections which denied the franchise to women for all future elections.[30] The act received the assent of the Governor General and in the ensuing general election women were for the first time excluded by law from the Lower Canada franchise.

The statutory disfranchisement of Lower Canadian women did not last long. The Colonial Office objected to a clause in the act which allowed select committees on controverted elections to continue beyond the prorogation of the Assembly. The Governor General was ordered to have the offending clause repealed or the act would be disallowed.[31] The Assembly complied with the request of the Colonial Office, but the Legislative Council disarranged their compliance by the addition of an amendment to which the Assembly refused to agree and the Colonial Office was obliged to disallow the act.[32] The disappearance of the brief statutory prohibition against women voting was of little moment. There was to be no recorded recurrence of women voting, for the destruction of the radical leaders in the rebellion of 1837 and the triumph of ultramontanism, as evidenced in Bourget's elevation to the episcopate of Montreal in the same year, effectively ended the practice. Social disapproval was to render statutory prohibition unnecessary.

In 1840 the Act of Union found both Lower and Upper Canada without any legislative enactment against women voting. Upper Canada had never enacted such a restraint and as no complaint of such voting ever reached its Assembly, we may conclude that the acceptance of the Common Law prohibition was sufficiently widespread that few if any women ever voted in that colony. Yet after union the first violation of the Common Law practice occurred in Canada West and not, as precedent might have suggested, in Canada East. In the general election of 1844 in the west riding of Halton County, the defeated Reform candidate, Durand, protested the receipt of the votes of seven women for his Tory opponent, Webster. The deputy returning officer, partial to Webster, had accepted these votes despite the objection of Durand, and Webster had thereby secured his return by a majority of four votes.[33] The Reformers were not to forget this incident. When they returned to power they took advantage of the opportunity to consolidate the election laws and to insert a clause excluding women from the franchise.[34] The Province of Canada thereby joined the colonies of Prince Edward Island and New Brunswick in debarring women from the vote by statute. The social reaction that had set in in the Canadas was to deny women political emancipation long after it had been conceded in most states of the United States. And that denial was to be most prolonged in the province of Quebec where the voting of women of property had in its colonial era reached the widest proportion of any of the colonies.

The confinement of women to the drawing room in England is less surprising than their confinement to the kitchen in the British North American colonies. The colonial women were as important economic units as their husbands or sons. The clearing, building, and establishment of farms and homes on the unfriendly frontier found the women full partners with their menfolk. It is this full partnership in every aspect of frontier life that makes it surprising that women were not granted and did not demand political equality. The activities of John Stuart Mill in favour of their political emancipation drew no response from the colonial women. They saw no "great improvement in the moral position of women to be no longer declared by law incapable of an opinion," nor any virtue in the claim that to "give the woman a vote [would bring her] under the operation of the political point of honour."[35] Editorializing on Mill's campaign, the *Acadian Recorder* of October 28, 1867, found no moral elevation likely to accrue from the political emancipation of women; it was rather of the contrary opinion, for "if women are to have votes we can never ask them to go to the poll in person or to mingle in the unavoidable strife of political contests. They must vote by proxy or by paper. . . ."

The general attitude towards women suffrage seems to have been more akin to the opinions of John Stuart Mill's father, who believed the close unity of interest within the family could allow the franchise to be confined to the heads of families and still achieve universality. To James Mill the best interests of the wife, sons, and daughters would be as wisely expressed in the composite vote of the father as by the vote of each individual.[36] The close unity of the frontier family, forged by isolation and economic necessity, made political unity a reality and few men or women looked upon the drive for women suffrage with anything but quiet amusement. The jocular manner in which

F*

the agitation was treated is reflected in an amusing digression on the subject by Mark Twain quoted in the *British Colonist* of May 27, 1867:

Think of the torchlight processions that would distress our eyes. Think of the curious legends on the transparencies: "Robins forever, vote for Sallie Robins, the only virtuous candidate in the field." And this: "Chastity, modesty, patriotism. Let the great people stand for Maria Sanders, the champion of morality and progress, and the only candidate with a stainless reputation." And this: "Vote for Judy McGinnies, the incorruptible. Nine children at the breast." In that day a man shall say to his servant. "What is the matter with the baby." And the servant shall reply. "It has been sick for hours." "And where is its mother?" "She is out electioneering for Sally Robins." And women shall talk politics instead of discussing the fashions; and they shall neglect the duties of the household to go out and take a drink with candidates; and men shall nurse the babies while their wives travel to the polls and vote. And also in that day the man who hath beautiful whiskers shall beat the homely man of wisdom for Governor, and the youth who waltzes with exquisite grace shall be chief of police in preference to the man of practical sagacity and determined energy.

III

There remains one sizeable group of British citizens, whose political status must be considered. This group was comprised of the native Indian peoples resident in the colonies. Only in Nova Scotia and British Columbia was the Indian population ever specifically disfranchised. The property or assessment qualification required for the exercise of the vote in the respective colonies was sufficient to exclude Indians whose property was the common holdings of their tribe. Thus it was not until the adoption of manhood suffrage in 1854 that Nova Scotia was led to exclude both Indians and paupers from the franchise by specific enactment.[37] Subsequently Nova Scotia, on reverting to an assessment franchise in 1863, dropped the ban against Indians voting although retaining the ban against paupers.[38] In British Columbia the universal franchise employed to select the popular nominees for the Legislative Council was at first so liberal as to comprehend "even the Red man with his painted face and string of scalps dangling from his wampum girdle," but it was subsequently curtailed to the exclusion of the Indians and Chinese.[39] From the election of 1866 on, the returning officers on the instructions of Governor Seymour gave notice in their proclamations of elections that the votes of Indians and Chinese would not be received.[40] It is not to be expected that a frontier mining community gave overmuch respect to official intimations, but the occasions on which Indians voted were few for the miners had learned from experience that the coastal Indians were not to be trifled with even for electoral purposes.[41]

Despite the common colonial barrier of a propertied franchise there were occasions in which Indians were recorded as voting. The notorious Richmond County election of 1840 in Nova Scotia was protested against because "wandering Indians of the forest and others not duly qualified voted for Mr. McKeagney and took the oath of qualification."[42] While this incident appears to have been an exception for Nova Scotia, the Indians resident in the parish of St. Ambroise de Jeune Lorette in Lower Canada appear to have voted regularly. The poll book of John Neilson records for the election of 1827 that five "chef sauvage" and ten "sauvage huron" voted for Neilson and his running mate.[43] As the defeated candidate, although no Indian cast a vote for him, did not protest the election, it may be concluded that these Indians customarily voted. These Indians, who were the remnant of the Huron nation (having been gathered to

Quebec by the Jesuits after the destruction of Huronia in 1649), were settled on farms outside the city and it was on these farms held under the equivalent of a ticket of location that they voted. The special footing on which the Indians of Jeune Lorette held their land may explain the recognition of their right to vote.

Turning to Upper Canada, we find John Brant, principal chief of the Six Nations reserve on the Grand River, elected to the Assembly in 1831 for the county of Haldimand. This county encompassed a large part of the territory originally granted by Sir Frederick Haldimand to the Mohawks although they had by 1831 conveyed a great deal of it away on 999-year leases. And it was on the grounds that leaseholders did not possess the franchise that the Assembly set aside Brant's return and awarded the seat to his opponent, a Colonel Warren.[44] As the Assembly did not deny Brant his seat on account of his race, we are left in doubt as to what would have been the Assembly's action if Brant had had a majority of legal votes.

These incidents do not detract from the fact that the bulk of the Indians were disfranchised because they lacked private ownership of real property. No attempt was made to remove this disability and to encourage their assimilation until John A. Macdonald, as Attorney General West, introduced a bill into the Canadian Provincial Parliament in 1857. This bill, which was passed by a near unanimous vote, was to allow Indians, subject to approval by a commission appointed by the Governor General, to acquire a freehold grant of fifty acres within their reservation together with a sum of money equivalent to the capitalized value of their share of the tribal revenues.[45] An Indian so circumstanced was to be eligible to acquire the franchise and to be subject to taxation.[46]

No Indian appears to have applied and qualified for the status of an "enfranchised Indian" between 1857 and Confederation and the intent of the act may be said not to have been achieved.[47] The political status of the Indians remained in this amorphous state at Confederation. They were specifically disfranchised in none of the colonies but they were seldom in an economic position to exercise the vote. The press and the public were divided and uncertain as to whether the Indians were denied the vote *per se* or were merely not qualified. For example in June, 1867, Dupont, the Superintendent of Indian Affairs in Algoma, informed the Indians on the Garden River Reserve that they were not eligible to vote on pain of the loss of their treaty rights, to which on July 16, 1867, the *Globe* thundered in reply: "We have the very best legal authority for stating that Indians and halfbreeds, both on the Government Reserves and elsewhere, have as good a right to vote as white men, not being in any way excluded by the terms of the Act [British North America Act 1867] and we need hardly say that if Mr. Dupont endeavours to prevent Indians from voting he will speedily discover his mistake. In like manner the returning officer who shall refuse their votes will be liable to be dealt with according to law." The *Globe* was partially right, for by law the Indians were not denied the franchise, but that they could qualify on tribal property was not conformable to the law. The returning officer took the latter view for the *Globe* was to report on September 6, 1867, that the returning officer had refused to open polls in the vicinity of Indian reserves or to receive Indian votes.

CHAPTER THIRTEEN

ALIENS AND NATURALIZATION

IN THE DEVELOPMENT of the franchise the colonies had to face a problem that was unknown to the Mother Country: the relationship of aliens to colonial political life. Were they to be allowed the franchise and take part in public life, or were they to be denied the franchise and remain outside the governing circle? This question posed a second. Could the colonies safely allow the growth of large settlements of aliens within their borders, when the population of such settlements might with time numerically exceed natural citizens? The answers to be given to these questions were of fundamental importance to the economic and political life of each colony, and in formulating the answers each colony faced the same paradox. They desired on economic grounds to share in the European emigration to America and in the American migration westward, but on political grounds they desired to confine power to British hands and British hearts.

If the alien question posed a paradox in the colonies, it was the cause also of a dichotomy in Whitehall between, on the one hand, the Board of Trade and the Colonial Office and, on the other hand, the Law Officers of the Crown and the Foreign Office. The former departments in their anxiety to encourage colonial settlement pursued a policy which encouraged the immigration of aliens. For instance, in 1730 the Board of Trade approved an Instruction to Governor Philipps which authorized him to grant a town lot and one hundred acres of land to each Protestant family settling in Nova Scotia from the Palatinate; and some years later the Board required the grantees of Prince Edward Island to settle their townships with foreign Protestants.[1] This policy of attracting alien settlers through the offer of land grants was contrary to the Common Law, whose legal maxims were *sancta sanctorum* to the Law Officers, for under the Common Law aliens were unable to hold real property or to vote in parliamentary elections. While Governor Cornwallis was, as regards the Lunenburg settlers, to point out to the Board of Trade the discrepancy between their policy and the Common Law, and while the Board were to agree, they nevertheless desired "that no interruption will be given to the foreign Protestants holding lands for the present, and in the meantime we will think of a method of determining this point for the future, and take the opinion of His Majesty's Attorney General upon it."[2] Although the Board were never able to devise a formula satisfactory to the Law Officers, they allowed the Lunenburg settlers to retain their lands and the dilemma was only resolved in 1758 on their naturalization. This incident did not deter the Board of Trade nor the Colonial Office from their settlement policy, nor did it shake the legal maxims of the Law Officers. The divergence was to continue and was to store up trouble for the future.

In Great Britain the prohibition against aliens holding real property, whether in fee simple or by lease, and the prohibition against their exercise of the franchise were never enshrined in statutory law during the colonial period. While the House of Commons had as early as 1698 confirmed the latter prohibition by unanimous resolution, the Common Law was not supplemented by statute until 1918 when legislation restricted the franchise to British subjects.[3] This neglect was understandable, for with a freehold suffrage aliens were effectively excluded by their inability to hold real estate. When the ban on holding real estate was lifted in 1844 with respect to leaseholds and in 1870 with respect to freeholds, the legislation specifically enacted that possession of real property was not to convey to aliens the right to exercise either the parliamentary or municipal franchises.[4]

In the Royal Commissions and Instructions to the respective colonies, the governors were obliged to require the oath of allegiance from all appointees to the Legislative and Executive councils and from all members of the assemblies, but in no case was it specified that the oath of allegiance was to be required of all electors. As the Law Officers of the Crown held that the Common Law was applicable to each colony, aliens should have been excluded from the colonial franchise regardless of the want of an Instruction or colonial enactment to that effect. The Constitutional Act's restriction of the franchise of the Canadas to British subjects may be taken as confirmation of this intent. But the constitutional precept which the Imperial authorities intended the colonies to adhere to, and the precepts which the colonial politicians and peoples did adhere to, were, needless to say, not always the same.

In the senior colony of Nova Scotia the constitutional precept was followed between the years 1758 and 1817 and subsequent to the year 1854. During the former period, minutes of Council and a statute barred aliens from the franchise by obliging electors to take the oath of allegiance at the option of any candidate.[5] In 1817 this requirement was dropped and there was no bar until 1854 when it was specifically enacted that an elector must be a British subject.[6] It would therefore appear that between the years 1817 and 1854 aliens could vote in Nova Scotia, but in the numerous controverted elections prosecuted before the Assembly during these years no complaint was ever made that aliens had voted.[7] The absence of alien voters undoubtedly resulted from the freehold franchise and the inability of aliens to hold real property in Nova Scotia. It was for this reason that the franchise act of 1854 which introduced manhood suffrage also confined the franchise to British subjects.[8] Of Nova Scotia it may be said that aliens to acquire the franchise had first to acquire British citizenship.

In Prince Edward Island as a consequence of the original intention to people it with foreign Protestants, there was no restraint on aliens voting until 1801 at which time legislation was passed to oblige electors to take the oath of allegiance at the option of any candidate.[9] This restraint disappeared in 1836 and from that time until 1853, when the franchise was specifically confined to British subjects, aliens were free to vote if they met the freehold or leasehold qualifications.[10] There seems no doubt that aliens in Prince Edward Island could not hold land in fee simple but it is less certain that they could not hold land by lease. The fact that the restriction of the Island franchise to British subjects in 1853 came some nine years after the Imperial Parliament allowed aliens to lease land in Great Britain would lead one to assume that the leasing of lands to aliens only emerged after its concession in Great Britain. Further credulity is lent to this assumption when it is realized that the restriction of the franchise to British subjects could have had no relation to alien freeholders, as the Island did not allow aliens to purchase real property until 1859.[11] It would nevertheless be presumptuous to assume that no aliens leased land and therefore no alien was eligible to vote on the Island. The laxity in the franchise between 1836 and 1853 might rather be attributed to the absence of any sizeable alien population, for fewer aliens settled in Prince Edward Island than settled in any of the other colonies. The emigration to the Island was almost exclusively drawn from the British Isles.

The above review of the situation in Nova Scotia and Prince Edward Island may make it appear that the status of aliens and the question of naturalization were less controversial than previously suggested and of minor significance in the colonial scene. The calm that surrounded these issues in Nova Scotia and Prince Edward Island is wholly deceptive. It was in the colonies bordering on the United States that the alien question was a contentious issue; and it was with these colonies that the Imperial authorities battled to safeguard, as an Imperial prerogative, the right to confer British citizenship. The importance of the issue in Upper Canada, Lower Canada, and New Brunswick was in direct proportion to the size of their alien populations. In Upper Canada, where it was estimated in 1820 that nearly half the population was alien and half the real property was in alien hands, the controversy was the most divisive.[12] The tempers and divisions that the controversy there aroused were to bring that colony to the brink of civil disobedience.

The dispute in Upper Canada concerned the status of the American settlers resident in the colony. Had these natural-born British subjects become aliens on the conclusion of the American Revolutionary War? If they had become aliens, at what moment had they lost their British citizenship? If they had ceased to be British subjects, were they ineligible to acquire real property on migration to a British colony? The answers to these questions were to determine the right of American immigrants to hold property, to exercise the franchise, and to control the political institutions of Upper Canada, and they involved the interpretation of the legal consequences attending the independence of the Thirteen Colonies.

The Common Law held that a natural-born British subject could not shed or lose his nationality by unilateral action of the subject or of the Crown.[13] But the Treaty of Paris to which the Crown and the rebellious colonists were both signatories was a formal recognition of the severance of allegiance. In Common Law the status of natural-born British subjects resident in the United States at the signing of the Treaty of Paris in September, 1783, was therefore clear; they became aliens and on subsequent migration to a British colony would be unable to hold property or participate in its political life. Their Common Law status was, however, beclouded by the effect of two Imperial statutes passed in 1731 and 1773.[14] These statutes had been enacted in order that children and grandchildren born abroad of British fathers might retain the status of British subjects. Did these statutes mean Americans born of British parents retained their British citizenship although they continued to reside in the United States after 1783? The question had to wait until 1824 for an authoritative ruling.

The legal niceties, however, did not trouble the public. In their mind, September, 1783, wrought no wizardry. The residents of New York, of Pennsylvania, of Ohio, remained the same friends and kinsmen, loyalists and non-loyalists, that they had been the day or month before. He who crossed with his family into Upper Canada the day or month or year after was welcomed without thought as to a divergence in nationality. The colonial administrators and the officials of the Colonial Office were no less indifferent than were the public to the consequences of September, 1783. The Colonial Office fostered the passage of an Imperial statute in 1790 to allow each American immigrant to bring in his personal property duty free.[15] Directed exclusively at the Americans, the Colonial Office sought to stimulate American settlement in the British colonies of North America. The lieutenant governors of the Canadas on the basis of this act issued identical proclamations offering land grants to settlers without distinction as to nationality.[16] Simcoe, the Lieutenant Governor of Upper Canada, had his proclamation published and circulated in New England and the northern states. Under its terms Americans coming to settle in Upper Canada were to be given land on the same conditions as any British settler. While the proclamation did not specify the rights the American settlers would have, the receipt of a grant of land implied they would possess full civil and political status. There seems no reason to believe that these proclamations were not made in good faith or that the American settlers did not accept them at their face value. Whatever difference the Treaty of Paris had made between Briton and American, Simcoe felt, was obliterated by the oath of allegiance which each recipient of a Crown grant had to take on receipt of his land.[17]

In the following years American settlers, availing themselves of the offer in the proclamation, came, received land grants, settled upon them, and voted in the legislative elections. The Constitutional Act, although it had confined the suffrage and membership in the Assembly to British subjects, was so loosely applied that the member returned for Lincoln fourth riding and Norfolk counties, Benjamin Hardison, had formerly been a soldier in the American Revolutionary Army and had for a time been held as a prisoner of war in Upper Canada.[18] While Hardison's right of admission to the Assembly was not challenged, the continuing influx of American settlers and their increasing political influence had nevertheless begun to create some disquiet in the minds of the older loyalist settlers. They had welcomed the first postrevolutionary immigrants as fellow subjects but as the years passed into decades and the immigration continued, they began to have serious doubts as to the loyalty and the nationality of the latecomers.

Actuated by these misgivings the Assembly, in the year prior to Hardison's election, took the first halting steps to curb the political influence of the more recent immigrants. Legislation was enacted which required all settlers who came from a non-British country to be seven years resident in the province before they were eligible for election to that body.[19] The Assembly, by requiring a probationary period of residence for prospective members, was trying to secure the protection the Constitutional Act should have afforded if the terms had not been nullified by the early confusion of the Colonial Office as to the nationality of the American settlers. The old settlers and the Upper Canada Executive were further alarmed some four years later when in a by-election for the riding of Ontario-Addington the Attorney General was defeated by American votes. The election defeat cannot be blamed entirely on the Americans for there was widespread hostility to the Administrator, Peter Russell, and to his extensive land grants to favourites; but there was always a tendency in Upper Canada to construe criticism of the regime's abuses as a lack of loyalty. As a consequence of this by-election the Assembly in the following year added a rider to a representation bill which established the same probationary period for voters that had been established for the members. All settlers who had ever sworn allegiance to or lived in the United States were to be required to have lived in Upper Canada seven years and to have taken the oath of allegiance before they could vote.[20]

The issue slumbered for the next decade. The Upper Canada Assembly had taken as strong steps to curb the political influence of the American settlers as its members thought advisable; and as for the Executive, it was not prepared to launch a frontal attack on the nationality of the American settlers at the risk of alienating friends who were land speculators and without the assurance of strong support from the Colonial Office. It was the War of 1812–14 and the ensuing defection of some members of the Assembly and of some American settlers that was to reawaken the British population of Upper Canada and the Colonial Office to the dangers inherent in their past failure to discriminate between subject and alien.[21]

The Assembly, frightened by the defections, hastily passed legislation in 1814 which denied all citizens the right to be elected to the Assembly unless they had been continuously resident in the colony for fourteen years,[22] and the Colonial Office, equally frightened by the consequences of its liberal immigration policy, hastily ordered the Administrator to prevent Americans from settling in the colony.[23] Thereupon all magistrates were ordered to desist from administering the oath of allegiance to persons coming from the United States, in order to prevent American settlers from obtaining title to lands they had secured in the colony.[24] These impetuous restraints generated just as impetuous an indignation. British immigrants were indignant at finding themselves excluded from the Assembly indiscriminately with the American immigrants; and Upper Canadians who had made brief sojourns in the United States were equally angered.[25] As a consequence the probationary period was in 1818 reduced to seven years.[26]

The British immigrants' indignation was mild, however, compared with the consternation among the land speculators. They saw their prosperity endangered if American settlers were denied the right to take the oath of allegiance and thereby secure title to Upper Canada lands. The largest and most influential speculators were to be found among members of the Executive and Legislative councils and their circle of friends, for these men had been the direct beneficiaries of the land-granting orgy conducted during the administration of Peter Russell. William Dickson, a magistrate, Legislative Councillor, and owner of a township of land on the Grand River, spearheaded the opposition with able assistance from Robert Nichol in the Assembly and Robert Gourlay in the country.[27] Dickson defied the Lieutenant Governor, for as a magistrate he continued to administer the oath of allegiance to Americans that they might secure land.[28] Nichol turned the Committee of Supply into a committee of grievances which censured the Lieutenant Governor for checking immigration from the United States and resolved "that subjects of the United States may lawfully come into and settle in this province, hold lands, and be entitled to all the privileges and immunities of natural born subjects therein," if they conformed to such formalities as taking the oath of allegiance.[29] Gourlay on his part used his oratorical powers to arouse the populace against the many sins of the Executive amongst which he listed the prohibition on the administration of the oath of allegiance.[30] The agitation bore fruit, for the Colonial Office was to declare the administration's refusal to administer the oath of allegiance illegal.[31]

The speculators would have had less reason for jubilance if they had known the full content of the Colonial Secretary's dispatch, for Bathurst had gone on to state that the receipt of the oath of allegiance did not entitle American citizens to hold lands in the province until they had become naturalized subjects under the Imperial Act of 1740; and he had instructed the Administrator of Upper Canada to "take the necessary legal measures for dispossessing those persons not entitled to the privilege of natural born subjects who shall since the War have possessed themselves of lands under any other circumstance than those admitted by Law."[32] Bathurst had placed the Administration in an untenable position. They were to allow, even to encourage, Americans to settle in the province; they were to administer to them the oath of allegiance; but they were to deny them the right to hold land until they were naturalized after seven years' residence.

If Bathurst did not realize the import of his order, the Executive Council certainly did. If they were to dispossess all Americans settled in the province since the War of 1812–14, what justification could be given for their action but the fact that these settlers were not naturalized subjects? If that reason was used, would it not be equally applicable to all settlers who had entered Upper Canada from the United States subsequent to September, 1783? For the Revolutionary War and not the War of 1812–14 had severed the allegiance of Americans to the British Crown. The Executive Council knew that the proclamation Bathurst contemplated would place the property of the late loyalist and recent immigrant alike in jeopardy. Since such a proclamation would have unsettled the greater part of the population of Upper Canada, the Executive Council decided to postpone action until the Colonial Secretary was made fully aware of the implications of his order.[33] Bathurst, alerted to the implications, did not reply; the proclamation was not issued; and the American settlers continued to come in and secure land in the province. The alarm occasioned by the War of 1812–14 was thereupon to subside and the American settlers were to remain undisturbed in their possession of civil and political rights. The economic self-interest of the old settlers had assuaged their misgivings as to the loyalty of the Americans.

As the nineteenth century entered its third decade, the alarm was to be renewed. Robert Gourlay's agitation against the Family Compact, the clergy reserves, and land jobbery had, together with the ferment of Jacksonian democracy, founded a radical party in Upper Canada which was securing its readiest response among the American settlers. The ruling families, finding their hegemony under increasing attack, were to discover that their self-interest could profitably make common cause with their loyalism. They came to the realization that the political destruction of the emergent radicalism could best be achieved by the disfranchisement of the American settlers and that the American settlers could be disfranchised by the revelation of their alien status. If the Tories hesitated to launch an immediate attack, it was not because they lacked strategy but because they lacked resolute leadership. When Sir Peregrine Maitland assumed the Lieutenant Governorship, the Tories were to find in him the resolute and autocratic leader they required.

A controverted election for Lennox-Addington in 1821 was made the occasion on which to reopen the alien question.[34] The member returned, Barnabas Bidwell, had been born a British subject but had remained in the United States after the Revolutionary War and had become successively Attorney General of Massachusetts and a member of Congress. In 1810 he had been forced to flee to Canada to escape imprisonment for the embezzlement of public funds and had in 1812 taken, somewhat reluctantly it was alleged, the oath of allegiance to the British Crown. The ensuing debate in the Assembly was to illustrate the general confusion in the public mind as to the status of the American settlers. While the Tories took the legal position that all Americans who had resided in the United States after the treaty of peace were aliens and by the Constitutional Act were ineligble to vote or sit in the Assembly, the moderate conservatives were to hold that past practice and past legislation which had allowed Americans to settle in Upper Canada, to hold land, to vote, and, after a probationary period, to sit in the House had overborne the legal niceties and had established the convention that the Americans were not aliens in Upper Canada. As a consequence of this confusion a motion to void Bidwell's election on the grounds he was an alien was defeated, while a subsequent motion to void his election on the general infamy of his character was to carry.[35]

The above controverted election did not resolve the national status of the American settlers but it brought the issue squarely before the public for the first time. Until this election, while disquieting rumours had occasionally reached the public, the nationality of the American settlers had never been openly challenged. The first Bidwell election case alerted the public to the issue and left them surprised, perplexed, and concerned. The *Upper Canada Herald* of March 12, 1822, reveals this state of mind:

A more interesting question was never agitated than that which has lately been started, whether all the inhabitants of this province who were either resident in the United States at the Treaty of Peace of 1783, or born there afterwards of British-born parents, are notwithstanding their residence here for seven years, to be deemed aliens, ineligible as members of Assembly, unqualified to vote at elections, and incapable of inheriting lands, or even holding them by purchase, except as tenants at will of the Crown.

They have heretofore not only considered themselves, but have been uniformly considered and treated by His Majesty and by the Provincial authorities and statutes, as subjects with respect both to enjoyment of rights and the performance of duties. As such they have, from the beginning, been permitted to take and hold lands, by descent as well as purchase, and to elect and be elected after seven years' residence. As such, also, they were required by law to serve in the militia, in defence of the Province during the late war, in common with European- and Canadian-born subjects, and are still, without distinction, enrolled and commissioned in the militia.

The new doctrine, if established and carried into execution, will have a most serious retrospective effect. It will disfranchise a large proportion of the freeholders of every district throughout the Province, to their grievous disappointment and injury; and will, in their view at least, be a breach of the public faith, under which many of them have received grants immediately from the Crown, and all of them have been encouraged to lay out their money and labour in the purchase and improvement of land. The Government surely did not intend to hold out false encouragement to American settlers; and it would be no less strange than unfortunate, if all parties, from His Majesty's Ministers and Representatives down to the settlers themselves, should be found to have been acting under a mistake on this essential point, for more than thirty years.

The Tories, having opened the alien question, were to find themselves unable to terminate the controversy until 1828. The Assembly, in the subsequent controverted elections involving Bidwell's son, Marshall Spring Bidwell, repeatedly showed its determination to accord the rights of British citizenship to the American settlers, and the Tories through their instrument, the returning officer for Lennox-Addington, as repeatedly showed their determination to treat these settlers as aliens. When the returning officer refused on two occasions to return Bidwell's son because he was an alien and when the Assembly voided the return and ordered another election,[36] it became obvious to Maitland that the Assembly could not be persuaded to accord the Americans alien status. The Executive then decided to transfer the issue to the Colonial Office and allowed Bidwell to be returned in the 1824 general election. With this decision began the series of Executive appeals and Assembly counterappeals to the Colonial Office that were to take up the better part of six years and were to profoundly agitate the province.

The prime object of Maitland and of the Tories' appeal to the Colonial Office was to secure an authoritative Imperial ruling that the American settlers were aliens; but they desired the public clarification of the national status of these settlers to be preceded by an Imperial enactment which would in Maitland's words secure this "numerous class of inhabitants in that property which they have now been permitted to enjoy for so long a period unmolested."[37] Maitland's benign concern for the property of the American settlers concealed the Tories' scheme to destroy their political opponents. What they wanted and what Maitland clearly stated was an Imperial act which would give the American settlers legal title to their lands but exclude them as aliens from the franchise. The foundations of the radical party would thereby be wiped away and the political attack that had been developing on the Family Compact, the clergy reserves, and the university could then be easily contained.

The Upper Canadian appeal to the Colonial Office coincided with the argument before the English courts of a test case as to the nationality of American citizens. The case involved the right of an American citizen born since the treaty of peace to inherit property in Yorkshire. Mrs. Frances Thomas (a kinswoman of George Ludlow, the first Chief Justice of New Brunswick) had been born in 1784 of natural-born British subjects. If her parents, who had continued to live in the United States after its independence, were considered aliens, Mrs. Thomas, as an alien, would not be able to inherit or hold property in Great Britain; but if her parents were considered to have retained their nationality, the plaintiff as child and grandchild of British subjects resident abroad would retain the right to inherit and hold property in Great Britain. The Court of King's Bench found that the plaintiff's father had by continuing to reside in the United States after September, 1783, become an alien and consequently could not inherit property in Great Britain.[38] The authoritative ruling Maitland had sought had now been given. It was of profound import to Upper Canada. It reversed the decision of the Assembly in the Bidwell cases, for both father and son were now aliens as were all the settlers in Upper Canada who had left America any time after September, 1783.

The scheme of Maitland and the Tories now received its first setback for Bathurst neglected to secure an enactment from the Imperial Parliament confirming the aliens of Upper Canada in the possession of their property and instead ordered Maitland to secure the necessary legislation from the Upper Canada Assembly.[39] To facilitate the settlement the Royal Instructions which forbade colonial legislatures to pass laws respecting aliens and naturalization were to be suspended for this occasion. Although the Tories were doubtless disappointed that their strategy had gone awry, they were quick to perceive that while a colonial naturalization act might secure the settlers in their property, it could not confer political privileges upon the settlers, for the Constitutional Act had explicitly limited the franchise and membership in the Assembly to natural-born subjects or subjects naturalized by act of the British Parliament. Unfortunately for the Tories the radicals in the Assembly were not without talent. After protracted debate and searching questioning the Assembly forced the Attorney General into the admission that a naturalization act of the Upper Canada Assembly would not confer political rights on its beneficiaries. The naturalization bill was consequently defeated, and the two parties turned once again to Whitehall. The episode had but served to profoundly disturb the greater part of the Upper Canadian population and to reveal to all the Tory conspiracy.[40]

Caught between Executive and Assembly, Tory and Radical, the Colonial Office sought to avoid offence to either party and tossed the issue back to Upper Canada. The Constitutional Act was amended at the instigation of the Colonial Under-Secretary to allow all persons naturalized by an act of the Upper Canada Parliament to vote and be eligible for a seat in the Assembly and Legislative Council.[41] The matter was not to be settled, however, for Bathurst, as Colonial Secretary, interfered. He informed Maitland that he would not tolerate a provincial act that declared all American settlers to be British subjects, nor would he approve any provincial enactment that established a general mode for naturalizing aliens who might in the future emigrate to Upper Canada.[42] He would only approve a provincial naturalization act with retrospective effect. The act might only naturalize aliens resident in Upper Canada at the date of the amendment to the Constitutional Act, who had taken an oath of allegiance to the British Crown and an oath of renunciation of allegiance to their country of origin.

Bathurst had badly misjudged the real temper of the Upper Canadian people. If it was impossible to grant them a declaratory act that they had always been British subjects, they would take nothing less than a declaratory act that they were now British subjects. Outraged loyalty would not allow them to subscribe at a cost of two shillings to an oath of allegiance before minions of the Family Compact in order to secure the citizenship that they believed they had always possessed.[43] When the Tories after the greatest difficulty managed to secure passage of legislation conformable to Bathurst's instructions, the Upper Canadian radicals appealed direct to the House of Commons. A central committee was set up at York to circulate a petition for signature throughout the province and to solicit funds to send an agent to London. Within two months several thousand signatures were secured, money was raised, and Robert Randal, member for Lincoln, was dispatched to present the petition to the Commons and to counter administrative influence at the Colonial Office.[44]

Fortunately for the success of Randal's mission there had been a change of ministry in Great Britain. Goderich had replaced Bathurst at the Colonial Office and the new Colonial Secretary was prepared without any persuasion from Upper Canada to disallow the naturalization bill.[45] Goderich found the bill's requirement that American settlers take an oath of renunciation of their allegiance to their country of origin repugnant to British foreign policy. As a former Lord of the Admiralty, Goderich knew of Britain's insistence during the Napoleonic Wars that British seamen could not repudiate their British citizenship by swearing allegiance to America.[46] The Colonial Office thereupon signified that they would approve new legislation which would declare all aliens resident in Upper Canada as of 1820 British subjects, and all aliens who had taken up residence in the province subsequent to that date British subjects on completion of seven years' residence and formal subscription to the oath of allegiance.[47] A declaratory bill was subsequently introduced into the Assembly by Marshall Spring Bidwell in conformity with Goderich's instructions and was carried against trifling obstruction from a band of Tory diehards. Sent home for royal assent, it was approved by Order in Council on May 7, 1828, and the American settlers were confirmed in the citizenship they believed they had always possessed.[48]

The alien controversy was closed and the doubt as to the nationality of the major part of the population of Upper Canada was resolved. All those resident in the province as of 1820 were to be automatically considered as British subjects *born within the United Kingdom*; and all emigrants settled in Upper Canada between 1820 and March 1, 1828, were to have the rights of British subjects *within the province of Upper Canada* after seven years' residence and after taking the oath of allegiance before a county registrar within a period of three years from the completion of the residence requirement.[49] The situation that the act resolved had arisen because of historical circumstances and the Colonial Office's desire to secure settlement by ignoring the legal status of the settlers. The Law Officers of the Crown had never deceived the Colonial Office but the Colonial Office with the best of intentions had deceived the settlers. It was virtually inevitable that the courts should rule as they did in the Thomas case; and alarming as the decision was to the settlers, it could have been resolved amicably if the Lieutenant Governor and his Council had not attempted to use the occasion to recover their political supremacy in the Assembly. Basic to their strategy was the determination that the American settlers were ineligible to exercise the franchise for on such a determination was to rest the balance of political power in the province. The decision went in favour of the settlers and the radicals consequently emerged from the struggle as the Reform party with its ranks extended and consolidated throughout the province.

In Lower Canada the relation of aliens to the political life of the colony was not as acute a problem as one might at first have expected. Although the great bulk of the population was not of British origin, the Constitutional Act, by confining the franchise and membership in the Assembly to British subjects or to subjects of His Majesty by the conquest and cession of the province of Canada, did not exclude the French Canadians from public life. There were, however, certain exceptions. The French Canadians who had withdrawn from Quebec with the French army or had been resident in France at the time of the Treaty of Paris in 1763 found themselves aliens on their return to Canada although their kin had become British subjects. Their number was not large, but they were influential persons being seigneurs or men of substance. Dorchester, aware of their predicament, had nevertheless urged that only residents of Quebec both before and following the conquest should automatically be considered British subjects and that the émigrés and other foreign immigrants should be naturalized by local enactment, a power he wished the Constitutional Act to confer on the legislatures of the new provinces.[50] The British Government did not follow Dorchester's advice; and as a result when the first Legislature of Lower Canada assembled, it contained twelve members who had returned to the colony since 1763, and whom the Legislature could not naturalize.[51]

Clarke, the Lieutenant Governor, was left to resolve the difficulty without any concession from the Colonial Office. The Assembly could not naturalize; the Imperial Naturalization Act of 1740 was of no assistance because the returned émigrés were Roman Catholics; and there was no time to secure letters of denization.[52] Clarke thereupon took the only course open to him; he decided to ignore the question of nationality and to treat all members as British subjects. In the Legislative Council, M. Lanaudière's desire to raise a debate on the question was frustrated, and in the Assembly the member for Cornwallis, P. L. Panet, was dissuaded from introducing an alien bill.[53] But Clarke's ultimate success in suppressing the issue was due to an apparent saw-off between the English members of the Assembly and Berthelot, the member for Quebec County. The English members appear to have dropped a petition against Lavaltrie's return for Warwick and a petition pending against Berthelot, both being returned émigrés, when petitions against the election of English members were discharged or withdrawn.[54] By designed disregard of the law the returned émigrés continued to hold their seats and their nationality was never again questioned.

Mention has been made that Clarke might have naturalized these members by letters of denization, an exercise of the royal prerogative which conferred British citizenship on the recipients by letters patent.[55] Denizens were allowed to hold land

and to vote, and generally possessed the same privileges as aliens naturalized by an act of Parliament. Letters of denization were granted without restraint as to race or religion and, aside from their restrictive cost, would have allowed French and Roman Catholics immigrants into Lower Canada to acquire citizenship. It was by this process that the émigré French Royalists were to have been settled in the Canadas following the French Revolution, and the Sulpicians of Montreal used the same process to secure citizenship for the French members of their order.[56]

The major alien immigration into Lower Canada was, however, neither French nor Catholic but American. While less numerous and more localized than in Upper Canada, the American settlers were estimated in 1828 to comprise one-half of the English-speaking population or about 40,000 souls.[57] As in Upper Canada, they had been encouraged to settle in the colony, they had been given land grants, and no question had been raised as to their right to vote. The Lower Canada Executive had welcomed their support and the Papineau party had sought to reduce their political influence not by challenging their national status but by depriving them of readily accessible polls.

By a happy coincidence, in the year the Assembly alleviated the territorial disfranchisement of the Eastern Townships through the creation of new counties, it also addressed the Crown for the right to naturalize alien residents by provincial legislation.[58] The motivation for the Address came from the predicament of a M. Moraud, a native of France, who had served in the British navy, taken up residence in Lower Canada, articled himself to a notary, and on completion of his legal apprenticeship had had his commission as a notary withheld on the grounds he was an alien.[59] His petition to the Assembly, coming at the moment when Upper Canada had just naturalized its alien population, led the Lower Canada Legislature to request that the British Parliament confer on it the power to naturalize all aliens seven years resident in the province. The request was endorsed by the Governor General and favourably received at the Colonial Office, and the Imperial Parliament passed an amendment to the Constitutional Act which allowed aliens naturalized by an act of the Legislature of Lower Canada to possess full political rights.[60] The permission came none too soon, for in the autumn of 1829 the elections in the new constituencies in the Eastern Townships had returned several members who could have been debarred from the Assembly on account of their nationality. Under the authority of the above amendment, the Assembly passed an act declaring that all persons resident in the province before 1823 (seven years previous) were to be considered natural-born British subjects and all other aliens resident in the province as of March 1, 1831, were to be British subjects within the colony when they had completed their seven years' residence.[61] This act, which was a copy of the Upper Canada Act of 1828, removed any question as to the nationality of the American settlers in the Eastern Townships. The passion aroused in the breasts of the French Canadian legislators by the wrong Moraud allegedly suffered had led them into a course of action whose benefit to the English-speaking alien population they would have been unlikely to countenance on its own merits.[62]

On the conclusion of the alien controversy in the Canadas it was evident that British subjects alone would be allowed to exercise the franchise in the future and that American immigrants who wished to obtain the vote would have first to acquire British citizenship. Yet the naturalization acts of the two colonies had only retrospective effect, and thus all new alien immigrants would have to secure citizenship via the Imperial act of 1740.[63] This act had certain limitations. It allowed naturalization of all aliens "born out of the ligeance of His Majesty" after seven years' residence, receipt of the Sacrament of the Lord's Supper in a Reformed Congregation, and subscription to the State Oaths before a colonial judge.[64] It was therefore of no value to Roman Catholics or to American immigrants who had been born within the dominions of the Crown. The latter limitation, if it ever was strictly observed, had become redundant with the passage of time. But the requirement that all aspirants for British citizenship must take the Sacrament of the Lord's Supper in a Reformed Congregation was a continuing limitation, even to the naturalization of Protestants, for an assumption had gained wide currency that the Sacrament had to be taken according to the rites of the Church of England,[65] and the evangelical sects, especially the Baptists and Methodists, were loathe to conform to a requirement which involved a secular employment of the Sacrament. In consequence after 1828 and 1831 in Upper and Lower Canada respectively there began to build up a new alien population which could not or would not employ the above act in order to secure British citizenship.

The build-up was most pronounced in Upper Canada and it led the Lieutenant Governor in some concern to enquire of the Colonial Office what the official attitude should be to the continued immigration and settlement of the large numbers of Americans.[66] Goderich's reply was less than helpful.[67] He suggested that the immigration might be checked if Colborne issued a proclamation to the effect that aliens could not hold land in a British colony until they had first acquired British citizenship. To give substance to the proclamation and to bring pressure on the resident American settlers to secure citizenship, Goderich suggested that Colborne might take steps to dispossess several prominent aliens. To the colony there was little question as to the more attractive remedy. The immigration must not be checked and steps must be taken to expedite the process of naturalization. Already the Legislative Council had originated a bill to provide for the general naturalization of all aliens resident in the province.[68] The Council had taken this step although it was contrary to the Royal Instructions and the repeated warnings of the Colonial Office that the Upper Canada declaratory act of 1828 was in no way to form a precedent. The Legislative Council did not press their general measure but rather undertook to concur in the particular bills that the Assembly was passing to naturalize batches of settlers. By their concurrence and Colborne's reservation of the bills it was hoped to force the Colonial Office to come to a decision on the future procedure for naturalization.[69] The Colonial Office was asked in effect to make up its mind whether colonial legislatures were to be allowed to grant British citizenship or whether that privilege was to remain the sole prerogative of the Imperial Parliament, and if the latter, what modifications it was willing to make to bring the antiquated act of 1740 into harmony with the actual conditions in the colonies.

Upper Canada was unfortunate to find a former Foreign Secretary at the Colonial Office. Aberdeen refused to change either the Imperial policy on naturalization or the Imperial legislation.[70] He believed such a change would be a repudiation of the British claim that the United States had no right to receive and protect the subjects of a foreign state on their unilateral disclaimer of allegiance to their natural Sovereign. He did, however, obtain royal assent to the particular naturalization bills forwarded by Colborne and intimated that the colonial Legislature might unofficially continue to naturalize in this manner aliens resident in Upper Canada.[71] While this surreptitious procedure allowed Roman Catholics and Protestant dissenters to be naturalized and secure political rights, it never did accommodate the bulk of the aliens in the two

Canadas, and its continuance was always at the mercy of the changing personnel of the Colonial and Crown Law offices.

The tacit right of the Upper and Lower Canada assemblies to naturalize continued in this unsatisfactory condition until union, at which time two ordinances of the Special Council of Lower Canada were disallowed on the recommendation of the Board of Trade who were of opinion that as the Legislature of Lower Canada never had the right to naturalize under the Constitutional Act, neither could the Special Council which superseded it.[72] Sydenham refused to accept this ruling and on the advice of his Attorney General he challenged the opinion of the Law Officers. He pointed out that the ordinances which the Law Officers had recommended be disallowed were merely rendering permanent two temporary ordinances which had been allowed in the previous year.[73] He went further and declared that the Constitutional Act had not denied the legislatures of the Canadas the right to pass naturalization acts but had merely limited the scope of such colonial acts by the proviso that political rights could only be conferred by Imperial legislation and that this proviso had been abolished as respects Lower Canada in 1830.[74] Sydenham was correct as far as the Constitutional Act was concerned but he ignored the Instructions to the governors that had accompanied the Act. The Law Officers, however, were routed; they revoked the order of disallowances and acknowledged that the local legislature could naturalize aliens subject to the limitation that they would be British subjects only within the limits of the colony.[75]

On the basis of this acknowledgment the first Parliament of the Province of Canada passed a retrospective naturalization act which allowed all aliens resident in the province on the proclamation of Union (February 10, 1841) to become British subjects after seven years' residence and, within the following twelve months, subscription to the oath of allegiance.[76] The legislation was prompted by the indignation of the Reformers who had seen the returning officers of Canada West reject many of their votes because they were tendered by Americans. There was considerable opposition in the Legislative Council to the measure but the opposition was only successful in substituting the seven-year period of residence which was required by the Imperial act of 1740 for the five-year period that the Assembly had specified and which was the time required by the United States.[77] The bill was allowed by the Colonial Office in 1842 after strong endorsement from Bagot.[78] Although the period of residence was subsequently reduced to five years in 1845, the American settlers continued to neglect to secure citizenship but persisted in exercising the franchise.[79] As a consequence to avoid antagonizing the Americans by enforcing their exclusion from the franchise, the Reformers, whose supporters they generally were, passed a declaratory act in 1849 which in fact made all aliens resident in the Canadas on the proclamation of Union British subjects.[80] Those aliens who had entered the province subsequent to Union were enabled by the same legislation to secure British citizenship on seven years' residence and subscription to the oath of allegiance; the period of residence was subseqently reduced to five years in 1854 and to three years in 1858.[81]

In the 1840's the tide of American migration had turned westward to California and the goldfields. The successive reduction of the residential qualification for citizenship was the Canadian Legislature's frail device to counter the attraction of the West. Its failure to divert the stream was to be evidenced in the absence of further declaratory naturalization acts. The American immigrants to Canada ceased to be numerous and with the deluge of British immigration ceased to be politically important. The public interest in aliens and naturalization flickered out.

There remains the need to consider the relationship of aliens to the franchise in New Brunswick. Although New Brunswick was contiguous to the United States, the influx of American settlers was less than might be expected. Several factors hindered the migration. There was a deeper antipathy between the Loyalists of New Brunswick and the Yankees of Massachusetts than there was between the Loyalists of Upper Canada and the residents of upstate New York; the suspension of Crown land grants in New Brunswick between the years 1790 and 1802 inclined the New England migrants westward to New York and Upper Canada or northward into Lower Canada; and later, immigration was retarded by the acrimony of the Maine–New Brunswick boundary dispute. To this antipathy may be attributed the early institution of the oath of allegiance as a prerequisite to the exercise of the franchise, and a closer adherence to the principle that aliens could not hold real property in a British colony. It is not suggested that some Americans did not secure Crown land grants in New Brunswick, but there was no outright abandonment of national distinction as in Upper Canada. The arrangements which American interests had to devise to secure timber lands is an illustration of this fact. It became necessary for them to buy the timber lands through resident British subjects who continued to hold the lands in trust for them.[82]

As regards the oath of allegiance New Brunswick specified that an elector could be required to subscribe to the oath before being allowed to vote. Instituted for the first election by a Minute of Council it was incorporated into the first election act and remained a component part of election procedure until its repeal in 1843.[83] It was then dropped along with other election oaths in order to facilitate polling on the introduction of single-day elections. When the Colonial Office brought the omission to the attention of the Lieutenant Governor, the Attorney General and Solicitor General argued successfully that the oath of allegiance had been replaced by a more effective qualification oath which required an elector to swear he was a British subject.[84] The latter oath was retained until 1855 when it was replaced by the specific enactment that all electors must be British subjects.[85]

While the oath of allegiance might or might not be invoked to bar aliens from the franchise, it remained a continuing possibility which aliens could only circumscribe by acquiring British citizenship. The sole avenue of access to this status was, in New Brunswick as elsewhere, conformity to the provisions of the Imperial act of 1740 which was a stern barrier not merely because it offended the religious scruples of many aliens but because the judges of the Supreme Court of New Brunswick refused while on circuit to accept the subscription to the oath of allegiance required by the Act and insisted all suppliants for naturalization must take the oath before them at Fredericton.[86] These two impediments discouraged or prevented most aliens from attempting to secure British citizenship.

It was, therefore, not surprising that New Brunswick should be interested in the events transpiring in the Canadas and that the Legislature should in 1829 forward a joint address to the Crown to secure the abolition of the Sacrament as a prerequisite to naturalization.[87] The address was favourably received but success of the appeal was ultimately frustrated by a change at the Colonial Office; for the appointment of a former Foreign Secretary as Colonial Secretary brought a refusal to modify the Imperial naturalization legislation because it might disrupt British relations with the United States.[88] When the Assembly continued to insist, the Colonial Office advised

New Brunswick to copy the example of the Canadas and pass a retrospective declaratory act to the effect that all aliens currently resident in the colony should become British subjects on completion of seven years' residence and the taking of the oath of allegiance.[89] On this authority the New Brunswick Legislature passed a retrospective act in 1836, and further retrospective acts were passed in 1841, 1845, and 1846 when fresh immigration continued to renew the alien population.[90] The frequency with which New Brunswick and the other colonies resorted to retrospective and private naturalization ultimately persuaded the Imperial authorities in 1847 to allow the colonies to enact prospective naturalization laws for the benefit of aliens who should immigrate in the future.[91] Subsequently the New Brunswick Legislature availed itself of this privilege and in 1850 passed an act to allow aliens to secure citizenship after seven years' residence.[92] When the scramble for emigrants began in earnest in the late 1850's, New Brunswick joined the competition and sought to outbid the Canadas and the neighbouring states by reducing the period of residence to one year.[93]

In Nova Scotia and Prince Edward Island the absence of any sizeable alien population reduced interest in the matter of naturalization. Prince Edward Island never solicited a change in the naturalization procedure prescribed by the Imperial act of 1740 and Nova Scotia did not request the right to naturalize by local legislation until 1845.[94] After the Imperial Parliament had granted this privilege to all the colonies, Nova Scotia and Prince Edward Island did not pass general naturalization acts but rather preferred to naturalize their aliens by private bill legislation.[95] It was not until 1863 that these two colonies passed permanent naturalization acts. In that year Prince Edward Island and Nova Scotia passed statutes which enabled aliens to acquire full civil and political rights *within the colony* after a residence of seven years and one year respectively.[96]

In conclusion the franchise of the three Maritime colonies may be said to have been closed to aliens while the franchise of the Canadas may be said to have been open. Although provisions existed in the Canadas to exclude aliens from the exercise of the suffrage, these provisions were seldom acted upon. When there were indications that they might be enforced steps were taken to naturalize the aliens en bloc. In some measure the laxity may be attributed to the ambiguous status of the Americans. But even if their status had been clarified, the laxity would likely have persisted, for a common origin, tongue, heritage, and environment did not fashion that conscious sense of divergency which the public mind required if the legal distinction was to be enforced in practice. The failure to disendow the Americans of British citizenship meant all aliens were holus bolus incorporated into the public life of the Canadas. Large alien communities divorced in sentiment from the colonies in which they lived did not therefore arise. The exercise of the franchise by all citizens maintained the constant pressure of the frontier at the seat of government. The old families, factions, and parties, in order to retain or secure power, had to reach out and acquire the support of the new; and political stratification on ethnical grounds could not endure.

CHAPTER FOURTEEN

CONTROVERTED ELECTIONS: THE MARITIME COLONIES

THE GROWTH AND MODIFICATION of the franchise cannot be treated purely as a study of change in the technical qualifications. The setting in which the franchise operated and its modifying influence have to be considered. Just as the availability of free land and the condition of county assessments had an important bearing on the effective as contrasted with the legal franchise, so too had the determination of controverted elections. Controverted elections were essentially a post-electoral modification of the franchise. These post-electoral reviews were initially instituted to correct evils that had crept into the exercise of the franchise during the elections, but as they were not always tempered with justice nor devoid of political manipulation they form an essential part of an account of the franchise.

I

From the foundation of representative government in Nova Scotia, it was always assumed that the Assembly should exercise a review over the qualification of its members and over the conduct of the elections. The assumption was based on the belief that the usages and conventions of the Imperial Parliament extended to its lowliest counterpart.[1] The resolution of the Governor and Council of January 3, 1757, which established the first Nova Scotian Assembly authorized the Provost Marshal to send the results of all scrutinies to the Assembly that any further disputation might be settled by the Assembly itself. This authority was reiterated by Minute of Council on August 22, 1759, and in the first election act in 1789. In the latter year the Assembly "resolved that the House has the sole and exclusive power of examining and determining the rights and qualifications of Electors and Elected together with return of writs and all matters incidental to elections."[2] This resolution was in effect a confirmation of past practice for the Assembly had been investigating disputed elections since 1759 and had been confirming or unseating the incumbent as it determined the merits of each case.

This right of the Assembly was not challenged until 1806. In that year the Lieutenant Governor refused to issue a new writ for Annapolis Township following the voiding of the previous election by the Assembly. In this particular case the election of Thomas Walker for Annapolis Township had been challenged by his opponent on the grounds, first, that Walker had won by polling illegal votes, and secondly, that Walker, by promising to discontinue a suit started in the Inferior Court at Annapolis, had used personal intimidation to influence the vote of one Jonathan Payson. In consequence of an investigation both by a select committee and by the whole House, the first charge against Walker was declared to be unfounded while the second charge of intimidation was found to be true.[3] The Speaker was then authorized to acquaint the Lieutenant Governor with the result and request him to issue a new writ to fill the vacancy.

When the Assembly met for its next session no writ had been issued and the Assembly requested the Lieutenant Governor to explain this neglect. The Lieutenant Governor in reply informed the Assembly that "as a writ had been issued for this purpose and returned, and the member sworn in, His Excellency requires that he should be informed by what means a vacancy has arisen, that he may be able to judge if, under the circumstances of the case, he may consider the seat as legally vacated."[4] The Lieutenant Governor was clearly seeking to extend executive control over controverted elections, just as his predecessors had exercised executive control over the franchise and over representation.

The assertion of executive control had been made by the Lieutenant Governor at the insistence of the Executive Council and in opposition to the advice of the Attorney General and Solicitor General.[5] In face of the difference of opinion between his Executive Council and his Law Officers, and in advance of the address from the Assembly, the Lieutenant Governor appealed to the Colonial Office for an authoritative ruling.[6] When the Imperial Law Officers were of the opinion "that the issuing of a new writ is the necessary consequence of the resolution of the House, and that such resolution cannot be appealed from, or questioned by or before any other authority or tribunal," the contention of the Assembly to determine the qualifications of its members and the propriety of their election was sustained and the pretensions of the Executive Council satisfactorily refuted.[7] The Walker case constitutionally confirmed the Assembly's right to determine controverted elections, a right that was a necessary adjunct of their right to determine the franchise.

The controversy attending the Walker case pointed out a defect that had long existed in the manner of dealing with controverted elections in Nova Scotia. There was no statute defining who should investigate controverted elections or the manner in which the investigations should be conducted. The Assembly had simply adopted over the years a variety of practices to suit the circumstances of the moment. In the first controverted election, the Assembly debated the petition, the petitioner spoke from the Bar of the House, and the sitting member championed his own suit.[8] This method of determining controverted elections by a general debate of the Assembly was subsequently abandoned and for the next fifteen years the disputed returns were determined by a committee of three or five members nominated by the House. In each case the Assembly on review agreed with the decision of the committee and the problem of controverted elections was in effect settled outside the Assembly proper.

The excitement accompanying the American Revolutionary War brought an end to the determination of disputed elections by select committees of the Assembly. In 1775 the Assembly reverted to dealing with controverted elections by Committee of the Whole. Although this manner of determination involved a considerable part of each session, the Assembly felt it advisable to require the entire membership to deal with the disputed elections on account of the questionable loyalty of individual members.

The political factions which were represented in the Assembly following the loyalist migration gave rise to partisan struggles over controverted elections in the Committee of the Whole. The two factions were led by members of the Executive Council; Solicitor General R. J. Uniacke, the "Cumberland Rebel," led the old settlers while the Attorney General, S. S. Blowers, led the loyalists. On three occasions these factions clashed over a controverted election, the election for Shelburne Township and two elections for Annapolis County.[9] Their bitter rivalry was not conducive to an impartial review of the true state of the franchise in these elections.

The factional rivalry and the difficulty in ferreting out the illegal votes which were occasioned by the fraudulent conveyances of property convinced the Assembly that some change in procedure was necessary. To avoid the time consumed in investigating disputed votes, the Assembly resurrected the instrument of select committees, and to maintain a degree of political impartiality the membership of these committees were selected by lot rather than by nomination.

The manner of choosing the membership of the committees was novel, but it was not a product of Nova Scotian ingenuity. The Assembly had simply copied the method of selecting controverted election committees that had been established in the Imperial Parliament by the Grenville Act of 1770.[10] The procedure as adapted to Nova Scotian requirements involved the selection by lot of fifteen members from the Assembly and the reduction of this number to five by the petitioner and sitting member each alternatively striking off a member. The five members remaining plus a member nominated by each of the contending parties were entrusted with the investigation of the disputed votes and possessed full power to call witnesses and acquire records.

This method was first used for the Kings County election of 1793.[11] But as the procedure was not regulated by law, the establishment of the select committee did not preclude the Assembly from first debating the case over a lengthy period and again debating the findings of the committee before affirming its decision. Although the lengthy controversy over the Kings County election led to the establishment of a committee to draft rules and regulations for the future use of select committees, the Assembly was sufficiently unwilling to renounce its freedom to interfere in disputed elections that the resultant draft bill was laid aside and the House for lack of a fixed procedure continued to hear most election cases itself.[12] The select committee method, however, continued to be used spasmodically and chiefly in those cases involving problems of technical investigation. The manner of selecting the personnel varied, being on occasions by lot and on other occasions by direct nomination. In all cases the House continued to exercise its privilege to review the decisions of the select committees. The resulting spectacle was not always edifying, as the Halifax Township election of 1800 illustrates. In this case the defeated candidate disputed the return on the ground that the sitting member was elected on a majority of illegal votes. The Assembly resolved to establish a select committee who were to gather the facts but were not to hear counsel for the contending parties. The select committee was established and was in the midst of its labours when its sittings were suddenly suspended by the Assembly which had decided to hear counsel for the disputants before the Bar of the House. The Assembly, after listening to the argument of counsel for some time, finally ordered the select committee to continue its investigation. When the committee reported the facts in favour of the sitting member, the Assembly in Committee of the Whole received the report and declared the sitting member duly elected. In formal session the House later refused to abide by its decision, reversed itself, and voided the election.[13]

While this Assembly had witnessed a larger number of controverted elections than had been customary up until that time, it set the pattern for the future.[14] Following each general election, the first session of the new Assembly was to be largely given over to the determination of the disputed elections, each session witnessing the same wrangling, the same procedural irregularities, and the same consumption of time. When, in 1819–20, two general elections followed hard upon one another, the patience of the Assembly became exhausted. The principles of the draft bill of 1793 were disinterred and the first act to regulate the procedure for settling controverted elections was passed.[15] The act was little more than a modified copy of the Grenville Act; like its prototype it required each controverted election to be finally determined by a select committee. To ensure an adequate representation of divergent political interests twenty-seven members (approximately two-thirds of the Assembly) were required to be present for the drawing of each select committee; their names were to be placed in a box and the Clerk of the House was to draw out fifteen names. From this number the contending parties were alternatively to strike off a member until seven remained; these members together with a member nominated by each of the disputants were to compose the select committee to try the merits of an election petition.

The new procedure was to relieve the Assembly of the unenviable and time-consuming task of handling each controverted election. To reduce the intrusion of partisan politics, the Assembly was to refer all disputed elections to a select committee whose determination was to be final. In the event that the decision was concurred in by less than five of the committee's members, the Assembly might, however, recommit a case for a retrial before a new select committee. The committees possessed the power to call for witnesses and records and to take evidence on oath. In this respect the committees were entrusted with a power which the Assembly itself did not possess. The closer approximation of the procedure to that of a judicial trial, the barrier to packing through selection of the personnel by lot, and the ability of the disputants to remove the more bigoted and partisan members were all designed to produce select committees in which an element of justice might govern the determination of disputed elections.

Over the years, various modifications were introduced to overcome weaknesses in the procedure. To prevent the prolongation of controverted elections, the above act had required the select committees to sit from day to day and they were not to adjourn nor their members absent themselves without first obtaining leave of the House. Yet when matters of political moment were before the Assembly the members found it necessary to adjourn the select committees repeatedly. This difficulty became most evident in the sixteenth General Assembly (1837–40) when the House was agitated by the demand for the separation of the Executive and Legislative councils. The political action in the Assembly so engaged the attention of its members that the consideration of four of the eight controverted elections had not been completed when the Assembly rose for its first prorogation. Following Imperial practice the four select committees ceased to be legally constituted on the prorogation of the House and following a decision of the Nova Scotian Assembly made under similar circumstances in 1828 the investigation of the disputed returns would have to begin *ab origine* at the next session.[16] In the technicalities governing legislative procedure a stratagem had been discovered which partisans could employ to thwart the resolution of disputed returns. To forestall its further exploitation an amendment to the controverted election act was subsequently passed which empowered controverted election committees to adjourn over periods of prorogation and to resume their deliberations at the next session.[17] This change was to ensure that an electoral mutilation of the franchise should not stand simply because a litigious disputant or partisanship within a committee had been able to prolong its deliberations beyond a prorogation of the House.

The independence of the controverted election committees was also increased by the new legislation, for the Assembly was denied the right to disallow a decision of a select committee on any grounds. Under the former Legislation, the Assembly, while it could not directly reverse such a decision, could in effect disallow it by ordering a new trial when the determination had not been concurred in by five members of the original committee. By their renunciation of this right the Assembly was establishing a principle which should have been of value in the partisan Houses that were to be common place with the achievement of responsible government. In theory controverted election committees, devoid of premeditated partisan swamping through the selection of their personnel by lot, possessed full power to summon witnesses and records, and endowed with a finality of judgment might have been expected to determine with detachment the disputed returns that came before them. In practice the expectation was most infrequently fulfilled; the all pervasive spirit of political partisanship corrupted the design. Their finality of judgment merely introduced the thrill of chance for no longer was a disputed return predetermined by the political complexion of the House, but rather was decided by the Clerk of the House as he intoned the name and political hue of the members which "Lady Lot" cast up to be the select committee.

If the above accusation against controverted election committees is true, the perversion of the franchise at the polls was unlikely to be overcome by an appeal to the Assembly. Many instances may be brought forward to show that the Assembly condoned and even inspired electoral abuses. In 1828 a select committee rejected a petition of William O'Brien against the undue return of Richard Smith for Hants County, yet the following year O'Brien secured a conviction for bribery against Smith to the extent of a £500 fine before the Supreme Court at Halifax.[18] In 1845 the Supreme Court at Antigonish convicted Patrick Power, member for Sydney County, of bribery and fined him £100 although a select committee had dismissed the same charge as unsubstantiated when it had been brought before them.[19] In 1852 Howe wrote privately to Hincks that he had been unseated for Cumberland because he had "had the bad luck to have four Tories and a violent anti-railroad man on my committee."[20] To ensure that these episodes are not isolated incidents it is only necessary to turn to the session following the bitter election campaign of 1860 for an illustration of the degree to which the political parties sought to pervert the expressed wishes of the electorate through the employment and manipulation of controverted election committees.

The Conservative administration of J. W. Johnston, which had emerged from the campaign as a minority government (Conservatives 26, Liberals 29), was determined to manufacture a majority in the Assembly and began the tactical manœuvres to accomplish this end long before the House had assembled and the first election petitions had been tabled. The plan devised involved the exploitation of the possibilities of legislation they had put on the statute books in the previous House. This act had made any person holding an office of profit under the Crown ineligible to sit in the Legislative Council or be nominated for a seat in the Assembly.[21] The act had excepted only the office of Executive Councillor, Queen's Council, and Justice of the Peace from its operation. It is doubtful if the Legislature had anticipated the limitless applicability of the act but the Conservative administration were now not adverse to its strictest enforcement. The election had terminated on June 1, the Conservatives had devised their tactics by July, and in November the public became aware of their design. The reappointment of seven legislative councillors to their seats in that body revealed that the Government had ruled that they had vacated their seats because they held provincial appointments.[22] This manœuvre was the first overt move in the plan to exclude all minor office holders from the Assembly of whom there happened to be nine, seven Liberals and two Conservatives. Johnston believed that the disability of the two Conservatives and two of the Liberals was questionable but that five of the Liberals came directly within the disqualifying terms of the act.[23] Johnston believed these office holders should be denied the right to sit until the Assembly had ruled on their cases and so advised the Lieutenant Governor. If the Lieutenant Governor had followed this advice and refused to swear in the offending members, the administration would have been provided with a majority in the Assembly. Realizing the political implications, Mulgrave applied to the Colonial Office for legal advice. The Law Officers of the Crown agreed with Johnston that the act rendered the occupants of these minor provincial offices ineligible to sit in the Assembly, but they did not agree that the offending members should be denied the right to take their seats in the Assembly. The Law Officers saw "nothing to prevent a member (returned by the Sheriff as duly elected) from sitting and voting altho' holding one of the offices in question until he has been unseated by the Assembly."[24]

The offending members were as a result seated, and Johnston at once moved the House into a consideration of their eligibility. The Liberals took the view that all questions of eligibility were by the Controverted Election Act of 1821 taken out of the hands of the Assembly and placed in the jurisdiction of select committees. The Conservatives took the stand that the act dealt only with elections protested by petition and that the Assembly could not be rendered impotent to consider the eligibility of members through lack of a petition. Johnston's motion was voted down on a majority provided by the offending members and the Conservative party resigned from office.

The Conservative offensive to retain the seals of office was not abandoned. On the day following their resignation, they tabled fourteen petitions protesting the election of eight Liberals. But the Liberals were not without guile; they tabled six petitions protesting the return of nine Conservatives.[25] The parties were setting the stage for the selection of the controverted election committees. While "Lady Lot" might determine the committee membership, the parties sought to circumscribe her choice. As no member whose election was protested was eligible to serve on a committee, the amassing of petitions served a twofold purpose; to dispute a return and to reduce the number of the foe available for committee service. Thereby the number of Liberals and Conservatives available to serve on the select committees had each been reduced to seventeen. The *Novascotian* of April 9, 1860, remarking on the political morality that sought to render the selections of controverted election committees a mockery, stated:

Exceptions were taken to the qualification of members returned by the then Opposition [Liberals] but there were just as many exceptions to be taken to Government members; and as fast as Mr. Johnston and his friends filed protests against their opponents, which had the effect of disqualifying them from sitting upon Election Committees, their opponents returned the fire and did the same thing. This was a game two could play at and if both parties had kept it on a little longer no scrutiny could be tried out at all, for all the members on both sides would have been disqualified.

Mr. Johnston then held his hand, and he and his friends signified that this warfare should cease. The Opposition who had become the Government Party ceased also. Then came the departmental elections in which the three members of the House who had accepted office, namely, the Attorney

General, Provincial Secretary, and the Financial Secretary went back to their constituents and were returned again with vastly increased majorities. Giving assurance, as far as such an ordeal could test it that the country was with them, that the change of government was acceptable to the people.

Now then, look at the mean miserable shift to which Mr. Johnston immediately resorted in order to get some unfair advantage. He and his henchman, Tupper, forthwith caused petitions to be preferred against the returns of all three of the Departmental Officers, solely for the purpose of disqualifying them from being drawn on committees to try the disputed elections. It had had its effect, and the moment the opposition succeeded, they abandon two of the three cases, and having obtained what they think a favorable committee against the Attorney General, decide to go on against him only.

The result of these political tactics was that the petitions against ten of the twenty disputed returns were abandoned either at the time of balloting for their committees or shortly thereafter; of the remaining disputed returns, seven involved seats held by Liberals and three seats held by Conservatives; and whereas the fortunes of balloting gave four Liberals a Conservative-dominated committee, it gave only one Conservative member a Liberal-dominated committee. At first glance the Conservatives believed the balloting had provided the means whereby they could retrieve the seals of office and the fact that a Conservative office holder had drawn a Conservative-dominated election committee certainly did not diminish this belief. The latter coincidence was, however, the undoing of the Conservative strategy. If they unseated the three Liberals for holding official appointments, they would have to be consistent and unseat their colleague who was Harbour Commissioner for Inverness, but should they be consistent they had no assurance that the three Liberal-dominated committees would follow suit. The Liberal committees simply waited; time was on their side. The Conservatives finally could delay no longer; they capitulated and sustained the eligibility of friend and foe alike. The Liberal committees then reported sustaining the eligibility of their colleagues. The manœuvre had boomeranged on the Conservatives, but it illustrates the purpose to which politicians believed controverted election committees could and should be put.

Aside from the nefarious influences of select committees on the expressed franchise of the people of Nova Scotia, the scrutinies, conducted by the sheriffs, could be equally effective in warping the political franchise of the electorate. From the first elections in Nova Scotia the sheriff had been given power to investigate votes that were objected to by a candidate. These investigations took place after the completion of each election and only on the request of a candidate. In the first instances, the sheriff was allowed to scrutinize any vote, but this freedom led to defeated candidates demanding an investigation of any and all votes of his successful rival out of sheer vindictiveness. In consequence the first franchise act of 1789 restricted the right of scrutiny to those votes which had been objected to at the time they were recorded in the poll book. This change restricted the scrutiny to those votes which the candidates had felt to be invalid at the time they were delivered and before the result could be accurately foretold.

In conducting a scrutiny the sheriff was obliged to hear witnesses pro and con for each of the votes contested. In order to check more easily the qualification of each voter the poll clerks were to record at the time of polling not merely the voter's name, but also his place of residence, and after 1839 the location of the property on which he voted. This information, together with the evidence recorded at the scrutiny, was returned to the Provincial Secretary to be the basis for any subsequent investigation by a committee of the House. A scrutiny was essential if the election was to be petitioned against, for as early as 1785 the Assembly refused to consider a petition dis-

G

puting the return for Hants County because the petitioner had never demanded a scrutiny.[26] In the beginning, the sheriff had no discretion as to the deductions to be drawn from his scrutiny; he was simply obliged to record the evidence and leave the deductions to the Assembly or a select committee. As time went on the Assembly, to ease their own burden, allowed the sheriff in certain circumstances to expunge votes proved illegal at the scrutiny and to return the candidate with the majority of legal votes.[27] The sheriff ceased to be purely an administrative officer and became an officer with judicial capacity.

The judicial power placed in the hands of the sheriffs enhanced the role of scrutinies in the struggles for political dominance. For this discretionary power to be satisfactorily exercised required men of ability and integrity. The office of sheriff, held for a year subject to reappointment by the Lieutenant Governor, did not necessarily provide men of this calibre. Aside from the dangers from political appointment, it is doubtful if sufficient men of the required impartiality could have been found to man the scrutinies, considering the partisan political atmosphere that permeated Nova Scotia after 1848. When the sheriffs approached their responsibility with marked political sympathies the search for justice was soon forsaken. Illustrative of this fact was the Victoria County election of 1851. In this case Victoria, having just been created out of the county of Cape Breton, lacked a sheriff. The election was conducted as a result by a deputy sheriff appointed by the sheriff of Cape Breton County. At the completion of the polling, the candidates stood Hugh Munro, 440; John Munro, 399; and C. J. Campbell, 393. A scrutiny was demanded and the deputy sheriff expunged the votes of seven ratepayers which reduced John Munro's vote to 392. The deputy sheriff then returned Campbell and Hugh Munro. The sheriff of Cape Breton County, however, on receiving the returns added them again and returned Hugh and John Munro. The Assembly by a party vote and without an investigation subsequently confirmed the juggling of the election returns.[28] Continued repetition of such incidents finally forced the Assembly to abandon the scrutinies and leave the scrutinizing of electoral returns to the Assembly alone.[29]

Deplorable as the conduct of some sheriffs may have been, and deplorable as its effect may have been on the purity of the franchise, their conduct at its blackest was no worse than that of their superiors, the members of the select committees of the Assembly. As long as the select committees to which election appeals lay were liable to support them on partisan grounds and in violation of the law, some sheriffs were encouraged by personal inclination, and others were pressured, into manipulating the expressed franchise of the people. Until the controverted election committees began to apply the law uniformly and impartially, the sheriffs could not be expected to be an oasis of virtue in this sea of partisan connivance.

It would be wrong to assume that all the sheriffs and all the controverted election committees did not discharge their responsibilities with a degree of impartiality, but from the records, as we have them, those who did were and had increasingly become the exceptions. In view of the fact that from 1830 on an average of 14 per cent of the seats were contested in each Assembly (in one critical Assembly the number went as high as 40 per cent), one can gauge the considerable effect a defective method of resolving controverted elections must have had on the franchise. The condition existed throughout the entire life of colonial Nova Scotia; the rise of parties and the attendant struggle for the spoils of office merely enhanced the evil. The achievement of Confederation was not to end the blight; it continued to flourish until the determination of the disputed returns was taken out of the hands of the politicians and made the responsibility of a judicial organ politically impartial.

II

In Prince Edward Island, following Imperial and Nova Scotia precedents, the Assembly constituted itself the sole judge of disputed elections. The Assembly set forward its claim in statutory form in 1780, but the disallowance of the act (for other reasons) meant that the claim did not have a statutory basis until 1801.[30] The Island Executive, however, had conceded the claim as early as 1787 when the Sheriff had returned no candidates in the general election of that year and the Lieutenant Governor in his dilemma had been led to enquire of the Executive Council whether it might not resolve the controverted election. Although the Attorney General was uncertain, the Chief Justice was of the firm opinion that "the House are the sole judges of the regularity and legality of the sheriff's return of members" and the Executive Council thereupon decided that the Lieutenant Governor in Council could not interfere with disputed elections.[31] The right was not again questioned until 1848 when the Lieutenant Governor on the advice of his Attorney General and Solicitor General refused to issue a writ for Prince County. The occasion arose when the sitting member accepted a seat on the Executive Council and the Assembly requested the issuance of a writ of election. As the position carried no remuneration, the Law Officers advised that the appointment was not covered by the local act of 1837 which vacated the seat of any member who accepted an office of emolument under the Crown. The Assembly challenged the Lieutenant Governor's refusal and the issue was taken to the Colonial Secretary who confirmed the jurisdiction of the Assembly when he replied that he could "entertain no doubt that the House of Assembly is the proper judge whether or not a vacancy exists . . . and . . . is the only judge on all questions touching the right of its members to their seats."[32]

The right to judge the legality of election returns having been conceded, the Assembly left their resolution to the Committee of the Whole on Privileges and Elections. On the occasion of the first controverted election reaching the Assembly in 1788, and on similar occasions in 1803 and 1806, the House devised the rules for their determination. The Committee on Privileges and Elections from its own numbers selected its chairman, heard evidence and questioned witnesses at the Bar, and by majority vote (the members whose seats were involved abstaining) determined the election cases. The Committee set a time limit on the receipt of petitions, ensured the good faith of the petitioners by insisting on the deposit of sureties, and sought to ensure their own good faith by swearing the members to adjudicate impartially the disputed returns that came before them.[33] These procedural rules were formalized into statutory form in 1836 and were continued by intermittent enactments down to Confederation.[34]

The Island Assembly during the colonial period decided more than 64 controverted elections.[35] Of this number the Assembly sustained 28 returns and voided or amended 36. Of the 28 elections sustained, 18 involved the seats of members of the majority party in the Assembly and 10 the seats of members of the minority party. Of the 36 returns voided or amended, 30 were modified in favour of the candidate of the majority party but only 6 in favour of a candidate from the minority party. While it cannot be assumed that all decisions made in favour of candidates of the majority party were

unjust, the statistics nevertheless make it clear that there was an undue affinity between the politics of the winning party to a controverted election and the politics of
the Assembly majority.

The difficulty that candidates of the minority party experienced in securing a favourable hearing is best illustrated by an incident in 1790. The election of four members
of the majority or Stewart party was petitioned against by their opponents. The petitioners, hearing rumours that the Assembly was going to prorogue without hearing
their petition, waited on the Lieutenant Governor, Edmund Fanning, and received his
assurance that the Assembly would not prorogue until the business of the session was
complete. Yet on the day the first petition was to be heard and while the witnesses
stood outside the chamber, the Assembly by a majority of three (three members petitioned against voting) requested the Lieutenant Governor to prorogue the House.
The Lieutenant Governor agreed to comply, but as he sat on the dais of the Legislative
Council awaiting the Assembly, the petitioners presented him with a request that the
prorogation be delayed until the controverted elections were determined. When Fanning wavered, the Stewart party informed him they would absent themselves from the
Assembly and reduce its numbers below a quorum if he complied with the request.
Fanning capitulated, the Assembly was prorogued, and the disputed elections whose
determination could have changed the political majority in the Assembly were never
to be decided.[36]

The Assembly always refused to place disputed elections in other hands. When
the Legislative Council was made elective in 1862, the Assembly refused to allow the
Council to refer its disputed elections to the Supreme Court for determination.[37]
The Assembly even refused to follow the British House of Commons when in 1868
it entrusted the settlement of controverted elections to the courts.[38] While it is true
that the political activities of the early Island judges had not created a tradition of
judicial detachment, the Assembly's reluctance to relinquish the resolution of controverted elections was conditioned by its desire to control the political repercussions
of such determinations.

The attitude of the sheriff toward controverted elections has to be examined more
closely in Prince Edward Island than in Nova Scotia. Whereas some sheriffs were partial in their conduct of elections and scrutinies in Nova Scotia, they may be said to
have been universally partisan in Prince Edward Island. In part the difference was
occasioned by the fact the Prince Edward Island did not create a sheriff for each county
until 1837 whereas Nova Scotia created county sheriffs as early as 1778. In both colonies
the duties of the office of sheriff were initially discharged by an Imperial officer known
as the Provost Marshal. On abolishing this office, Nova Scotia had created a sheriff
for each county but Prince Edward Island replaced the Provost Marshal in 1786 by a
single sheriff for the whole Island.[39] In part the difference was due to the intensity of
Island politics whose fury engulfed lieutenant governors no less than judges and
sheriffs. For instance in the general election of 1784, the Lieutenant Governor,
Walter Patterson, found himself actively campaigning against the Stewart party led
by the son of his Chief Justice, Peter Stewart, and before the election was over the
councillors and the Provost Marshal were all involved. The Provost Marshal's conduct
was so partial to the candidates of the Patterson party that his conduct was the subject of complaints to the Colonial Secretary,[40] for when the candidates of the Stewart
party demanded a scrutiny, the Provost Marshal "declared we might have scrutineers
or not but he held himself the sole judge in the matter. And notwithstanding any

scrutiny that might be taken he would return the members he thought proper, and accordingly returned the candidates who opposed us as duly elected, they having the greatest number of votes; but tho' his oath bound him to return such candidates as should have the greatest number of legal votes he chose to overlook or omit the word legal in his return."[41] In contrast Patterson had found the Provost Marshal's assistance so helpful that he was able to report to Sydney "that notwithstanding every opposition which could be made, there has been chosen by a great majority the most respectable and best intentioned House of Representatives which have ever met on this Island, and accordingly a perfect harmony subsisted between all branches of the Legislature from the commencement to the end of the session; nor was there a dissenting voice on any matter which related to the public."[42]

When the Provost Marshal subsequently resigned, Patterson, fearful of a less amenable Imperial replacement, had the Legislature abolish the office and create a sheriff for the Island. Following English precedent the legislation required the Chief Justice to nominate annually three fit persons from which list the Lieutenant Governor was to select the sheriff.[43] In order to secure a compatible list of nominees Patterson suspended Chief Justice Stewart from his post and nominations were then made by the senior puisne judge who was a friend of Patterson. This partisan inauguration of the office of sheriff founded the tradition that Island sheriffs were to be political partisans of the governing clique and were to exercise their function as returning officers to the advantage of their political friends.

Despite frequent criticism of the political activities of the sheriffs, the Assembly took few steps to discourage their partisanship. When a majority hostile to the Executive secured control of the Assembly in 1801, the Assembly did terminate the power of the sheriffs to decide the legitimacy of disputed votes.[44] They were henceforth to limit their scrutiny to the gathering of evidence against disputed votes and to leave the decision as to their validity to the judgement of the House. But in 1806 with harmony restored between the Executive and the Assembly, the deputy sheriffs were allowed to be candidates for the Assembly, and in 1848 this privilege was extended to the sheriffs.[45] The Assembly was in fact not adverse to encouraging the sheriffs, the returning officers, and the poll clerks to be active partisans.

Several incidents in the 1850's illustrate how the franchise was distorted by the partisanship of the sheriffs and how little the Assembly cared. In 1853 the Liberal Government was defeated when their leader was not returned although he had received a majority of votes; the sheriff, after holding a scrutiny and being of opinion that the Liberal leader did not have a legal majority, had taken the law into his own hands and returned the Liberal leader's Conservative opponent.[46] The Liberals on their next assumption of office took steps not to eradicate partisanship but rather to ensure that when it next occurred it would be to their benefit. They decided to place the office of sheriff directly at the disposal of the party in power. Accordingly the nomination of three fit persons by the Chief Justice and the Lieutenant Governor's personal appointment of one as sheriff was abolished in favour of nomination and appointment by the Lieutenant Governor in Council.[47] Consequently the Conservatives experienced the hostility of the sheriffs at the following general election. Being returned to power, however, the Conservatives were able to rectify the damage and to revert to the former method of nominating and appointing the sheriffs.[48] The office of sheriff was not neutralized thereby; and the Administrator in 1870 was still able to complain that such breaches of propriety had been committed by the returning officers that the returns for five districts could be invalid.[49] At any particular moment the franchise of Prince Edward Island may therefore be said to have been the interpretation that the partisan sheriffs and the Assembly Committee on Privileges and Elections chose to put on the electoral qualifications as specified by law.

III

In the eighty years that New Brunswick existed as a distinct colony, the Assembly resolved eighty-seven controverted elections. While this number represented an average of only four controverted elections per Assembly, there were occasions when a substantial proportion of the returns were disputed, as for instance during the Fourth Assembly (1803–8) when 42 per cent of the seats were challenged. This Assembly and the Seventeenth Assembly (1856–57) were the sole occasions when controverted elections were numerous enough to change the political balance in the House. On the former occasion the Government forces won the decisions on the controverted elections and remained in power, while on the latter occasion they lost the struggle for control of a controverted election committee and thereby lost control of the House.[50]

While the above incidents illustrate that controverted elections and their resolution could be as important as elsewhere in determining the composition of the New Brunswick Legislature, it must be stated that their determination was less influenced by party politics than in the other colonies. The lack of political parties and their attendant partisanship may explain the large number of New Brunswick election petitions which were withdrawn or not pressed to a conclusion. Of the 87 elections disputed the petitions protesting 35 were withdrawn, the returns of 34 were confirmed, and the returns of a mere 18 were voided. In New Brunswick, party lines were firmly drawn for little more than the decade, between 1854, the establishment of responsible government, and 1864, the break-up of the parties under the impact of the Confederation movement. It nevertheless should not be assumed that the absence of strong parties meant controverted elections were resolved in a more impartial manner, for there was partiality in the New Brunswick Assembly even if it did not arise from political parties. The political situation in New Brunswick was unique, for it was long dominated by personality cults. The Assembly was divided into spheres of influence centring on specific personalities, and the fate of election petitions depended on the relationship of the contestants to these personalities.

Let us take for an example the controverted election of 1838 for Sunbury County. A controverted election committee, after considering the case for a year, had concluded that the petitioner had a majority of the vote and should be seated in lieu of the sitting member. The committee had reached this conclusion because it had invalidated the votes of residents on the Nerepis Road that had been tendered at the Sunbury poll. The Nerepis Road at the time of the election had been in Queens County but subsequent to the election a new survey had been completed and the road had been placed in Sunbury County. If the Nerepis Road residents were taken to have been within Sunbury at the time of the election, their votes were valid and the sitting member was duly elected, but if the traditional boundaries were accepted the votes were invalid and the petitioner should have been returned. The select committee had accepted the traditional boundaries, but the Assembly refused to acquiesce in their decision and reversed the ruling, thereby confirming the sitting member in his seat.[51] Why was the decision of the select committee reversed? Because the sitting member was a kinsman of John R. Partelow and John R. Partelow was the dominating political personality in that Assembly.

On his entrance into the Assembly, Partelow had secured the chairmanship of the Committee on Public Accounts. This committee controlled the allocation of public funds for local improvements and Partelow skilfully exploited his power as committee chairman. Consequently, during his tenure as chairman from 1828 to 1850 he was always able to muster a sizeable following in the Assembly. Of the nine controverted elections in which he took sides during this period he lost but two. His first defeat came at the hands of Charles Simonds, another political personality, and his second defeat at the hands of Lemuel A. Wilmot.[52] The second defeat marked the commencement of Partelow's political eclipse for it was shortly to be followed by the termination of his chairmanship of the Committee on Public Accounts.

Against what procedural background did these political personalities exercise their influence on the determination of controverted elections? From 1786 to 1828 when disputed elections were resolved before the whole Assembly, these individuals were able to influence the results from the floor of the House; after 1828 when the Grenville system of select committees was adopted, these individuals were usually appointed to the committees as nominees of one of the contending parties.

The resolution of controverted elections before the Assembly proper was instituted in the first session of the first Assembly. The election for the city and county of St. John, having precipitated a riot, was protested and the Executive Council's refusal to interfere in a sphere it considered rightly to belong to the Assembly forced the latter body to evolve a method for determining such protests.[53] The Assembly decided that all petitions must be tabled within fourteen days of the commencement of the session, that the evidence would be presented to the House in Committee of the Whole by counsel and witnesses questioned at the Bar, that no votes would be reviewed unless the petitioners had demanded their scrutiny by the sheriff, and that the validity of the return would be determined by a vote of the Assembly, the interested parties abstaining.[54] These rules, amplified as experience dictated, served as the basis of the Assembly's conduct for the following forty years.

The determination of controverted elections by the Committee of the Whole was time-consuming. In 1820 a disputed return for the county of Sunbury consumed seventeen days, over one-half of the session;[55] so when in 1828 the Assembly was faced with the prospect of seven disputed elections, the House decided to change the procedure. A select committee appointed to investigate the matter reported in favour of select committees, as employed by the House of Commons. For its own controverted elections the Assembly adopted this procedure by resolution and future disputed elections established the procedure by law.[56]

The procedure prescribed by the new legislation required the Clerk of the Assembly to draw by lot the names of eleven members from a House whose quorum for this purpose was set at twenty. From the list of members selected by lot, the counsel for the contending parties had alternatively to strike off a name until the list was reduced to five; these five members together with a nominee appointed by each of the contending parties were to form the controverted election committee with power to summon witnesses and records, take evidence on oath, and determine by majority vote the disputed election. To ensure the sincerity of each petition, the petitioner was required to enter into a surety of £200 to cover the expenses of his witnesses and to pay the expenses incurred by the sitting member if the petition was subsequently abandoned or was found to be frivolous. To ensure adequate time for investigation and for the business of the session, the controverted election committees were allowed to adjourn their proceedings over prorogation and to resume them with the next session.

New Brunswick had already employed the latter procedure on two occasions, and if these occasions were to serve as precedents they did not augur well for the innovation, for the two controverted election cases had never been resumed.[57] The augury proved all too correct for, of the numerous controverted elections which were adjourned over prorogation, 60 per cent were never brought to a conclusion. Few petitioners, for instance, had the financial resources or the pertinacity revealed by the petitioners in the Charlotte County and Carleton County cases of 1851 and 1854 respectively who had to endure the vexatious deliberations of controverted election committees over three sessions before their cases were brought to a conclusion.

The hazards which beset the path of any candidate who wished to correct injuries that he had suffered through faulty exercise of the franchise were for most candidates insurmountable barriers. The public and the politicians knew that many of these hazards were contrived but from long usage they had become reconciled to their continuance. The puritanism which emerged in the decade of the 1850's and was associated with the temperance movement showed signs for a time of challenging this state of mind. For instance a petitioner against a return for Albert County took his complaint against the political interference of the sheriff to the courts after a controverted election committee had dismissed his petition and had the court award him damages against the sheriff to the amount of £125.[58] Although the legislation under which a conviction was secured had been on the statute books since 1791, this occasion was the first on which it had been invoked. That the statute had been successfully invoked at a jury trial was an indication of the new temper abroad.

In the same General Assembly, adherents of the new puritanism, exasperated at the prolonged deliberations of the controverted election committees on the Westmorland County and Charlotte County elections (two and three sessions respectively), sought to terminate the determination of disputed elections by the Assembly or by its select committees. Gray, an Executive Councillor and the petitioner's nominee on the Westmorland committee, was led to introduce a bill to facilitate the trial of controverted elections and reduce their partisan component.[59] The bill would have taken the controverted elections outside the Assembly and have placed them in the hands of a commission of five barristers appointed for life by the Lieutenant Governor.[60] The bill was sidetracked in an unsympathetic House and although the Lieutenant Governor, Sir Edmund Head, felt that the circumstances surrounding the determination of disputed elections were so deplorable that he brought the subject to the attention of the House at its next session, the Assembly remained unsympathetic and buried the issue in a general discussion of the election law, the merits of the ballot, and the voters' register.[61] In consequence the determination of controverted elections remained with the Assembly until after Confederation, but in fairness to New Brunswick, it may be said that it was almost unique in having contemplated the removal of controverted elections from the House of Assembly.

The role of the sheriffs in New Brunswick politics seems to have approximated the Nova Scotia pattern, where they were intermittently partisan, rather than that of Prince Edward Island, where they were uniformly partisan.[62] This degree of political activity among New Brunswick sheriffs was nevertheless surprising considering the absence of organized political parties. The reason for their political activity appears to stem from two factors, the existence of a ruling class in New Brunswick and the political nature of the tasks assigned the sheriffs at elections. Throughout the colonial period the Executive Council of New Brunswick was dominated by the loyalists and their conservative traditions. From their number all official appointments were drawn and there existed a unity of social and political outlook within the administration seldom equalled in the other English-speaking colonies. From the lowest to the highest office holder they uniformly interpreted all criticism and all agitation for change as a manifestation of democracy, the progenitor of republicanism. The sheriffs drawn from this class and background were instinctively hostile to political radicalism and therefore repeatedly took it upon themselves to interfere in the elections to destroy the advocates of democracy.[63] The sheriffs, however, did not look upon their conduct as partisan, for they conceived it to be their duty to guard British institutions and traditions against democratic radicalism.

In New Brunswick the sheriffs possessed discretionary power to concede or refuse a scrutiny and were empowered, as a result of their findings, to modify the election return. This practice was contrary to that allowed in Nova Scotia and Prince Edward Island where the sheriffs had to grant scrutinies on request and the Assembly, except for short intervals, was alone empowered to draw conclusions from the evidence accumulated at a scrutiny.[64] There was considerable virtue in the New Brunswick practice for it allowed a disputed election to be decided in the light of the evidence produced at the scrutiny and avoided the needless repetition of evidence and argument which accompanied any appeal to the Assembly. The labour and expense spared the candidates and the Assembly may be deduced from the general election of 1854 when sixteen elections were scrutinized but only seven were appealed to the Assembly. Useful as this discretionary power undoubtedly was, it nevertheless placed the sheriffs under continuous political pressure to accommodate this or that candidate. Although the scrutiny was finally abandoned on the introduction of the voters' register and the ballot in 1855, the discretionary power of the sheriffs was not ended, for they were entrusted with the power to destroy all damaged ballots immediately and the remaining ballots after the count had been completed.[65] The imposition of these discretionary as well as administrative functions on the New Brunswick sheriffs inevitably jeopardized the political neutrality of their office and thereby imperilled the franchise.

IV

The franchise of the colony of British Columbia was not distressed by controverted elections. As the elective and non-elective members of the Legislative Council owed their places to appointment by the Governor, the validity of their tenure was not open to dispute. The elections, attendant on the popular selection of the elective members, were properly nominations, a colonial example of the modern American primary. The populace were inclined, however, to ignore the legal status of these popular nominations and to treat them as real parliamentary elections. New Westminster presents us with the spectacle of a defeated candidate demanding and securing a scrutiny.[66] As the scrutiny confirmed the initial standing, we shall never know

G*

what attitude the Governor would have taken to the intrusion of parliamentary electoral procedure into these popular nominations.

It was only during the ten-year independent existence of the Legislative Assembly of Vancouver Island that controverted elections could and did arise. During this period twelve election returns were challenged. Of these challenges three were not proceeded with because the required sureties were not lodged, one was withdrawn, and eight were resolved. The result was decisions sustaining five and voiding three returns.

The Vancouver Island Assembly adopted the British procedure for determining controverted elections.[67] The then current British practice, a modified version of the Grenville Act, had been established in 1848; it required the Speaker every session to nominate six members to form a General Committee on Elections which scrutinized the legitimacy of all election petitions, saw to the deposit of the required sureties, and advised the House if the petition warranted investigation and should therefore be referred to a select committee.[68] If such advice was tendered, the House, following the procedure of the Grenville Act, chose a select committee by lot to determine the disputed election. The Vancouver Island Assembly, while anxious to follow the procedure of the House of Commons, found its sparsity of members a handicap. The difficulty was especially acute in the first Assembly. A House of seven members was faced with three disputed returns which eliminated three members, and a fourth and fifth member were eliminated since one was a petitioner and the other was the Speaker.[69] The Assembly found itself incapable of staffing a controverted election committee until one petitioner withdrew his petition and allowed the Speaker to appoint a three-member election committee to resolve the remaining controverted elections.

The difficulty was overcome following the next general election when the membership of the Assembly was virtually doubled. With the larger resources the practice of the House of Commons was more closely followed. The Speaker appointed a five-member General Committee on Elections to review each election petition and on their satisfactory report a select election committee of five was chosen by ballot to determine each disputed return.[70]

The select committees appear to have determined the disputed elections in a judicious manner. Their failure to subvert the franchise may in large measure be attributed to the absence of political parties and of responsible government. There is evidence that the Vancouver Island Assembly would not have been adverse to the subversion of the franchise if party loyalties or crucial issues had been present. Amor de Cosmos, intent on securing the passage of resolutions in favour of legislative union with British Columbia, attempted to eliminate his opposition by charging three members with having forfeited their seats through the acceptance of government contracts and a government appointment.[71] The charges were not sustained but the manoeuvre sufficiently disorganized the opposition to union that De Cosmos secured the approval of the Vancouver Island Assembly to its own liquidation. The incident serves to suggest that controverted elections in similar circumstances would have been exploited by artful politicians.

CHAPTER FIFTEEN

CONTROVERTED ELECTIONS: THE CANADAS

I

IN THE ADDRESS TO THE CROWN based on that compendium of grievances, the ninety-two resolutions, the Legislative Assembly of Lower Canada charged the returning officers with partiality and corruption at elections.[1] Bereft of objectivity the Assembly could see the shortcomings of the administration and of the administration's servants, but it was never able to perceive that its own failure to resolve controverted elections was an equally important contribution to the corruption at elections. It never considered that the condoning of wrongs might be as productive of evil as acts of commission.

The Assembly's accusation that the returning officers were agents of the administration entrusted with the manipulation of elections for the administration's advantage is not borne out by facts. It is not to be understood that the returning officers were always impartial, but their partiality was seriously limited by the lack of a real contest in most ridings. In most counties the elections went by default to the Papineau party, and where contests did develop the partiality of the returning officers was influenced more by personal factors than by the administration. For example, in the 1834 general election a stiff fight developed in Montreal West Ward between the French party, whose candidates were Papineau and Nelson, and the English-Irish party, whose candidates were Walker and Donnellan. After the French party had seized control of the hustings and had put their candidates at the head of the poll, it was agreed that to prevent further disorder the returning officer, Dr. Lusignan, should alternatively receive the votes of an equal number of electors from each party until the votes of one party were exhausted. After seventeen days' polling the supporters of Papineau and Nelson showed signs of exhaustion and it became evident that should the poll remain open Walker and Donnellan would be returned. But on the eighteenth day when Walker and Donnellan's supporters arrived to continue the polling, they found that the returning officer, on the pretext of apprehension for his personal safety and without coming to the hustings, had terminated the election and returned Papineau and Nelson.[2]

The above case illustrates the prejudice of the returning officer, but it does not justify the charge that the returning officers were the instruments of the administration. Although they were appointed by the Governor General, the Assembly never challenged or removed this power although it had the right to do so. The Constitutional Act had given this responsibility to the Governor General for a period of two years; the Assembly had continued to vest the power in the Governor General by temporary enactments until 1807 when it permanently bestowed the responsibility on him.[3] The Assembly in fact turned down a bill put forward by the Legislative Council in 1793 which would have taken the appointment of the returning officers out of the hands of the Governor General and placed it in the hands of the electorate.[4]

If the partiality of the returning officers was not inspired by the administration, it certainly was not discouraged by the attitude of the Assembly towards their misdemeanours. On the two occasions when the Assembly did take steps to discipline the returning officers, it reprimanded them for being too conscientious rather than too partial. For instance, in 1816 the Assembly took the returning officer for Bedford County into custody because he had closed the poll and made no return (thereby necessitating a new election) when a candidate complained that he had not notified all localities of the election.[5]

While the Assembly could find time to reprimand two returning officers who had taken their responsibilities too seriously, it could never find time to reprimand returning officers who sought to influence the outcome of an election. In the election for Montreal West Ward, the Assembly refused even to investigate the charges. This refusal to resolve controverted elections was characteristic of the Lower Canada Assembly; of the petitions protesting elections which were submitted to the Assembly, a scant 28 per cent were ultimately investigated and determined, 8 per cent were dismissed or withdrawn, and 64 per cent were never concluded. Since one-quarter of the petitions that were determined found in favour of the sitting member, it may be said that a candidate petitioning against a corrupt election had but a slight chance of securing the disallowance of a return made by a returning officer. The impartiality of the returning officers was therefore of fundamental importance.

The tradition that members returned at an election retained their seats, regardless of the means they employed to secure their return, was established early in the history of the elective institutions of Lower Canada. The foundations of the tradition were laid in the first Assembly. Petitions challenging six returns were presented to this Assembly, but that body failed to investigate any. Four of the petitions were against the return of English candidates for the ridings of Quebec County, Quebec Upper Town, Quebec Lower Town, and Leinster County; the fifth petition was put forward by the defeated English candidate in Warwick County against his French opponent, the seignior of Lavaltrie, on the grounds the latter was an alien, having been absent in France at the time of the signing of the Treaty of Paris.[6] The election for Quebec County had ended at Charlesbourg in a riot when Lynd had jammed the poll with sailors and ne'er-do-wells, Grant had carried Quebec Upper Town through the lavish provision of houses of entertainment, and Young had carried Quebec Lower Town by similar largesse.[7] Yet the Assembly investigated none of these petitions; they were either tabled or dismissed on the pretext of the insufficiency of the charges, although they had been signed by 2,000 citizens and had in some cases been authenticated by the signature of priests.[8]

The decision of the Assembly appears to have been the result of a saw-off between the English and French members; the English would not press their petition against de Lavaltrie if the French dropped their petitions against the English members.[9] Again in 1797 Young after some difficulty got the House to discharge the petition to void the election of two English members for Buckinghamshire and in 1805 his friends managed to prevent the House considering a petition against his own election for Quebec Lower Town.[10] In consequence of the political maneouvring, no election petition was ever investigated by the Assembly during its first fifteen years. During this formative period a tradition of disregard for mutilations of the franchise committed at the elections was firmly established.

The struggle to dismiss the petition against Young's election in 1805 had brought to the Assembly's attention the total absence of legislation to regulate the trial of controverted elections. As a result, in 1808 an act was passed establishing a procedure for such trials.[11] If the Assembly had on the passage of the act intended to reverse the practice of previous years, it did not have the opportunity to do so. The next two assemblies were dissolved in such rapid succession that no controverted elections could be determined. It was not until the threat of an American invasion and the moderating influence of Governor General Prevost had reduced racial wrangling in the Assembly that the House gave some encouraging signs that it meant to retrieve the elections from the corruption and excess into which they had fallen. In 1815 the Assembly investigated and set aside the election for Leinster, which had shown that the intimidation, bribery, and open houses that had featured the electoral practices of the English candidates in Quebec had now been copied by their French-speaking compatriots.[12] In 1818 the Assembly set aside a by-election for Quebec County and in 1821 an election for Bedford.[13] The new attitude of the Assembly was also reflected in the passage of legislation which was designed to be more effective in preventing bribery and corruption and which enhanced the powers of the returning officers.[14] The returning officers were granted the powers of a magistrate, were given the authority to call upon the police and militia for assistance in the maintenance of order at the hustings, and were empowered to summarily commit to gaol any disturber of the peace.

With the advent of Dalhousie as Governor General, the relations between the two races again deteriorated and what appeared to have been a genuine move on the part of the Assembly to judiciously handle controverted elections came to an end. For the remaining years of its life the Assembly of Lower Canada dealt with controverted elections in an erratic manner. Justice was diverted or perverted by partisan animosity or partisan friendship, each strengthened by the all-pervasive malevolence of racial ill will. Cases were set aside on legal technicalities as in the Richelieu County election in 1825 when the uncertainty as to the boundary between Richelieu County and Buckinghamshire allowed the location of the property posted as surety by the petitioners to be challenged;[15] they were prolonged until the petitioners wearied as in the Northumberland case in 1825–26, or until the House was dissolved as in the Three Rivers case in 1827. While undoubtedly some of this neglect was due to the preoccupation of the Assembly with other inflammable political issues, much of the neglect was due to design.

This inability or unwillingness to determine controverted elections existed in an Assembly which had provided in some respects better legal machinery to handle election cases than had any other of the colonial legislatures. By the first controverted election act, the Assembly was empowered to appoint three commissioners to proceed to the locale of a controverted election and examine witnesses.[16] The commission was initially instituted to overcome the expense to petitioners attendant on bringing witnesses to Quebec to appear before the Bar of the House, but the Assembly realized, following the Quebec County election case of 1817 when the petitioner threatened to call 189 witnesses, that the examination of all witnesses by commission could relieve it of much tedium. As a result legislation was passed in 1818 authorizing the Assembly to nominate commissions to gather evidence in all controverted election cases.[17]

The institution of commissions to gather evidence was not an unqualified success. It was difficult to find suitable men willing to serve as commissioners. As the Assembly made a point of drawing at least one member of each commission from the Bar, the work of investigation was often stalled by the enforced absence of a commissioner during the terms of court as in the Montreal East Ward election case of 1832–34. The latter difficulty meant the evidence was seldom presented by the commissioners in the same session in which the election was protested. Delay was also encouraged by the sheer convenience of the commission which led the contending parties to examine multitudes of witnesses to the needless duplication of evidence.[18] Furthermore as the Assembly still had to determine the election, the commission did not preclude prolonged debate or renewal of evidence before the Assembly. In 1815 the Assembly to relieve itself and speed the consideration of controverted elections began the practice of referring disputed returns to *ad hoc* select committees of five members. For a time the decisions of the select committees were ratified by the House, but with the deterioration of political relations under Dalhousie the Assembly reasserted its power over elections and the select committees were relegated to minor matters such as checking the authenticity of signatures and the validity of the sureties. The select committees ultimately disappeared when these technical matters were handed over to the standing committee on privileges which, enlarged to eleven members in 1831, became known as the standing committee on privileges and elections.

A decade and a half after the determination of controverted elections had reverted to the Assembly, that body became both fatigued and exasperated with the amount of time lost in the futile discussion of election cases. A three-session wrangle over a Bonaventure election case, which ended only in the petition's dismissal, and a two-session wrangle over a Montreal East election, which was only brought to an end by the dissolution of the House, convinced the members that the use of the full House in the resolution of disputed elections should be abandoned. The result was the statutory adoption of a version of the Grenville system of select committees which, modified by Papineau's refusal to render the findings of the select committee final, did not preclude the Assembly from opening a full hearing of any disputed election either before or after its reference to a select committee.[19]

While it is doubtful if this change in procedure would have facilitated the decision of controverted elections, no opportunity was given to try the new procedure for the act was disallowed.[20] It had authorized the Assembly to sustain the investigations of controverted election committees beyond prorogation, and the Colonial Secretary saw dangerous implications in this power. It would have enabled

the Assembly to give a kind of permanency to their own sittings and so to render the royal prerogative of prorogation ineffectual to arrest the progress of agitation. Nothing would be more easy than to keep on foot during every recess one or more election committees. The members of those bodies would never be at a loss to use the large and indefinite powers which belong to them, for purposes the most remote from their professed and legitimate object. Such committees might be made the rallying point and the shelter for all persons desirous to excite popular discontent.[21]

Considering the obstreperous nature of the Lower Canada Assembly, the Colonial Office was probably wise in not wishing to imperil the power of the Crown to close a rebellious session by prorogation. But as a result of this disallowance the determination of controverted elections remained with the Assembly proper until that body's suspension following the rebellion of 1837.

The tradition of electoral depravity which had grown up in Lower Canada was strengthened by several other factors besides the failure to properly determine controverted elections. For instance, the election law had never set any limit to the days of polling, which were limited only by the date set for the return of the writs, or upon the common agreement of the candidates, or the failure of any elector to appear to vote for a period of one hour.[22] As a result elections were in many cases unduly prolonged; for example, the election for Missisquoi County in 1834 lasted eighteen days, and that for Montreal West Ward in 1832 lasted twenty-four. The prolonged excitement encouraged corruption and excesses, and undoubtedly led to the riot which closed the latter election, where it became necessary to call out the soldiery who quelled the riot at the cost of the lives of three civilians, and thereby created the first martyrs to inspire the extremists of the Papineau party.[23]

A final factor in establishing this tradition was the corrupt means which were used on several occasions by the Law Officers to secure their own election. Several glaring incidents occurred during the governorships of Craig and Dalhousie that went far to confirm in the minds of the French Canadians the growing belief that elections were contests to be won without regard to means. In the general election of 1809 the tax collector for the seigniory of Laprairie de la Magdelaine, a part of the Jesuit Estates then held by the Crown, used his influence to have the occupants vote for Stephen Sewell, the Solicitor General; the name of Sir John Johnson was invoked to order the Iroquois to vote and the votes of the Indians, aliens, and residents of an adjacent county were recorded for Sewell, the returning officer neglecting to record their qualifications in order to prevent a scrutiny of these votes. All this was accompanied by bribery, houses of entertainment, and a bailiff armed with an iron ramrod posted at the door of the poll to intimidate and impede voters opposed to the Solicitor General.[24] In 1827 James Stuart, the Attorney General, was defeated in an election for the borough of William Henry by Wolfred Nelson, a Papineau lieutenant, although the greatest exertions were made to secure his election. Dalhousie took up residence in the borough and used his prestige and that of his aides to influence the electors in Stuart's favour; Stuart broadcast threats of prosecution and the pillory for perjury against Nelson's electors but was himself not above seizing the hand of an elector and holding it on the Bible when that elector turned reluctant on Nelson's challenging his right to vote.[25] The Assembly took up Stuart's behaviour in the Select Committee of Grievances and Stuart was in consequence required to explain his conduct to the Colonial Secretary. Subsequently the Colonial Secretary felt obliged to remove Stuart from the office of Attorney General.[26]

Such corrupt and coercive tactics used by the Law Officers were not the only official interference with the freedom and purity of elections. Previous to the general election of 1827 Dalhousie dismissed all the officers of the militia who were opposed to the administration; new commissions of the peace were issued from which the names of magistrates who were the administration's political opponents were dropped;[27] and diatribes appeared in the Government press against the interference of the Roman Catholic clergy in the elections although in reality they were being assailed because they had not interfered on the side of the administration.[28] The practice of the officers of the garrisons at Quebec, Montreal, and William Henry voting for the administration's candidates, the practice of employees of the civil departments and of the occupants of Crown seigniories being dragooned to vote for the same candidates, created an attitude in the public mind fatal to the purity of elections and subversive of the franchise.[29] When it is considered that these breaches of public morality were committed by English-speaking administrators and Law Officers, and when it is recalled that the distribution of largesse at elections and the Assembly's avoidance of the investigation of controverted elections were initiated by English-speaking members, a large part of the responsibility for the corruption of public morality in Lower Canada must rest with them. The English officials and electors of Lower Canada had a duty to introduce an alien people to the best traditions of representative government; instead they showed the French Canadian people that the franchise was merchandise to be bought and sold, that controverted election laws were to be circumvented, that electoral honesty meant political failure and electoral dishonesty success, public office, and power. In the formative years of Lower Canada's public life a tradition of political and electoral immorality was laid that has not yet been eradicated.

II

The Upper Canada experience with controverted elections is one of contrast with Lower Canada. Where 64 per cent of the Lower Canada petitions were never determined by its Assembly, 87 per cent of the Upper Canada petitions that complied with the rules of submission were determined.[30] Where the odds were heavily in favour of the sitting member in a Lower Canada controverted election, the reverse was true in Upper Canada. In the latter colony 70 per cent of the petitions were sustained, that is to say, the return in dispute was voided or the petitioner was awarded the election. The lack of deep racial and party divisions in Upper Canada had much to do with the more peaceful elections and the greater zeal of the Assembly in resolving disputed returns. Indeed it was not until 1821, with the eighth General Assembly and the development of definite party lines under the impact of the alien controversy, that disputed returns became numerous. To the less rancorous racial and political divisions of Upper Canada cannot be attributed the entire divergence in the attitude of the two assemblies to controverted elections; allowance must be made for the tradition of public morality that the peoples of Upper Canada brought to their political life. They were not the political novices that formed the electorate of Lower Canada.

Certainly the superior record of the Upper Canada Assembly cannot be attributed to the procedure employed to determine controverted elections for it did not materially differ from that of Nova Scotia or Lower Canada. Until 1824 the Assembly determined disputed elections in Committee of the Whole or in a formal session after having heard counsel and witnesses for the contending parties at the Bar of the House; after 1824 the Grenville system of select committees was employed except for a brief reversion to formal sittings of the House between 1831 and 1833 when the Assembly neglected to renew the temporary legislation on which the Grenville procedure rested.[31] As in Lower Canada the Assembly was empowered to appoint commissions of three to gather evidence at the scene of disputed elections for the benefit of the select committees trying such returns. The Assembly adopted this convenient instrument following difficulties which it experienced in maintaining at York the witnesses for a disputed election for Durham County in 1825.[32] Commissions were employed much less frequently than in Lower Canada because the Assembly of Upper Canada disliked passing the questioning of witnesses over to an outside body, and it never employed them as a device to prolong unduly the determination of a controverted election as its Lower Canadian counterpart was prone to do. As a consequence the Assembly considered the use of commissions in five cases only and employed them in two, both involving disputed elections for the town of Brockville.[33]

Since the procedure governing the determination of controverted elections in Upper Canada was not fundamentally different from that in Nova Scotia and Lower Canada, the impressive record of that colony as respects controverted elections must be attributed to the spirit in which the procedure was employed. The higher public morality attributed to Upper Canada was due less to any unique endowment of virtue Upper Canadians might have possessed than to the fact that for the first several decades their Assembly was able to resolve disputed elections in a legislature devoid of partisan and factional rancour. Their population possessed an initial unity of outlook and interest which the populace of Nova Scotia did not. Nova Scotia's political traditions were laid following the American Revolutionary War when bitterness and jealousy between the pre- and post-revolutionary settlers corroded her political morality, a contamination from which the exercise of her franchise and the determination of her controverted elections were not spared. When political parties emerged in Upper Canada after the general election of 1820, a tradition of political conduct was in existence which the new partisanship was not able to destroy.

In the face of the above assertion, the accusation of partisanship laid against the Assembly by William Lyon Mackenzie and his biographer[34] concerning the controverted election for the second riding of York has to be examined. Mackenzie had been defeated by his Tory opponent in the riding in the general election of 1836 and he had petitioned against the return. The House on January 4, 1837, had discharged his petition because he had not entered into the required surety within the fourteen-day period specified by law. The petition, which had been tabled in the Assembly on December 20, had been read to the House on December 22, and Mackenzie claimed that, as it had been the practice to calculate the fourteen days from the day on which the petition was read to the House, the period should not have elapsed until January 5. As the statute stated the days should be calculated from the date of presentation of the petition to the House, there was ground for claiming the period could be dated either from the time of tabling or from the time of reading and both sides were able to claim the sanction of the law. Mackenzie, as was his habit, unceasingly and unsparingly condemned the Assembly and its Tory majority for the discharge of his petition, but there is evidence to indicate that the Assembly had not been ungenerous to him.

There was a rule of the Assembly, adopted in a previous Parliament at the instigation of Mackenzie himself, which declared no election petition was to be entertained by the House unless it had been presented within the first fourteen days of the session.[35] As he had been ill, Mackenzie had not been able to table his petition within the time specified, but he had requested and the Assembly had granted him an extension of time to December 20, a full six weeks after the commencement of the session. If Mackenzie could not lodge his security within a further two weeks, the Assembly can hardly be accused of partisanship, especially as Mackenzie had found time to squander his energy in lining up 172 witnesses. The incident is less a reflection on the morality of the Assembly than on Mackenzie's lack of balance. The Assembly, having waived the time limit on presentation, might nevertheless have been better advised to have followed precedent and dated the fortnight from the day the petition was read to the House.

If the Assembly's handling of controverted elections was more just than that of other British North American assemblies, it is not implied that Upper Canadian elections were paragons of purity. Intimidation, provision of entertainment, and illegal voting did occur, but they never reached the intensity to require the Assembly to pass laws to regulate election procedure. Upper Canada is peculiar in this respect, for in no colony was the election procedure less formalized. It was not until 1808 that a statutory time limit was placed on elections.[36] The hours of polling were never defined and as a consequence two controverted elections occurred in which the polls had not closed until midnight.[37] It was not until 1824, in order to prevent voting on fraudulent conveyances, that electors were required to possess their deeds registered three months previous to the election, or to have been in actual possession or receipt of the rents and profits for twelve months.[38] The form of the poll book and the fees of the returning officers and poll clerks were not formalized until 1833.[39] Although Mackenzie tried to end this informality by his "Election Law Amendment Bill of 1836," the bill failed to clear the Legislative Council and the life of the Parliament of Upper Canada closed without the electoral procedure and the nature of corrupt practices being adequately defined by statute.[40]

The problems of Executive interference in elections arose in Upper Canada as elsewhere, but it never reached serious proportions until the last general election in 1836. Although Simcoe said his residence at Kingston in 1792 enabled Attorney General White to be elected for Leeds-Frontenac, and in 1799 the Administrator, anxious to secure legal talent in the Assembly, offered to pay White's expenses if he would stand for election in Addington-Ontario, the main influence of the Executive in elections had until 1836 been through the number of office holders (judges, registrars, sheriffs, custom officers) who sought and won election on their own merits.[41] The returning officers do not appear to have been used to secure the election of Government candidates, for although their appointment rested with the Lieutenant Governor, the Assembly never lost confidence in the Executive's impartiality, as was illustrated by its continual renewal of the statute conferring this power on the Lieutenant Governor.[42]

On the occasion of the general election of 1836 there is no doubt that the Lieutenant Governor of Upper Canada, Sir Francis Bond Head, threw the weight of his office and administration against the Reform party. Bond Head pursued the path Craig and Dalhousie had plotted in Lower Canada and he achieved a success denied them. Bond Head, personally, took it upon himself to destroy public confidence in the Reform party. By tours, speeches, and the replies to seventy-two addresses he sought to create in the public mind the belief that the Reform party was a Toronto and an American party whose secret objective was to seduce Upper Canada from allegiance to the Crown.[43] After having built up in the public mind doubts as to the loyalty and objectives of the Reformers, he dissolved the General Assembly and in the ensuing general election drew from the loyal heart of Upper Canada a majority for the Tories.

Bond Head had not confined his interference in the partisan politics of Upper Canada to a verbal onslaught on the Reformers. He had patent deeds to the number of 1478 issued to the occupants of Crown lands between the prorogation of the Assembly on April 20, 1836, and the close of the elections on July 2. Since property derived from the Crown was exempt from the statute requiring that titles to property be registered three months before the owner could vote, the possessors of these patent deeds were enfranchised the moment the deeds came into their possession. Bond Head subsequently denied that these patent deeds had been issued with his connivance, claiming that "from the date of my arrival in this province to the present hour, in no one instance have I ever withheld from any individual my signature to that patent or title to his land, which bearing the signature of the Attorney General, has thus been officially declared to me to be his due; and on the other hand, in no one instance have I ever affixed my signature to a patent which did not carry on its face that mark of authenticity."[44] Bond Head's claim was probably true but he did not state or explain why the Attorney General had sent forward for his signature more patent deeds in a ten-week period than had ever been issued in any year prior to 1835.[45]

The inspiration for this outpouring of patent deeds may not have been conceived personally by the Lieutenant Governor, but it was more than mere coincidence that

a short time previous to the election for the County of Simcoe, I [the Clerk of the Crown in Chancery] selected from the shelves of the Secretary's office, every patent for land, situate in that county ... some of them had been completed ten or fifteen years before but not called for by the grantees ... and took upon myself the responsibility of transmitting them to the place where the election was appointed to be held, to be issued to the respective grantees by a Mr. Ritchie, a resident Government Agent and Surveyor.[46]

Similarly Jessop, the agent for the Commissioner of Crown Lands at the Perth settlement, was surprised to receive 77 title deeds for the emigrants who had settled in the Bathurst District in 1823-25. As these title deeds had come unsolicited on Jessop's part, the motivation of the Commissioner of Crown Lands must remain suspect, especially as the Commissioner had neglected to issue the title deeds three years previously when Jessop had informed his office that these settlers had completed their settlement duties.[47] In any event a clerk in the Crown Lands Office, fearful that Jessop might not grasp the significance of this outpouring of title deeds, accompanied the deeds with a suggestion that Jessop distribute them with an eye to the re-election of Captain Lewis, a supporter of the Tory party. Likewise in the village of Port Credit a sudden boom in the sale of village lots, a quick payment of the selling price, and a quick issue of the patent deeds aroused legitimate suspicion of the administration's motives when the unanimous opposition of the new owners to the candidature of William Lyon Mackenzie became evident.

Bond Head was to declare that in no case had he "ever stopped for a moment to consider what might be the political opinion of him whose name inscribed upon a parchment was demanding from me a right which I am proud to feel I am not entitled to withhold; for my station of Lieutenant Governor would be despicable indeed if my powers enabled me to deprive a British subject of his rights."[48] Bond Head's claim was again probably true but the officers of his administration felt inspired to deliver only those patent deeds whose recipients would vote for the Tory party. Jessop, in the Perth settlement, finding the Irish Roman Catholic settlers to be so anti-England as to be anti-Government, delivered only 27 patent deeds and returned the others to the Crown Land Office to the fury of the Reform candidates.[49] In Simcoe the agent for the Commissioner of Crown Lands, also a man of discriminating taste, was able to deliver only 30 patents out of the several hundreds sent him.

There is no reason to doubt the charge levelled at Bond Head that his administration issued the patent deeds with the object of influencing the election. There were sufficient deeds issued to have changed the results in six ridings returning a total of ten members.[50] But the results were unchanged from the previous election in all ridings save two, the Tory party gaining a seat from the Reformers in Simcoe and in Hastings, while in Middlesex the issuance of title deeds may have enabled the Tories to capture the representation for the county town when the county itself continued to return two supporters of the Reform party. The destruction of the Reform majority in the Assembly cannot therefore be attributed to the distribution of patent deeds but their distribution was part and parcel of that wider campaign of vituperation and misrepresentation launched by Bond Head to destroy the political following of the Reformers.[51] The electorate of Upper Canada, which until 1836 had been spared the worst electoral abuses that had characterized the exercise of the suffrage in the other colonies, experienced during its last election as widespread and as conscientious an attempt to subvert the franchise as any colonial administration had up to that moment engaged in.

III

Large in number and seldom settled in a judicious manner, controverted elections in the Province of Canada played as important a part in the outcome of the elections as did the exercise of the franchise itself. After each general election never less than 10 per cent of the returns were disputed and following the general election of 1857–58 the figure rose to 27 per cent. The large number of returns disputed after the latter election may be explained in part by the intense partisanship of the campaign, for George Brown and Antoine Dorion were at the zenith of their popularity and had led their parties in a bitter contest against the Conservatives under Macdonald and Cartier. But the record of the Canadian Assembly in settling controverted elections was so defective that party workers were encouraged to try to win elections by foul means when they could not win them by fair means.

A tradition had been established in Lower Canada that as long as a member was returned at an election, regardless of how that return was secured, he would be certain to retain his seat against all proceedings. This tradition was retained in the United Legislature as regards Canada East. The Act of Union had stated that all laws which at the time of its passage were in force in Upper Canada, and all laws which at the time of the passage of the act suspending the Lower Canada Legislature were in force in that province relating to the trial of controverted elections, were to be applied to the election of members to serve in the United Legislature for the respective parts of the Province of Canada for which such laws had been originally passed. It was a moot question as to what laws were in force in Lower Canada at the time of the suspension of its Legislature. The controverted election procedure as set forth in 48 Geo. III, c. 21 (1808), had been amended and continued by subsequent enactments "until the first day of May one thousand eight hundred and thirty-six, and thence until the end of the then next session of the Provincial Legislature and no longer."[52] The Legislature had met in two brief sessions subsequent to May 1, 1836, although it has passed no legislation, and the consensus was that legislation governing controverted elections had expired by February 10, 1838, the day on which the Imperial Act, suspending the constitution, had passed.[53]

It was against this background that petitions protesting nine returns for Canada East were lodged following the first general election. The racial tension and the determination of the English to carry the elections in the district of Montreal had resulted in riots in six counties with deaths in three, while in a seventh county a riot had only been forestalled by the withdrawal of the French candidate. None of the petitioners against the Montreal elections had conformed to the procedure set forth by the defunct legislation, and the Assembly had to decide what attitude to take.

In a tumultuous debate some members contended that the Lower Canada law had not expired because there had been no session of Parliament after May 1, 1836, the date the controverted election act was scheduled to expire. Though the Legislature had met twice and been twice prorogued, it was contended that as no bill had passed the two Houses of the Legislature and received the royal assent there had been no session, although there might have been a convention of Parliament. Other members contended that whenever there had been a prorogation, there had been a session. In the words of the Montreal *Gazette* of July 3, 1841:

The naked question before the House was, has the law regulating contested elections in Lower Canada expired, or not? But the ulterior consequences of their discussions, is what the members seem to have uppermost in their minds, and as they are for or against members sitting for counties where the election is disputed, so, in the same light, they naturally view the question. The decision of the House will be an important one, because all the petitions except one (Mr. Gugy against the return of the member for St. Maurice) have not complied with the terms of the statute in question by giving security, on the supposition that it had expired. The time has now gone by for entering the security and therefore the sitting members (if the law is still in force) remain undisturbed in their seats.

The Francophobe members were able to raise sufficient doubts about the validity of the two sessions that the Assembly ruled the controverted election law was still in effect and all petitions which had not conformed to its procedural requirements were invalid.[54] As only one petition, that against Turcotte's return for St. Maurice County, had conformed to this procedure, this petition was alone determined by the House.[55]

The decision of the Assembly confirmed the sitting members in seats secured by mobs of bullies armed with sticks, axes, shillelaghs, and stones, or, as in Beauharnois, by the conversion of a large mill into a tavern distributing liquor, and by the use of armed individuals, many wearing the uniform of volunteers in Her Majesty's service, who converted or intimidated the electors before they reached the polls.[56] The consequences of this decision outraged the sense of justice of sufficient members from Canada West that a bill cleared the Assembly which would have allowed the petitioners to resubmit their petitions in accordance with the procedure required by the law of Lower Canada. The Legislative Council, undoubtedly desiring to accommodate Sydenham, refused to give the bill second reading; the Assembly, in consequence, had to content itself with a resolution to engage the House in a public enquiry into the disputed elections at its next session.[57]

In the following sessions a select committee of enquiry was constituted but made little progress because of the turmoil of the events surrounding the defeat of the Draper ministry and the formation of the first Baldwin-Lafontaine coalition. The investigations of the committee became increasingly academic in the third session, for the sitting members for four of the disputed seats had already resigned, three to accept Government appointments. The Reformers' preoccupation with the committee's investigations and with the struggle for responsible government unfortunately prevented them giving any attention to the passage of new legislation to regulate the trial of controverted elections. When the next general election was fought, it was fought with the knowledge that no provision had been made to resolve the disputed elections that should result from the contest in Canada East.

The Draper ministry, sustained in the election by a narrow majority of six, was immediately confronted with the necessity of devising an avenue for the disposal of the petitions which would not endanger its slender hold over the Assembly. When the Reformers pressed for an investigation of the disputed returns, the Tories sought to delay a decision through a series of adjournments until they had contrived a way out of their dilemma. The irrepressible and indomitable Ogle Gowan, Grand Master of the Orange Order, finally pointed the way when he moved the discharge of a petition on the grounds that the Act of Union had required that until the provincial parliament should otherwise decree all Lower Canada controverted election petitions were to conform to the laws in force in that colony at union.[58] Dubious as the first extension of the controverted election law had been, this attempt to extend it to the second Parliament of the united province was manifestly unconstitutional; nevertheless through a unity born of desperation the Tory ranks held and the motion for discharge was carried by a slender majority of two. This decision reached in the first instance on the petition against the notorious election for Montreal City was subsequently applied to all election petitions from Canada East and marked the end of any attempt to deal with the disputed returns from that quarter. The tradition of inaction on disputed elections established by the Assembly of Lower Canada had now been continued and confirmed by the Parliament of Canada, and when the third general election came and left its deposit of election petitions those from Canada East were again discharged unresolved. The decline in the number of elections disputed in Canada East during the second, third, and fourth parliaments was not a reflection of improved electoral morality but the result of a recognition of the futility of petitioning.

The situation with respect to the determination of controverted elections originating in Canada West was much better, quantitatively at least, for the Parliament of Canada did investigate and resolve the disputed returns from that quarter. There was no doubt in the mind of the public or of the politicians that the trial of controverted elections from Canada West was governed by the Upper Canada acts of 1824 and 1827. These acts, based on the Grenville act, declared that a select committee of nine together with a nominee from the petitioner and from the sitting member were to resolve each dispute. The legislation required each select committee to be initially drawn to the number of twenty-three members from a House whose quorum for this purpose was thirty. The twenty-three members selected by ballot had to exclude all members whose return was disputed, or who were themselves petitioners, or had voted at an election now disputed, while those members over sixty years or who were serving on election committees might be excluded on request or on direction of the House. From this roster of twenty-three members, the contending parties by alternately striking off a member's name reduced the list to nine, the number that constituted the trial committee.

An inability on the part of the United Legislature to handle the above procedure imperilled for a time the resolution of controverted elections from Canada West, and the indisposition to resolve disputed returns which characterized Canada East almost did engulf the western segment of the new province. The danger arose when the Legislature found itself unable to muster sufficient personnel to operate the procedure for the selection of the election committees. That the larger membership of the new Parliament should prove unable to operate procedure which the smaller membership of the Upper Canada Assembly had been able to manage satisfactorily may seem surprising. The larger number of disputed returns and therefore the larger number of members (seventeen in all) debarred from serving on the select committees was a handicap, but the real difficulty was due to the fact that members from Canada East absented themselves from the House whenever an election committee was to be drawn. Unwilling to resolve their own controverted elections, they withdrew from the House when it became apparent that the contending parties to the disputed returns from Canada West were showing a predilection to put them on the select committees.[59] In consequence the Parliament of Canada had more disputed elections and fewer members available to resolve them than had the Upper Canada Assembly. Although the difficulty had already become apparent, it was intensified when the Legislature, desirous of more closely approximating Imperial practice and of relieving members from an excess of committee work, resolved that no member should serve on more than one controverted election at a time.[60]

The crisis involving the survival of the traditions of the Upper Canada Assembly came when an attempt was made to draw the fourth select committee. This committee, to try the disputed return of Robert Baldwin for Hastings County, failed to be constituted on four separate occasions. Should the House have remained unable to draw this committee, the committees for the remaining four disputed returns would not have been drawn. The House stood at the parting of the ways. The controverted election act of 1824 came at this point to the rescue of tradition. It required the House to adjourn from day to day until the select committee was drawn and the business of the entire session was thus brought to a standstill. The House was ultimately forced to break the stalemate by ordering a roll call of the members and the arrest of those who absented themselves.[61] By this means the Hastings election committee was drawn on the fifth attempt and the tradition was saved. This action of the House put an end to absenteeism as a device to prevent the determination of controverted elections, and following the next two general elections, although the number of disputed returns from Canada West was to continue to rise, there was no occasion on which the House was unable to draw a select committee. What difficulty there may have been was further eased by the House's reversal to former practice wherein members were allowed to serve simultaneously on more than one committee.[62]

If stalling had been overcome as a means to prevent the determination of disputed returns from Canada West, a more sinister disease began to trouble the determinations. Partisanship, of which Upper Canada election committees had been relatively free, emerged strongly in the second Parliament. There were fourteen returns disputed, involving the seats of seven Conservatives and seven Reformers. Of these disputed returns eleven were disposed of by the end of the first session with a resultant gain of one for the Draper ministry. The ministry, therefore, met the second session with a majority of eight, but with three Conservative returns still in doubt. The ministry did not fail to realize that if they retained these seats their tenure of the executive offices would be rendered secure for that Parliament, but should they lose them their tenure would be precarious.

Of the three select committees for Middlesex, Halton West, and Oxford counties, the Conservatives possessed a majority on all but the latter. When the commissions appointed by the House to gather evidence on the Middlesex and Halton West elections reported evidence unfavourable to the sitting members, the select committees refused to receive the reports on the ground the proceedings of the commissions had been invalidated by the failure of the commissioners to observe certain formal technicalities.[63] The select committees then confirmed the returns without gathering any further evidence.[64] Brazened by success the Conservatives next undertook to secure the the defeat of the petition against the Conservative member for Oxford. On this committee the Reformers possessed a majority of one, and as the committee worked its way through the disputed votes it became clear that the petitioner, Francis Hincks, would secure a majority and be seated by the committee. Although the enforced absence of a Reform member was to wipe out the Reform majority and its Conservative members were to devise various stratagems to discharge the committee, the Reform chairman on his casting vote managed to keep the committee relentlessly at work. For the comfort of the ministry the investigations of the committee had to be stopped, and the Government was forced to devise the means. The means were found in governmental patronage, and Roblin, a Reform member of the committee for Prince Edward County, was the willing recipient. In return for the offices of Collector of Customs at Picton, Registrar of Prince Edward County, and Agent for Crown Lands in Prince Edward District, Roblin resigned his seat in the House and vacated thereby his seat on the select committee. The Conservatives, having acquired a majority on the committee, then brought its investigations to a halt and sustained the return of the sitting member.[65] By the manipulation of these election committees the Draper ministry had retained control of the Assembly.

Just as the tradition of relative impartiality which had characterized Upper Canada's determination of disputed elections was in decline in Canada West, so the relative freedom of elections from violence which had typified Upper Canadian contests was also on the wane in Canada West. The violence and immorality which had marred Lower Canada elections was rapidly spreading from Canada East to Canada West. As Ricardo had discerned in the field of economics, so in politics there could not exist side by side two standards of political morality.

There were politicians in Canada West who were concerned at the spread of electoral violence and immorality. Since the Reformers on the whole suffered more than did the Conservatives from the debasement of the political coinage, it was not surprising that the Reformers made the first attempts to check the contagion. Baldwin, after an abortive attempt in 1841, managed in 1842 to secure the passage of an act to regularize election procedure and specify corrupt practices, thereby overcoming a deficiency that had always existed in Upper Canada law.[66] The legislation, while it did little more than re-enact the Lower Canada statute of 1825 and extend it to Canada West, did outlaw incitements to public disorder such as the exhibiting of party flags and colours, treating at public places, carrying of firearms, assault and battery, and bribery; it also conferred upon the returning officers the powers of a conservator of the peace which allowed them to swear in special constables and to summarily arrest those disturbing the electoral contests. The Reformers on their next return to power were further to consolidate and extend the category of election offences.[67] But Baldwin was aware that the creation of statutory offences was of little avail in purifying elections as long as the Assembly continued in its election committees to countenance these very violations. To correct this evil, Baldwin was to undertake a complete revision of the law regulating the trial of controverted elections.

In drafting the legislation, Baldwin modelled his measure on the law regulating the trial of controverted elections in Great Britain with interpolations from the law relating to the trial of Irish elections. Since the feature drawn from the legislation relating to Ireland, the power given select committees on controverted elections to appoint a commission to gather evidence on the spot, had long been familiar practice in Lower and Upper Canada, the novel features of the Baldwin act came from the British statute of 1848.[68] The Baldwin measure abolished the practice of drawing the names of twenty-three members from those present in the House and leaving the contending parties to reduce the number to nine which together with a nominee from each contestant would constitute a select committee to try the disputed return. While this procedure had removed the determination of a disputed election from the whole House, it had been open to certain difficulties. The large number of members required to operate the procedural aspects of selection as well as staff the select committees was difficult for the Legislature to provide; absenteeism could forestall or influence the composition of a select committee; and there was no assurance that each committee would contain a member experienced in the conduct of the trial of a controverted election.

The statute[69] secured by Baldwin required election petitions to be tabled within fourteen days of the commencement of each session or of the day of the return of the writ, unless the petition complained of bribery when twenty days were allowed. The petition was to be accompanied by a recognizance to the amount of £200, the Speaker to determine the validity of the recognizance. A General Committee of Elections of six members, appointed by the Speaker, was to make up the select committees to try each election petition referred to them by the House. The act indicated the procedure the General Committee of Elections was to follow. It was first to select from the personnel of the House four, six, or eight members skilled in trial procedure, who were to form the chairman's panel from which was to come the chairman for each election committee. The General Committee was then to divide the remaining members into three equal panels from whose number the rank and file of each election committee were to be drawn.

On the reference of an election petition, the General Committee of Elections was to set a day for the selection of the committee. On the day assigned and from the member panel serving for that particular week, the General Committee of Elections selected four members, while the chairman's panel from its own number selected the chairman for the committee. An absolute majority of the General Committee of Elections was to agree on their choice of personnel for each committee, while the chairman's panel was to be unanimous on its choice, but if unanimity could not be secured the chairman was to be selected by lot. The contending parties might object to personnel of the select committee and if an absolute majority of the General Committee on Elections sustained their objection, a new committee would be constituted. The select committee on its formation was to proceed from day to day to hear witnesses on oath and examine records. It was not dissolved by a prorogation of the Assembly, but was adjourned to recommence hearings on the Legislature's next assembling. On the basis of evidence heard and on evidence gathered by a commission when such was appointed, the select committee was to determine by majority vote the disputed return and, if warranted, award costs. The determination of the select committees was to be final.

Baldwin appears to have hoped his measure would improve the handling of disputed returns. The law, being applicable to both sections of the province, was to end the total failure of the Assembly to deal with disputed returns from Canada East. By concentrating responsibility on the Speaker, on the General Committee of Elections, and on smaller select committees, Baldwin believed partisanship would be curtailed. Interference from the House was reduced to two occasions: it might disapprove in whole or in part the personnel selected by the Speaker to form the General Committee of Elections, and it was required to authorize the reference of petitions, once the Speaker had cleared their recognizances, to the General Committee of Elections. Undoubtedly Baldwin expected the British precedents would be followed and the Speaker would appoint members to the General Committee of Elections equally from the ministerial and opposition benches, and that these men working under the absolute majority rule would select able men to staff the chairman's panel. If Baldwin was hopeful that the new procedure would improve the handling of election cases, John A. Macdonald was sceptical. The instability of ministerial majorities and the chronic ministerial crises had permeated the Canadian political scene with intense partisanship. In consequence it was Macdonald's belief that no ministry would risk the loss of any seat regardless of how it was secured and that both honour and integrity would have to be sacrificed to political survival. Macdonald had most acutely gauged Canadian political realities, and his estimate was only rendered more accurate by the departure of Baldwin and Lafontaine from public life. The loss of their stabilizing influence not only intensified the internecine party strife but left the implementation of the new procedure to alien hands.

Following the next election the procedure appeared to work satisfactorily for Canada West. All cases were tried and to all appearances properly determined. But for Canada East the measure was a total failure, not one case being determined. In the Richelieu County case, for example, the Speaker, John Sandfield Macdonald, ruled the recognizance objectionable on a technical point and prevented an investigation of an election which on the face of its poll books was blatantly illegal.[70] The poll books showed that the sitting member, Antoine N. Gouin, owed his election to the parish of St. Pierre de Sorel. This parish had given Gouin 1,278 votes but none to his adversaries, and this vote was larger than the total adult male population of the parish which had numbered 746 in the census of the same year.[71] In the Kamouraska and Megantic cases, a rash of absenteeism from their select committees and protracted adjournments to secure additional evidence by commission were to prolong the determination of these disputed elections beyond the life of that Parliament.

In the next Parliament there was some improvement in the trial of the controverted elections. The Canada West cases were dealt with promptly and properly, and for the first time since union some disputed elections from Canada East were investigated and voided on the findings of the select committees. It was none too soon, for the padding of the poll books which had occurred at the previous election in Richelieu County had in this election been resorted to in four counties of Canada East. In Saguenay County more votes were polled than the entire population of the county, 14,319 voters being recorded in a county whose population at the late census had been 12,965;[72] in Kamouraska the votes cast in five parishes were larger than their adult male population, while in Argenteuil one township and in Lotbinière two parishes shared the same distinction.[73] The elections for Saguenay, Kamouraska, and Argenteuil were voided and the offending deputy returning officers in the two former counties were brought to the Bar of the House, interrogated, reprimanded, and the worst offenders confined to jail for brief periods.

This creditable showing was, however, marred by the determination of the Lotbinière controverted election committee. This committee, which was staffed by a majority of the sitting member's political friends and was chaired by Joseph Cauchon, a political chameleon, was to sustain the return.[74] While the committee members were to admit that violence had occurred at the election and illegal votes had been polled, they declared that they were unable to judge whether these irregularities had occurred to such an extent as to nullify the sitting member's majority. This declaration was made in the face of the evidence that O'Farrell, the sitting member, had polled

1,033 votes and his opponent, Laurin, 99 votes from a parish whose population at the late census had consisted of 736 Irish males and that from a second parish O'Farrell had gathered 228 votes and Laurin 8 although the male population had stood at 91. Influenced by partiality the committee had been led to condone villainy with the consequence that both candidates were emboldened to employ the same tactics at the next general election.

Notwithstanding the Lotbinière case, the above Parliament had the best record of any Parliament since union in the handling of controverted election cases. The improvement was not sufficient, however, to check the ravages of an affliction which had become widespread and popularly accepted, at least in Canada East, as concomitant with elections. The country was to learn that the depths of electoral corruption and the legislators' determination to pervert justice for partisan ends had not yet been reached. The general election of 1858 was to plumb those depths and the ensuing Parliament was to condone the excesses by confirming in their seats the beneficiaries of the corruption.

The excesses of the sixth general election and of the sixth Parliament differed not in kind but in extent from their predecessors. The determined drive of the forces of Brown and Dorion against the Macdonald-Cartier entente was to produce a violent campaign which was to accord the ministry a narrow margin of victory and was to leave the elections of one-quarter of the membership of the House disputed. It would serve no purpose to record for each case the stratagems that were devised and the duplicity that was employed to enable the Government to escape from the intent of the law governing controverted elections while seeming to abide by its procedural requirements. Let it suffice to say that the manipulation began at the commencement of the new Parliament when Macdonald and Cartier secured the transfer of their cabinet colleague Henry Smith from the office of Solicitor General West to the office of Speaker and closed some three sessions later when a select committee after an interminable investigation finally became convinced that the return of three ministerialists for Quebec City, one of whom was a cabinet minister, was invalid.

From the duration of their investigation the members of this Conservative-dominated election committee would appear to have found great difficulty in determining the validity of the Quebec City election, although the poll of some 15,000 votes had been larger than the adult population of the city and although the editor of *Le National* had on examining the poll books found inscribed therein the names of Lord Palmerston, the Earl of Elgin, Sir Edmund Head, Napoleon III, Bishop de Charbonnel, Charles Gavan Duffy, Bishop Hughes of New York, and General Havelock. The name of the late Daniel O'Connell appeared "not less than one hundred times" in the poll books as did the names of "several illustrious gentlemen who had been dead for a very long time."[75] But the General Committee of Elections had doubtless exercised as scrupulous care in the selection of the membership of this and the other select committees as the Speaker had shown in the selection of the General Committee and in the validation of the recognizances that were required to accompany each election petition. For the Speaker in appointing the bipartisan General Committee of Elections had somehow managed to include one ailing and one chronically absent Reformer which had left that committee in effective Conservative control. With the same unerring instinct the Speaker had been able to find flaws in the recognizances accompanying nine of the thirty-three petitions and by plausible coincidence seven of the nine petitions, dismissed as a result, had challenged the return of Conservatives.

Among this number had been the petitions against the return of George Cartier and John Rose, Attorney and Solicitor Generals East respectively.

There had been one change in the law governing the investigation of the 1858 controverted elections that should be mentioned, particularly as it was employed to prevent the investigation of some of the disputed returns. The change, fathered by William Lyon Mackenzie, had concerned the commissions of enquiry which the select committees had the power to appoint to gather evidence at the locale of an election. It may be recalled that Lower and Upper Canada had both made provision for the appointment of commissions of enquiry in order to facilitate the gathering of evidence and the termination of controverted elections. While good in concept, these commissions had proved disappointing in practice on account of the difficulty of securing competent commissioners and the abuse of the lax rules of evidence. For example, in 1841 the contestants had attempted to call 212 witnesses before the commissioners for the Hastings County election, 289 before the commissioners for the Huron County election, 709 for the Frontenac County election, and the absurd number of 3,079 before the commissioners for the Oxford County election. These defects of the commissions of enquiry had persisted after union until they were largely eradicated by Baldwin's revision of the legislation relating to controverted elections in 1851. This revision had required the controverted election committees to appoint a single commissioner who was to be a judge of either the circuit or county courts unless the contending parties could mutually agree on a commissioner satisfactory to the select committee. While the reduction in the number of commissioners and their increased competence and prestige had improved the efficiency of commissions, the determination of disputed returns continued to extend over more than one session. The delays in the constitution of the controverted election committees and the time consumed in their preliminary investigations meant that it was always late in the first session before a warrant appointing a commission of enquiry would be issued. It was to overcome these delays and to hasten the determination of the disputed returns that Mackenzie had secured a change in the controverted election law.

The change required any person desiring to dispute an election for any reason not evident by a scrutiny of the poll books to give notice to the member-elect within two weeks of the election's termination that his return was to be disputed.[76] The written notice was to specify the grounds on which the return was to be disputed and no subsequent petition was to be received by the Assembly levying other charges, nor was an election petition to be received by the Assembly unless such a notice had been served. The member upon whom the notice was served was required to reply within two weeks, admitting or denying the charge and setting forth in his rebuttal any relevant facts. At this point one of the parties might apply to a circuit or county judge that he constitute himself a commission of enquiry to take evidence respecting the allegations in the notice and reply. The legislation required the judges to lay aside their other judicial duties on receipt of such an application, to conduct the enquiry, and to transmit the evidence adduced to the Clerk of the Assembly where it would be laid before the controverted election committee when that body was subsequently appointed. It was intended that this preliminary investigation, while not ruling out the possibilities of a select committee issuing a warrant for its own commission of enquiry, would provide them at the commencement of their deliberations with sufficient tangible evidence to determine expeditiously the disputed return.

First coming into operation following the election of 1858 the above procedure was used not to facilitate but to prevent the determination of disputed elections. Although the procedure was mandatory only for elections whose offences were not evident on the face of the poll books the Assembly insisted that the legislation was applicable to all disputed elections and dismissed those petitions in which the petitioner had not employed the procedure. On this pretext the petition against Fellowes' return for Russell County was dismissed, although the poll books revealed this Conservative owed his election to the votes of some three hundred residents of New York State whose names and places of residence had been extracted from a New York State directory and boldly inscribed in alphabetical order in the Cambridge Township poll book by some American deer hunters visiting the district. The legislation was no less exploited to the disadvantage of those petitioners who had sought to follow the procedure. The County Judge for Durham refused to conduct an investigation into the election of the Conservative member for Durham East because the notice required had not been personally served on the member-elect. This ruling was made although the petitioner had employed every effort to serve the notice but had been thwarted by the disappearance of the member and his family from their home in Port Hope and their failure to reappear until the fourteen days had elapsed.[77] Similarly the controverted election committee on the Ottawa disputed return ruled that the Conservative member-elect had not been given proper notice and thereupon set aside the findings of the Commissioner and dismissed the petition although it was revealed that the petitioner had had to search diligently before he uncovered the absconded member and his family lodged some sixty miles distant at Prescott.[78]

The intent of the legislation was further thwarted by the reluctance of the judges to abandon their judicial duties and undertake the interrogation of election witnesses. Mr. Justice Mondelet denied the constitutionality of legislation which peremptorily required him to attend upon the investigation of an election and to substitute another judge or a barrister-at-law to fulfil his judicial functions; and he thereupon refused act as Commissioner to investigate the charges against Attorney General Cartier's election for Verchères.[79] While Mr. Justice Badgley agreed to conduct such investigations he delayed the interrogation of witnesses against Solicitor General Rose's election for Montreal City for nearly four months, and thereby destroyed the utility of the advance investigation.

The concerted and sustained efforts of the Conservative ministry and its friends to pervert the judicious determination of the disputed elections were the desperate strivings of a party determined to salvage victory from defeat. In a Parliament which was to witness the formation and collapse of the Brown-Dorion ministry followed by the device of the "double shuffle," the margin of political survival was so narrow that no artifice was left untried in the struggle to retain political dominance.

The Assembly's blatant confirmation of the disputed elections, following hard upon the equally blatant corruption by which those elections had been secured, did not escape public indignation. The outspoken remarks of the Chief Justice of Canada East to the Montreal Grand Jury, the public appeal in the archdiocese of Quebec for signatures to a petition against the electoral corruption, and the mutterings of disapproval from sections of the ministerial press created an uneasiness among Government supporters in the House that finally led to open disaffection.[80] In consequence the ministry felt obliged to reopen several controverted elections for show trials before the Bar of the House, to unseat and thereby sacrifice the Conservative member for Lotbinière, and to commit several of that county's election officers to the

York County Gaol.[81] Ministerial contrition was, however, of short duration. After the public's indignation had subsided, the ministry resumed its old ways, voiding the elections of enemies and confirming the elections of friends; where the corruption was too flagrant to be condoned, select committees unduly protracted their investigations. Beyond repealing Mackenzie's legislation, this Parliament took no further steps to correct the method of handling controverted elections.[82] As a consequence the disputed returns attendant upon the two general elections remaining to the Province of Canada were to be determined with no perceptible improvement over the practices employed to resolve the disputed elections of 1858.

It was not that the politicians did not give occasional consideration to the raising of the standards for the determination of controverted elections. When Baldwin passed his controverted election act in 1851, John A. Macdonald had expressed himself in favour of placing their trial in the hands of the judiciary.[83] When a measure to more effectively prevent corrupt practices was before the House in 1860 he expressed the same opinion, yet as Attorney General he did not throw his weight behind the private bill introduced by William McDougall in the same year which would have established a single select committee presided over by a judge to hear and determine all disputed elections.[84] Like Baldwin in 1851, Macdonald justified his opposition on the grounds that the character of the Bench might be damaged and public confidence in the judiciary impaired if the judges were required to adjudicate disputed elections. To this criticism McDougall's bill was especially vulnerable as the judicial chairman would have but served to mask reality, for the adjudication would have remained with the political members of the committee.

The same criticism could not be levelled against a bill introduced by Sicotte, Macdonald's colleague, later in the same session which would have placed the trial of disputed elections within the sole jurisdiction of the courts.[85] Although the advocates of this measure could point to its successful operation in the field of municipal elections, for the judges of the county court in Canada West and the circuit court in Canada East had been required since 1849 and 1855 respectively to determine all disputed municipal elections,[86] and although it was the consensus of opinion that the practice had improved the tone of municipal contests and reduced the number of disputed returns, Macdonald and the legislators generally could not be persuaded to extend the practice to provincial elections. The members were reluctant to depart from a system in which "parties," in Mowat's words, "were encouraged to commit violations of the law by the hope of securing impunity from a partisan committee"; while John Sandfield Macdonald was of opinion that "it was a dangerous experiment, which he was not yet prepared to make, to transfer from the control of the Legislature to an irresponsible set of men the trying of election contests. The judges were not responsible to the people, except insofar as sensible to public opinion. . . . It was too great a power to be committed to two or three judges to influence the complexion of the Legislature for a whole Parliament."[87] The old cliché of responsibility was dragged out to cloak the real opposition to the proposal which was the reluctance of the politicians to lose control of controverted elections.

In subsequent years, attempts continued to be made to pass the determination of controverted elections over to the courts but the reform was never accomplished.[88] As if to ease guilt-stricken consciences the legislators, who could not bring themselves to adopt the requisite reform, busied themselves instead with the passage of merely palliative legislation. Electoral laws were introduced and in some cases passed augmenting the number of acts classified as corrupt practices and increasing the penalties attached to their commission.[89]

Corrupt practices had, since Baldwin's consolidation of the legislation governing elections in 1849, been defined in considerable breadth and detail but the laxity of the controverted election committees had nullified this breadth and the severity of the penalties attached thereto. In no case was the discrepancy between the law and reality more evident than in the provision of entertainment, food, and liquor to electors. Although a candidate or his well-wishers were forbidden to promote his election by the provision of food and drink, the public universally expected candidates to ignore the prohibition. George Brown, when he carried Toronto in 1858, found himself presented after the election with large bills for entertainment which he had not authorized but which his supporters had felt compelled to provide if the election was to be carried.[90] Various candidates in the same election were charged with maintaining numerous houses of entertainment; for example, the winning candidate in Drummond-Arthabaska was accused of maintaining thirteen, in Missisquoi with eleven, in Renfrew with ten, but none had their elections voided on this account.

The legislation provided the requisite loophole, for it was not an offence for any person to provide entertainment for electors at his own expense and at his own residence. Consequently many were the private citizens who in theory unstintingly dipped into their own pockets to turn their homes into a dispensary of liquor and victuals for the benefit of a candidate. So universal was this private and unsolicited "hospitality" that in all the Canadian controverted elections, one select committee alone found the partisan heart to void a return on grounds a candidate had provided entertainment.[91] The temperance advocates had even to succumb to this universal hospitality. In 1858 William Lyon Mackenzie charged his temperance opponent, Malcolm Cameron, with carrying the Lambton election with whisky. As a correspondent to the *Globe* of January 5, 1858, related:

Mr. Cameron had the support of the "Temperance Advocate" and has always been spoken of as the great temperance champion, and yet his election was carried by the influence of whiskey [sic]! There was no lack of money, hard as the times are, and on the second day of polling, it looked as if half the county had come to worship at the shrine of Bacchus. Men in a beastly state of intoxication were marched up to the polling booths to vote as they were bidden and the perjury committed in the townships of Sombra, Moore and Sarnia that day will not soon be forgotten.

The offence of bribery had similarly long been sufficient in law to void an election but, although bribery was often charged, no election was ever voided on this grounds. The law, by making it an offence both to give and to receive a bribe, closed the mouths of both parties. It was only when friends fell out that evidence could be secured to substantiate charges in court. Such a case transpired in 1857 when the defeated candidate in the Missisquoi East by-election of 1845 refused to redeem a note for £150 that he had given to his agent to cover the costs of bribing and corrupting the electors. His agent thereupon sued, and in the Superior Court and before the Appeal Division of the Court of Queen's Bench, the uses to which the money was put were amply proved.[92]

While the final spate of legislation was to contain more elaborate provisions defining bribery and intimidation, while the conveyance of electors to the polls was to be made an election offence, and while the evidence given before a court, a select committee, or a commission was to cease to incriminate a witness, the new legislation does not appear to have made any perceptible improvement in the few years remaining before Confederation.[93] In truth all such legislation would remain ineffective until the public became aroused against such election practices. In the words of the *Globe* of December 3, 1858, such evils came "more properly within the range of direct public action rather than of legislative enactments." The public gave no evidence of moral indignation, and by 1867 the only hopeful sign was the growing concern of many of the members at the mounting costs of election campaigns.

In conclusion it might be said that the conduct of elections in Canada had progressively deteriorated following union. The tradition of violence and corruption inherited from Lower Canada had been accentuated after union by racial and partisan antagonisms. The worse features of this corruption were for a time confined to the district of Montreal where racial and commercial friction was the more sharp. The district of Quebec initially avoided the worst excesses largely on account of the influence of John Neilson, for he threw the weight of his influence in favour of electoral honesty and racial harmony, and while he lived his political followers adhered to his code. On his death the noxious humour seeped eastward from Montreal, aided by the sharpening political contest between the Rouge party and the French Conservatives, until the corruption had permeated the conduct of elections throughout Canada East. Canada West was not immune to the contagion and as the years passed there was an increasing provision of liquor, use of bribery, and violence. But these practices never became as commonplace as in Canada East and were never accepted as the norm. The difference between the two sections was a matter of degree, but this difference in historical inheritance has had some bearing on the current disparity in the purity of elections between Ontario and Quebec.

While the spread of electoral corruption was undoubtedly assisted by the intense political partisanship, by the patronage at the disposal of the government and in later years by the political designs of railway promoters,[94] it was encouraged most of all by the reluctance of the Legislature to adjudicate disputed elections. On January 19, 1857, the *Daily Colonist* concluded that "Parliament had indeed become a sort of court for the acquittal of wrongdoers. Its majorities systematically sanctify rascality and rascality in return systematically whitewashes majorities. Let a Parliamentary supporter of a ministry get into a mess, or abuse his position or fail in a contract, or defraud the public and straightway the struggle is not to find out the facts that would vindicate public morality, but to get just such a committee together as would most effectively conceal, misinterpret or disbelieve the truth."

THE STATE OATHS AND THE DECLARATION AGAINST TRANSUBSTANTIATION

I. The State Oaths

The State Oaths were established by English statute 13 & 14 Wm. III, c. 6, in 1701 and were renewed on the accession of each sovereign. They were three in number, consisting of the Oath of Allegiance, the Oath of Supremacy, and the Oath of Abjuration. These oaths together with the Declaration against Transubstantiation were required to be taken by recipients of official appointments, civil or military, by teachers, by the clergy, by members of Parliament, and by the electors. They were made applicable in varying degree to the colonies by the Instructions issued to each governor. The Oaths quoted are taken from the British statute 1 Geo. I, stat. 2, c. 13 (1714); the Oath of Abjuration was modified slightly in 1766 (6 Geo. III, c. 53) on the death of the Old Pretender.

The Oath of Allegiance

"I, A.B., do sincerely promise and swear, That I will be faithful and bear true allegiance to His Majesty King George. So help me God."

The Oath of Supremacy

"I, A.B., do swear, That I do from my heart abhor, detest and abjure, as impious and heretical, that damnable doctrine and position, That Princes excommunicated or deprived by the Pope, or any authority of the See of Rome, may be deposed or murthered by their subjects, or any other whatsoever. And I do declare, That no foreign Prince, Person, Prelate, State or Potentate hath or ought to have any jurisdiction, power, superiority, pre-eminence or authority, ecclesiastical or spiritual, within this Realm. So help me God."

The Oath of Abjuration

"I, A.B., do truly and sincerely acknowledge, profess, testify and declare in my conscience, before God and and the world, That Our Sovereign Lord King George is lawful and rightful King of this Realm, and all other His Majesty's Dominions and Countries thereunto belonging. And I do solemnly and sincerely declare, That I do believe in my conscience, that the person pretended to be Prince of Wales, during the life of the late King James, and since his decease, pretending to be, and taking upon himself the Stile and Title of King of England, by the name of James the Third, or of Scotland, by the name of James the Eighth or the Stile and Title of King of Great Britain, hath not any right or title whatsoever to the Crown of this Realm or any other the Dominions thereto belonging; and I do renounce, refuse and abjure any allegiance or obedience to him. And I do swear, That I will bear faith and true allegiance to His Majesty King George, and him will defend to the utmost of my power, against all traiterous conspiracies and attempts whatsoever which shall be made against His Person, Crown or Dignity. And I will do my utmost endeavour to disclose and make known to His Majesty and His Successors all treasons and traiterous conspiracies which I shall know to be against him or any of them. And I do faithfully promise, to the utmost of my power, to support, maintain and defend the succession of the Crown against him the said James, and all other persons whatsoever, which succession, by an Act, intituled, An Act for the further Limitation of the Crown, and better securing the Rights and Liberties of the Subject, is and stands limited to the Princess Sophia, Electoress and Duchess Dowager of Hanover, and the Heirs of Her Body, being Protestants. And all these things I do plainly and sincerely acknowledge and swear, according to these express words by me spoken, and according to the plain and common sense and understanding of the same words, without any equivocation, mental evasion or secret reservation whatsoever. And I do make this recognition,

H

acknowledgment, abjuration, renunciation and promise heartily, willingly and truly, upon the true faith of a Christian. So help me God."

II. The Declaration against Transubstantiation

This declaration is to be found in English statute 25 Chas. II, c. 2 (1672):

'I, A.B., do declare, That I do believe that there is not any transubstantiation in the Sacrament of the Lord's Supper, or in the elements of Bread and Wine, at or after the consecration thereof by any person whatsoever."

NOTES

CHAPTER ONE

1. L.C., *Ass. J.*, Nov. 23, 1832.

2. Professions about the universality of the franchise come from many sources. See L. C., *Leg. Co. J.*, Feb. 13, 1827; Poulett Thomson to Russell, Jan. 22, 1840 (confidential), Jan. 22, 1840, P.A.C., Q270.1, 118; Campbell to Grey, June 26, 1850, P.A.C., P.E.I. G49, 276; Craig to Liverpool, May 1, 1810, Q112, 147.

The statistics of populations and vote returns are fragmentary and do not permit a conclusive assertion. The data that the author has been able to compile when compared with a recent federal election would seem, bearing in mind the physical difficulties of travel, to support the claim that the colonial franchises were by no means restrictive.

Colony	Franchise	General election	Vote as percentage of population
Nova Scotia	freehold	1826	8·0
	manhood & freehold	1855	19·9
	manhood	1859	21·6
Prince Edward Island	freehold, leasehold, & household	1850	11·2
	statute labour	1870	22·3
New Brunswick	freehold	1850	12·5
	assessment	1861	11·6
Upper Canada	freehold	1836	5·6
Canada (Province)	freehold	1854	8·7
	freehold & assessment	1858	15·4
	assessment	1861	9·5
Canada (Dominion)	manhood	1965	19·71

For purposes of comparison, the 1965 vote for Canada has been reduced to manhood suffrage by eliminating the women's vote, assuming their vote to be the same proportion of the total as the proportion of women in the 1965 adult population. Returns have been eliminated from the above computations where the election was subsequently voided.

3. The electors of the Irish Parliament were by law to be 40s. freeholders as in England but the practice had long prevailed to treat leases for lives as equitable freeholds and to allow their possessors to vote. See T. D. Ingram, *A History of the Legislative Union of Great Britain and Ireland* (London, 1887), 23 f.

4. See U.C., *Ass. J.*, Nov. 21, 1832, Jan. 26, 1835; L.C., *Ass. J.*, Nov. 26, 1832; N.B., *Ass. J.*, Jan. 28, 1840, March 12, 1842; N.S., *Ass. J.*, 1844, App. 87; *New Brunswick Courier* (henceforth referred to as *Courier*), April 16, 1853.

5. *L'Avenir*, May 21, 1851; Can., *Bills*, sess. 1863, Bill no. 62.

6. *Examiner*, March 20, 27, 1850.

7. Can., Ass. Debates, May 11, 1858, quoted in *Globe*, May 12, 1858.

8. N.B., Ass. Debates, Feb. 24, 1855. See John, Earl Russell, *An Essay on the History of English Government and Constitution* (new ed., London, 1865), 252, 263.

9. *Montreal Gazette*, April 25, 1849.

10. Can., Ass. Debates, April 27, 1857, quoted in *Globe*, April 28, 1857.

11. Howe to Newcastle, July 8, 1863, P.A.C., Howe Papers, XXXVII; *Novascotian*, May 29, 1865. For the opinions of other Nova Scotian leaders, see *Novascotian*, May 31, 1854, and *Acadian Recorder*, May 5, 12, 1860, and March 24, 1865.

12. See *British Columbian*, Oct. 3, 1863.

13. The newspapers carried the occasional article pointing out the excesses of manhood suffrage in the United States and of Australian dissatisfaction with the same franchise. See *Courier*, July 18, 1863, and *British Colonist*, Feb. 28, 1871.

14. *The Spirit of the Laws*, trans. Thomas Nugent with intro. by Franz Neumann (New York, 1949), I, 155.

15. N.B., Ass. Debates, Feb. 24, 1855.

16. L.C., *Ass. J.*, Dec. 4, 1828.

17. For conflict between the views of the franchise as a privilege and as a right of freemen in the Putney debates of the Cromwellian army, see A. S. P. Woodhouse, ed., *Puritanism and Liberty* (London, 1938), 53f, 55f, and C. B. Macpherson, *The Political Theory of Possessive Individualism* (Oxford, 1962), 107–36.

18. See Edmund Burke, "An Appeal from the New to the Old Whigs", in the *Works of the Right Honourable Edmund Burke*, F. C. & J. Rivington, eds. (London, 1808), vi, 265.

19. Thomas Paine, "The Rights of Man, pt. I," and "Dissertation on First Principles of Government," in P. S. Foner, ed., *The Complete Writings of Thomas Paine* (New York, 1945), I, 314; II, 579.

20. See C. F. Adams, ed., *The Works of John Adams* (Boston, 1856), X, 267.

21. N.B., Ass. Debates, Feb. 28, 1855.

22. W. Blackstone, *Commentaries on the Laws of England*, ed. R. M. Kerr (4th ed., London, 1876), I, 138.

23. See *Colonial Advocate*, Sept. 25, 1834. See also *Ibid.*, June 20, Sept. 19, 1833, and Feb. 8, 1834.

24. P. L. Ford, ed., *The Works of Thomas Jefferson* (New York, 1904), IV, 85f.

25. For a similar but a more extreme view, see Daniel Defoe, *The Original Power of the Collective Body of the People of England*: "I do not place this right [of government] upon the inhabitants, but upon the freeholders; the freeholders are the proper owners of the country; it is their own and the other inhabitants are but sojourners, like lodgers in a house, and ought to be subject to such laws as the freeholders impose upon them, or else they must remove; because the freeholders having a right to the land, the others have no right to live there but upon sufferance." In W. Hazlitt, ed., *The Works of Daniel Defoe* (London, 1843), III, 12.

CHAPTER TWO

1. Commission to Governor Cornwallis, May 6, 1749, P.A.C., N.S. E7.

2. Belcher to Pownall, Jan. 16, 1755, P.A.C., N.S. A57, 53.

3. Report of Attorney and Solicitor General to the Board of Trade, April 29, 1755, N.S. A57, 118.

4. Board of Trade to Lawrence, May 7, 1755, N.S. A57, 134f.

5. See Lawrence to Board of Trade, Oct. 18, 1755, A58, 134; Nov. 3, 1756, A60, 107; and Nov. 9, 1757, A61, 214.

6. Lawrence to Board of Trade, Dec. 8, 1755, N.S. A58, 166f.

7. Board of Trade to Lawrence, March 25, 1756, N.S. A59, 21.

8. Instructions to Governor Lawrence, March 2, 1756, No. 11, N.S. E2.

9. Instruction No. 86 to Hopson dated April 23, 1752, N.S. E2.

10. Proposal of Chief Justice Belcher on Convening an Assembly, Oct. 24, 1755, N.S. A58, 142.

11. N.S., *Ex. Co. Min.*, Dec. 3, 1756, P.A.C., B9, 2.

12. Lawrence to Board of Trade, Dec. 8, 1755, N.S. A58, 166.

13. Board of Trade to Lawrence, March 25, 1756, N.S. A59, 24.

14. N.S., *Ex. Co. Min.*, Jan. 3, 1757, B9, 12. See also Report of Lawrence to Board of Trade, Jan. 3, 1757, N.S. A61, 1.

15. Executive Council to Board of Trade, March 12, 1757, N.S. A61, 109.

16. Petition of Ferdinando J. Paris on behalf of the Freeholders of Halifax to the Board of Trade, Jan. 26, 1758, N.S. A62, 1, 47, 48. This petition was signed by 204 freeholders, most of whom were New Englanders, and of whose number eleven were members of the first Assembly.

17. See Minutes of Board of Trade, Jan. 31, 1758, N.S. A62, 53.

18. *Ibid.*, 59f.

19. *Ibid.*, 63–64.

20. Board of Trade to Lawrence, Feb. 7, 1758, N.S. A62, 99–100.

21. N.S., *Ex. Co. Min.*, May 20, 1758, B9, 83–92.

22. Lt. Gov. Monckton, in Lawrence's absence on a military expedition, dispatched Zouberbuhler,

a Justice of the Peace, to Lunenberg to naturalize the German settlers. Zouberbuhler carried a letter to Rev. Mr. Moreau, the S.P.G. missionary, ordering him to administer the Sacrament to the settlers in order that they might fulfil the legal requirements to become British subjects. Monckton to Capt. Faesch and to Rev. Mr. Moreau, July 5, 1758, P.A.C., Monckton Papers, XI.

23. Memorial of Robert Sanderson to Board of Trade, Jan. 14, 1761, N.S. A65, 42. The danger had been anticipated, for the Executive Council authorized the Provost Marshal to proceed to determine the election even if votes from the townships of Annapolis Royal and Cumberland had not been received eight days before the expiration of the election writ. N.S., *Ex. Co. Min.*, May 20, 1758, B90.

24. Sanderson, Speaker of the first Assembly, writing to the Board of Trade stated: "And to effect his purposes the Governor granted away large tracts of the best lands in these countys and towns . . . to such persons as he thought proper, to make them freeholders therein and qualify them to choose members or to be chosen to represent the said uninhabited countys and towns." Memorial of R. Sanderson to Board of Trade, N.S. A65, 43f.

25. Details of the organization of the elections remained much as set forth in the Minute of Council to Board of Trade, Jan. 3, 1957, and as adopted for the election of the first Assembly, The few changes that did occur reduced the amount of notice the Provost Marshal had to give of the time and place of election from twenty to five days, and involved the replacement of the two-day and four-day elections for township members and the members for the province at large respectively to a single polling day (6 A.M. to 6 P.M.) for both town and county. N.S., *Ex. Co. Min.*, Aug. 22, 1759, B9, 221–27.

26. Board of Trade to Lawrence, March 25, 1756, N.S. A59, 25f.

27. N.S., *Ass. J.*, March 19, 1759, P.A.C., D2.

28. N.S., *Ex. Co. Min.*, Jan. 30, 1765, B13, 147.

29. See Belcher to Board of Trade, Jan. 11, 1762, N.S. A67, 83; N.S., *Ex. Co. Min.*, Aug. 28, 1762, B12, 96f; and W. S. MacNutt, "The Beginnings of Nova Scotia Politics 1758–66," *Canadian Historical Review*, XVI (1935), 41.

30. N.S., *Ex. Co. Min.*, June 1, 1765, B13, 172.

31. N.S., *Ass. J.*, May 30, 1765, D6, 15. The Executive Council's issuance at this time of a writ for the election of two members from the newly created county of Sunbury on the St. John River increased the fears of the outsettlement members as its principal proprietor was Joshua Mauger, a former Halifax merchant.

32. *Ibid.*, June 1, 1765, D6, 20.

33. In 1767 the Board of Trade had before it acts from five colonies increasing the representation in the assemblies of Nova Scotia, New Hampshire, Massachusetts, New York, and South Carolina. See L. W. Labaree, *Royal Government in America* (New Haven, 1930), 179–88 for a detailed discussion of the problem.

34. N.S. A79, 189. For a copy of the statute disallowed see N.S., *Stat.*, 5 Geo. III, c. 10 (1765).

35. Instructions to Legge, Aug. 3, 1773, No. 13, N.S. E4.

36. Legge to Dartmouth, No. 17, 1774, N.S. A91, 159, and enclosure, A91, 155; Dartmouth to Legge, Jan. 27, 1775, N.S. A93, 121.

37. N.S., *Ex. Co. Min.*, June 29, 1775, B16, 97–98.

38. Petition of the Province of Nova Scotia to the King and Parliament (secret) June 24, 1775, N.S. A94, 11–30.

39. See N.S. A95, 254–68, for copy of bill as amended. For amendments see N.S., *Ass. J.*, July 11, 1775, D11, 132ff.

40. "An Act for limiting the duration of the General Assembly in this Province," P.A.N.S., Unpassed Bills, 1780.

41. Board of Trade to the King, March 20, 1781, N.S. A101, 76a.

42. N.S., *Stat.*, 18 Geo. III, c. 2 (1778).

43. N.S. A94, 25.

44. Secretary of State to Parr, July 7, 1784, N.S. A105, 163. Cape Breton was reannexed to Nova Scotia in 1820. During the thirty-six years of separate existence it never possessed representative institutions and as a result no problem of a franchise ever arose.

45. Joseph Alpin to Chief Justice Smith, March 6, 1784, N.S. A104, 137. Alpin described Halifax as "that source of republicanism from whence many towns in the Province occasionally draw fresh supplies."

46. Germain to Hammond, May 9, 1781, N.S. A101, 107; North to Parr June 24, 1783, N.S. A103, 112f.

47. Parr to Sydney, Aug. 13, 1784, N.S. A105, 185.

48. Instructions to Parr, Sept. 11, 1784, No. 15, N.S. E4.

49. N.S., *Stat.*, 25 Geo. III, c. 5 (1784).
50. N.S., *Ass. J.* June 7, 14, 1766, D6, 79f, 101.
51. N.S., *Ex. Co. Min.*, April 2, 1770, B15, 26.
52. N.S., *Ass. J.*, Dec. 7, 1785, D15.
53. N.S., *Ass. J.*, March 31, 1789, D17.
54. N.S., *Stat.*, 29 Geo. III, c. 1 (1789).
55. Reduced to ten days in 1817 (57 Geo. III, c. 7).
56. Remonstrance of Freeholders of Sunbury County, April 30, 1783, P.A.N.S., Assembly Papers, IA.
57. N.S., *Ex. Co. Min.*, Nov. 3, 1785, P.A.N.S., E5, 70.
58. N.S., *Ass. J.*, April 1, 1789, D17.
59. N.S., *Ass. J.*, Feb. 21, 1800, D28.
60. N.S., *Ex. Co. Min.*, Oct. 19, 1820, P.A.N.S. The governing statute was the consolidation act of 1817 (57 Geo. III, c. 7).
61. See R. Brown, *A History of the Island of Cape Breton* (London, 1869), 445.
62. N.S., *Stat.*, 1 & 2 Geo. IV, ϩ. 5 (1820–21).
63. *Ibid.*, 4 & 5 Geo. IV, c. 22 (1824). Residents of Cape Breton had been officially encouraged to treat their tenures as equivalent to grants in fee simple, and conveyances had been made on lands held by lease or licence. See enclosure in Kempt to Gordon, Feb. 11, 1825, N.S. A166, 20f.
64. Bathurst to Kempt, April 15, 1826, P.A.C., N.S., C.O. 218, vol. 30, 115f.
65. Kempt to Horton (private and confidential), Sept. 19, 1826, N.S. A168, 132.
66. N.S., *Stat.*, 32 Geo. III, c. 10 (1792); Wentworth to Dundas, Oct. 25, 1792, N.S. A117, 232. The life of the Assembly was restricted to a maximum of four years in 1840 (3 Vic., c. 4).
67. N.S., *Ass. J.*, March 21, 22, 1793, D20.
68. *Ibid.*, March 25. 1793.
69. *Ibid.*, March 28, April 26, 1793.
70. N.S., *Stat.*, 37 Geo. III, c. 3 (1797).
71. N.S., *Ass. J.*, Feb. 25, 1800, Nov. 21, 1806.
72. N.S., *Ass. J.*, Dec. 14, 1820, Feb. 12, 1819, Feb. 6, 1812.
73. N.S., *Stat.*, 4 & 5 Geo. IV, c. 22 (1824).
74. See "An Act in amendment of an Act for the better regulating of Elections," P.A.N.S., Unpassed Bills, 1790.
75. N.S., *Ass. J.*, April 1, 1790. The petition stated that Digby and Clare were 40 and 60 miles distant from the county town for Annapolis.
76. Parr to Grenville, May 3, 1790, N.S. A114, 104.
77. N.S., *Stat.*, 32 Geo. III, c. 8 (1792).
78. Wentworth to Dundas, Oct. 25, 1792, N.S. A117, 232.
79. N.S., *Stat.*, 57 Geo. III, c. 7 (1817); 4 & 5 Geo. IV, c. 22 (1824); 5 Wm. IV, c. 25 (1834–35); N.S., *Ex. Co. Min.*, Oct. 9, 1820, April 19, 1826. The practice was not extended to Cape Breton by statute until 1831 (1 Wm. IV, c. 5). See N.S., *Stat.*, 3 Vic., c. 31 (1840) for a consolidation of the polling circuits.
80. N.S., *Ex. Co. Min.*, Oct. 16, 1811, E7, 448; Thomas Cutter to Cogswell, Jan. 20, 1814, P.A.N.S., vol. 227, doc. 3.
81. Dalhousie to Bathurst June 10, 1819, N.S., A160, 154f.
82. Bathurst to Dalhousie July 10, 1819, N.S., C.O. 218, vol. 29, 252.
83. See N.S., Unpassed Bills, 1821.
84. N.S., *Leg. Co. J.*, Feb. 21, 1821.
85. The situation was prevented from becoming intolerable as respects Halifax County solely because a convention had grown up that Pictou and Truro should each return one of the four county members. Pictou returned Edward Mortimer from 1800 until his death in 1819 and then George Smith; Truro returned James Fulton in 1800 and on his death S. G. W. Archibald. See *Acadian Recorder*, Nov. 27. 1819.

CHAPTER THREE

1. The mixed motives are revealed in thirty petitions that reached the fifteenth General Assembly (1830–36) desiring the subdivision of counties.

2. *Novascotian*, March 10, 1830.

3. N.S., *Ass. J.*, April 10, 1833. By 1 Wm. IV, c. 5 (1831), the election for Cape Breton had to adjourn to four places, Sydney, Arichat, Port Hood, and Cheticamp, and thirty-four days exclusive of Sundays and holidays were required to complete it. The period would have been extended to forty-two days by the addition of Little Bedeque in 1833 (3 Wm. IV, c. 43) if the county had not been divided in 1836.

4. N.S., *Ass. J.*, Dec. 17, 1830, Feb. 10, 1832.

5. In 1835 four bills were introduced to divide and adjust the representation of Halifax, Annapolis, Shelburne, and Cape Breton counties. After the Halifax bill had cleared the Assembly, the Halifax faction carried amendments to prevent the division of the other counties resulting in any increase in representation. Shelburne and Annapolis refused to accept the bills as amended, and Annapolis by petition to the Colonial Office was able to prevent the immediate confirmation of the Halifax bill. Chastened, the Halifax faction in the following year allowed Shelburne and Sydney counties to be divided with a net increase in representation but refused to apply the same principle to Annapolis until 1837.

6. N.S., *Ass. J.*, Dec. 22, 1834. For a copy of the bill see "An Act for preventing charge and expense in elections of Representatives to serve in General Assembly." P.A.N.S., Unpassed Bills, 1834–35.

7. N.S., *Stat.*, 5 Wm. IV, c. 25 (1835–35). In the Lunenburg County election of 1836, there seems to have been some division of opinion as to the efficacy of the legislation. See *Novascotian*, Dec. 21, 28, 1836.

8. See N.S., *Ass. J.*, Nov. 29, 1830, Feb. 19, 1833, Feb. 16, 1837, Jan. 23, 1839. The last select committee produced a draft bill which would have required the magistrates in General Session to appoint assessors to prepare a voters' register. See *Novascotian*, April 11, 1839, for a copy of the bill.

9. N.S., *Stat.*, 2 Vic., c. 35 (1839).

10. *Novascotian*, Jan. 31, 1839.

11. E. M. Saunders, *Three Premiers of Nova Scotia* (Toronto, 1909), 203.

12. N.S., *Ass. J.*, 1844, App. 87.

13. *Ibid.*, March 8, 1845.

14. C. Seymour, *Electoral Reform in England and Wales* (New Haven, 1915), 115ff.

15. N.S., *Stat.*, 10 Vic., c. 1 (1847). The act specified the polling subdivisions for some counties, but the remainder were left to be subdivided by their sheriff, subject to review and alteration, first by the Grand Jury, and secondly by the Court of General Sessions.

16. *Ibid.*, 14 Vic. c. 2 (1851).

17. N.S., *Rev. Stat.*, 1851, c. 46.

18. Report on General State of Nova Scotia, 1847, P.A.C., Howe Papers, VI, 161.

19. The above increase is open to error from the limited nature of the comparable statistics. It was arrived at from a comparison of the vote in four counties, Hants, Pictou, Lunenburg, and Colchester, and in three townships, Lunenburg, Pictou, and Shelburne.

20. N.S., *Rev. Stat.*, 1851, c. 46. s. 10.

21. N.S., *Ass. Debates*, Feb. 18, 1856; J. A. Chisholm, *Speeches and Public Letters of Joseph Howe* (Halifax, 1909), I, 60.

22. N.S., *Ass. Debates*, March 19, 1855.

23. N.S., *Ass. J.*, March 20, 1851.

24. *Ibid.*, 1852, App. 87.

25. *Ibid.*, Feb. 2, 1854.

26. *Acadian Recorder*, Feb. 11, 1854.

27. In 1839 a rider to a bill respecting polling places had sought to establish a tenant franchise, but the Legislative Council rejected the bill on a secondary issue. See N.S., *Leg. Co. J.*, March 27, 1839.

28. *Acadian Recorder*, Feb. 11, 18, 1854; N.S., *Stat.*, 17 Vic., c. 6 (1854).

29. See Howe to Harvey and Bourke to Howe, Aug. 4, 1847: Howe Papers, I, 246; VI, 180.

30. J. Bartlet Brebner, "Joseph Howe and the Crimean War Enlistment Controversy between Great Britain and the United States," *Canadian Historical Review*, XI (1930), 300–27.

31. N.S., *Leg. Co. Debates*, April 9, 1858, in *Acadian Recorder*, June 19, 1858.

32. N.S., *Stat.*, 21 Vic., c. 37 (1858).

33. *Acadian Recorder*, Aug. 2, 1862. This action is evidenced by letters in the Howe correspondence. See Howe to McKinnon and McDonald, May 28, 1862, Howe Papers, VIII, 292. McKinnon was member for the county of Sydney and brother of the Bishop of Arichat.

34. N.S., *Stat.*, 26 Vic., c. 28 (1863). A vestige of manhood suffrage was allowed to remain; teachers

might vote if they had been teaching six months and had resided three months in the riding before issuance of the writs.

35. See *Acadian Recorder*, March 28, 1863, and April 4, 11, 1863, for Assembly debate on the assessment franchise bill.

36. See N.S., *Leg. Co. Debates*, April 17, 1860.

37. A. C. MacDonald to Howe (private), June 2, 1863. "The extraordinary defeat we have sustained fully proves to my mind the soundness of your views as regards the franchise bill. This was perhaps the strongest element in our defeat. Next to this was the strong tide of feeling against the government for their alleged inactivity about railway extension. . . . The *subsidium* of the Protestant platform and your letters to MacKinnon and McDonald also operated to some extent among the ignorant class of Presbyterians who severed their old political ties at the last election on that ground, but this was a minor matter." Howe Papers, VII, 779.

38. N.S., *Ass. Debates*, Feb. 8, 1864. Tupper expressed similar sentiments in the following year, *ibid.*, Feb. 17, 1865.

39. There were 72 petitions presented to the Assembly during the sessions of 1865 and 1866 demanding the appeal or amendment of the education act.

40. N.S., *Ass. Debates*, March 7, 1865. In a by-election in Lunenburg County in December, 1865, for which the assessment franchise was first operative, the vote declined by approximately 49 per cent from the 1863 vote under manhood suffrage. See *Novascotian*, Jan. 8, 1866.

41. N.S., *Stat.*, 19 Vic., c. 20 (1856).

42. To allow for the neglect the effective date of the assessment franchise was deferred a further year to June, 1865. See *ibid.*, 27 Vic., c. 20 (1864).

43. N.S., *Ass. Debates*, Feb. 17, 1865.

44. *Ibid.*, Feb. 8, 1864.

45. Howe to Newcastle, July 8, 1863, Howe Papers, XXXVII, n.p. See N.S., *Ass. Debates*, Feb. 25, 1861, for similar opinions of Howe and Archibald.

46. See Musquodoboit petition to the King enclosed in Campbell to Glenelg, May 13, 1836, N.S., A183. 2, 567f, and *Acadian Recorder*, April 10, 1847, for complaints.

47. N.S., *Stat.*, 12 Vic., c. 33 (1849), abolished the representation of Onslow Township and expanded the remaining townships of Truro and Londonderry for representative purposes to encompass the whole of Colchester County. *Ibid.*, 15 Vic., c. 17 (1852), erected the rural county of Victoria to relieve the strain between the miners of Sydney Township and the farmers and fishermen of Cape Breton County. *Ibid.*, 19 Vic., c. 66 (1856) abolished the representation of Liverpool Township and gave it to the county at large while the two county members were henceforth to be returned from the southern and northern halves of the county.

48. See N.S., Unpassed Bills, 1858, "An Act for better Equalizing the Representation in the House of Assembly." *Novascotian*, Feb. 12, 22, 1858, and N.S., *Ass. Debates*, Feb. 12, 1858, and March 1, 1859.

49. See N.S., *Stat.*, 22 Vic., c. 1 (1859).

50. *Novascotian*, March 7, 21, 1859.

51. N.S., *Leg. Co. Debates*, March 21, 1859.

CHAPTER FOUR

1. Commission to Patterson, Aug. 4, 1769, P.E.I., Commissions and Instructions 1766–1839, P.A.C., M593, 27.

2. Hillsborough to Patterson, Aug. 7, 1772, Dartmouth to Patterson, Nov. 4, 1772, P.A.C., P.E.I. A2, 69, 76.

3. Patterson to Dartmouth, May 1, 1774, P.E.I. A2, 215.

4. P.E.I., *Ex. Co. Min.*, Feb. 17, 1773, P.A.C., B1, 47. See also Patterson to Dartmouth, Feb. 17 1773, P.E.I., A2, 91f.

5. Dartmouth to Patterson, Dec. 1, 1773, P.E.I., A2, 169.

6. Stewart to [Sydney], June 2, 1784, P.E.I. A5, 161.

7. P.E.I., *Ex. Co. Min.*, Nov. 27, 1784, Dec. 3, 1784, B3, 119–32, B4, 13–24.

8. See D. C. Harvey, "The Loyal Electors," *Proceedings and Transactions of the Royal Society of Canada*, XXIV (1930), 101–10, and F. MacKinnon, *The Government of Prince Edward Island* (Toronto, 1951), 53–56, 61ff, for a discussion of the early party system.

9. In 1791 when certain merchants, outraged by the confiscation of their cargoes, brought charges against Lieutenant Governor Fanning before the Privy Council Committee on Plantations, they did charge Fanning with an unconstitutional modification of the representation. Fanning easily obtained local petitions to justify his action and the Privy Council exonerated him of any impropriety. See Fanning to Privy Council [1791], Answer to Charge No. 1, P.A.C., Fanning Papers, vol. 1.

10. P.E.I., *Ex. Co. Min.*, July 18, 1787, B6, 163–69; Aug. 20, 1787, B6, 208.

11. P.E.I., *Stat.*, 41 Geo. III, c. 4 (1801). Through the courtesy of the Dominion Archivist copies of Prince Edward Island statutes which are unavailable in Canada were secured from the records of the Colonial Office. These copies are now available in the Public Archives of Canada.

12. See Memorandum of Arrangement signed by Fanning and John Patterson on Oct. 10, 1797, in which Fanning makes important concessions to achieve a rapprochement with the Patterson party. Fanning Papers, vol. 1.

13. P.E.I., *Stat.*, 47 Geo. III, c. 3 (1806). The statute is rather vague; it states "qualification if in land" was to be registered three months before the issuance of the writs but it does not make clear whether this applies to both freeholders and leaseholders or merely the former.

14. In the early election writs, candidates were required to be "actually" resident on the Island but when this phrase was used in the election of 1788 to exclude candidates in Prince County and Royalty because they were out fishing, Fanning, on the advice of Charles Stewart, dropped the word "actually" from the election writ of 1790. The act of 1801, passed by an Assembly hostile to the Stewart party, restored this restrictive qualification but the 1806 act now dropped it. See Affidavit of Charles Stewart, Dec. 7, 1791, Fanning Papers, I.

15. Ready to Huskisson, May 27, 1828, P.E.I. A45, 207.

16. See copy of bill, P.E.I. A45, 223.

17. P.E.I., *Stat.*, 10 Geo. IV, c. 12 (1829),

18. Murray to Ready, Aug. 30, 1829, P.A.C., P.E.I. G6, 298.

19. P.E.I., *Stat.*, 11 Geo. IV, c. 8 (1830).

20. P.E.I., *Ass. J.*, Jan. 24, 1833.

21. *Ibid.*, Feb. 14, 1834.

22. *Ibid.*, Feb. 8, March 28, 1833. The indiscretion of the petitioners in advocating the abolition of the rotten boroughs of Princetown and Georgetown led the Assembly initially to dismiss the petition.

23. *Ibid.*, Feb. 14, 1834.

24. P.E.I., *Leg. Co. J.*, March 15, 1834.

25. P.E.I., *Ass. J.* March 19, 1834.

26. P.E.I., *Stat.*, 6 Wm. IV, c. 24 (1836).

27. P.E.I., *Ass. J.*, Feb. 3, 1837, Jan. 24, 1838.

28. *Ibid.*, March 27, 30, 1838.

29. Petition to the Legislative Council [March 6, 1838], P.E.I. A56. 2, 665; Address to Lt. Gov. Fitzroy [March 1838], P.E.I. A56. 1, 322; Observations on the Election Act to the Colonial Office, P.E.I. A56. 2, 676–77. See also Attorney General Hodgson's Report on the Laws, March 10, 1838, P.E.I. A55.1, 144.

30. Fitzroy to Glenelg, April 9, 1838 (separate), P.E.I. A55.1, 235.

31. P.E.I., *Stat.*, 1 Vic., c. 9 (1838); Glenelg to [Fitzroy], May 28, 1838, P.E.I. G11, 247.

32. P.E.I., *Stat.*, 5 Vic., c. 24 (1842). Doubts had arisen as to whether leaseholders could vote who held land by an agreement which was not a formal lease, or who had not paid their rent. Doubts had also arisen as to whether owners of premises in a royalty could vote on property which was normally productive of £10 yearly rent if the premises were vacant. The act declared all citizens so circumstanced were eligible to vote.

33. Huntley to Grey, March 23, 1847, P.E.I. G48, 395. Three electors were killed in the riot which marred the first by-election.

34. Grey to Campbell, Nov. 12, 1847, P.E.I., G17, 369f; P.E.I., *Ass. J.*, Feb. 1 and March 15, 1848; and P.E.I., *Stat.*, 11 Vic,, c. 21 (1848). The act amended the franchise to the extent that leaseholders whose rent was less than 40s. a year might vote if their lease was for a minimum of twenty-one years, the value of the leased farm was not less than £100 and its extent not less than fifty acres.

35. Campbell to Grey (confidential), June 1, 1848, in W. R. Livingston, *Responsible Government in Prince Edward Island* (Iowa City, 1931) App. IV.

36. Campbell to Grey, June 26, 1850, P.E.I. G49, 275–84; Campbell to Grey (confidential), June 28, 1850, in Livingston, App. VIII.

37. P.E.I. G49, 278.

H*

38. This was the second such appeal that had emanated from the Island. In 1841, 700 Island house-holders had petitioned the Crown to secure Imperial legislation to raise the qualifications of members of the Assembly. Prompted by identical motives, the first appeal had been made at a time when the escheat party controlled the Assembly. The petition had sought to raise the property qualification in order ostensibly to secure men of independent means and thereby allow the cessation of the ses-sional indemnity accorded members since 1825. Under the cloak of economy, the proprietary interests behind the petition had sought to exclude from the Assembly members accustomed to seduce the leaseholders with promises of escheat. See Petition of 700 Householders to H.M. Queen, 1841, P.A.C., C.O. 226, vol. 62, n.p.

39. Grey to Campbell, July 18, 1850, G19, 479.

40. P.E.I., *Ass. J.*, April 26, 1851.

41. See Assembly Debates in *Haszard's Gazette*, Feb. 12, 1852.

42. P.E.I., *Ass. J.*, March 11, 1852. Whereas a candidate was to possess a freehold or leasehold of £50 value twelve months before the test of the writ, Whelan's qualification of seventy acres of land had not been transferred to him until after the election and the purchase price had not been fully paid until 1852, a year after his appointment to the Executive Council.

43. P.E.I., *Leg. Co. J.*, March 27, 1852. The Legislative Council divided six to five against the bill. Rice resigned from the Executive Council two days later.

44. P.E.I., *Stat.*, 15 Vic., c. 13 (1852). See Bannerman to Pakington, Aug. 31, 1852, P.E.I. G50, 145, for petition against the education bill. The petition signed by fourteen proprietors and proprie-tors' agents declared the bill was another device to force the proprietors' lands onto the market through the agency of taxation.

45. *Ibid.*, 16 Vic., c. 9 (1853).

46. *Ibid.*, 14 Vic., c. 16 (1851).

47. Assembly Debates, Feb. 16, 1853, in *Haszard's Gazette*, Feb. 26, 1853.

48. Bannerman to Newcastle, June 20, 1853, P.E.I. G50, 241; Newcastle to Bannerman, July 27, 1853, P.E.I. G22, 231.

49. Petition of Landowners, Merchants, Shipowners, etc., to the Queen [1853], P.E.I. G22, 299.

50. Bannerman to Newcastle, Aug. 30, 1853, and enclosures, P.E.I. G50, 277; Newcastle to Banner-man, Dec. 27, 1853, P.E.I. G22, 371.

51. P.E.I., *Stat.*, 24 Vic., c. 34 (1861).

52. *Ibid.*, 29 Vic., c. 10 (1866).

53. See F. MacKinnon, *The Government of Prince Edward Island* (Toronto, 1951), 99 *et seq.*

54. See Can., *Stat.*, 19 & 20 Vic., c. 140 (1856). Candidates for the Canadian Legislative Council were required to be British subjects, thirty years of age and owners of property valued at £2,000 currency over and above all encumbrances.

55. P.E.I., *Stat.*, 24 Vic., c. 8 (1861).

56. Newcastle to Dundas, Feb. 4, 1862, P.E.I. G31, 45–46.

57. *Ibid.*, 47–48.

58. P.E.I., *Stat.*, 25 Vic., c. 18 (1862).

59. P.E.I., *Ex. Co. Min.*, June 4, 1787, B6, 120.

60. This is borne out by the election results. The total vote is given at the conclusion of each poll.

	Princetown	St. Peters	Charlottetown
Richmond Bay list (Stewart faction)	45	72	113
Capt. Fletcher's list (Patterson faction)	15	45	182

See P.E.I., *Ex. Co. Min.*, July 17, 1787, B6, 141ff.

61. *Ibid.*, July 18, 1787, B6, 154ff.

62. *Ibid.*, Feb. 18, June 27, Aug. 16, 1774, P.E.I., B1, 69, 77f, 79f.

63. P.E.I., *Stat.*, 14 Geo. III, c. 2 (1774). The act was continually renewed until it was superseded in 1801.

64. Fanning's Supplementary Remarks to the Charge of Malfeasance (1791), Fanning Papers, I, 81. An act was passed requiring twenty days' notice of election but it was disallowed because it ex-tended the immunity of arrest accorded members of Assembly to their servants. See P.E.I., *Stat.*, 20 Geo. III, c. 4 (1780); Lords of Trade to the King, June 20, 1781, and Germain to Patterson, Aug. 2, 1781, P.E.I. A4, 199f, 210.

65. P.E.I., *Ex. Co. Min.*, Feb. 8, Feb. 25, March 16, 1785, B5, 10, 12f, 15f. This action had two consequences; it marked the first occasion on which polling lasted more than one day, and the polling was not completed until the day after the writ was officially returnable.

66. P.E.I., *Stat.*, 41 Geo. III, c. 4 (1801).

67. See writs enclosed in MacGowan to DesBarres, No. 5, 1806, P.E.I. A21, 185.

68. MacGowan to DesBarres, Oct. 29, 1806, P.E.I. A21, 176.

69. DesBarres to MacGowan, Oct. 31, 1806, P.E.I. A21, 178.

70. MacGowan to DesBarres, Nov. 5, 1806, A21, 183–84.

71. P.E.I., *Stat.*, 47 Geo. III, c. 3 (1806).

72. P.E.I., *Ass. J.*, Jan. 4, 1832.

73. P.E.I., *Stat.*, 11 Geo. IV, c. 8 (1830). Having a suspending clause, the act was not given royal assent until Feb. 6, 1832.

74. *Ibid.*, 2 Wm. IV, c. 9 (1832).

75. *Ibid.*, 1 Vic., c. 9 (1838).

76. The act required forty days between teste and return of the writ, and ten days' notice to the electors. The sheriff's court was to open at the county court house between 10 A.M. and 4 P.M. to receive nominations for all the electoral districts within the county. It then adjourned until after the election when it reassembled and the sheriff would open the poll books, tabulate the vote, and declare the return. The hours of polling between April 1 and October 1 were from 8 A.M. to 7 P.M. and for the rest of the year were from 9 A.M. to 5 P.M.

CHAPTER FIVE

1. [Sydney] to Carleton, Aug. 20, 1784, P.A.C., N.B. A1, 32.

2. N.B., Instructions to Carleton, July 28, 1784, No. 12; N.B., *Ex. Co. Min.*, Oct. 11, 1785, P.A.C.

3. N.B., *Ex. Co. Min.*, Oct. 11, 21, 1785.

4. Carleton to Sydney, Oct. 25, 1785, N.B. A2, 216. Sydney, while approving of Carleton's arrangement, was of opinion that the franchise should have been confined to those in possession of land, regardless of tenure, and thus eliminate "the most refractory and disorderly" electors. It was the inclusion of this class of electors that Sydney blamed for the riot at St. John which accompanied the general election. Sydney to Carleton, April 19, 1786, N.B. A3, 39.

5. N.B., *Ass. J.*, Jan. 9, 1786.

6. N.B., Instructions to Carleton, July 28, 1784, No. 15.

7. N.B., *Stat.*, 26 Geo. III, c. 62 (1786), N.B., A69, n.p.

8. C. F. Bishop, *History of Elections in the American Colonies* (New York, 1893), 75.

9. Carleton to Grenville, March 19, 1790, N.B. A4, 129.

10. Enclosure in Grenville to Carleton, Aug. 25, 1790, N.B. A4, 197; Grenville to Carleton, Aug. 26, 1790, N.B. A4, 198.

11. N.B., *Stat.*, 31 Geo. III, c. 17 (1791).

12. N.B., *Ex. Co. Min.*, July 24, 1795.

13. Charter of the city of St. John, May 18, 1785, N.B. A2, 47–51. There were over five hundred freemen admitted in the year of the city's incorporation. See E. C. Wright, *The St. John River* (Toronto, 1949), 36.

14. This uncertainty was not removed until the consolidation act of 1843 (6 Vic., c. 44) when it was made plain the freehold electors of the city of St. John were required to fulfil the same qualifications as the freehold electors of the county.

15. N. Macdonald, *Canada 1763–1841, Immigration and Settlement* (London, 1939), 98, infers that the land was valued at about 2*s.* an acre.

16. See N.B., Instructions to Col. Thomas Carleton, July 28, 1784, Nos. 41, 48, 52, and 55; Instructions to Sir Guy Carleton, Aug. 23, 1786, No. 57; Additional Instructions to Dorchester, March 6, 1790, to Carleton, Sept. 4, 1802, to Prescott March 14, 1807.

17. Baillie to Douglas, Dec. 2, 1825, N.B. A34.2, 446. In 1822–23, the Crown Land Office reduced the customary grant to two hundred acres for married men and a hundred acres for single men.

18. Grenville to Carleton, March 10, 1790, N.B. A4, 120.

19. N.B., Committee of Council to Knox, June 23, 1800, N.B., A14.2, 225.

20. See N.B., *Ex. Co. Min.*, Aug. 5, 1803. This Minute states the Royal Instruction ordering the resumption of grants was issued on April 7, 1803, although there exists an additional Royal Instruction to Carleton ordering the resumption which is dated Sept. 4, 1802. The fees on a grant of two hundred acres amounted in 1818 to £12/8/4. See N.B., *Ass. J.*, Feb. 20, 1818.

21. Baillie to Douglas, Dec. 2, 1825, N.B. A34.2, 446.

22. N.B., *Ass. J.*, March 13, 1828.

23. N.B., *Stat.*, 9 Geo. IV, c. 36 (1828).

24. See N.B., *Ass. J.*, Feb. 27, 28, March 3, 1828, for the report of the controverted election committee on the lack of a proper register of the freemen of St. John.

25. See *Courier*, Feb. 15, 1834. Election procedure which was governed by the act of 1791 required the sheriff, if a poll was demanded on nomination day, to commence polling on the same or the following day and to continue to poll from day to day for a maximum of fifteen days unless the electors were sooner exhausted. The poll was to be kept open for seven hours each day between 8 A.M. and sunset, the fifteenth day only excepted, when the poll was to close at 3 P.M. The fifteen-day poll was to be completed within the forty days that were to elapse between the teste and return of the writ. Within this period the sheriff was to give public notice of the election, taking care that each parish constable would have a six-day interval in which he was to post a public notice in his parish. The sheriff was to determine the time and place of nomination and election, guided by the proviso that he should hold his court "at the most usual and public place of election within the county." The first two general elections had been conducted under the Minute of Council of Oct. 11, 1785. This Minute had specified an interval of forty days between teste and return of writ, and had required each sheriff to give fifteen days' notice of election, but had left the place and length of poll unspecified. The sheriffs appear to have held the poll at the most populous place in their county, polled by open vote, and continued the poll until the electors were exhausted. See W. H. Davidson, *An Account of the Life of William Davidson* (St. John, 1947), 44, for report on the first election in Northumberland County.

26. The 1791 act allowed the poll to move around the county on the request of a majority of the candidates but the sheriff had to acquiesce and the candidates had to agree on the place of adjournment. In 1826 a bill to make it mandatory for the sheriff to grant such a request passed the Assembly but failed to clear the Legislative Council. Consequently polls were seldom held outside the county town in New Brunswick. In Nova Scotia, on the other hand, it was common practice after 1792 to adjourn the poll around the county; on the request of a single candidate, the sheriff was required to adjourn the poll from the county town to one or more places in the county specified by law.

27. J. Hannay, *History of New Brunswick* (St. John, 1909), I, 368f.

28. See *Courier*, Feb. 18, 1837, for Assembly debate of Jan. 9, 1837.

29. N.B., *Ass. J.*, Feb. 10, 1835. The petitioners not only wanted the franchise confined to freeholders as by law established but also wanted to exclude the freeholders of the city of St. John from voting in the county.

30. N.B., *Stat.*, 7 Wm. IV, c. 55 (1837).

31. See N.B., *Ass. J.*, Feb. 8, 1842, for petition from York County.

32. Quoted in E. C. Wright. *The Miramichi* (Sackville, N.B., 1944) 49–50. The riot was ended only by the arrival of a detachment of troops.

33. N.B., *Stat.*, 6 Vic., c. 44 (1843).

34. N.B., *Ass. J.*, Feb. 10, 1826; Douglas to Bathurst, March 8, 1826. N.B. A36.1, 36.

35. See 1824 Census in Baillie to Murray, Aug. 1, 1829, N.B. A42.2, 281.

36. N.B., *Stat.*, 7 Geo. IV, c. 31 (1826).

37. *Ibid.*, 1 Wm. IV, c. 50 (1831).

38. *Ibid.*, 4 Wm. IV, c. 47 (1834).

39. *Ibid.*, 7 Vic., c. 51 (1844), 8 Vic., c. 104 (1845); Colebrooke to Stanley, April 29, 1844; C.O. 188, vol. 202, 268. See Gesner Report in the *Courier*, Jan. 7, 1843.

40. The lands were sold at an upset price of 2s. 6d. per acre, one-quarter of the purchase money to be paid at the time of purchase and the remainder in three annual instalments. A lessee was to pay a yearly rent equivalent to 5 per cent of the value of the land. To accommodate the poorest settlers, the Lieutenant Governor in Council was authorized on unsurveyed land to grant licences of occupancy for two hundred acres. See Bathurst to Commissioner of Crown Lands, March 1, 1827, in N.B., Ex. Co. Papers, P.A.C., M.G.9, A1, vol. 16; and the evidence before Durham's Committee on Crown Lands and Emigration (Quebec, 1839) on New Brunswick.

41. Colebrooke to Stanley, Aug. 9, Sept. 13, 1842, P.A.C., C.O. 188, vol. 202, n.p.

42. N.B., *Ass. J.*, Jan. 28, 1840, Jan. 21, 1842.

43. *Ibid.*, Feb. 27, 1844, Jan. 30, 1845, Feb. 6, 1846, Feb. 10, 1847, Feb. 10, 1848.

44. N.B., *Stat.*, 5 Vic., c. 41 (1842).

45. G. E. Fenety, *Political Notes and Observations* (Fredericton, 1867) I, xix.

46. *Ibid.*, I, 220.

47. *Ibid.*, I, 220.

48. Baillie to Colebrooke, Dec. 15, 1847, in N.B., *Ex. Co. Min.*, Feb. 2, 1848.

49. *Chronicle*, Feb. 15, 1850.

50. *Courier*, June 8, 1850

51. N.B., *Ass. J.*, March 15, 1851. These petitions, in addition to the ballot and a registry of voters, endorsed annual elections.

52. See election ads in the *Chronicle*, June 14, 1850, and June 2, 1851.

53. N.B., *Stat.*, (local), 14 Vic., c. 38, 14 Vic., c. 15 (1851). The former act to allow counties to establish municipal corporations was permissive and was adopted by only three counties, Carleton in 1852, York in 1855, and Sunbury in 1856.

54. *Courier*, Oct. 11, Oct. 25, 1851.

55. N.B., *Ass. J.*, March 30, 1852; *Courier*, Feb. 14, 1852, March 26, 1853.

56. *Courier*, March 5, 19, 1853.

57. *Ibid.*, April 16, 1853.

58. *Ibid.*, Feb. 25, 1854.

59. N.B., *Stat.*, 17 Vic., c. 13 (1854). Supporters of the bill had circulated the rumour that the Roman Catholic bishop intended to qualify subscribers to funds for the cathedral and cemetery by making them joint owners of the property. See *Courier*, April 15, 1854.

60. *Courier*, April 9, 16, 1853.

61. *Ibid.*, March 19, 1853.

62. *Chronicle*, Nov. 3, 1854.

63. *Courier*, April 1, 1854, April 18, 1857.

64. *Ibid.*, June 17, 1854. The editor is referring to citizens of the county who were required to pay a poll tax.

65. N.B., *Ass. Debates*, Feb. 28, 1855.

66. *Ibid.*, Feb. 24, 1855, Feb. 27, 1855.

67. N.B., *Stat.*, 18 Vic., c. 37 (1855).

68. N.B., *Rev. Stat.*, c. 53, s. 11 (1854).

69. *Courier*, March 31, 1855.

70. *Ibid.*, March 24, 1855.

71. In 1858 the act was amended to allow the ballot box to be opened, counted, and results announced at each poll. See N.B., *Stat.*, 21 Vic., c. 33 (1858).

72. N.B., *Ass. J.* 1857 (1st sess.), App.

73. *Ibid.*, March 7, 1857.

74. N.B., *Ass. J.* Feb. 23, 1857.

75. *Ibid.*, March 13, 1857.

76. N.B. *Stat.*, 20 Vic., c. 2 (1857).

77. *Courier*, Aug. 29, 1857. The increase in the potential electorate for St. John County as contrasted with the actual voters in the late election was probably due to the season. The election had been held at the end of April at a time when rural communications were poor and the farmers busy. At the next general election in June, 1861, the vote cast for St. John County was up only 25 per cent.

78. N.B., *Ass. Debates*, May 3, 1865. See N.B., *Ass. J.*, Feb. 13, 1863, Feb. 20, 1864, May 1, 1865.

79. N.B. Census 1861; see N.B., *Leg. Co. J.*, 1862, App.

80. *Courier*, July 18, 1863.

CHAPTER SIX

1. Draft of Particular Instructions to Carleton, 1786, No. 3, in A. Shortt and A. G. Doughty, eds., *Documents Relating to the Constitutional History of Canada 1759-1791* (Ottawa, 1918), 814.

2. Dorchester to Sydney, June 13, 1787, P.A.C., Q27.2, 983; Sydney to Dorchester, Sept. 3, 1788, Q36.2, 469.

3. See enclosure, Grenville to Dorchester, Oct. 20, 1789, Q42, 96.

4. In a petition five years previously, the English residents had expressed a desire for an assembly open to His Majesty's "Old and New Subjects." See Petition of the Ancient and New Subjects, Inhabitants of the Province of Quebec, Nov. 24, 1784, Q24.1, 1.

5. Dorchester to Grenville, Feb. 8, 1790, Q44.1, 24; see Second Draft of the Constitutional Act 1790, in Shortt and Doughty, 1010f.

6. Grenville to Dorchester, June 5, 1790, Q44.1, 155.

7. Br., *Stat.*, 31 Geo. III, c. 31 (1791).

8. Shortt and Doughty, 753.

9. Grenville considered the qualification required in the above New Brunswick bill too low; see Grenville to Carleton, Aug. 26, 1790, P.A.C., N.B. A4, 198.

10. *The Parliamentary History of England* (London, 1817), XXIX, 106f.

11. Anon., *Thoughts on the Canada Bill* (London, 1791), 22f, P.A.C., Pamphlet Collection No. 741.

12. W. B. Munro, *The Seigniorial System in Canada* (New York, 1907), chaps. IV–VII.

13. Lymburner to Grenville, July 24, 1789, Q43.2, 777.

14. Additional Instruction to Carleton, July 2, 1771, and Instructions to Carleton, Jan. 3, 1775, No. 38, Shortt and Doughty, 423, 608.

15. Additional Instruction to Haldimand, July 16, 1783, *ibid.*, 730ff. This Additional Instruction to Haldimand was incorporated in the Instructions to Dorchester, Aug. 23, 1786, *ibid.*, 829–31.

16. Dorchester to Sydney, June 13, 1787, Q27.2, 983.

17. Ordinance Establishing Civil Courts, Sept. 17, 1764 and Patents Creating New Districts, July 24, 1788, Shortt and Doughty, 205, 953.

18. See *Thoughts on the Canada Bill*, 19.

19. *Parliamentary History of England*, XXIX, 427.

20. *Ibid.*, 428. Fox was also able to have the life of the Assembly reduced from seven to four years.

21. L.C., *Ass. J.*, Nov. 23, 1832.

22. *Édits. Ordonnances royaux, Declarations et Arrêts du Conseil d'État du Roi concernant le Canada* (Québec, 1854), I, 585–86.

23. By the Custom of Paris, lands held *en roture* were divided equally among all the family, while of lands held *en fief* the manor house and one-half of the seigniory went to the eldest son and the other half went to the rest of the family in equal proportions. See C. de Ferriere, *Nouveau Commentaire sur la Coutume de la Prévôté et Vicomté de Paris*, revised by S. D'Aramon, vol. I, arts. xv, xvi, and vol. II, art. cccii (Paris, 1770).

24. Craig to Liverpool, May 1, 1810, Q112, 147.

25. See *Quebec Gazette*, July 12, 1824.

26. *Quebec Gazette*, Jan. 10, 1831.

27. Craig to Liverpool, May 1, 1810, Q112, 147.

28. Strachan to [Bathurst], June 5, 1823, Q165, 20; Campbell to Murray, Oct. 20, 1828, Q186.1, 136.

29. See First Annual Report of the Constitutional Association of Quebec (Quebec, 1835), 21, General Report of the Commissioners for Investigation of all Grievances affecting His Majesty's Subjects of Lower Canada, 1836, Q234, 260.

30. L.C., *Stat.*, 4 Wm. IV, c. 28, s. 27 (1834).

31. L.C., *Ass. J.*, Jan. 27, 1834.

32. Papineau in the Assembly debate of Feb. 5, 1836, as reported in the *Quebec Mercury*, Feb. 9, 1836, stated Neilson was the author of the clause to disfranchise the commercial interests. This inaccuracy is corrected in an anonymous letter dated Quebec, Feb. 12, 1836, and published in the *Montreal Gazette*, Feb. 18. 1836. Neilson had been in favour of disfranchising not co-proprietors but shareholders in joint stock companies.

33. See *Petition of the Constitutional Association of Montreal*, March, 1836, Q.227.1, 66.

34. Glenelg to Aylmer, June 29, 1835, P.A.C., G29.2, 609.

35. See L.C., *Ass. J.*, Jan. 8, 1836; *Quebec Mercury*, Jan. 21, 1836; and Glenelg to Gosford, July 20, 1836 G.32.1, 35. Unaware of the disallowance, the London agent of the Constitutional Association of Montreal at the time of the reunion of the Canadas advised the Colonial Office to remove the prohibition against co-partners, claiming it would increase the English vote in Montreal and Quebec by 50 to 100 votes. Gillespie to Russell, June 11, 1840, Q276.1, 74.

36. L.C., *Ass. J.*, Jan. 17, Jan. 21, Feb. 5, 1834.

37. *Ibid.*, March 28, April 4, 1793.

38. *Ibid.*, March 18, 24, 26, 1800. Lt. Gov. Milne writing to Portland stated: "Very few of the seigneurs . . . have sufficient interest to ensure their own election or the election of anyone to whom they give their support . . . and the uneducated habitant has even a better chance of being nominated (though he cannot perhaps sign his name) than the first officer under the Crown." Milne to Portland (separate & secret), Nov. 1, 1800, Q85, 232. See also Black to Kent, Oct. 9, 1806, Q106.2, 565.

39. Craig to Liverpool, May 1, 1810, Q112, 146–47.

40. *Ibid.*, 130.

41. Dalhousie to Bathurst (confidential), Nov. 21, 1823, Q166.3, 506; Draft Union Bill, June, 1822, Q163.1, 9.

42. Campbell to Murray, Oct. 20, 1828, Q186.1, 137.

43. Br., *Stat.*, 3 & 4 Vic., c. 35, s. 28 (1840). See Thomson to Russell, (confidential), Jan. 22, 1840, Q270.1, 111. From 1710 (9 Anne, c.5) until its abolition in 1858 (21 & 22 Vic., c. 26) the Imperial Parliament required its members to be possessed of real property of an annual value of £600.

44. L.C., *Ass. J.*, 1828–29, App. H.H.

45. The township residents in Buckingham lived anywhere from 90 to 120 miles from a poll, in Richelieu County 100 miles and in Bedford a mere 20 to 30 miles. In York County, which extended along the entire eastern back of the Ottawa River from the county's southern limits opposite the Island of Montreal, the settlers at Hull were placed 100 miles distant from a poll. In addition the returning officers tended to confine the notification of elections to the vicinity of the poll and one elector for the township of Eaton in Buckinghamshire complained before a controverted election committee that during his twenty-three years' residence in the township he had never known the township to be notified as to the date of polling. See L.C., *Ass. J.*, Jan. 18, 1822; Jan. 9, 1824, and App. TTT; and Feb. 18, 1825.

46. L.C., *Stats.*, 40 Geo. III, c. 1 (1800), 47 Geo. III, c. 16 (1807). A twelfth county was given a second poll in 1825 (5 Geo. IV, c. 33). By the act of 1800, the returning officers were required to post a notice of election between fifteen and eight days before the election on the door of each parish church, or other public place, on pain of forfeiture of £10 for neglect. In 1803 (43 Geo. III, c. 5) it was decided to supplement the practice of penalizing returning officers by a schedule of financial enticement to encourage them to fulfil their duty. The returning officer was to be paid £3 for each election, 5s. for each notice of election posted, and 1s. per league for travel involved in posting notices. In 1807 (47 Geo. III, c. 16) while the financial enticement was retained, the financial penalty for neglect was raised to £30.

47. By 1816 the townships surrounding Hull had begun to fill in with English and Irish settlers drawn by the lumber trade. These settlers, through the agency of Philemon Wright, made representation to the Assembly in 1823–24 to secure better polling facilities and the division of York into three counties. See L.C., *Ass. J.*, 1823–24, App. TTT.

48. Milne to Camden, Aug. 1, 1805, Q98, 109.

49. Opinion of the Attorney General, May 10, 1805, Q98, 123.

50. Craig to Liverpool, May 1, 1810, Q112, 121. If control of the Assembly could not be secured by redistribution, Craig recommended its abolition or union with Upper Canada. His recommendations were the foundation of the union bill introduced into the House of Commons by the Under-Secretary of State, Wilmot Horton, in 1822. See Q163.1, 9.

51. See Craig to Liverpool, May 1, 1810, Q112, 145f; Dalhousie to Bathurst, April 5, 1825, Q172.1, 113f; Felton to Horton, Jan. 21, 1826, Q178.1, 221; and Dalhousie to Gale, Jan. 25, 1828, Q182.1, 1.

52. The township population estimated at 5,000 in 1805 had risen to an estimated 26,000 in 1823. Milne to Camden, Aug. 1, 1805, Q98, 109; L.C., *Ass. J.*, 1823–24, App. T.T.T.

53. [Liverpool] to Craig, Sept. 12, 1810 (confidential), Q113, 51; and Draft Union Bill, 1822, Q163.1, 9.

54. L.C., *Ass. J.*, March 10, 1823, March 4, 1824, March 4, 1825, March 11, 1826, Feb. 6, 1827; L.C., *Leg. Co. J.*, March 19, 1823, March 9, 1824, March 17, 1825, March 15, 1826, March 2, 1827; *Quebec Gazette*, March 3, 1825, Jan. 5, 1826.

55. Dalhousie to Gale, Jan. 25, 1828, Q182.1, 7–9; Felton to Horton, Jan. 21, 1826, Q178.1, 224f.

56. See Stephen to Murray, Sept. 3, 1828, Q184.4, 567–80, for the arguments presented to the select committee.

57. See U.C., *Stat.*, 60 Geo. III, c. 2 (1820), which gave one representative to each county containing 1,000 citizens and two representatives to each county whose population was in excess of 4,000.

58. See N. Hoskins, *A History of the State of Vermont from its discovery and settlement to the close of the Year 1830* (Vergennes, 1831); and Z. Thompson, *History of the State of Vermont from its earliest settlement to the close of the Year 1832* (Burlington, 1833).

59. L.C., *Ass. J.*, 1828–29, App. H.H. It should be said the Colonial Office was prepared to consider intervention if the townships were not enfranchised. See Murray to Kempt, Sept. 29, 1828, G17, 260f.

60. L.C., *Stat.*, 9 Geo. IV, c. 73 (1829). See L.C., *Ass. J.* 1828–29 App. G.G.; L.C., *Leg. Co., J.*, March 9, 1829; *Quebec Gazette*, Feb. 2, 1829.

61. The Assembly retrieved its honour by frenchifying the names of the counties. The effect of the act was to increase the French representation by twenty-five and the English by nine.

62. See Walker to Glenelg, June 17, 1835, and Neilson to Glenelg, July 10, 1835, Q232, 19v–21v.

63. L.C., *Ass. J.*, 1831–32, App. OO. The census showed that fifteen counties whose population ranged from 2,000 to 10,000 sent thirty members to the Assembly, while eleven counties with a population range of 10,000 to 15,000 sent twenty-two, and ten counties with a population between 15,000 and 20,000 sent twenty.

64. General Report of the Commissioners for the Investigation of all Grievances affecting His Majesty's Subjects of Lower Canada, Part II, The Representation of the People, Nov. 15, 1836, Q234, 8–12. Sir Charles Grey conceived this suggestion.

65. Moffatt and Badgley to Durham, April 5, 1838, Q255.2, 458. This letter of the agents of the Montreal Constitutional Association and a similar letter from Moffatt to Durham, April 16, 1838, Q246.1, 21, are full of false criticisms of the representation act of 1829.

66. See L.C., *Ass. J.*, Feb. 2, 1831, Nov. 16, 1832, Jan. 20, 1834.

67. L.C., *Stats.*, 3 Wm. IV, c. 22 (1833); 4 Wm. IV, c. 6 (1834).

68. M. M. Quaife, ed., *John Askin Papers* (Detroit, 1928), I, 416ff. The last vestige of seigniorial tenure did not disappear until 1821 when Grand Island near Kingston was regranted in freehold.

69. U.C., *Ass. J.*, Feb. 5, 21, 22, 1821.

70. *Ibid.*, March 5, 1821.

71. See *York Weekly Post*, March 12, 1821, and *Kingston Chronicle*, March 30, 1821 (supplement), for Attorney General Robinson's speech in the Assembly debates on the question.

72. By Minute of Council, Oct. 20, 1818, U.C. Land Book J., 469, no patents were to be issued unless the ticket holder had erected a habitable house and cleared and fenced five acres in every hundred.

73. Assembly Debates, March 5, 1821, in *Kingston Chronicle*, March 30, 1821 (supplement).

74. *Ibid.*

75. Maitland to Bathurst, July 21, 1821, Q329, 281.

76. Maitland to Bathurst, Nov. 9, 1824, Q336.2, 512.

77. See Chas. Jones to Hillier, March 20, 1824; Hamnett Pinhey to Hillier, April 9, 1824; W. Morris to Hillier, June 4, 1824: P.A.C., U.C. Sundries.

78. Copley and Wetherall to Bathurst, Sept. 9, 1826, Q342, 55, enclosed in Huskisson to Maitland, Nov. 25, 1827, G63.2, 408.

79. U.C., *Ass. J.*, Nov. 26, 30, 1832, Jan. 11, 16, 1833.

80. *Ibid.*, Feb. 17, 1827, Nov. 10, 1836.

81. Nov. 25, 1836. Wm. Buell, a former Reform M.P.P., was the editor of this paper.

82. Richardson to Joseph, May 16, 1836, U.C. Sundries.

83. See Sir C. P. Lucas, ed., *Lord Durham's Report on the Affairs of British North America* (Oxford, 1912) II, 229; and U.C. Land Book P., Minute, May 24, 1832, 181–82. The abolition of settlement duties on these grants in 1832 led to the disappearance of location tickets.

84. U.C., *Ass. J.*, Feb. 1, 1831.

85. *Ibid.*, Nov. 21, 1832, Jan. 26, 1835.

86. *Ibid.*, Dec. 8, 1831, Dec. 10, 1832. The members for York tried over a considerable number of years to secure a vote for urban leaseholders of commercial lots and premises, and at times attempts were made to apply this extension to rural leaseholders. See *ibid.*, Jan. 14, 1831, Nov. 6, 1832, Nov. 26, 1833, Jan. 16, 1836; U.C., *Leg. Co. J.*, Dec. 7, 1832, Feb. 18–26, 1836; and *British Colonial Argus*, Jan. 11, 1834, for Assembly Debates of Dec. 8, 1833.

87. U.C., *Stat.*, 40 Geo. III, c. 3 (1800). For the election immediately following the passage of the act, a period of only four years' residence in Upper Canada and subscription to the oath of allegiance was required.

88. Gray to Hunter, July 16, 1800, Q287.2, 242.

89. U.C., *Ass. J.*, June 3, 1801, Feb. 21–25, 1804, Feb. 21–26, 1805, Feb. 7–19, 1806.

90. See below chap. XIII.

91. Memorial in Mackenzie to Goderich, July 24, 1832, Q376.1, 85.

92. Goderich to Colborne, Nov. 8, 1832, G69, 371–73; U.C., *Stat.*, 4 Wm. IV, c. 14 (1834).

93. U.C., *Ass. J.*, Feb. 2, 1838, Dec. 11, 1839. The bills would have disfranchised members of Hunters' Lodges. See *Brockville Recorder*, Dec. 26, 1839.

94. U.C., *Stat.*, 35 Geo. III, c. 2 (1795); Simcoe to Portland, Aug. 22, 1795, Q281.2, 451.

95. *Ibid.*, 54 Geo. III, c. 4 (1814).

96. U.C., *Ass. J.*, Feb. 25, March 3, 1817.

97. U.C. *Stat.*, 58 Geo. III, c. 9 (1818). In 1822 an act (2 Geo. IV, c. 4) was passed to exclude for all time from membership in the Assembly any person who had taken an oath of abjuration of his allegiance to the Crown or held any public office in the United States federal or state governments.

98. See U.C., *Ass. J.*, Feb. 11-12, 1818.

99. This convention had been summoned by Robert Gourlay to discuss the grievances under which the people of Upper Canada laboured. The resolution was rescinded by the Assembly on March 2, 1821.

100. Simcoe to Dundas, Aug. 20, 1792, enclosing proclamation of July 16, 1792, Q278, 197-200.

101. U.C., *Stats.*, 38 Geo. III, c. 5 (1798); 40 Geo. III, c. 3 (1800). See report on the former bill by Chief Justice Elmsley in Russell to Portland, Aug. 11, 1798, Q285, 85-90.

102. In 1808 six additional members were distributed equally between the eastern and western sections of the province, and in 1817 representation was accorded the new counties of Halton and Wentworth which had been created in 1816 out of townships detached from the west riding of York, the first riding of Lincoln, and Haldimand. See *ibid.*, 48 Geo. III, c. 11 (1808), 57 Geo. III, c. 1 (1817).

103. *Ibid.*, 60 Geo. III, c. 2 (1820); for comment on act see Maitland to Bathurst, May 7, 1821, Q329, 151.

104. A proviso declared no county should return fewer members than it was then returning in order to safeguard Lincoln which was returning four. The act for the first time assigned representation to urban centres. All towns which were the site of the Quarter Sessions for each judicial district were to return a member once their population reached 1000. Since there were only ten judicial districts the privilege was limited, and York and Kingston were the only towns to qualify immediately. Representation was authorized for the contemplated provincial university. See U.C., *Ass. J.*, June 22, 1819, for Maitland's Message to the Assembly.

105. See C. Lindsey, *Life and Times of Wm. L. Mackenzie* (Toronto, 1862), I, 190ff; Assembly Debates, Feb. 12, 1831, in *Kingston Chronicle*, March 5, 1831; and Memorial in Mackenzie to Goderich, July 24, 1832, Q376.1, 107f.

106. U.C., *Ass. J.* Jan. 21, 25, 1831.

107. Memorial, Mackenzie to Goderich, July 24, 1832, Q376.1, 113; Lindsey, 201.

108. See *Kingston Chronicle*, March 5, 12, 1831, for Assembly Debates of Feb. 12, 1831.

109. Goderich to Colborne, Nov. 8, 1832, G69, 308.

110. U.C., *Ass. J.*, Nov. 25, 1831.

111. *Ibid.*, 1832, App.: Select Committee on Grievances, First Report, 196.

112. U.C., *Stat.*, 3 Wm. IV, c. 15 (1833); 4 Wm. IV, c. 45 (1834). The Lieutenant Governor asked the Assembly to consider the creation of Huron County. See U.C., *Ass. J.*, Nov. 30, 1833.

113. See *St. Thomas Liberal*, Dec. 16, 1832, for Assembly Debates of Nov. 16, 1832.

114. Robinson to Hillier, June 28, 1824, U.C. Sundries.

115. R. Leonard to S. P. Jarvis, Oct. 25, 1830, in U.C., *Ass. J.*, 1831, App. 213.

116. Memorial, Mackenzie to Goderich, July 24, 1832, Q376.1, 113. See U.C., *Ass. J.*, Nov. 25, 1831, for Vaughan Township petitions.

117. The only legislation secured was a temporary measure to establish polling subdivisions for the second Leeds by-election. See U.C., *Stat.*, 6 Wm. IV, c. 32 (1836).

118. U.C., *Ass. J.*, March 1-April 16, 1839, Dec. 4-24, 1839, Jan. 2-9, 1840. The bill was subjected to eight divisions on Jan. 9, 1840. See *Brockville Recorder*, Dec. 19, 1839 for a copy of the bill.

CHAPTER SEVEN

1. Br., *Stat.*, 3 & 4, Vic., c. 35 (1840); see also C. P. Lucas, ed., *Lord Durham's Report on the Affairs of British North America* (Oxford, 1912), II, 307.

2. Thomson did suggest an educational test might be useful. As it would have been a limiting factor especially in Lower Canada, he suggested it should not be applied until the end of a specific period of eight or ten years. Thomson to Russell (confidential), Jan. 22, 1840, P.A.C., Q270.1, 117. Poulett Thomson, who became Governor of Canada in 1839, was raised to the peerage as Baron Sydenham in 1840. He will henceforth be referred to as Sydenham.

3. The North American Colonial Association was an organization of London merchants trading to Canada; the Montreal Constitutional Association was a group of Montreal merchants. For their representations, see Carter to Glenelg, Jan. 26, 1839, Q266.1, 93; Badgley to Normandy, April 12, 1839, Q268.1, 116; Robinson to Labouchere, July 12, 1839, P.A.C., C.O. 42, vol. 468, 247.

4. Gillespie to Russell, April 3, 1840, Q276.1, 55.

5. See above, p. 87.

6. Q268.1, 126; Q266.1, 96; Q270.1, 140. The Upper Canada Assembly did not specify the form the qualification should take. See U.C., *Ass. J.*, March 27, 1839.

7. Q163.1, 9.

8. Carter to Glenelg, Jan. 26, 1839, Q266.1, 94.

9. Lucas, *Lord Durham's Report*, II, 299.

10. *Ibid.*, 324.

11. *Ibid.*, 288f.

12. G. de T. Glazebrook, "Representation by the Act of Union of 1840," *Canadian Historical Review*, X (1929), 252-56.

13. The first draft bill sent by Normanby to Colborne on June 12, 1839, had been prepared but never introduced into Parliament. It has been impossible to obtain a copy of this bill but an informed letter which appears to reveal its general contents appeared in the Cobourg *Star* and was copied by the *Quebec Gazette*, July 15, 1839. The second draft bill sent by Normanby to Colborne, on July 5, 1839, is printed in the *Quebec Gazette*, July 29, 1839.

14. U.C., *Ass. J.*, Dec. 7, 1839.

15. Lucas, II, 299. The token opposition in the House of Commons allowed the equal representation clause to pass through committee without a division. The opposition to the clause was more vociferous in the Lords; a division was called and on third reading Ellenborough entered a formal protest against this injustice. See *Hansard's Parliamentary Debates*, 3rd Series (London, 1840), March 23, April 13, May 29, June 12, June 30, and July 13, 1840.

16. Colborne estimated the French population at 520,000 and the English at 680,000; Thomson estimated the population of Upper Canada at 400,000 and of Lower Canada at 650,000 leaving the English with an over-all majority. Colborne to Normanby, Aug. 19, 1839, Q260.1, 41; Thomson to Russell (confidential), Dec. 24, 1839, Q262, 141.

17. Gillespie to Russell, May 22, 1840, Q276.1, 66-67.

18. Lucas, II, 324.

19. Can., *Ass. J.*, March 20-21, 1849, June 28, 1850, and July 29, 1851. The bill introduced was essentially the same in all cases. See Can., *Bills*, sess. 1849, Bill no. 147; sess. 1850, Bill no. 95; and sess. 1851, Bill no. 231.

20. Quoted in *Montreal Gazette*, Jan. 24, 1849.

21. Can., *Stat.*, 14 & 15 Vic., c. 5 (1851).

22. *Ibid.*, 16 Vic., c. 152 (1853). The previous year the Hincks-Morin ministry had tried by 16 Vic c. 1 (1852) to adjust the old representation to the new county structure.

23. The year after the passage of the Morin-Hincks representation act the Imperial Parliament by 17 & 18 Vic., c. 118 (1854), amended the Act of Union to abolish the two-thirds majority required to secure adjustments to the representation.

24. The counties were L'Acadie, Beauharnois, Chambly, Laprairie, Richelieu, Rouville, St. Hyacinthe, Terrebonne, Two Mountains, and Verchères. See C.O. 42, vol. 468, 251; Q266.1, 96.

25. Gillespie to Russell, April 3, 1840, Q276.1, 55.

26. *Ibid.*, May 27, 1840, Q276.1, 69. "Bear" Ellice advocated these views in the House of Commons and was largely responsible for their adoption. See also Sydenham to Russell (private), Feb. 24, 1841, in P. Knaplund, ed., *Letters from Lord Sydenham to Lord John Russell* (London, 1931), 118.

27. Sydenham to Russell (confidential), Feb. 26, 1841, P.A.C., G12, vol. 56, 171. Sydenham, born into a mercantile family and having served as M.P. for Manchester and as an officer of the Board of Trade, was by nature sympathetic to mercantile interests. See G. P. Scrope, *Memoir of the Life of the Right Honourable Charles, Lord Sydenham* (London, 1843).

28. Sydenham to Russell, March 6, 1841, G12, vol. 56, 178.

29. See Can., *Ass. J.*, 1841. App. NN.

30. Can., *Stat.*, 6 Vic., c. 16 (1842).

31. See *Quebec Gazette*, April 9, 1841, for list of old and new polls.

32. *Le Canadien*, March 29, 1841.

33. See Can., *Ass. J.*, 1841, App. Y., for the correspondence. It was widely published in the newspapers during the course of the election; see *Quebec Gazette*, March 29, 31, 1841.

34. Can., *Ass. J.*, 1841, App. Y.

35. The counties were Montreal, Rouville, Beauharnois, Vaudreuil, Chambly, Terrebonne, and Berthier. The first six counties returned administration candidates, the latter returned an Englishman, but one who opposed the administration. Montreal and Rouville returned two French Canadian supporters of the administration but the other four counties returned Englishmen despite the fact that only in Beauharnois were the French Canadians in a minority.

36. See *Quebec Gazette*, April 6, 1841, for letter from J. A. Berthelot, Lafontaine's law partner.

37. The editor of the *Montreal Herald* was the secretary of the trustees charged with improving the Montreal roads and the Irishmen were in their employ.

38. For electoral purposes the county of Montreal included the freeholders of city and county whose joint population by the 1844 census was 64,306 and whose electors were estimated at 3,300.

39. It should be realized that the French and English parties in the Assembly from Canada East were not exclusively French or English. The former party included such English members as Neilson, Aylwin, and Armstrong, and the latter party included such French members as de Salaberry and DeLisle. All English members who supported the French party were returned from French electoral districts.

40. Knaplund, *Letters*, 110f. Major Campbell married a daughter of M. Duchesnay, seignior of Gaudarville and Fossembault, following this general election and on his retirement from the army returned to Canada, purchased the seigniory of St. Hilaire, and was subsequently elected to the Legislative Assembly for the county of Rouville. See P. G. Roy, *La Famille Juchereau Duchesnay* (Lévis, 1903), 324ff.

41. See *Montreal Gazette*, Aug. 5, 1841 and *Quebec Gazette*, Sept. 1, 22, 1841.

42. Jackson to Stanley, No. 30, 1841, G12, vol. 59, 95f.

43. Bagot to Stanley, Nov. 11, 1842, G12, vol. 63, 361f.

44. Can., *Stat.*, 6 Vic., c. 1 (1842).

45. The poll, which was to open at 9 A.M. each day, was on no account to close until 5 P.M. on the second day. The Act did not specify the time of closing on the first day. Under Lower Canada law the poll had been limited to eight hours a day between 8 A.M. and 5 P.M.; but in Upper Canada there had been no legal limit on the daily hours of polling, which had depended upon agreement among the candidates or on the decision of the returning officer. As a result the hours of closing and the duration of polling had been irregular. For example, in 1841, the poll for Kent County had not closed until midnight on the sixth day of polling, and the election for Stanstead which had begun on March 22 had not terminated until April 6, a total of fifteen polling days.

46. Can., *Ass. J.*, Dec. 11, 1844. See also J. C. Dent, *The Last Forty Years: Canada since the Union of 1841* (Toronto, 1881), I, 376, and Sir F. Hincks, *The Political History of Canada between 1840 and 1855, a lecture* (Montreal, 1877), 35f.

47. See Can., *Ass. J.*, Feb. 6, 1845, April 6, 1846; *Montreal Gazette*, Feb. 8, 1845; and *Le Canadien*, April 20, 1846.

48. Can., *Stat.*, 12 Vic., c. 27 (1849).

49. Can., *Stat.*, 29 & 30 Vic., c. 13 (1866). To curtail political exuberance the act abolished the "show of hands" on nomination day, and the public proclamation of the return. George Brown deplored these features of the legislation as likely to destroy the spirit and fervour of Canadian elections. See *Globe*, Aug. 13, 1866.

50. Can., *Ass. J.*, Sept. 29, 1854; Can., *Bills*, sess. 1860, Bill no. 83; sess. 1862, Bills no. 63, 64; sess. 1864, Bill no. 57; and sess. 1866, Bill no. 10. Dorion, when Attorney General, secured the passage of the measure through the Assembly in 1864 but it perished in the Legislative Council.

51. Can., *Ass. J.* March 13, 1848. See also *Globe*, Jan. 15, 19, 1848.

52. The 1844 general election provides two illustrations. In Lanark, the returning officer neglected to establish polls in four townships and in Grenville an over-zealous officer established polls in two townships of the adjacent county. See Can., *Ass. J.*, Dec. 6, 9, 1844.

53. Doctors, postmasters, millers, former returning officers, and persons sixty years and upwards were not obliged to serve if requested.

54. Can., *Ass. J.*, Feb. 12, 1849.

55. Can., *Stat.*, 7 Vic., c. 65 (1843).

56. *Ibid.*, 6 Vic., c. 1 (1842).

57. *Ibid.*, 20 Vic., c. 22 (1857).

58. *Ibid.*, 22 Vic., c. 82 (1858).

59. P.E.I., *Stat.*, 47 Geo. III, c. 3 (1806). This ban also applied to all members of the Executive Council as in the early years its membership was synonymous with that of the Legislative Council. In 1838 (1 Vic., c. 9) the ban was limited to members of the Legislative Council.

60. V.I., *Stat.*, Franchise Act, 1859.

CHAPTER EIGHT

1. Can., *Stat.*, 12 Vic., c. 27 (1849). These qualifications were those of the Constitutional Act first

modified for local currency by L.C., *Stat.*, 2 Geo. IV, c. 4 (1822). Besides specifying tenure *en fief* and *en roture* the 1849 act specified tenure *en franc alleu*. Tenure *en franc alleu* was analogous to freehold tenure and by the Commutation of Tenure Act, Can., *Stat.*, 8 Vic., c. 42 (1845) those holding land *en roture* could commute to *franc alleu* on agreement with the seignior. The act also specified that, unless an elector's property had been acquired by descent or marriage, it had to be registered three months before the teste of the writs. These restraints had existed in Lower Canada since 1822 when property had to be held six months before the teste of the writs, and since 1824 in Upper Canada when property had to be possessed for twelve months and the deed of conveyance (Crown patents excepted) registered three months prior to the election. The exception as respects Crown patents was now ended because the privilege had been abused not merely by Bond Head in the 1836 general election but in the 1848 election in Waterloo County. In the latter case the patents had been issued to settlers on the Owen Sound Tract for the benefit of the Conservative candidate. See Can., *Ass. J.*, March 13, 1848, Feb. 8, 1849.

2. *Montreal Gazette*, April 6, 1849. The British American Land Company possessed approximately 800,000 acres in the Eastern Townships. See O. D. Skelton, *The Life and Times of Sir Alexander Tilloch Galt* (Toronto, 1920), 32 *et seq*.

3. *Montreal Gazette*, April 25, 1849.

4. *Ibid.*, April 20, May 15, 1849; Can., *Ass. J.*, April 18, 1849.

5. The increase cannot all be attributed to the improved facilities, for the vote actually declined in some counties. For instance in Dorchester the vote cast in 1844 at fifteen polls was 50 per cent less than the vote cast in 1841 at a single poll gathering votes for six days. The drawing power of rousing political contests cannot be overlooked. Whereas Dorchester was in 1841 convulsed by a political feud between an uncle and nephew of the Taschereau family, the election in 1844 went by virtual default.

6. See I. A. Stewart, "The 1841 Election of Dr. William Dunlop, as Member of Parliament for Huron County," *Papers and Records, Ontario Historical Society*, XXXIX (Toronto, 1947), pp. 51–62. It would appear the officer was less exacting when it came to Strachan's supporters, for a controverted election committee unseated Strachan when it was found the votes of minors and non-freeholders had given him a majority. Can., *Ass. J.*, June 16, Aug. 20, 1841.

7. Census of the Canadas 1851–52 (Quebec, 1853), I, pp. xi–xii.

8. *Examiner*, March 20, 27, 1850. See also G. M. Jones, "The Peter Perry Election and the Rise of the Clear Grit Party," *Papers and Records, Ontario Historical Society*, XII (Toronto, 1914), 164–75.

9. See *L'Avenir*, May 21, 1851, for platform of the Parti Rouge.

10. Can., *Stat.*, 16 Vic., c. 153 (1853). In local currency £1/4/4 was equivalent to £1 sterling. It should be noted that Canadian assessment laws assessed rural property at its actual value, and urban property at its yearly value. This accounts for the franchise in the counties being ascribed to property of an assessed actual value or of an assessed yearly value, while in representative cities and towns it was ascribed only to property of a specific assessed yearly value.

11. There was considerable criticism of the special liability imposed on tenants and occupants of Crown lands, it being argued that the Government sought to use the franchise to enforce the payment of monies due the Crown Land Office. The Crown, however, put itself in the same position as a private landlord in respect of those seigniories which were in its possession where failure to pay seigniorial dues was not to disfranchise the occupant. See *Pilot*, Feb. 26, 1853.

12. Can., *Stat.*, 13 & 14 Vic., c. 67 (1850). The assessment laws for Canada West were consolidated following the passage of the assessment franchise; see *ibid.*, 16 Vic., c. 182 (1853). By the latter act the assessment rolls in Canada West were not required to be finally revised until July 15 each year. They were thus in the process of preparation when the ministry was defeated on June 20, 1854.

13. See *Montreal Gazette*, July 7, 10, Aug. 2, 1854.

14. Can., *Stat.*, 18 Vic., c. 7 (1854).

15. Feb. 22, 1858.

16. See Can., *Bills*, sess. 1854–55, Bill no. 180, for a private member's attempt to reduce the assessment.

17. Can., *Stat.*, 18 Vic., c. 87 (1855). The temporary franchise extension act of 1854 had slightly modified the franchise prescribed by the act of 1853. These changes were continued by the above act.

18. See *Montreal Gazette*, April 25, 1855, for Assembly debates on the bill. The attempts of the Rouges and Clear Grits to use the municipal tax rolls as a makeshift voters' register by equating the provincial and municipal franchise through the extension of the vote to all who paid municipal taxes was curtly dismissed by the Assembly. See Can., *Ass. J.*, May 25, 1855.

19. Can., *Ass. J.*, 1858, App. 28, for the election returns for 1854 and 1858. In using these returns,

all ridings have been eliminated for which there was a disputed return or an acclamation in either general election. The percentages have been derived from twenty-three ridings in Canada East and thirty-five ridings in Canada West.

20. *Globe*, Jan. 7, 1858. Describing the election *Le Journal de Quebec* of Jan. 12, 1858, stated, "votes are given, at the different polls, in the names of the living and the dead of all nations."

21. See *Pilot*, March 24, 1858.

22. Draft petition enclosed with the "Circulaire au Sujet des Élections", March 8, 1858. See H. Têtu and C. O. Gagnon, éds. *Mandements, Lettres, Pastorales, et Circulaires des Évêques de Québec* (Québec, 1888), IV, 321ff. As a result of this circular, eighty-three petitions reached the Assembly from seventeen ridings in the district of Quebec. The first signature on seventy-two petitions was that of the parish *curé*, and Archbishop Turgeon led off the petition from the city of Quebec.

23. *Leader*, Jan. 15, 1858.

24. Can., *Ass. J.*, Feb. 26, 1858.

25. See Can., *Bills*, sess. 1858, Bills no. 20 and 26.

26. See *Globe*, Jan. 9, 1857, and Can., *Ass. J.*, April 27, 1857.

27. In 1837 the Legislative Council of Upper Canada incorporated a voters' register into the charter of the city of Toronto and in the following year the Assembly included a voters' register in the Act establishing the town of Kingston for municipal elections. In 1839–40 the Tories made attempts to establish a voters' register for provincial elections. See U.C., *Stats.*, 7 Wm. IV, c. 39 (1837), 1 Vic., c. 27 (1837–38); U.C., *Leg. Co. J.*, March 2, 1837; U.C., *Ass. J.*, Dec. 24, 1839. Jan. 9, 1840.

28. Can., *Stat.*, 22 Vic., c. 82 (1858).

29. Can., *Stat.*, 18 Vic., c. 100 (1855).

30. *Ibid.*, 24 Vic., c. 25 (1861). The act, while passed prior to the 1861 election, was passed too late to effect the voters' registers for that election. If no complaints were lodged against a list prepared by a municipal clerk such list was to be considered the voters' register despite the failure of the municipal council to correct and revise.

31. *Ibid.*, 27 Vic., c. 8 (1863). Municipal assessments in Canada East were quinquennial until 1860 and thereafter triennial; *ibid.*, 19 & 20 Vic., c. 101 (1856).

32. *Ibid.*, 22 Vic., c. 10 (1859), 29 & 30 Vic., c. 13 (1866).

33. See *Globe*, April 28, June 5, 1858, for the debate on the establishment of the voters' register. The oath required a voter to swear that he was the person designated on the register, that he was a British subject, twenty-one years of age, and had received no corrupt consideration for his vote.

34. Can., *Stat.*, 16 Vic., c. 158 (1853), set the rate at $4 to £1 sterling, and by 20 Vic., c. 18 (1857), the dollar was made the official currency of the province as on Jan. 1, 1858.

35. Can., *Ass. J.*, Aug. 12, 1858; *Globe*, May 12, June 9, 1858.

36. *Globe*, April 28, 1858.

37. See Can., *Ass. J.*, Dec. 13, 1844, March 2, 1848.

38. *Ibid.*, June 15, 1841. In similar activity at Cornwall see *ibid.*, Dec. 9, 1844, and March 2, 1848.

39. *Ibid.*, Jan. 31, Feb. 7, 10, 1845. See *Quebec Gazette*, Feb. 12, 1845, and *Montreal Gazette*, Feb. 13, 1845, for discussion on the bill.

40. The statistics are drawn from the returns from twenty-three ridings in Canada East and forty-four ridings in Canada West. The returns from all ridings experiencing an acclamation or a disputed return in the general elections of 1858 and 1861 are excluded. See Can., *Ass. J.*, 1862, Sess. Paper 24.

41. Can., *Stat.*, 22 Vic., c. 10 (1859).

42. Can., *Ass. J.*, April 14, 1859.

43. *Globe*, April 15, 1859.

44. Can., *Stat.*, 27 Vic., c. 8 (1863).

45. In 1864 Geoffrion (M.P.P. Verchères) and in 1865 Antoine Dorion (M.P.P. Hochelaga) sponsored bills which would have confined the franchise in all cases to the assessed actual value on which taxes were levied. These bills desired to strike off the voters' register all those whose assessment was less than $200 actual value, even if the annual value of the property might be assessed at $20.

46. U.C., *Con. Stat.*, 1859, c. 54, ss. 75, 76.

47. Can., *Stat.*, 29 & 30 Vic., c. 53, s. 30; c. 51, s. 76 (1866).

48. *Ibid.*, c. 51, s. 81 (1866).

49. See Can., *Ass. J.*, Aug. 10, 1866; *Globe*, Aug. 11, 1866, and Dec. 17, 1867. Of the members from urban ridings the motion was supported by the members for Brockville and Hamilton, but opposed by the members for Kingston, Cornwall, and Niagara. The Toronto members, it being Friday, were absent.

CHAPTER NINE

1. Instructions to Blanshard, July 16, 1849, P.A.C., M.G. 11, B2, vol. 18, 1.
2. Commission to Blanshard, July 16, 1849, M.G. 11, B2, vol. 1, 6.
3. Blanshard to Grey, April 8, 1850, P.A.C., C.O. 305, vol. 2, 49; ibid., May 12, 1851, C.O. 305, vol 3, 18.
4. Resolutions of the Hudson's Bay Company [March, 1849], C.O. 305, vol. 1, 641f. See also W. N. Sage, "Early Days in British Columbia," Canadian Historical Review, III (1922), 145f.
5. A. S. Morton, A History of the Canadian West to 1870–71 (London, 1939), 752. H. H. Bancroft, History of Oregon, II, 1848–88 (San Francisco, 1888), 260–63.
6. Blanshard to Grey, Nov. 18, 1850, C.O. 305, vol. 2, 95, and Aug. 30, 1851, C.O. 305, vol. 3, 38.
7. Douglas to Pakington, Nov. 11, 1852, C.O. 305, vol. 3, 147.
8. Douglas to Newcastle, Jan. 7, 1854, C.O. 305, vol. 5, 15; Cockburn and Bethill to Grey, Dec. 28, 1854, C.O. 305, vol. 5, 184; Grey to Douglas (confidential), April 5, 1854, C.O. 305, vol. 5, 193.
9. [Merivale] to Governor of Hudson's Bay Company, April 5, 1855, C.O. 305, vol. 5, 199. Douglas had informed the Colonial Office in 1854 that there were but fifty-six freeholders on the Island and the Company in two reports on the progress of colonization stated the adult male population was 417 in 1855 of whom 54 possessed freeholds of twenty or more acres. A census conducted by Douglas in 1855 set the adult male population at 307. See Douglas to Grey, Dec. 11, 1854, C.O. 305, vol. 5, 133; Colville to Pakington, Nov. 24, 1852, C.O. 305, vol. 5, 468; Colville to Russell, June 9, 1855, C.O. 305, vol. 6, 255; Douglas to Russell, Aug. 21, 1855, C.O. 305, vol. 6, 126 v.
10. Colville to Merivale, April 16, 1855, C.O. 305, vol. 6, 247.
11. Labouchere to Douglas, Feb. 28, 1856, P.A.C., J. 1, vol. 1, 315. Their misgivings as to population did lead them to suggest that Douglas might adopt the practice devised in the smaller islands of the West Indies and fuse the Assembly and the Council into one chamber.
12. See Douglas to Labouchere, July 22, 1856, C.O. 305, vol. 7, 59, and three enclosures.
13. Br., Stat., 1 & 2 Vic., c. 48 (1838).
14. British Colonist, Dec. 18, 27, 1858.
15. Douglas to Labouchere, Aug. 20, 1856, C.O. 305, vol. 7, 82; see also V.I., Ass. J., Aug. 26, 28, 1856.
16. V.I., Ass. J., May 6, 1857. See also Douglas to Labouchere, May 22, 1856, C.O. 305, vol. 7, 45; Br. Parliamentary Papers, 1854, Reports of Select Committees on Public Petitions' App. 277; Labouchere to Douglas, Aug. 23, 1856, J.1., vol. 1, 485.
17. V.I., Ass. J., May 28, 1857; see copy of "An Act to enfranchise the Town of Victoria," C.O. 305, vol. 8, 101.
18. See V.I., Council Minutes, March 23, 25, April 11, 16, 1859.
19. British Colonist, Feb. 19, March 5, 1859.
20. Ibid., May 25, July 6, 8, 1859, for bill drafted by the select committee, and as amended by the Assembly.
21. V.I., Stats., "An Act to increase the number of Representatives of the People of this Colony in the House of Assembly 1859"; "An Act to Amend the Law Relating to the Representation of Vancouver Island and its dependencies 1859."
22. See British Colonist, May 20, June 8, Sept. 21, 23, and Oct. 3, 1859.
23. Ibid., Jan. 22, May 20, Oct. 3, 1859.
24. See Douglas to Lytton, Oct. 13, 1858, C.O. 305, vol. 9, 197.
25. Morton, History, 755. With the enfranchisement of these farm managers the right of the freeholders to vote by proxy which had been adopted for the first election was dropped.
26. Merivale to [Douglas], March 1, 1856, J.1, vol. 1, 373. De Cosmos' advocacy of a taxpaying franchise seems to have been motivated by his belief that the tax collectors' records could serve as a voters' register. See British Colonist, Jan. 22, 1859.
27. British Colonist, Oct. 5, 1859.
28. V.I., Stat., "An Act to make provision for the Registration of Voters, and for other purposes relating thereto, 1859."
29. The preliminary voters' list prepared for the 1859 general election listed 228 electors for Victoria Town, 59 for Victoria County, 37 for the Lake District, 21 for Saanich, 55 for Esquimalt and Metchosin County, and 28 for Esquimalt Town, whereas the preliminary lists for 1861 contained 179 electors for Victoria Town, 37 for Victoria County, 23 for Esquimalt, etc., See British Colonist, Dec. 1, 3, 1859, Feb. 2, 1861.
30. Ibid., Jan. 5, 19, 1860. When the time to receive names expired on Nov. 30, there were eight

or nine names registered for the above district, but on Dec. 21 the same district showed twenty-one names registered. On Nov. 22, 1860, the same newspaper stated, "The revised list of voters for Victoria Town at the expiration of the period for registration was 220; the day following 222, and when the Revisor certified to the list there were 234, a more miraculous feat than the miracle of the loaves and fishes."

31. *Ibid.*, July 24, 26, 1860.

32. *Ibid.*, Nov. 22, 1860.

33. V.I., *Stat.*, "An Act to amend the Registration of Voters' Act 1859" (1860). See *British Colonist*, Nov. 29, 1860, Nov. 15, 1862.

34. See *British Colonist*, Nov. 14, 1862, and McLure to Newcastle, Feb. 11, 1863, C.O. 305, vol. 21, 366.

35. V.I., *Stat.*, "An Act to increase the number of Representatives for Victoria Town District, and to alter the limits of the said District" (1862).

36. *British Colonist*, Feb. 25, Oct. 16, 1863.

37. Cary to Wakeford, July 7, 1864, C.O. 305, vol. 23, 418.

38. Kennedy to Cardwell, Aug. 24, 1865, C.O. 305, vol. 26, 325 v.

39. See *British Colonist*, Feb. 16–May 31, 1865, and Dec. 5, 1865–Jan. 17, 1866, for Assembly debates on the move to change the franchise. The same bill was introduced on both occasions.

40. V.I., *Stat.*, 28 & 29 Vic., c. 16 (1865).

41. Kennedy to Cardwell (confidential), Dec. 16, 1865, Jan. 24, 1866, C.O. 305, vol. 26, 578, vol. 28, 63.

42. Douglas to Lytton, Dec. 11, 1858, July 20, 1859, C.O. 305, vol. 9, 253, vol. 10 265.

43. *Ibid.*, July 19, 1859, C.O. 305, vol. 10, 217; Douglas to Newcastle, March 28, 1860, C.O. 305, vol. 14, 130; Newcastle to Douglas, June 28, 1860, P.A.C., G8c, vol. 2, 292.

44. Douglas to Newcastle, Dec. 17, 1859, C.O. 305, vol. 11, 387; Douglas to Newcastle, April 25, 1861, C.O. 305, vol. 17, 161.

45. *British Colonist*, Oct. 5, 1859. Land held by pre-emption did not convey the franchise.

46. See *British Colonist*, Nov. 29, 1859.

47. V.I., *Stat.*, "An Act to provide for naturalization of Aliens" (1861). See also *British Colonist*, Jan. 10, July 24, 26, 1860.

48. *British Colonist*, Nov. 29, 1861.

49. Kennedy to Cardwell, May 4, 1865, C.O. 305, vol. 25, 376 v.

50. *Daily Chronicle*, Dec. 16, 1865.

51. Kennedy to Cardwell (confidential), March 23, 26, 1866, C.O. 305, vol. 28, 317, 323.

52. Br., *Stat.*, 21 & 22 Vic., c. 99 (1858).

53. Lytton to Douglas, July 31, Aug. 14, 1858, J.1, vol. 1, 610, 630.

54. See Douglas to Newcastle, April 23, 1860, J.2, vol. 2, 102; *ibid.* (separate), Feb. 28, 1861, J.2, vol. 2, 277; and *ibid.* (separate), May 29, 1862, J.2, vol. 3, 196.

55. Douglas to Newcastle, Aug. 4, 1860, C.O. 60.8, 29.

56. Memorial to Newcastle, June, 1860, C.O. 60.9, 316; New Westminster Memorial to Newcastle, Feb. 20, 1861, C.O. 60.10, 192; Hope Memorial to Newcastle, Sept. 11, 1861, C.O. 60.11, 50. See *British Columbian*, Feb. 13, 1861.

57. Douglas to Newcastle, July 28, 1862, J.2, vol. 3, 216.

58. Newcastle to Douglas (separate), June 15, 1863, C.O. 60.17, 159; the Order in Council is to be found in J.1, vol. 10, 478.

59. Douglas to Newcastle, Feb. 2, 1864, J.2, vol. 3, 431.

60. Douglas to Newcastle, July 28, 1862, J.2, vol. 3, 216.

61. *British Columbian*, Sept. 26, Oct. 3, 7, 1863.

62. *Ibid.*, Oct. 21, 31, Nov. 14, 1863. There were slight differences. The main change was the establishment of a qualification for the candidates of British citizenship and ownership of £500 real property.

63. Br., *Stat.*, 29 & 30 Vic., c. 67 (1866).

64. Kennedy to Cardwell (separate), March 21, 1865, C.O. 305, vol. 25, 152.

65. Kennedy to Cardwell (separate), March 21, 1865; Kennedy to Cardwell (confidential), Jan. 24, 1866: C.O. 305, vol. 25, 198; vol. 28, 63.

66. Seymour to [Cardwell], April 29, 1865, May 17, 1865, J.2, vol. 4, 188, 222.

67. Seymour to [Carnarvon], Jan. 17, 1867, J.2, vol. 4, 444.

68. See *British Colonist*, Dec. 11, 1866. The elections were held as previously on a single day in each of the three districts. In District no. 2, which combined the six former rural electoral districts, a poll was held simultaneously in each of the former districts.

69. *British Columbian*, Sept. 15, Oct. 17, 20, 1866. All other aliens including sixteen Polynesians voted in the New Westminster district.

70. Seymour in a dispatch to Carnarvon on Jan. 17, 1867, stated that Chinese and Indians were not allowed to vote in all districts. This statement is open to question especially as respects the Chinese who formed one-quarter to one-third of the population of British Columbia. Seymour had made a similar statement to the Colonial Office when the Act of Union was under discussion, although the Cariboo West by-election was in direct contradiction. The Chinese and Indians did not desire to vote but the contending candidates always felt obliged to secure their "voluntary" support. Seymour to [Carnarvon], Jan. 17, 1867, J.2, vol. 4, 444; Seymour to Cardwell, d. Paris, Feb. 17, 1866, in Papers relating to the Proposed Union of British Columbia and Vancouver Island, *Br. Parliamentary Papers*, 1866.

71. High Sheriff's Notice of Election, Oct. 17, 1868, in *British Colonist*, Oct. 19, 1868.

72. See *British Columbian*, Dec. 19, 1868, for petition from 100 British subjects at Victoria against the abandonment of the Island franchise.

73. Br., *Stat.*, 33 & 34 Vic., c. 66 (1870).

74. *Ibid.*, 28 & 29 Vic., c. 63 (1865).

75. Enclosed in Kimberley to Musgrave, Aug. 22, 1870, J.1, vol. 17, 309.

76. Musgrave to Grenville, Feb. 23, 1870, J.2, vol. 6, 104.

77. Musgrave to Kimberley, Oct. 17, 1870, J.2, vol. 6, 229. This election was the first occasion aliens were denied the franchise on the mainland. It might be noted that it had been possible since 1867 to secure British citizenship after one year's residence in the colony and the subscription to the necessary oaths. See B.C., *Rev. Stat.*, 1871, c. 93.

78. Musgrave to Kimberley, Dec. 22, 1870, J.2, vol. 6, 278; Musgrave to Kimberley, Feb. 18, 1871, vol. 6, 301.

79. B.C., *Rev. Stat.*, 1871, cc. 156, 157, 158, and 167.

80. *Ibid.*, c. 156. The legislation, establishing a voters' register at a cost of 50 cents to each claimant, erecting polling subdivisions in each electoral district, defining corrupt practices, and placing controverted elections in the hands of the courts, belongs to the history of the new province.

81. Musgrave to Kimberley, April 5, 1871, J.2, vol. 6, 339.

82. See *British Colonist*, Sept. 25, Nov. 19, Nov. 25, 1870.

CHAPTER TEN

1. *Eng. Stat.*, 30 Car. II, Stat. 2, ss. 7, 8 (1677); 7 & 8 Wm. III, c. 27, s. 19 (1696); and 11 & 12 Wm. III, c. 4, s. 4 (1700).

2. Commission to Lawrence, Jan. 7, 1756, P.A.C., N.S. E7. The former act contained three oaths; the oath of allegiance, the oath of supremacy, and the oath of abjuration. These oaths will henceforth be referred to as the State Oaths. The latter act required a denial of the mystery of the Mass and will henceforth be referred to as the Declaration against Transubstantiation. For the State Oaths and Declaration against Transubstantiation see Appendix, p. 215f.

3. A. E. McKinley, *The Suffrage Franchise in the Thirteen English Colonies in America* (Philadelphia, 1905), 74f.

4. N.S., *Ex. Co. Min.*, Jan. 3, 1757, P.A.C., B9, 12. Recusants were those who refused to attend the services of the Church of England; refusal was punishable by law in England.

5. N.S., *Stat.*, 32 Geo. II, c. 5 (1758). The statute was designed to curb French influence among the Acadian remnant.

6. *Ibid.*, 32 Geo. II, c. 2 (1758).

7. "An Act for regulating Elections of Members to serve in the General Assembly of this Province, and for the preventing irregular proceedings of the Provost Marshal, Sheriffs and other officers in the electing and returning such members and for other purpose therein mentioned." N.S., Unpassed Bills, 1775, P.A.N.S.

8. P.E.I., *Ex. Co. Min.*, Feb. 17, 1773, B1, 47.

9. Instructions to Patterson, Aug. 4, 1769, no. 26, P.A.C.

10. P.E.I., *Stat.*, 20 Geo. III, c. 4 (1780), P.A.C., C.O. 228, vol. 1, 7.

11. Br., *Stat.*, 14 Geo. III, c. 83 (1774).

12. Treaty of Paris 1763, art. IV, in A. Shortt and A. G. Doughty, *Documents Relating to the Constitutional History of Canada 1759–1791* (Ottawa, 1918), I, 115.

13. Commission to Murray, Nov. 21, 1763, in Shortt and Doughty, I, 173.

14. Instructions to Murray, Dec. 7, 1763, nos. 3, 29, in Shortt and Doughty, I, 181.

15. Murray to Lords of Trade, Oct. 29, 1764: "Little, very little will content the New Subjects but nothing will satisfy the licentious fanatics trading here, but the expulsion of the Canadians who are perhaps the bravest and the best race upon the Globe, a race who could they be indulged with a few privileges which the Laws of England deny to Roman Catholics at home, would soon get the better of every national antipathy to their conquerors and become the most faithful and most useful set of men in this American Empire." Shortt and Doughty, I, 231.

16. Petition of Quebec Traders to H.M. the King, n.d., Shortt and Doughty, I, 235.

17. Norton and De Grey to Lords of Trade, June 10, 1765, C.O. 42, vol. 2, pt. 1, 120. Besides Quebec, the Treaty of Paris ceded Grenada and the Floridas to Great Britain, colonies which possessed large Roman Catholic populations.

18. Lords of Trade to H.M. the King, Sept. 2, 1765, Shortt and Doughty, I, 247.

19. P.A.C., Q56, pt. 1, 126f, 146f.

20. Instructions to Carleton, n.d. (1768), no. 2, Shortt and Doughty, I, 301.

21. Shortt and Doughty, I, 266–67n.

22. Instructions to Governor of Grenada, 1768, in L. W. Labaree, *Royal Instructions to British Colonial Governors 1670–1776*, no. 621 (New York, 1935). See *Edward's Civil and Commercial History of the British West Indies: An Abridgdement* (London, 1794), I, 256f.

23. Report of the Lords Commissioners for Trade and Plantations relative to the state of the Province of Quebec, July 10, 1769, Shortt and Doughty, I, 383f. The Board proposed that the Quebec Assembly be composed of twenty-seven members: city of Quebec, 7; district of Quebec, 6; city of Montreal, 4; district of Montreal 4; town of Trois Rivières, 3; and district of Trois Rivières, 3. All members were to take the State Oaths but only the members for the cities of Quebec and Montreal and the town of Trois Rivières were also to take the Declaration against Transubstantiation.

24. Report of Solicitor General Wedderburn, Dec. 6, 1772, Shortt and Doughty, I, 426.

25. Br., *Stat.*, 14 Geo. III, c. 83 (1774). The new Instructions to Sir Guy Carleton of Jan. 3, 1775, necessitated by the passage of the Quebec Act, contained the names of eight Canadian Roman Catholics appointed to the Council. See Shortt and Doughty, II, 594.

26. See Petition for House of Assembly, Nov. 24, 1784, Q24, pt. 1, 3; also *Quebec Gazette* (supplement), March 8, 1792, which stated: "Too much praise cannot be bestowed on the British Parliament for the enlarged and liberal plan upon which they have decreed the House of Assembly shall be formed, as well with regard to the Electors as the Representatives and Officers."

27. Br., *Stat.*, 31 Geo. III, c. 31 (1791).

28. Br., *Stat.*, 18 Geo. III, c. 60 (1778); 31 Geo. III, c. 32 (1791). See P. Hughes, *The Catholic Question 1688–1829: A Study in Political History* (London, 1929), 152–72.

29. Hughes, 183–90; see also D. Gwynn, *The Struggle for Catholic Emancipation 1750–1829* (London, 1928), 86–93.

30. Ir. *Stat.*, 33 Geo. III, c. 21 (1793).

31. R. J. S. Hoffman and P. Levack, eds., *Burke's Politics* (New York, 1949), 500. Burke has ignored the continued loyalty of Nova Scotia and Prince Edward Island, two Protestant colonies of the first Empire.

32. N.S., *Stat.*, 29 Geo. III, c. 1 (1789).

33. Parr to Sydney, April 11, 1789, P.A.C., N.S. A111, 4; N.S., *Ass. J.*, April 1, 1789, P.A.C., N.S. D17.

34. See below, p. 144. It should be remembered the first English relief bill was passed in 1778.

35. N.S., *Stat.*, 23 Geo. III, c. 9 (1783).

36. N.B., *Ex. Co. Min.*, Oct. 11, 21, 1785, P.A.C.

37. N.B., *Ass. J.* Jan. 13, 20, 1786.

38. N.B., *Stat.*, 31 Geo. III, c. 17 (1791). The 1786 act (26 Geo. III, c. 62) was disallowed by Grenville to Carleton, Aug. 25, 1790, P.A.C., N.B., C.O. 190, vol. 2, A4, 196; the 1791 act was confirmed by Portland to Carleton, June 4, 1795, P.A.C., N.B. A6, 264.

39. N.B., *Ass. J.*, Feb. 18, 1796.

40. *Ibid.*, Feb. 18, 21–23, 1791.

41. A copy of the bill enclosed in Lyman to King, April 15, 1795, N.B. A6, 224–30.

42. N.B. *Stat.*, 50 Geo. III, c. 36 (1810). This act contained a suspending clause. It was confirmed by Order in Council dated June 22, 1811. See Liverpool to the Administrator, July 5, 1811, N.B., C.O. 188, vol. 151, 231.

43. A. B. Warburton, *A History of Prince Edward Island 1534–1831* (St. John, N.B., 1923), 257.

44. Smith to Bathurst, Oct. 1, 1814, P.A.C., P.E.I., G44, 81. See also McEachern to Bathurst, Nov. 26, 1818, P.E.I. A33.2, 121, and Petition of the Bishop of Charlottetown, Feb. 29, 1832, in Campbell to Goderich, March 20, 1832, N.B. A46, 208f.

45. P.E.I., *Ex. Co. Min.*, July 18, 1787, B6, 168f; Lt. Gov.'s writ to Sheriff, Feb. 8, 1785, enclosed in Fanning to Sydney, Oct. 3, 1787, P.E.I., A9, 129ff.

46. P.E.I., *Ass. J.*, March 30, 31, 1790. Walter Berry, the member for Prince County, who sponsored the bill, left the Island before the next session, which may account for the failure of the relief bill to be reintroduced. See *ibid.*, Nov. 11, 1790.

47. P.E.I., *Stat.*, 41 Geo. III, c. 4 (1801); C.O. 228, vol. 3; 47 Geo. III, c. 3 (1806).

48. P.E.I., *Ass. J.*, July 22, 23, 1801, P.A.C., D8.

49. *Ibid.*, Oct. 18, 1825.

50. *Ibid.*, March 29, 1827.

51. *Ibid.*

52. D. Campbell, *History of Prince Edward Island* (Charlottetown, 1875), 73.

53. P.E.I., *Ass. J.*, April 25, 1828.

54. Br., *Stat.*, 10 Geo. IV., cc. 7, 8 (1829).

55. P.E.I., *Stat.*, 10 Geo. IV, c. 12 (1829); C.O. 228, vol. 4. See Murray to Ready, Aug. 30, 1829, P.E.I. G6, 298, for the fate of this bill.

56. Murray to Ready, May 4, 1829, P.E.I., G6, 267. Enclosed was the Imperial act, 10 Geo. IV, c. 7.

57. P.E.I., *Stat.*, 11 Geo. IV, c. 7 (1830).

58. Murray to Douglas, May 4, 1829, enclosed in N.B., *Ex. Co. Min.*, Feb. 13, 1830.

59. N.B., *Stat.*, 10 & 11 Geo. IV, c. 33 (1830).

60. See N.B., *Leg. Co. J.*, Feb. 27, 1830.

61. Bathurst to Kempt, Aug. 15, 1820, N.S., C.O. 218, vol. 29, 313.

62. N.S., *Ex. Co. Min.*, Oct. 9, 1820, P.A.N.S.

63. Kempt to Goulburn (private) Nov. 15, 1821, N.S. A162, 85.

64. Bathurst to Kempt (private and confidential), Dec. 21, 1821, N.S. A162, 89.

65. "An Act entitled an Act to remove certain disabilities which His Majesty's subjects professing the Roman Catholic religion now labor under in this Province." N.S., Unpassed Bills, 1822.

66. N.S., *Leg. Co. J.*, Feb. 28, March 1–11, 1822; N.S., *Ass. J.*, Feb. 20–28, March 1–6, 1822.

67. Kempt to Bathurst, March 20, 1822, N.S. A163, 4; Bathurst to Kempt, May 8, 1822, N.S., C.O. 218, vol. 29, 376. Bathurst's caution was doubtless enhanced by the acute political divisions at Westminster on the Catholic question.

68. N.S., *Ass. J.*, April 2, 3, 1823. See *Acadian Recorder*, April 5, 1823, for details of the debate, but the division recorded in the newspaper on April 12, 1823, is incorrect.

69. N.S., *Stat.*, 7 Geo. IV, c. 18 (1826).

70. *Acadian Recorder*, Feb. 17, 1827.

71. *Acadian Recorder*, March 10, 1827.

72. N.S., *Stat.*, 11 Geo. IV, c. 1 (1830).

73. *Ibid.*, 32 Geo. II, c. 2 (1758).

74. Halifax to Wilmot, June 9, 1764, N.S. A74, 73. The dispatch was followed up by an additional instruction to the same effect. See Additional Instruction to Wilmot, July 16, 1764, P.A.C., M.G. 11, Supp. II.

75. Francklin to Shelburne, Feb. 20, 1768, N.S. A81, 125.

76. Hillsborough to Lt. Gov. of Nova Scotia, June 21, 1768, N.S. A82, 136. Belcher, Chief Justice of Nova Scotia, entertained a similar opinion. See enclosure in Francklin to Shelburne, Feb. 20, 1768, N.S. A81, 131.

77. Legge to Dartmouth, May 24, 1774; Legge to Dartmouth, July 13, 1774; N.S. A90, 105, 187.

78. Dartmouth to Legge, Sept. 7, 1774, N.S. A91, 2.

79. Instructions to Legge, Aug. 3, 1773, no. 45, Feb. 3, 1774, no. 26.

80. N.S., *Leg. Co. J.*, June 26, 29, 1782, P.A.C., C12. See N.S., Unpassed Bills, 1782, for "An Act to repeal certain clauses in two Acts of the General Assembly of this Province, which have been found to be injurious and oppressive to that part of His Majesty's Subjects professing the Romish religion." Draft to the Lord President, May 12, 1783; North to Governor of Nova Scotia, June 24, 1783: N.S. A103, 70, 108.

81. N.S., *Stat.*, 23 Geo. III, c. 9 (1783).

82. P.E.I., *Stat.*, 26 Geo. III, c. 8 (1786). This act had a suspending clause and was confirmed by Order in Council on Aug. 18, 1790. See Grenville to Lt. Gov. of St. John's Island, Aug. 25, 1790, P.E.I. All 69.

83. Fanning to Nepean, Oct. 4, 1787, P.E.I., A9, 152. It should be noted that Fanning gave licences of occupation on the sole authority of himself and his Council without prior consent of the proprietors concerned nor of the Crown. Fanning was forced to take this arbitrary action because the Acadians in their petition threatened to leave the Island and go to Nova Scotia or Cape Breton unless their request for land was granted. It might also be noted that Fanning in his dispatch to Nepean said he had given licences of occupation "during Pleasure" whereas in his reply to the petitioners, he promised to give them "permanent leases." See Petition of Acadian Inhabitants of Fortune Bay to Fanning, P.E.I. A9, 66, 83.

84. N. MacDonald, *Canada 1763–1841: Immigration and Settlement* (London, 1939), 103f.

85. [Bathurst] to Smith, May 20, 1818, P.E.I. A34.1, 21.

CHAPTER ELEVEN

1. A. E. McKinley, *The Suffrage Franchise in the Thirteen English Colonies in America* (Philadelphia, 1905), 476.

2. See N.S., *Ex. Co. Min.*, May 20, 1758, Aug. 22, 1759, P.A.C., B9.

3. N.S., Unpassed Bills, 1775, P.A.N.S.

4. W. S. MacNutt, 'The Beginnings of Nova Scotia Politics 1758–66," *Canadian Historical Review*, XVI (1935), 41–53.

5. N.S., *Stat.*, 29 Geo. III, c. 1 (1789).

6. N.B., *Ex. Co. Min.*, Oct. 11, 21, 1785.

7. N.B., *Stat.*, 31 Geo. III, c. 17 (1791).

8. *Ibid.*, 50 Geo. III, c. 36 (1810).

9. P.E.I., *Ex. Co. Min.*, Feb. 17, 1773, Feb. 18, 1774, B1; Writ to Sheriff, Feb. 8, 1785, P.A.C., P.E.I. A9, 129.

10. P.E.I., *Stat.*, 41 Geo. III, c. 4 (1801), P.A.C., C.O. 228, vol. 3, 14.

11. *Ibid.*, 11 Geo. IV, c. 8 (1830).

12. N.S., *Leg. Co. J.*, Feb. 15, 1836, March 25, 1836, March 29, April 16, 1838; N.S., *Ass. J.*, April 16, 1838.

13. Law Officers to Glenelg, June 12, 1838, N.S. A189.1, 260f (their italics); for opinions of Colonial Office officials, see N.S. A187.2, 710f.

14. Russell to Campbell, Sept. 29, 1839, N.S. A195, 39.

15. Sydenham to Russell, May 25, 1841; P.A.C., G12, vol. 57, 243. The Act of Union, like the Constitutional Act, did not require the State Oaths of electors or members of the Assembly, but the Royal Commission to Sydenham required the State Oaths to be taken by all executive councillors who were not Roman Catholics.

16. Day to Murdock, May 14, 1841; Baldwin to Murdock, May 15, 1841: G12, vol. 58, 6, 7.

17. Pollock and Follett to Hope, April 9, 1842, G12, vol. 101, 180.

18. N.S., *Ass. J.*, March 20, 1846; N.B., *Ass. J.*, April 6, 1846.

19. Gladstone to Falkland, May 5, 1846, N.S., vol. 85, 188; Gladstone to Colebrooke, June 2, 1846, N.B., C.O. 188, vol. 174, n.p.

20. See Joseph Tassé, "Droits politiques des Juifs en Canada," *Revue Canadienne*, VII (Montreal, 1870), 409f.

21. See L.C., *Ass. J.*, Feb. 12, 1808, for Hart's petition to the Assembly.

22. T. E. May, *Treatise on the Law, Privileges, Proceedings and Usage of Parliament* (5th ed. rev., London, 1863), 406. It was not until 1838 that Parliament removed all doubts as to the manner of administering oaths when it declared they were to be taken in the manner binding on the conscience of the swearer. See Br., *Stat.*, 1 & 2 Vic., c. 105 (1838).

23. L.C., *Ass. J.*, Feb. 17, 1808.

24. Quoted in Tassé, 419.

25. L.C., *Ass. J.*, March 4, 1808.

26. L.C., *Ass. J.*, May 5, 1809. The struggle of Charles Bradlaugh, an atheist, to be admitted to his seat in the British House of Commons is a latter-day (1880–86) parallel to the Hart case. See H. B. Bonner and J. M. Robertson, *Charles Bradlaugh, a Record of His Life and Work* (London, 1908).

27. Br., *Stat.*, 31 Geo. III, c. 31, s. 23 (1791). The Executive Council were of the above opinion when they advised Craig that Jews were eligible to seats in the Assembly. See L.C., *Ex. Co., Min.*, May 0, 1809, P.A.C., State Book E.; Craig to Castlereagh, June 5, 1809, P.A.C., Q109, 138f.

28. L.C., *Ass. J.*, April 24, 1809.

29. *Ibid.*, May 8, 1809. Benjamin G. Sack in his history of Canadian Jewry asserts that Craig's abrupt dissolution of the Assembly on May 15, 1809, was to prevent the Assembly giving third reading to the Jewish disabilities bill. As the bill had not passed committee stage such an assertion appears groundless. The bill that was to be read a third time on that date and on whose account the Assembly was dissolved was the judges' exclusion bill. That Craig had contemplated dissolving the Assembly over the Hart controversy is without doubt, but the Executive Council had advised him against such a step until the legality of the Assembly's action had been submitted to the Colonial Office. See B. G. Sack, *History of the Jews in Canada* (Montreal, 1945), I, 93f; L.C., *Ex. Co. Min.*, May 10, 1809, State Book E.

30. [Castlereagh] to Craig (private), Sept. 7, 1809, Q109, 221.

31. The Jewish population of Lower Canada, although never large, was the largest in the British North American colonies. The first Jewish congregation in Canada was organized at Montreal in 1768. See Sack, I, 59f, 103.

32. L.C., *Ass. J.*, Jan. 31, Feb. 7, 1831.

33. L.C., *Stat.*, 1 Wm. IV, c. 57 (1831).

34. W. C. Braithwaite, *The Second Period of Quakerism* (London, 1919), 15, 182.

35. McKinley, *The Suffrage Franchise*, 475.

36. F. H. Miller, "Legal Qualifications for Office in America 1619–1899," *American Historical Association, Annual Report*, I (1899), 106f.

37. Br., *Stat.*, 7 & 8 Wm. III, c. 34 (1696). This statute was continued for a term of years and made perpetual in 1714; see *ibid.*, 1 Geo. I, stat. 2, c. 6 (1714).

38. *Ibid.*, 22 Geo. II, c. 46 s. 36 (1749).

39. N.S., *Stat.*, 33 Geo. II, c. 2 (1759). The act denied use of an affirmation in criminal cases. N.B., *Stat.*, 26 Geo. III, c. 19 (1786). This act was a virtual transcript of the Nova Scotian legislation. L.C., *Stat.*, 33 Geo. III, c. 4 (1793). This act denied Quakers the right to hold offices of profit under the Crown, to sit on juries and to testify in criminal cases, and exempted them from militia service.

40. P.E.I., *Stat.*, 25 Geo. III, c. 10 (1785). See *ibid.*, 14 Geo. III, c. 8 (1774); Jackson to Lords of Trade, Nov. 13, 1775, and Callbeck to Germain, May 18, 1776, P.E.I. A3, 32, 137.

41. A. G. Dorland, *A History of the Society of Friends (Quakers) in Canada* (Toronto, 1927), 30–33.

42. Hartshorne was appointed to the Legislative Council in 1801 and a fellow Quaker, Joseph Fitzrandolph, was appointed in 1838. See N.S., *Ex. Co. Min.*, Aug. 15, 1801, P.A.N.S., E6; N.S., *Leg. Co. J.*, Jan. 25, 1838.

43. Desbrisay to Dartmouth, Dec. 10, 1774, P.E.I., A2, 260; Smith to Bathurst, July 29, 1814, P.A.C., P.E.I. Lt. Gov.'s Letterbrook 1813–17, 60.

44. See Robinson to Wilmot, July 1, 1822, Q322.2, 436.

45. U.C., *Ass. J.*, Sept. 19, 1792.

46. Capt. Chas. Stevenson to Dundas, July 31, 1793, in E. A. Cruickshank, ed., *The Correspondence of Lieut. Governor John Graves Simcoe*, I, *1789–93* (Toronto, 1923), 412.

47. Dundas to Simcoe, Oct. 2, 1793, Q278A, 33.

48. U.C., *Leg. Co. J.*, June 24, 1801, Feb. 19, 1806. U.C., *Ass. J.*, March 1, 1817, Dec. 5, 1825.

49. Memorial of Mackenzie to Goderich, July 24, 1832, Q376.1, 82f.

50. Goderich to Colborne, Nov. 8, 1832, G69, 365ff.

51. Br., *Stat.*, 3 & 4 Wm. IV, c. 49 (1833).

52. Can., *Leg. Co. J.*, Nov. 8, 1843. See *La Minerve*, Nov. 13, 1843, and Quebec *Gazette*, Nov. 15, 1843.

53. Metcalfe to Stanley, Jan. 27, 1844, G12, vol. 64, 230f.

54. Stanley to Metcalfe, March 27, 1844, G1, vol. 107, 229; Can., *Stat.*, 7 Vic., c. 65 (1843).

55. Can., *Ass. J.*, Dec. 5, 9, 12, 1844. Under the act any common informer who instituted proceedings against a clergyman who voted in violation of the law was entitled to recover £500 from the offender.

56. Can., *Stat.*, 8 Vic., c. 10 (1844–45). An act was also passed to stop all legal proceedings to recover damages from clergymen who had voted at the late election. See *ibid.*, 8 Vic., c. 9 (1844–45).

57. Can., *Ass. J.*, Jan. 15, Feb. 3, 1845.

58. Br., *Stat.*, 41 Geo. III, c. 63 (1801). This statute had been necessitated by the return of a former clergyman, Horne Tooke, for Old Sarum and his demand to be seated. See *Annual Register*, 1801 (London, 1802), 184. The proscription was specifically extended to Roman Catholic priests when Roman Catholics were emancipated in 1829.

59. In 1810 the Assembly of Upper Canada interpreted the exclusion to include Methodist lay preachers and voided the elections of the two members from the counties of Lennox-Addington and Prince Edward. See U.C., *Ass. J.*, Feb. 6, March 3, 7, 1810.

60. N.B., *Stat.*, 58 Geo. III, c. 24 (1818). The act was not confirmed by the Crown until Feb. 6, 1821.

61. Smyth to Bathurst, Aug. 13, 1819, Dec. 7, 1819, N.B., A28, 39, 56.

CHAPTER TWELVE

1. See Eng., *Stat.*, 7 & 8 Wm. III, c. 25 (1696); T. E. May, *Treatise on the Law, Privileges, Proceedings and Usage of Parliament* (5th ed. rev., London, 1863), 33.

2. General James Murray, "Report of the State of the Government of Quebec in Canada, June 5, 1762," in A. Shortt and A. G. Doughty, *Documents Relating to the Constitutional History of Canada 1759–1791* (Ottawa, 1918), I, 52ff. For discussion of minors under the Roman Law, see M. Guyot, ed., *Repertoire de Jurisprudence* (Paris, 1785), XI, 517–30.

3. N.S., *Stat.*, 14 Vic., c. 2 (1851); also see N.S., *Ex. Co. Min.*, Jan 3, 1757, Aug. 22, 1759, P.A.C., B9, 12, 221.

4. N.S., *Ass. J.*, Feb. 16, March 16, 1841. The Richmond County election was not voided specifically because minors voted but rather on the grounds that the returning officer by his failure to insert the qualifications of the electors in the poll book had prevented the controverted election committee ruling on the validity of their votes.

5. N.S., *Ex. Co. Min.*, Oct. 9, 1820, P.A.N.S.

6. P.E.I., *Stat.*, 6 Wm. IV, c. 24 (1836), P.A.C. C.O. 228, vol. 6; 47 Geo. III, c. 3 (1806).

7. Election writ to Sheriff, Feb. 8, 1785, P.A.C., P.E.I. A9, 130f.

8. N.B., *Ex. Co. Min.*, Oct. 11, 21, 1785, P.A.C.; N.B., *Stat.*, 31 Geo. III, c. 17 (1791).

9. Br., *Stat.*, 3 & 4 Vic., c. 35, s. 27 (1840).

10. Can., *Ass. J.*, Sept. 3, 1852.

11. Can., *Stat.*, 16 Vic., c. 153 (1853).

12. L.C., *Stat.*, 4 Wm. IV, c. 28 (1834); P.E.I., *Stat.*, 6 Wm. IV, c. 24 (1836); N.B., *Stat.*, 6 Vic., c. 44 (1843); Can., *Stat.*, 12 Vic., c. 27, s. 46 (1849); N.S., *Stat.*, 14 Vic., c. 2 (1851).

13. Br., *Stat.*, 2 Wm. IV, c. 45, ss. 19, 20, 27 (1832).

14. Edward Coke, *Institutes of the Laws of England* (London, 1817), part IV, 5.

15. *Chorlton* v. *Lings*, 4 C.P., 394 (1868).

16. A. E. McKinley, *The Suffrage Franchise in the Thirteen English Colonies in America* (Philadelphia, 1905), 473f.

17. N.B., *Ex. Co. Min.*, Oct. 11, 1785.

18. N.S., *Ass. J.*, Nov. 20, 24, 1806.

19. B. Murdoch, *Epitome of the Laws of Nova Scotia* (Halifax, 1832), I, 68.

20. "Plan for a House of Assembly Nov. 1784," Shortt and Doughty, II, 754.

21. "Les Femmes electeurs," *Bulletin des Recherches historiques*, XI (1905), 222.

22. Bedard to Neilson, July 1, 1820, P.A.C., John Neilson Collection, III, 412.

23. L.C., *Ass. J.*, Dec. 30, 1820.

24. *Ibid.*, 1820–21, App. W.

25. *Ibid.*, Dec. 31, 1821.

26. *Ibid.*, Dec. 4, 1828.

27. *Ibid.*, Dec. 4, 1828.

28. W. R. Riddell, "Woman Franchise in Quebec, a Century Ago," *Royal Society of Canada, Transactions*, Ser. 3, XXII (1928), 93.

29. *Quebec Gazette*, Jan. 29, 1834.

30. L.C., *Stat.*, 4 Wm. IV, c. 28, s. 27 (1834).

31. Glenelg to Aylmer, June 29, 1835, P.A.C., G29.2, 609.

32. Glenelg to Gosford, July 20, 1836, G32.1, 35.

33. Can., *Ass. J.*, Dec. 2, 1844. A partisan select committee, appointed to investigate the disputed return, threw the protest out after two sessions. See *ibid.*, April 30, May 6, 1846.

34. Can., *Stat.*, 12 Vic., c. 27 (1849).

35. J. S. Mill, *On Representative Government* (Oxford, 1947), 223f.

36. James Mill, *An Essay on Government* (Cambridge, 1937), 45.

37. N.S., *Stat.*, 17 Vic., c. 6 (1854).

38. *Ibid.*, 26 Vic., c. 28 (1863).

39. *British Columbian*, Oct. 3, 1863.

40. See Seymour to Colonial Secretary, Jan. 17, 1867, P.A.C., J.2, vol. 4, 447; *British Columbian*, Sept. 15, 1866, Oct. 10, 1868; *British Colonist*, Oct. 12, 19, 20, 1868.

41. See *British Colonist*, Nov. 4, 1868, for an occasion on which Indians voted.

42. N.S., *Ass. J.*, Feb. 16, 1841. Some ten years later Lawrence O'Connor Doyle during the debate on the assessment franchise bill stated that ten Indians voted in the Richmond election. As McKeagney only carried the election by a majority of six, the Indian vote may be said to have returned him. See *Acadian Recorder*, March 8, 1851.

43. Poll Book of John Neilson, candidate for county of Quebec, July 30, 1827. John Neilson Collection, M.G. 27/81, P.A.C.

44. U.C., *Ass. J.*, Jan. 12, Feb. 1, 1831. See W. L. Stone, *Life of Joseph Brant* (New York, 1838), II, 533f; *Canadian Freeman*, Feb. 3, 1831.

45. Can., *Stat.*, 20 Vic., c. 26 (1857). Wm. Lyon Mackenzie, sitting for Haldimand, was the only member to oppose the bill; see Can., *Ass. J.*, May 22, 1857, and *Daily Colonist*, May 16, 1857, for debate on second reading.

46. The commissioners were instructed to examine periodically all Indians who were desirous of becoming enfranchised. If they were of the male sex, twenty-one years, free of debt, of good moral character, and able to speak, read, and write either the French or English languages, the commission was to approve their enfranchisement. The commissioners could also grant probational status to any male Indian between twenty-one and forty years of age who, although unable to read or write, could speak French or English and was in good moral and economic standing. If after three years' probation the Indian was still in good standing the Governor General on the recommendation of the commissioners could proclaim him an "enfranchised Indian."

47. This act was continued by Can., *Rev. Stat.*, 1859, c. 9, and was affirmed with modifications as applicable to the new Dominion by Can., *Stat.*, 32 & 33 Vic., c. 6 (1869).

CHAPTER THIRTEEN

1. Additional Instructions to Governor Philipps [March 25, 1730], P.A.C., M.G. 11, Supp. II; Minutes of His Majesty's Commissioners for Trade and Plantations, July 8, 1767, *Canadian Archives Report 1905* (Ottawa, 1906), I, part II, 6–9.

2. Board of Trade to Cornwallis, March 6, 1752, P.A.C., N.S. A46, 143.

3. Viscount Hailsham, ed., *Halsbury's Laws of England* (2nd ed., London, 1931), I, 453; Br., *Stat.*, 7 & 8 Geo. V, c. 64 (1918).

4. Br., *Stat.*, 7 & 8 Vic., c. 66 (1844), 33 Vic., c. 14 (1870).

5. N.S., *Ex. Co. Min.*, May 20, 1758, Aug. 22, 1759, P.A.C., B9, 80, 221; N.S., *Stat.*, 29 Geo. III, c. 1 (1789).

6. N.S., *Stat.*, 57 Geo. III, c. 7 (1817), 17 Vic., c. 6 (1854).

7. In the year 1793 there had been a complaint of an alien voting in Kings County but the sheriff had struck off the vote at the scrutiny. The loyalty of the votes appears to have been a prime requisite in Nova Scotia as evidenced by the action of the Assembly in disfranchising the townships of Onslow, Truro, and Londonderry in 1777 when their sympathy for the American Revolution led them to refuse to take the oath of allegiance. See Report of the Sheriff of Kings County, 1793, N.S., *Assembly Papers*, IV, P.A.N.S.; N.S., *Ass. J.*, June 11, 13, 1777, P.A.C., D12.

8. In the same year aliens were allowed to acquire real estate; see N.S., *Stat.*, 17 Vic., c. 19 (1854).

9. P.E.I., *Stat.*, 41 Geo. III, c. 4 (1801), P.A.C., C.O. 228, vol. 3.

10. *Ibid.*, 6 Wm. IV, c. 24 (1836), C.O. 228, vol. 6; 16 Vic., c. 9 (1853). When in 1862 the Legislative Council was made elective, the legislation did not specify its electors must be British subjects. After the Colonial Secretary pointed out the omission, a correction was made. See Newcastle to Dundas, Sept. 20, 1862, P.A.C., P.E.I. G31, 377; Dundas to Newcastle, Oct. 15, 1862, P.E.I. G52, 341; Newcastle to Dundas, Nov. 4, 1862, P.E.I. G31, 421.

11. *Ibid.*, 22 Vic., c. 4 (1859).

12. Maitland to Dalhousie, n.d., 1820, P.A.C., Q328.2, 217.

13. W. Blackstone, *Commentaries on the Laws of England* (4th ed., Oxford, 1770), I, 369f.

14. Br., *Stat.*, 4 Geo. II, c. 21 (1731); 13 Geo. III, c. 21 (1773).

15. Br., *Stat.*, 30 Geo. III, c. 27 (1790).

16. See Proclamation dated Quebec, Feb. 7, 1792, in A. G. Doughty and D. A. McArthur, *Documents Relating to the Constitutional History of Canada 1791–1818* (Ottawa, 1914), 60ff.

17. Simcoe to Dundas, Feb. 16, 1792, Q278, 48f.

18. C. C. James, "The Second Legislature of Upper Canada 1796-1800," *Royal Society of Canada, Proceedings and Transactions*, Ser. 2, IX (1903), 145.

19. U.C., *Stat.*, 35 Geo. III, c. 2 (1795); see also Simcoe to Portland, Aug. 22, 1795, Q281.2, 451.

20. *Ibid.*, 40 Geo. III, c. 3 (1800). For the first general election subsequent to the passage of the act, a four-year rather than a seven-year residence in Upper Canada was required. The act passed the Assembly by a vote of seven to five, and the proponents were all loyalists, five having been officers in loyalist regiments and now on half pay.

21. Brock to Liverpool, March 23, 1812, Q315, 5f.

22. U.C., *Stat.*, 54 Geo. III, c. 4 (1814).

23. Bathurst to Drummond, Jan. 10, 1815, G1, vol. 57, 86.

24. U.C., *Ex. Co. Min.*, Oct. 7, 1815, P.A.C., State Book F.; see also Gore to [Bathurst], April 7, 1817, Q322.1, 129.

25. See U.C., *Ass. J.*, Feb. 25, March 3, 1817, for the voiding of the election of Moses Gamble for Halton County under the above act.

26. U.C., *Stat.*, 58 Geo. III, c. 9 (1818).

27. Nichol, member for Norfolk County, was a kinsman of the Hon. Wm. Dickson, the Hon. Thomas Clark, and the late Hon. Robert Hamilton. Clark, a Legislative Councillor, had extensive holdings on the Grand River and Hamilton had bequeathed his family 100,000 acres of land on his death. Nichol had also been an agent for Col. Thomas Talbot of the Talbot Settlement. Gourlay, a Scottish agitator, was by marriage a nephew of the late Hon. Robert Hamilton and a cousin of the Hon. Wm. Dickson and of the Hon. Thomas Clark. Gourlay had himself come to Upper Canada with the intention of securing a substantial grant of land. See E. A. Cruikshank. "A Sketch of the Public Life and Services of Robert Nichol, a Member of the Legislative Assembly and Quartermaster General of the Militia of Upper Canada," *Ontario Historical Society, Papers and Records*, XIX (Toronto, 1922), 6-81; E. A. Cruikshank, "The Government of Upper Canada and Robert Gourlay," *Ontario Historical Society, Papers and Records*, XXIII (Toronto, 1926), 65-103.

28. U.C., *Ex. Co. Min.*, April 8, 1817, State Book F.

29. "Resolutions of the Committee on the State of the Province of the Assembly of 1817" enclosed in Gore to [Bathurst], April 7, 1817, Q322.1, 137.

30. Robert Gourlay to the Resident Landowners of Upper Canada, Feb. 1818, Q324.1, 26.

31. Bathurst to President Smith, Nov. 30, 1817, G58, 242. The prohibition was ruled illegal because it conflicted with the procedure of the Imperial Naturalization Act of 1740 (13 Geo. II, c. 7) and the Act to encourage new settlers in His Majesty's American colonies of 1790.

32. Bathurst's directive was based on the opinion of the Law Officers of the Crown. Similar opinions had been given to his predecessors, Portland, Hobart, and Camden, which they had thought wise to ignore in practice. See Shepherd and Gifford to Bathurst, Nov., 1817, Q323, 18f.

33. Smith to Bathurst, Feb. 25, 1818, Q324.1, 21; same to same, April 20, 1818, Q324.1, 102; enclosed in latter dispatch Attorney General Robinson's Report to Mr. President Smith, n.d., 1817, Q331, 96; and *Ex. Co. Min.*, April 16, 1818, U.C., State Book F.

34. U.C., *Ass. J.*, Nov. 24, 29, Dec. 31, 1821.

35. *Ibid.*, Nov. 29, 1821, Jan. 2-4, 1822.

36. *Ibid.*, Feb. 13, 14, Nov. 13, Dec. 8, 1833. Bidwell, senior, was unable to stand as a candidate after his expulsion as the Assembly passed legislation which declared any resident of the province who had abjured allegiance to the Crown, held an executive or political office in Congress or any of the States, or had committed an offence abroad which, if committed within the province, would have been a criminal act, was ineligible to sit in the Assembly. See U.C., *Stat.*, 2 Geo. IV, c. 4 (1822).

37. Maitland to Bathurst, April 15, 1822, Q331, 93.

38. *Doe d. Thomas* v. *Acklam* (1824), 26 *Rev. Reports* 544.

39. Bathurst to Maitland, July 22, 1825, G61, 223.

40. See Editor of the *Canadian Freeman* [Francis Collins], *An Abridged View of the Alien Question Unmasked* (York, 1826), P.A.C., Pamp. no. 1196.

41. Br., *Stat.*, 7 Geo. IV, c. 68 (1826).

42. Bathurst to Maitland, Aug. 31, 1826, G62, 266.

43. See *Canadian Freeman*, March 1, 1827.

44. See *First Report of the Central Committee of the Inhabitants of Upper Canada* (York, 1827), P.A.C., Pamp. no. 1221; Petition to the Commons, Q345.1, 169.

45. Horton to Maitland (private & confidential), July 6, 1827, G63.1, 136.

46. See "Report of the Royal Commissioners for Inquiring into the Laws of Naturalization and

Allegiance," *Br. Parliamentary Papers*, XXV, 1868–69, for discussion of the principle. The Chesapeake affair was a consequence of the application of the principle.

47. Goderich to Maitland, July 10, 1827, G63.1, 144.

48. Maitland to Huskisson, March 6, 1828, enclosed Robinson to Hillier, March 5, 1828, Q346.1, 216, 219; Huskisson to Maitland, May 10, 1828, Q327A, 22; Order in Council, May 7, 1828, Q350.1, 16.

49. U.C., *Stat.*, 9 Geo. IV, c. 21 (1828). In 1831 the period in which the oath might be taken was extended to 1835 and in 1839 the period was reopened and extended to 1841. See *ibid.*, 1 Wm. IV, c. 7 (1831); 2 Vic., c. 20 (1839).

50. Dorchester to Grenville, Feb. 8, 1790, enclosing Second Draft of the Constitutional Act, Q44.1, 20, 30; Dorchester to Grenville, Sept. 25, 1790, Q46.1, 2.

51. Grenville to Dorchester, June 5, 1790, Q44.1, 152; Monk to Clarke, Nov. 9, 1792 (and enclosure), Q61.2, 444, 449.

52. Clarke to Dundas, Aug. 11, 1792, Grenville to Clarke, Nov. 8, 1792, Q60, 10, 212.

53. Monk to Nepean (private), May 8, 1793, Q66, 283.

54. Monk to Nepean, Jan. 3, 1793, Q66, 261; Clarke to Dundas, July 3, 1793, Q63.2, 307; draft petition against Berthelot, 1793, in P.A.C., John Young Papers, and L.C., *Ass. J.*, Jan.–March, 1793.

55. Blackstone, *Commentaries*, I, 374.

56. [Camden] to Hunter, Aug. 2, 1804, Q299, 51; Bathurst to Dalhousie, June 5, 1823, G12, 200. The Colonial Office at one time contemplated conferring on colonial governors the power to grant letters of denization.

57. Observations on various clauses of the Petition of the Counties in the District of Quebec, 1828, Q184.2, 383.

58. L.C., *Ass. J.*, March 12, 1829.

59. *Ibid.*, Nov. 28, 1828; *Quebec Gazette*, Jan. 5, 1829.

60. See Kempt to Murray, April 7, 1829, Q188.1, 76; Kempt to Murray, Jan. 12, 1830, enclosure Stuart to Yorke, Jan. 11, 1830, Q193.1, 120, 123; Murray to Kempt, March 22, 1830, G20, 378; Br., *Stat.*, 1 Wm. IV, c. 53 (1830). This act gave the same authority to the Lower Canada Legislature that had been given to the Legislature of Upper Canada in 1826.

61. L.C., *Stat.*, 1 Wm. IV., c. 53 (1831).

62. *See* Cochran to Hillier (private), Dec. 25, 1827, P.A.C., U.C. Sundries.

63. Br., *Stat.*, 13 Geo. II, c. 7 (1790). There had been some doubt whether the act applied to the conquered colony of Quebec. In 1792, 43 European tradesmen who had complied with the requirements of the act petitioned Lieutenant Governor Clarke as to the validity of their naturalization under it. The Crown Law Officers thereupon confirmed the applicability of the act to Quebec. See Clarke to Dundas, March 10, 1792, enclosing Memorial to Clarke, March 3, 1792, Q58.1, 231, 233; Report of His Majesty's Attorney and Solicitor General, July 6, 1792, Q61.2, 383.

64. It was on these terms that the Lunenberg settlers were admitted to citizenship and the franchise for the first Nova Scotian election in 1758. See Monckton to Faesch, July 5, 1758, and Monckton to Rev. Moreau, July 5, 1758, P.A.C., Monckton Papers, XI.

65. Stephen to Hay, Aug. 20, 1828, P.A.C., N.B. A40.1, 299.

66. Colborne to Hay (private), Nov. 25, 1831, Q357.2, 178.

67. Goderich to Colborne (confidential), Jan. 10, 1832, G29, 1.

68. U.C., *Leg. Co. J.*, March 2–17, 1829.

69. *Ibid.*, Feb. 28, 1834. Colborne to Stanley, April 10, 1834, Q381.3, 583. When the alien controversy first broke in Upper Canada, Bathurst had asked Maitland to suggest a more convenient process of naturalization than the act of 1740. The Executive Council thereupon prepared a draft bill which would have allowed any aliens regardless of religion to become British subjects after seven years' residence and subscription to the oath of allegiance before a judge of the Court of King's Bench. Bathurst did not welcome the draft and brusquely announced that the Colonial Office would not at that time consider any change in the naturalization procedure. The decision may have been occasioned by the crisis within the Home Government over Catholic emancipation. See Bathurst to Maitland, July 22, 1825, G61, 223; U.C., *Ex. Co. Min.*, Feb. 3, 1826, State Book H; Maitland to Bathurst, March 15, 1826 (enclosing draft bill), Q340.2, 368, 382; Bathurst to Maitland, Aug. 31, 1826, G62, 266.

70. Aberdeen to Colborne, Dec. 26. 1834, G72, 393; Aberdeen to Colborne (private), Dec. 26, 1834, G72, 398.

71. See U.C., *Rev. Stat.*, local and private, 3 Wm. IV, c. 60 (1833), 4 Wm. IV, c. 54 (1834).

72. Russell to Sydenham, April 3, 1841, G1, vol. 97, 4; enclosed Law Officers to Russell, Nov. 13, 1840, Q275.1, 160.

73. L.C., *Ordinances*, 2 Vic., c. 11 (1839), 2 Vic., c. 12 (1839), 3 Vic., c. 12 (1840), 3 Vic., c. 21 (1840).

74. Sydenham to Russell, April 26, 1841; enclosed Ogden to Murdock, April 26, 1841, G12, vol. 56, 298, 299.

75. Russell to Sydenham, June 30, 1841; enclosed Campbell and Wilde to Russell, June 17, 1841, G1, vol. 98, 59, 62.

76. Can., *Stat.*, 4 & 5 Vic., c. 7 (1841).

77. Can., *Leg. Co. J.*, Aug. 20, 24, 1841.

78. Bagot to Stanley, April 9, 1842, G12, vol. 62, 212; Stanley to Bagot, Aug. 5, 1842, G12, vol. 102, 240.

79. Can., *Stat.*, 9 Vic., c. 107 (1845).

80. *Ibid.*, 12 Vic., c. 197 (1849).

81. *Ibid.*, 18 Vic., c. 6 (1854), 22 Vic., c. 1 (1858).

82. See Campbell to Stanley, Jan. 7, 1834, C.O. 188, vol. 49, 27. In 1855 the Assembly rejected a bill to allow aliens to hold real property because it was feared that the Americans by block buying would monopolize land ownership to the exclusion of native sons. See N.B., *Ass. Debates*, Feb. 20, March 27. 1855.

83. N.B., *Ex. Co. Min.*, Oct. 21, 1785; N.B., *Stat.*, 31 Geo. III, c. 17 (1791), 6 Vic., c. 44 (1843).

84. Stanley to Colebrooke, July 31, 1843, C.O. 188, vol. 171, n.p., and Peters and Street to Odell, Aug. 29, 1843, C.O. 188, vol. 83, 361.

85. *Ibid.*, 18 Vic., c. 37 (1855).

86. Douglas to Huskisson, May 20, 1828, N.B. A40.1, 295.

87. Douglas to Maitland, Jan. 2, 1826, U.C. Sundries; N.B., *Ass. J.*, Jan. 29, 1829. The sponsor of the address was the member for Charlotte County in which Americans of the Baptist and Methodist persuasions were most numerous.

88. Murray to Black, June 24, 1829, C.O. 188, vol. 157, n.p.; Campbell to Goderich, Sept. 18, 1832 N.B. A46, 344; Goderich to Campbell (confidential), Nov. 8, 1832, C.O. 188, vol. 159, n.p.

89. N.B., *Ass. J.*, March 2, 1833; Aberdeen to Campbell, Dec. 20, 1834, C.O. 188, vol. 161, 667.

90. N.B., *Stat.*, 6 Wm. IV, c. 75 (1836), 4 Vic., c. 45 (1841), 8 Vic., c. 106 (1845), 9 Vic., c. 6 (1846).

91. Br., *Stat.*, 10 & 11 Vic., c. 83 (1847). This act allowed the colonies to confer British citizenship within the colony. To secure citizenship throughout the Empire it was still necessary to conform to the act of 1740.

92. N.B., *Stat.*, 13 Vic., c. 41 (1850).

93. *Ibid.*, 24 Vic., c. 54 (1861).

94. Falkland to Stanley, May 1, 1845, P.A.N.S.

95. Nova Scotia, for instance, passed twenty-one acts to naturalize a total of 184 aliens.

96. P.E.I., *Stat.*, 26 Vic., c. 14 (1863); N.S., *Stat.*, 26 Vic., c. 36 (1863). The Colonial Office had refused to confirm a Prince Edward Island naturalization act of the previous year because it conferred on the alien the right of British citizenship within the Empire. See Newcastle to Dundas, Sept. 20, 1862, P.E.I. G31, 373.

CHAPTER FOURTEEN

1. In Great Britain controverted elections were decided by the King in Chancery until 1604, by the House of Commons from 1604 to 1868, and subsequently by a judge of a superior court. See W. R. Anson, *The Law and Custom of the Constitution* (4th ed., Oxford, 1909), I, 168–71.

2. N.S., *Ass. J.*, March 31, 1789.

3. *Ibid.*, Nov. 21, 29, Dec. 11, 1806.

4. *Ibid.*, Jan. 9, 1808.

5. N.S., *Ex. Co. Min.*, April 28, 1807, P.A.N.S., E6. The Attorney General, R. J. Uniacke, was a former Speaker of the Assembly.

6. Wentworth to Windham, May 20, 1807, P.A.C., N.S. A139, 15; and N.S., *Ass. J.*, Jan. 14, Feb. 1, 1808.

7. Law Officers of the Crown to Castlereagh, July 7, 1807, N.S., A139, 274. In 1860 the Colonial Office had to reaffirm this decision. See Newcastle to Mulgrave (separate), Aug. 30, 1860, P.A.C., N.S., vol. 104.1, 278f.

8. N.S., *Ass. J.*, April 7, 9, 1759.

9. *Ibid.*, Dec. 7, 8, 16, 17, 1785, June 12, 15, 23, 1786.

10. Br., *Stat.*, 10 Geo. III, c. 16 (1770). Under this act the House of Commons selected a commit-

I

tee of forty-nine by lot, from which the contending parties alternatively struck off members until the committee was reduced to thirteen. These members together with a nominee for each of the contenders were responsible for determining the controverted election.

11. N.S., *Ass. J.*, March 25, 1793.

12. *Ibid.*, March 30, April 26, 1793.

13. *Ibid.*, Feb. 21, 28, March 1–5, 12–15, 1800; see also Report of the Select Committee on Halifax Town Election, 1800, *Assembly Papers*, VII, P.A.N.S.

14. Eleven petitions were tabled protesting seven elections and the first month of the session was consumed in their determination. See Wentworth to King (private), April 6, 1800 and Wentworth, to Portland, June 21, 1800, N.S., A131, 80, 199.

15. N.S., *Stat.*, 1 & 2 Geo. IV, c. 17 (1820–21).

16. N.S., *Ass. J.*, Feb. 5, 1828.

17. N.S., *Stat.*, 2 Vic., c. 31 (1839).

18. See N.S., *Ass. J.*, March 4, 1828; *Acadian Recorder*, Oct. 31, 1829. The amount of the bribe was £1 and was expended on the purchase of seed oats. The Court convicted on a British statute of 1729 (2 Geo. II, c. 24) which had been made applicable to Nova Scotia by local statute, 57 Geo. III, c. 7, s. 6 (1817).

19. See N.S., *Ass. J.*, April 16, 1844; *Acadian Recorder*, July 26, 1845.

20. Howe to Hincks, Feb. 29, 1852, P.A.C., Howe Papers, VII, 16. And see Brown to Howe, Oct. 21, 1851, *ibid.*, I, 868.

21. N.S., *Stat.*, 21 Vic., c. 36 (1858).

22. N.S., *Ex. Co. Min.*, July 20, 1859; *Acadian Recorder*, Nov. 5, 1859. The legislative councillors had resigned their provincial offices before their reappointment to the Council. See N.S., *Leg. Co. J.*, Jan. 26, 1860.

23. N.S., *Ass. J.*, Feb. 3, 1860. Of these five Liberals two were way office keepers, one a coroner, one a health officer, and one a commissioner of relief for insolvent debtors and a commissioner of affidavits for bail.

24. Law Officers to Newcastle, Dec. 7, 1859, P.A.C., N.S., vol. 103, 428.

25. N.S., *Ass. J.*, Feb. 8, 1860.

26. N.S., *Ass. J.*, Dec. 9, 1785.

27. N.S., *Stat.*, 10 Vic., c. 1 (1847).

28. N.S., *Ass. J.*, Nov. 6, 10, 1851.

29. N.S., *Stat.*, 26 Vic., c. 28 (1863). During the colonial period five elections were voided because of the conduct of the sheriff.

30. P.E.I., *Stat.*, 20 Geo. III, c. 4 (1780), 41 Geo. III, c. 4 (1801); P.A.C., C.O. 228, I, 7; III, 14.

31. P.E.I., *Ex. Co. Min.*, July 17, 1787, P.A.C., B6, 147.

32. P.E.I., *Ass. J.*, Feb. 1, 18, 1848 and App. O.

33. P.E.I., *Ass. J.*, Jan. 23, 1788, March 22, 24, 1803, Dec. 2, 1806.

34. P.E.I., *Stat.*, 6 Wm. IV, c. 20 (1836), 3 Vic., c. 25 (1840), 7 Vic., c. 23 (1844), 11 Vic., c. 17 (1848), 18 Vic., c. 17 (1855), and 29 Vic., c. 5 (1866).

35. The statistics are compiled from the Assembly Journals, but they are incomplete as the Journals are missing for ten sessions.

36. P.E.I., *Ass. J.*, April 5, 1790; Abstract of Charges against Fanning, Nov. 18, 1791, P.E.I.. A11, 179, 182; Fanning to Lords of Trade [1791], P.A.C., Fanning Papers, I, 19–21, 31–35.

37. P.E.I., *Leg. Co. J.*, April 11, 16, 1862.

38. Br., *Stat.*, 31 & 32 Vic., c. 125 (1868).

39. N.S., *Stat.*, 18 Geo. III, c. 2 (1778); P.E.I., *Stat.*, 26 Geo. III, c. 15 (1786), 7 Wm. IV, c. 2 (1837).

40. Roberts to Sydney, Dec. 8, 1785 (4 encl.); P.E.I. A7, 130, 13, 43, 55, 66.

41. P.E.I., A7, 55f.

42. Patterson to Sydney, April 20, 1785; P.E.I. A7, 61, 27.

43. The appointment was tenable only for one year whereas in Nova Scotia an appointment could be continued unless the magistrates in Quarter Session petitioned against a reappointment. As a result the incumbents of some Nova Scotia shrievalties became life appointees; for instance, that of Lunenburg was in the Kaulbach family for near a century.

44. P.E.I., *Stat.*, 41 Geo. III, c. 4 (1801); C.O. 228, III, 14. On the introduction of simultaneous polling in 1848, the sheriffs were allowed to adjudicate the validity of votes on two grounds, double voting and voting in the wrong polling subdivision. In all other cases they were to continue merely to record the evidence and leave the final determination to the Assembly. P.E.I., *Stat.*, 11 Vic., c. 21 (1848).

45. P.E.I., *Stat.*, 47 Geo. III, c. 3 (1806), 11 Vic., c. 21 (1848). There was one limitation on this privilege: neither the sheriff nor deputy sheriff could be a candidate in the county or riding for which he served as a sheriff or as a returning officer.

46. See P.E.I., *Ass. J.*, 1854, App. L.

47. P.E.I., *Stat.*, 18 Vic., c. 7 (1855). After the establishment of responsible government, Nova Scotia had also changed its method of appointing sheriffs. A nomination committee of two judges and two executive councillors was to nominate three fit persons and the Lieutenant Governor in Council was to make the appointment from this list. See N.S., *Stat.*, 12 Vic., c. 3 (1849).

48. P.E.I., *Ass. J.*, April 19, 1859; P.E.I., *Stat.*, 23 Vic., c. 41 (1860). Some years later the puisne judges were required to participate with the Chief Justice in the preparation of the nominations. P.E.I., *Stat.*, 32 Vic., c. 14 (1869).

49. Hodgson to Kimberley, Aug. 9, 1870, P.A.C., P.E.I. G54, 212.

50. The crucial return was for Gloucester County. The ballot gave the Oppositon control of the select committee which unseated the Government member and seated an Opposition member in his stead. This reduced the Government majority from three to one, and forced the immediate prorogation of the House to save the Government from defeat. While the Government tried to meet the Assembly at its next session, they were unable to control it, and ultimately had to recommend its dissolution. See N.B., *Ass. J.*, July 24, 26, 1856, March 26, 1857.

51. N.B., *Ass. J.*, Dec. 29, 1837, Jan. 26, 1838, Feb. 21, 22, 1839.

52. *Ibid.*, Feb. 22, March 8, 1833, Feb. 26, March 8, 1847.

53. N.B., *Ex. Co. Min.*, Dec. 16, 1785, P.A.C.

54. N.B., *Ass. J.*, Jan. 20, 24, 1786. It later became customary to adopt these rules formally at the commencement of each new Assembly. See *ibid.*, Jan. 31, 1821.

55. *Ibid.*, Feb. 21–March 15, 1820.

56. *Ibid.*, Feb. 16, 18, 1828. Two controverted elections were referred to ad hoc select committees. The Assembly appointed five members to each committee and debated their findings on their reporting to the House. See N.B., *Stat.*, 9 Geo. IV, c. 37 (1828).

57. See N.B., *Ass. J.*, March 2, 1803, Feb. 19, 1820.

58. *Ibid.*, Oct. 21, 1854, Feb. 20, March 19, 1855. See the *Courier*, July 24, 1858, for *Stiles* v. *Gilbert*.

59. N.B., *Ass. J.*, Feb. 23, 1852.

60 *Courier*, March 6, 1852.

61. N.B., *Ass. J.*, Feb. 24, 1853.

62. There was no statute establishing or regulating the office of sheriff until 1836. The sheriffs were appointed by the Lieutenant Governor in Council without any prior nomination by the Bench or Quarter Sessions. Their appointment was for one year but it was customary to reappoint year after year. When a statutory basis was given to the office in 1836, the legislation was no more than a codification of past practice. See N.B., *Stat.*, 6 Wm. IV, c. 1 (1836).

63. See W. H. Davidson, *An Account of the Life of William Davidson* (St. John, 1947), 44, and J. Hannay, *History of New Brunswick* (St. John, 1909), I, 310, for examples.

64. The powers of New Brunswick sheriffs were the same as those conventionally exercised by the sheriffs in England until modified by the first Reform Bill.

65. N.B., *Stat.*, 18 Vic., c. 37 (1855). Although no occasion is recorded on which a sheriff denied a scrutiny, the right to refuse such a request was abolished in 1843. See *ibid.*, 6 Vic., c. 44 (1843).

66. *British Columbian*, Oct. 17, 20, 1866.

67. The Assembly adopted the British procedure by incorporating it into the Standing Orders of the Assembly. It has not been possible to find these Standing Orders but their general content can be deduced from the Assembly Journals.

68. Br. *Stat.*, 11 & 12 Vic., c. 98 (1848).

69. V.I., *Ass. J.*, Aug. 19, 26, 1856; Douglas to Labouchere, Aug. 20, 1856, C.O. 305, vol. 7, 82.

70. V.I., *Ass. J.*, March 12, 30, April 27, May 10, 1860.

71. *Ibid.*, Oct. 4, 1864, in *British Colonist*, Oct. 5, 1864.

CHAPTER FIFTEEN

1. L.C., *Ass. J.*, March 1, 1834.

2. *Quebec Gazette*, Nov. 19, 1834, Nov. 11, 1835. The 1804 Northumberland election provides another example of irregularity. The returning officer closed this election without adjourning to the second county poll for an alleged gift of £100; see L.C., *Ass. J.*, Jan. 22, 1805.

3. L.C., *Stat.*, 47 Geo. III, c. 16 (1807). The temporary acts were 33 Geo. III, c. 7 (1793), 37 Geo. III, c. 5 (1797), 38 Geo. III, c. 5 (1798), 39 Geo. III, c. 1 (1799), 40 Geo. III, c. 1 (1800), and 43 Geo. III, c. 5 (1803).

4. See Monk to Nepean (private), May 8, 1793, P.A.C., Q66, 286, for copy of the Legislative Council bill.

5. L.C., *Ass. J.*, Jan. 26, 29, 30, 1816. The second occasion was the Stanstead by-election of 1833. See *Quebec Gazette*, April 5, 1833; *Quebec Mercury*, March 8, 1834.

6. *Ante.*, 171. The sixth petition was against the return for Gaspé County and was dismissed for an insufficiency of signatures.

7. See "Petition of Electors of Lower Town of Quebec Dec. 15, 1792," in which the petitioners, led off by two priests, declared "That the said John Young did also before and during the said election open and caused to be opened several taverns particularly one near the place chosen by him to hold the poll, where hams were sliced and strong liquors given to tradesmen and labourers, who were also influenced by sundry other unwarrantable acts of his servants or hirelings. That he treated them by these blameable disbursements, distributing to them cockades to distinguish his party, got them conducted to the poll by his creatures, where ribbons and oranges were again given to them to induce them to vote for him, in order to exclude other candidates. That by several promises to employ tradesmen, labourers and others to work at a higher price than customary, he endeavoured to obtain their votes; that assaults, insults and battles contrary to peace and liberty were the results thereof." Also see "General Account of the Expenses of the Election for the Lower Town of Quebec June 1792," where there is listed the sum of £93/14/10 paid three tavernkeepers. P.A.C., John Young Papers, II.

8. *Quebec Gazette*, March 7, 1792.

9. Evidence of this deal appears in the John Young Papers, II; a draft petition against the return of a French member because he was an alien bears the endorsement, "Quebec 1793 Copy of an intended petition against the election of Berthelot d'Artigny had he persisted in his petition against others."

10. L.C., *Ass. J.*, Feb. 13, 18, 20, 1797, Jan. 21, March 1, 6, 1805.

11. L.C., *Stat.*, 48 Geo. III, c. 21 (1808).

12. L.C., *Ass.. J.*, Jan. 25, March 21, 1815.

13. *Ibid.*, Jan. 14, Feb. 6–18, 1818; 1820–21, App. W; Dec. 29, 1821.

14. L.C., *Stat.*, 2 Geo. IV, c. 4 (1822). An elector convicted of perjury for falsely swearing at the hustings that he had not been bribed was among other penalties to be disfranchised. Any candidate who gave bribes was to be disfranchised and debarred from a seat in the Assembly, as were all electors who gave bribes on his behalf. The act also made it clear that wages paid by candidates to electors, ostensibly as compensation for the loss of time or expense of going to vote, were bribes. It should be noted that perjury, bribery, intimidation, and maintenance of houses of entertainment had first been made election offences subjecting the wrongdoer to a fine in 1800, and that in 1807 the penalty had been extended to a disqualification from a seat in the Assembly. In the latter year fraudulent conveyances of land to create votes had also been made an election offence as well as wearing of ribbons, carrying flags, and impeding access to the polls. *Ibid.*, 40 Geo. 111, c. 1 (1800), 47 Geo. III, c. 16 (1807).

15. L.C., *Ass. J.*, Jan. 19, Feb. 4, 7, 1825.

16. L.C., *Stat.*, 48 Geo., III, c. 21 (1808). The idea of the commission was borrowed from Great Britain where in 1802 the Imperial Parliament, in order to obviate the expense of bringing witnesses from Ireland, empowered the controverted election committees on Irish cases to appoint three barristers to examine the witnesses to the election and record their evidence on the spot. See Br., *Stat.*, 42 Geo. III, c. 106 (1802).

17. L.C., *Stat.*, 58 Geo. III, c. 5 (1818).

18. Papineau in the Assembly debates for Jan. 27, 1834, reports an election case at Three Rivers where 300 witnesses were called. See *Quebec Gazette*, Jan. 29, 1834.

19. L.C., *Stat.*, 4 Wm. IV, c. 28 (1834).

20. Glenelg to Gosford, July 20, 1836, P.A.C., G32.1, 35.

21. Aberdeen to Aylmer, Jan. 19, 1835, G29.1, 98ff.

22. The election act of 1800 (40 Geo. III, c. 1) fixed the daily hours of polling at eight hours between 8 A.M. and 6 P.M., and in all counties with two polling places the poll at the first place was to remain open a maximum of four days. In 1825 (5 Geo. IV, c. 33) the returning officer was permitted to keep the poll open at the first place of election for six days, and for eight hours between 8 A.M. and 5 P.M. There was no time limit on the duration of an election in counties with one poll, and in counties with two polls there was no time limit on the duration of the polling at the second place of election.

23. See *Montreal Gazette*, May 24, 1832, and L.C., *Ass. J.*, Nov. 23, 1832.

24. L.C., *Ass. J.* Feb. 9, 1810. For other examples, see *ibid.*, Jan. 17, 1825, Feb. 2, 1827.

25. *Ibid.*, Dec. 9, 1828. Dalhousie was accused of having threatened to report the rector of Sorel to his bishop unless he curbed his father's campaign against Stuart's election. See *ibid.*, 1828–29, App. EE.

26. Goderich to Aylmer, Nov. 20, 1832, G25, 165. See L.C., *Ass. J.*, 1828–29, App. EE; 1831–32, App. A, for Memorial of Stuart to Goderich, April 14, 1831, Memoir of Stuart to His Majesty, Aug. 6, 1831, and Remarks of D. B. Viger, July 21, 1831.

27. *Quebec Gazette*, Jan. 8, Feb. 16, Nov. 5, 1829. In the Assembly following this election there were nineteen members returned who had been dismissed from their commissions in the militia. The Assembly, being unable to avenge itself on Dalhousie, voided the election of Robert Christie for Gaspé County five times because he, as Chairman of the Quarter Sessions for the Quebec District, had co-operated with Dalhousie in the removal of four Opposition members from the list of magistrates.

28. See *Quebec Mercury*, Jan. 16, 1827, and *Quebec Gazette*, Aug. 16, Sept. 13, 1827.

29. *Quebec Gazette*, Aug. 16, Aug. 20, 1827.

30. Compiled from the Upper Canada Journals of Assembly subject to the limitation that the Journals are missing for seven sessions; Gen. Ass. I, sess. III, IV, and V; Gen. Ass. II, sess. I; Gen. Ass. V, sess. I; and Gen. Ass. VI, sess. I and II. From the fact that the third General Assembly had to establish rules to handle controverted elections, it would seem that there were no disputed elections until that time.

31. The determination of controverted elections by a formal session of the House was not established by statute until 1805; prior to that time an *ad hoc* procedure was followed which usually involved the examining of witnesses and the determination of the issue before the Committee of the Whole. See U.C., *Ass. J.*, June 3, 1801, Feb. 8, 1805; U.C., *Stat.*, 45 Geo. III, c. 3 (1805), 4 Geo. IV, c. 4 (1824), 8 Geo. IV, c. 5 (1827), 3 Wm. IV, c. 11 (1833), and 2 Vic., c. 8 (1839).

32. U.C., *Ass. J.*, Feb. 7, 1825; U.C., *Stat.*, 8 Geo. IV, c. 5 (1827).

33. U.C., *Ass. J.*, Jan. 18, 1831, Feb. 13, 1835. The House considered the use of a commission for the controverted elections in Prince Edward County in 1831, Leeds in 1835, and York in 1836. In the latter case the commissioners were appointed but the petition lapsed when the petitioner failed to lodge his surety.

34. C. Lindsey, *The Life and Times of Wm. Lyon Mackenzie* (Toronto, 1862) I, 382–86, 394.

35. U.C., *Ass. J.*, March 14, 1829.

36. U.C., *Stat.*, 48 Geo. III, c. 11 (1808).

37. See U.C., *Ass. J.*, Jan. 17, 1825, Jan. 17, 1835, for Essex County and Lincoln, third riding, elections.

38. U.C., *Stat.*, 4 Geo. IV, c. 3 (1824). Estates acquired by a grant from the Crown, by descent, devise, or marriage were exempt from this provision.

39. *Ibid.*, 3 Wm. IV, c. 11 (1833). This act made the provincial Treasury responsible for the fees of the returning officers, poll clerks, etc. Up to this time they had been borne by the candidates and while most of the electoral officers had followed the scale of fees established by British statute, some set their own value on their services. Mackenzie had complained of this to the Colonial Secretary when in England in 1832 and Goderich ordered Colborne to reduce the cost of elections within the narrowest limits. The above act was the Assembly's reply. See Goderich to Colborne, Nov. 8, 1832, G69, 407.

40. See U.C., *Ass. J.*, 1836, App. IV.

41. Simcoe to Dundas, Nov. 4, 1792, Q279.1, 79; Russell to Portland (separate) June 1, 1799, Q287.1, 1. White was defeated but Russell kept his promise and White's election expenses were paid to the amount of £23/10/3.

42. The Assembly first conferred this power by temporary statute 33 Geo. III, c. 12, in 1793 and repeatedly renewed it until the statute was made permanent by 3 Wm. IV, c. 11, in 1833.

43. Head to Glenelg, July 8, 1836, Q390.3, 743v–4. For some addresses and replies, see *St. Catharines Journal*, March 24, 31, 1836.

44. Head to Glenelg, Feb. 4, 1837, Q396.4, 644 f.

45. U.C., *Ass. J.*, 1836–37, App. 5 (341).

46. *Ibid.*, App. 5 (351).

47. Petition of Jessop to Head, Jan. 1, 1837, Q397.1, 217.

48. Head to Glenelg, Feb. 4, 1837, Q396.4, 644v.

49. Petition of Jessop to Head, Jan. 1, 1837, Q397.1, 217.

50. The constituencies were Hastings, Simcoe, Middlesex, Kent, Cornwall, and London. See U.C., *Ass. J.*, 1836–37, App. 5 (36J1, 50S).

51. For Bond Head's exoneration by the Tory-dominated select committee of the Upper Canada Assembly and for the Earl of Durham's opinion of Bond Head's conduct see U.C., *Ass. J.*, 1836-37, App. 5, and C. P. Lucas, ed., *Lord Durham's Report on the Affairs of British North America* (Oxford, 1912) II, 157, 161f.

52. L.C., *Stat.*, 4 Wm. IV, c. 9 (1834). An act of the same session (4 Wm. IV., c. 28) would have amended the controverted election procedure and have sustained the legislation until May 1, 1840, but this act was disallowed and therefore the aforementioned act was the operative statute.

53. See Colborne to Glenelg, April 24, 1838, Q244.2, 456.

54. Can., *Ass. J.*, July 30, 1841.

55. *Ibid.*, Aug. 12, 16, 1841.

56. *Ibid.*, June 17, 1841.

57. See *ibid.*, July 14, 16, 19, Sept. 13, 1841. See *Montreal Gazette*, July 21, 1841, for an angry denunciation of the bill.

58. Can., *Ass. J.*, Jan. 16, 1845. See also *Quebec Gazette*, Jan. 20, 27, 1845.

59. The first two select committees drawn, those for Lennox-Addington and Huron counties, each had seven out of their nine members drawn from Canada East. See Can., *Ass. J.*, July 1, 5, 1841; *Montreal Gazette*, July 12, 1841.

60. Can., *Ass. J.*, July 9, 1841. In the Assembly of Upper Canada in which the former procedure had first been in effect the House had been able to staff five select committees because six members had served on three committees and ten members on two committees.

61. *Ibid.*, July 9-12, 1841. See a private letter describing the dilemma from Sydenham to Russell dated July 12, 1841, in P. Knaplund, ed., *Letters from Lord Sydenham, Governor General of Canada, 1839-41 to Lord John Russell* (London, 1931), 149f.

62. Can., *Ass. J.*, Jan. 9, 1845.

63. *Ibid.*, April 6, 21, 23, 24, 27, 30, 1846.

64. *Ibid.*, April 29, May 5, 6, 15, 1846. The select committee for Middlesex confirmed the sitting member's election although the House had ordered the appointment of a new commission to gather evidence.

65. *Ibid.*, May 27, 1846. See also Sir Francis Hincks, *Reminiscences of His Public Life* (Montreal, 1884), 140.

66. Can., *Stat.*, 6 Vic. c. 1 (1842). The dying Sydenham had reserved assent to the 1841 bill; see Can., *Ass. J.*, Sept. 18, 1841.

67. *Ibid.*, 12 Vic., c. 27 (1849). Fraudulent conveyances to create votes and malicious destruction or damage of poll books, writs, etc. were made offences, the latter a penal offence.

68. Br., *Stat.*, 11 & 12 Vic., c. 98 (1848). This act was an improved version of an act of 1839 (2 & 3 Vic., c. 38) which had sharply modified the practice established under the Grenville act in 1770.

69. Can., *Stat.*, 14 & 15 Vic., c. 1 (1851).

70. The petitioners subsequently lodged £200 cash with the Clerk of the House in place of the recognizance declared objectionable by the Speaker but the attempt to reactivate the petition failed on an adverse vote of the House. Feeling ran so high that Laurin, the member for Lotbinière, tried to secure a private bill to validate the recognizance in the belief "justice and equity require that relief should be afforded to the petitioners." See Can., *Bills*, sess. 1852-53, Bill no. 151.

71. Can., *Ass. J.*, Aug. 27, 1852.

72. *Ibid.*, Sept. 5, 21, 1854. For a description of the election see *Montreal Gazette*, Sept. 9, 1854.

73. Can., *Ass. J.*, Sept. 15, 21, Nov. 17, 1854. See *ibid.*, 1854-45, App. N, for the votes and population of each poll.

74. *Ibid.*, April 10, 1855.

75. *Le National*, Jan. 2, 1858. See also *Le Journal de Québec*, Jan. 12, Feb. 20, 1858.

76. *Ibid.*, 20 Vic., c. 23 (1857). The change Mackenzie introduced was an adaptation of the procedure practised by the United States Congress. He first sponsored the change when two months of the fifth Parliament had elapsed before any select committee had begun to try a disputed return. The Macdonald-Morin ministry gave his measure scant sympathy and it was not until the investigations of the Quebec City and Argenteuil elections had dragged on for two years that the ministry changed its attitude. When in the last session of the same Parliament Mackenzie reintroduced his measure, John A. Macdonald gave the bill his support and it became law. See Can., *Bills*, sess. 1854-55, Bill no. 32; see also Assembly Debates for Oct. 27, 1854, and March 30, 1857, in the *Montreal Gazette*, Oct. 31, 1854, and the *Globe*, March 31, 1857, respectively.

77. *Globe*, Feb. 2, 1858; see also Can., *Ass. J.*, March 4, 1858.

78. *Globe*, Jan. 19, June 12, 1858.

79. *Ibid.*, Feb. 1, 1858; Can., *Stat.*, 14 & 15 Vic., c. 1, s. 101 (1851). For a review of the judicial decisions on the controverted elections see *Globe*, Feb. 23, 1858.

80. The disaffection was led by Sicotte who as Commissioner of Crown Lands was a member of the ministry. See Assembly Debates, March 11, 1858, on the reception of the Russell petition, *Globe*, March 12, 1858.

81. Can., *Ass. J.*, May 10, 12, 1858.

82. Can., *Stat.*, 22 Vic., c. 11 (1859).

83. See *Montreal Gazette*, July 25, 1851, for Assembly Debates of July 18.

84. Can., *Bills*, sess. 1860, Bill no. 143. This bill was inspired by a measure proposed by Lord Brougham in 1834 which would have placed all disputed elections in the hands of a jury of twelve whose members selected from both Houses of Parliament would have sat under the presidency of a judge.

85. *Ibid.*, Bill no. 167. See *Globe*, April 14, 1860, for the debate on the bill.

86. See Can., *Stat.*, 12 Vic., c. 81 s. 146 (1849), and 18 Vic., c. 100 s. 35 (1855).

87. Assembly Debates, April 13, 1860, in *Globe*, April 14, 1860.

88. See Can., *Bills*, sess. 1860, Bill. no. 167; sess. 1861, Bill no. 31; sess. 1862, Bill no. 43; sess. 1863, Bill no. 137. The first three bills were sponsored by Sicotte and were identical, the latter bill was sponsored by Dorion.

89. See Can., *Bills*, sess. 1859, Bill no. 28; sess. 1860, Bills no. 23 and 25; and Can., *Stat.*, 23 Vic., c. 17 (1860).

90. See Assembly Debates, Feb. 17, 1859, in *Globe*, Feb. 18, 1859.

91. *Globe*, July 15, 1858.

92. See *Pilot*, Jan. 23, 1857. On appeal, the judges reversed the decision of the lower court, and voided the note, because the money guaranteed by the note was to be used for purposes illegal in law. Justice Caron stated: "Equity is in favour of the plaintiff [the agent] but the law, the inflexible law, is with the defendant and the duty of the Court is to give him the advantage of his right."

93. See Can., *Stat.*, 23 Vic., c. 17 (1860).

94. Incidents of the interference of railways in the elections are numerous. There was the bitter battle between the Montreal and Bytown Railway and the Grand Trunk to secure the representation of Argenteuil in the elections of 1854 and 1858; in Hamilton, the directors of the Great Western closed their workshops and marched their men to the polls in military order to vote against Isaac Buchanan in the general election of 1858, and in the same year the Grand Trunk was able to secure the election of John Rose in the Rouge stronghold of Montreal City.

INDEX

Lightning Source UK Ltd.
Milton Keynes UK
UKHW030614210722
406167UK00006B/638

9 781487 598891